Facing the Past

Facing the Past

Policies and Good Practices for Responses to Illegal Intercountry Adoptions

Editors:
Elvira Loibl
David M. Smolin

eleven

Published, sold and distributed by Eleven
P.O. Box 85576
2508 CG The Hague
The Netherlands
Tel.: +31 70 33 070 33
Fax: +31 70 33 070 30
e-mail: sales@elevenpub.nl
www.elevenpub.com

Sold and distributed in USA and Canada
Independent Publishers Group
814 N. Franklin Street
Chicago, IL 60610, USA
Order Placement: +1 800 888 4741
Fax: +1 312 337 5985
orders@ipgbook.com
www.ipgbook.com

Eleven is an imprint of Boom (Den Haag).

ISBN 978-90-4730-188-2
ISBN 978-94-0011-365-7 (E-book)

Foreword

On 8 February 2021, Sander Dekker, then Minister for Legal Protection in the Netherlands, apologized to the victims of illegal intercountry adoption. It was the first time that an official apology was offered to illegally adopted individuals. The then minister followed the recommendation of the Joustra Committee that was set up to investigate past intercountry adoptions and whose report uncovered and described systemic abuses which took place with the knowledge of Dutch government officials. In other countries too inquiries into past intercountry adoptions took place (Switzerland, Belgium and Guatemala) or have been commissioned (Sweden, France, Norway and South Korea). Many adoptees, who have requested the governments to deal with past adoptions for years, feel that the harm that they and their birth families had suffered is finally being recognized.

However, these developments only mark the beginning of a long journey of reconciliation. Numerous adoptees that have been adopted illegally request remedies for the human rights violations and for the costs that they experienced as a result of searching for their families. Others have reasonable grounds to believe that they have been victims of an illegal adoption and demand that their individual cases be investigated by the state. Yet, so far, governments have been reluctant to offer reparation to victims or to assist adoptees in their individual root searches. When abuses in intercountry adoptions are exposed, the stakeholders of the adoption system would often only promise reforms for future adoptions but fail to properly respond to the wrongs in past adoptions.

Whereas (inter)national standards exist aiming to ensure ethical international adoptions that respect the rights of children and their natural parents, there is a wide gap in adequate regulations regarding remedies and reparations for intercountry adoptions that violate these standards. Also, academic literature has so far widely neglected the aftermath of illegal adoptions. A rich body of scholarly work has described and analysed abusive adoption practices and discussed the legitimacy of intercountry adoptions as well as possible ways to reform the system. Yet considerably less attention has been paid to the question as to how past illegal adoptions should be addressed and responded to. The aim of this book is to fill this gap and to assist in the process of reconciliation. The contributions in this volume present and discuss measures that the stakeholders in the intercountry adoption system in both the sending and the receiving countries can use in an effort to repair the injustices inflicted on the victims of illegal adoptions.

Elvira Loibl Maastricht, August 2023

Contents

1 Introduction

David M. Smolin

PART 1: Out of the Fog: Responses and Remedies for the Illegal Separation of Children from their Families in the Context of Intercountry Adoption

The Fog and Confusion Surrounding Discussions of Illegal Adoption

Adoptee literature speaks of the process of coming out of the fog, which can be described as moving from a naive and entirely positive view of adoption to a more realistic perspective that acknowledges the inherent loss and pain in adoption, including separation from the first family.[1] I am using the phrase in a related but different way.

First, the fog about adoption envelops not only adoptees but also adoptive parents, sometimes even first families, and also the general society. The fog has enveloped us all within the romanticized mythology of adoption as a saving, selfless act of rescue, making it difficult for us to live with and legislate about real adoption with all of its multilayered complexities.

Second, even for those who acknowledge the inherent emotions and complexities of adoption and have thus moved out of what is commonly termed the adoption fog, there is often scant or no awareness of the prevalence of illegal adoption. We are enveloped within the fog of presuming that adoption systems, including intercountry adoption systems, have generally operated in accordance with legal and ethical standards. Given the necessary governmental approvals in two countries, the involvement of 'adoption professionals', applicable international treaties and specialized international bodies, and various bureaucratic processes and seemingly endless paperwork, many presume that seriously illegal or unethical practices are kept to a minimum. This is an additional level of ignorance and confusion, I would argue, that has made it very difficult to discuss, enact and implement remedies and responses to illegal and unethical adoptions.

---

1 See, e.g., L. MacFarquhar, 'Living in Adoption's Emotional Aftermath', *New Yorker*, 3 April 2023, https://www.newyorker.com/magazine/2023/04/10/living-in-adoptions-emotional-aftermath; S.F. Branco, J. Kim, G. Newton, S. Kripa Cooper-Lewter and P. O'Loughlin, 'Out of the Fog and into Consciousness: A Model of Adoptee Awareness', *ICAV*, 2022, https://intercountryadopteevoices.com/wp-content/uploads/2022/06/adoptee-consciousness-model.pdf.

Dispelling the fog concerning illegal adoptions is not about taking a negative stance towards intercountry adoption as a political or ideological matter, but rather about realizing the degree to which systemic violations of legal and ethical standards have occurred in intercountry adoption systems over the entire modern history of intercountry adoption. Dispelling the fog is about using that awareness and accompanying clarity as a foundation for action and narratives concerning remedies and responses.

I have spent nearly a quarter-century personally and professionally responding to illegal intercountry adoption.[2] This chapter is a reflection on identifying and overcoming the severe obstacles to the provision of remedies for illegal intercountry adoption, based on a clear and realistic assessment of those barriers and obstacles.

Out of the Fog: Reconceptualizing Illegal Adoption as Usually Involving the Illegal Separation of Children from their Families

A foundational step in moving out of the fog is reconceptualizing illegal adoption as usually involving the illegal separation of children from their families.[3] While not all illegal adoptions involve this wrong, the most important – and in many instances the most widespread – forms of illegal adoption commonly do involve the illegal and wrongful separation of a child from the child's family. Illegally separating children from families is a wrong easily understandable to the general public. Parents normally have an intrinsic fear of losing their children. Modern societies have created organized response systems that treat a missing or stolen child as an emergency requiring an immediate response. The fact that not all missing or stolen children receive the same publicity and effort – often based on race, ethnicity or socioeconomic status – is broadly understood as a wrong to be rectified, not a difference to be embraced.[4] In order to dispel the fog, in addressing illegal adoptions we should constantly speak of the illegal and indeed cruel separation of children from their families.

Second, once the focus is on illegal separation of children from their families, the opportunity arises to explain how adoption systems incentivize, facilitate and hide such wrongs. Adoption systems have unfortunately caused the needless separation of

2 Many of my writings on intercountry adoption are available for free download here: https://works.bepress.com/david_smolin/.

3 UN Human Rights Treaty Bodies, Joint Statement on Illegal Intercountry Adoptions, 29 September 2022, https://www.ohchr.org/sites/default/files/documents/hrbodies/ced/2022-09-29/JointstatementICA_HR_28September2022.pdf, para. 3.

4 G. Barton, 'What Happens When a Child Disappears in American', *CNN*, 26 August 2022, https://www.usatoday.com/in-depth/news/investigations/2022/08/26/racial-disparities-abound-efforts-find-missing-children/10331706002/.

children from their families.[5] Adoption systems have unfortunately exacerbated rather than remedied separations of children from their families that otherwise could have been remedied.[6] Intercountry adoption further exacerbates separations through the geographical, linguistic and cultural distances it creates between children and their original families.[7] Such an understanding counters the common view of adoption as an inherent good and sets the premise for limiting, reforming and regulating adoption.

Third, a focus on the illegal separation of children from their families clarifies the question of remedies. Where illegal adoptions include an illegal separation of children from their families, the remedy should normally involve a restoration of that relationship.[8] Yet, depending on the facts of the case, remedies for illegal adoptions should also take into account the time and events between the separation and the reunion, including the relationships the child has formed due to the adoption. Remedies commonly should be 'additive' rather than 'subtractive', or 'both/and' remedies, meaning that remedies should acknowledge the importance of the child's relationships with both the original family and the adoptive family, as well as the child's complex cultural, racial and national identities. In practice, remedying illegal adoptions turns out to be an exceedingly complex process over time.[9]

Fourth, a clear focus on how intercountry adoption systems have incentivized, facilitated, exacerbated and hidden the illegal and unethical separation of children from families, in combination with the grave difficulties in supplying even partially effective remedies, strengthens the case for ending the modern era of intercountry adoption. On a systemic level, the harm to benefit ratio of intercountry adoption is

---

5 See, e.g., Committee Investigating Intercountry Adoption, *Consideration, Analysis, Conclusions, Recommendations, and Summary*, February 2021, https://www.government.nl/documents/reports/2021/02/08/summary-consideration-analysis-conclusions-recommendations; see Chapters 2, 3, 4, 5, 6, 7, 8, 9; E.C. Loibl, *The Transnational Illegal Adoption Market: A Criminological Study of the German and Dutch Intercountry Adoption Systems*, The Hague, Eleven International, 2019; D.M. Smolin, 'Child Laundering: How the Adoption System Legitimizes and Incentivizes the Practices of Buying, Trafficking, Kidnapping, and Stealing Children,' *Wayne Law Review*, Vol. 52, No. 1, 2006, pp. 113-200.

6 See, e.g., S.A. Jafri, 'Missing Girl Among Children Rescued in Tandur', *Rediff*, 1 May 2001, https://m.rediff.com/news/2001/may/01ap1.htm; D.M. Smolin, 'The Two Faces of Intercountry Adoption: The Significance of the Indian Adoption Scandals', *Seton Hall Law Review*, Vol. 35, 2004, pp. 403-493; Smolin, 2006, pp. 121-122.

7 Compare United Nations Convention on the Rights of the Child (1989) 1577 UNTS 3, Art. 20(3): "due regard shall be paid to the desirability of continuity in a child's upbringing and to the child's ethnic, religious, cultural and linguistic background."

8 See Art. 8(2) UNCRC; UN Human Rights Treaty Bodies, 29 September 2022, paras. 15-18.

9 On the complexities of reunions, in general, and the complexity of kinship post reunion and long term, see G. Clapton, 'Close Relations? The Long-Term Outcomes of Adoption Reunions', *Genealogy*, Vol. 2, No. 4, 2018, p. 41; L. Long, 'ICAV Perspective Paper: The Experiences and Views of Intercountry & Transracial Adoptees', July 2016, https://intercountryadopteevoices.com/wp-content/uploads/2016/07/search-and-reunion-icav-perspectives-july-2016-v12.pdf.

much worse than has been recognized. Most interventions with such a poor record as to systemic abuses over such a long period of time would have been discontinued long ago. The difficulties involved in even partial remedies underscore this need to end the modern era of intercountry adoption.[10]

Fifth, reviewing the accuracy of past predictions about intercountry adoption systems, I will make new predictions on how recent efforts to remedy illegal intercountry adoptions will likely proceed. While, of course, no one can predict the future, it is often possible to make reasonable hypotheses about the future based on the past and on the nature of the systems involved. These predictions can serve as an important reality check.

Legal Premise: Children Normally Have the Right to be Raised by Their Original Family

As a matter of children's rights, the child has a right to "know and be cared for by his or her parents" (Art. 7(1) UNCRC). The child also has rights to 'a name' and a 'nationality' and to "preserve his or her identity, including nationality, name and family relations…" (Art. 8(1) UNCRC). Hence, many separations of a child from parents violate the rights of the child and require remedies; indeed, the United Nations Convention on the Rights of the Child (UNCRC) states: "Where a child is illegally deprived of some or all of the elements of his or her identity, State Parties shall provide appropriate assistance and protection, with a view to speedily re-establishing his or her identity" (Art. 8(2)). As will be discussed later, Article 9 requires further actions from the state where the separation results from "any action initiated by a State Party…", and Article 10 requires states to accommodate international travel for purposes of 'family unification'.

As a technical matter, the right of the child to "know and be cared for by his or her parents" is limited by two contingencies: "as far as possible" (Art. 7(1) UNCRC) and the "best interests of the child" (Art. 3(1) and Art. 20-21 UNCRC). These are explained in what follows.

'As far as possible'

Under the UNCRC, where it is not 'possible' for the child to be raised by their original family, the child's rights have not been deprived when the child is not raised by the

10 I make the case at greater length for ending the modern era of intercountry adoption in D.M. Smolin, 'The Legal Mandate for Ending the Modern Era of Intercountry Adoption', *in* N. Lowe and C. Fenton-Glynn (eds.), *Research Handbook on Adoption Law*, Cheltenham, Edward Elgar, 2023, pp. 384-407, draft version available at https://works.bepress.com/david_smolin/24/.

original family. The African Charter on the Rights and Welfare of the Child (hereinafter ACRWC) has a similar provision, stating that "[e]very child ... shall, whenever possible, have the right to reside with his or her parents" (Art. 19(1)). These provisions make it important to distinguish between a tragic loss and the deprivation of a right.

Practically speaking, there are some tragic circumstances that cannot be avoided by either the state or society, and thus since no one has committed a deprivation of a right, there is no deprivation of a right. For example, if the parents die from an illness, despite receiving appropriate medical care, and thus neither state nor society nor any individual is liable, then there is great loss but technically no rights deprivation. Psychologically, of course, loss occurs regardless of whether there is a rights deprivation or not.

The distinction is foundational to the legality of adoption. Where it was not possible for the child to remain and be raised by their family, and it is not possible to remedy that separation, a subsequent adoption may be legal. On the other hand, an adoption built on top of an illegal separation that could have been avoided or remedied is an illegal adoption, which constitutes the deprivation of the rights of the child. An adoption built on an illegal separation is an illegal adoption no matter how many legal procedures were followed at later stages of the adoption process, and even if the adoptive family was unaware of the illegal separation – although the adoptive family would not be legally or ethically responsible for such illegality if the adoptive family neither created nor knew of the illegal separation. An adoption built on an illegal adoption exacerbates the deprivation of the child's rights in relationship to the original family, because the adoption makes it more difficult to remedy the illegal separation.

'Best interests of the child'

The principle of the best interests of the child is often misunderstood. As Nigel Cantwell has pointed out, the term 'best interests of the child' can be and has been misapplied to justify deprivations of the rights of the child, and, indeed, of the *human rights* of the child.[11] To the contrary, the term best interests of the child should be understood as a shorthand for respecting all of the rights of the child.[12] Beyond that, a best interests of the child determination is an important procedure for making what are often fact-intensive and complex decisions about the child.[13]

11 N. Cantwell, *The Best Interests of the Child in Intercountry Adoption*, UNICEF, 2014, https://www.unicef-irc.org/publications/712-the-best-interests-of-the-child-in-intercountry-adoption.html.

12 Cantwell, 2014, pp. 54, 60, 81; United Nations Committee on the Rights of the Child, 'General comment No. 14 (2013) on the right of the child to have his or her best interests taken as a primary consideration (Art. 3, para. 1)', 29 May 2013, CRC/C/GC/14, para. 4.

13 Cantwell, 2014, pp. 54-60; United Nations Committee on the Rights of the Child, 'General comment No. 14 (2013) on the right of the child to have his or her best interests taken as a primary consideration (Art. 3, para. 1)', 29 May 2013, CRC/C/GC/14, pp. 12-20.

The term 'best interests of the child' also embodies the balancing between the rights of the child and the rights of adults implicated in specific situations. Hence, the UNCRC specifies that "in all actions concerning children ... the best interests of the child shall be a primary consideration" (Art. 3(1)). This 'primary consideration' test prioritizes the rights of the child while leaving significant room for consideration of the rights of others, including adults, who may be impacted by decisions.[14] By contrast, the UNCRC insists that, as to adoption, the best interests of the child should be 'the paramount consideration' (Art. 21). 'The paramount consideration' as compared with 'a primary consideration' elevates the priority of the rights of the child as compared with adults[15] and counters longstanding tendencies to create and employ adoption for the interests of adults, such as the wishes of adults for children.[16] This tendency to create adoption systems in order to fulfil the wishes and demands of adults continues all the way to the present day, despite the contrary provisions of the UNCRC.[17]

The UNCRC refers specifically to children "in whose best interests cannot be allowed to remain in [his or her family environment]" (Art. 20(1)). This standard follows immediately after Article 19 concerning abuse, neglect, negligent treatment, exploitation and sexual abuse, and in context refers to circumstances where the life and safety of a child are seriously endangered (see also Art. 25, 34, 35, 36 UNCRC). Certainly, the UNCRC does not permit the removal of a child merely because the state might view another family as 'better' or 'best' for a child as compared with the original family. To the contrary, from a child rights point of view, absent significant harm, the 'best interests' of a child reside in being cared for and raised by the child's original family, particularly given the child's identity rights (see Art. 7, 8, 9 UNCRC; Art. 18, 19, 20 ACRWC).

This understanding of the concept of 'best interests of a child' is embedded in a child rights and human rights understanding of the relationship of children to their parents and families. From a child rights perspective, children do *not* have a right to be raised in 'a family', but, rather, each child has the right to know and be cared for by their specific family (see Art. 7, 8, 9 UNCRC; Art. 18, 19, 20 ACRWC). Children and families are

14 United Nations Committee on the Rights of the Child, 'General comment No. 14 (2013) on the right of the child to have his or her best interests taken as a primary consideration (Art. 3, para. 1)', 29 May 2013, CRC/C/GC/14, paras. 36-40.

15 Ibid., para. 38.

16 C. Baglietto, N. Cantwell and M. Dambach, 'Responding to Illegal Adoptions: A Professional Handbook', *International Social Services*, 2016, https://iss-ssi.org/wp-content/uploads/2023/04/Illegal_Adoption_ISS_Professional_Handbook.pdf, sections 7.1.2b, c, d.

17 See, e.g., Committee Investigating Intercountry Adoption, 2021, pp. 8-11 (acknowledging that, despite invoking constantly the best interests of the child, in practice intercountry system primarily served adoptive parents and the demand for children).

not fungible and parent-child relationships are not like dating relationships. There is a certain 'givenness' to original parent-child relationships that is permanent, no matter what happens subsequently; the relationship is literally written into our bodies, as DNA reveals. Children, of course, are not clones of their parents and have an original and unique humanity; but that humanity arises in and from specific relationships.

The recognition of the importance of parent-child and family bonds is not a mere sentiment and is not based on a romanticized understanding of family life. Family life indeed is often difficult and a mix of beautiful, mundane, foundational, frustrating and toxic. Nonetheless, procreation and family life are constitutive of our humanity; family life is where we come from in the literal physical sense of human procreation, genetic and gestational, as well as in the bonding in early childhood necessary to normal development.[18] We may in adult life grow away from our original families and parts of our original identities, but the very significance of those choices is based on the constitutive and formative nature of family life for human development. We are never blank slates insofar as we are human. Our stories always begin somewhere and with specific parents and family. To treat children as fungible objects that can simply be re-matched at will to a different family is to strip the child of a part of the human dignity that is the foundation of human rights, as it fails to recognize the child as a unique person.[19]

Hence, the 'best interests' exception to the child's right to be cared for and raised by the original parents and family is narrow.

Adoption, Children's Rights and the Separation of Children from Families

Adoption – particularly full adoption – is a legal transfer of a child from the original family to the adoptive family and hence involves a modification of identity.[20] Hence, every adoption involves a significant loss. The child loses the identity and experience of

---

18 See, e.g., R. Karen, *Becoming Attached: First Relationships and How They Shape Our Capacity to Love*, New York, Oxford, Oxford University Press, 1998; B. van der Kolk, *The Body Keeps the Score: Brain, Mind, and Body in the Healing of Trauma*, London, Penguin Books, 2014, pp. 107-124; M. van IJzendoorn, 'Attachment At An Early Age (0-5) and Its Impact on Children's Development', *Encyclopedia on Early Child Development*, September 2019, Rev. ed.

19 Universal Declaration of Human Rights, preamble & Art. 1; C. Baglietto, L. Bordier, M. Dambach and C. Jeannin, *Preserving "Family Relations": An Essential Feature of the Child's Right to Identity*, Geneva, Child Identity Protection, 2022, https://child-identity.org/images/files/CHIP-Preserving-Family-Relations-EN.pdf.

20 M. Dambach and C. Jeannin, *Policy Brief 1: Respecting the Child's Right to Identity in INTERCOUNTRY adoption*, Geneva, Child Identity Protection, https://child-identity.org/images/files/CHIP-Policy-Brief-Adoption-EN-V2.pdf.

being raised by (or continuing to be raised by) the original family; the original family loses the experience of raising the child (or continuing to raise the child) within the original nuclear and extended family.[21]

Adoption in this sense is not so much 'lesser' as it is additive; adoption necessarily builds on the procreative acts and family life that preceded the adoption. Whoever 'parents' a child day to day and over a significant portion of childhood and adolescence also becomes constitutive of the identity and humanity of the child, as human beings developmentally require parenting and family life in order to mature into mature adulthood. To be adopted in that sense is intrinsically complex and multilayered. Everyone who procreated and gestated and loved and parented that child counts; nothing goes to waste, and all of it matters. Although children can be resilient to different degrees, the fact that it all counts means that deficits all matter as well, including the losses intrinsic to adoption and neglect or abuse at any stage.[22]

Adoptive parenting, then, is also 'real parenting'. However, to the degree that adoption is based on an understanding of negating and completely replacing all that went before, adoption itself becomes a self-contradiction and contrary to human nature. Such self-contradiction complicates the life and development of adoptees, who are asked to deny a part of who they are as the price for the family life of the present and future that they need and enjoy. Too often, adoption has been conceived of as a Faustian bargain in which adoptees must betray either original or adoptive family; to the degree adoptees care about both the original and adoptive family, they are understood to be betraying both.[23]

Adoption, however, can be lived in a more open and additive way. Rather than subtracting the original family, adoption as additive self-consciously recognizes and builds on the original family's foundational roles. Adoption when done in this way can be legal and compatible with the rights and human dignity of the adoptee, so long as the prior separation of the child from the original family was legal and ethical.

21 Child Welfare Information Gateway, Helping Adopted Children Cope with Grief and Loss, https://www.childwelfare.gov/topics/adoption/adopt-parenting/helping/ ("Loss is a central theme to adoption, and it is experienced by all constellation members.").

22 See, e.g., H.D. Grotevant, A.Y.H. Lo, L. Fiorenzo and N.D. Dunbar, 'Adoptive Identity and Adjustment from Adolescence to Emerging Adulthood: A Person-Centered Approach', *Developmental Psychology*, Vol. 53, No. 11, 2017, pp. 2195-2204, https://www.ncbi.nlm.nih.gov/pmc/articles/PMC5679095/; Intercountry Adoptee Voices (ICAV), various resources about identity, https://intercountryadopteevoices.com/?s=identity.

23 See, e.g., B.J. Lifton, *Twice Born: Memoirs of an Adopted Daughter*, Other Press, 1975/2006; L. Dusky, *Hole in My Heart*, Tempe Arizona, Grand Canyon Press, 2015/2022.

Parental Responsibility and Rights and the Separation of Children from Families

Parental Rights and Responsibilities

Parents and families also have rights – and responsibilities – in relationship to their children. Hence, the separation of a child from the child's original family can also constitute serious deprivations of the rights of parents and families, as recognized in the September 2022 Joint Statement on illegal intercountry adoptions (Joint Statement).[24] The Joint Statement has particular weight, having been issued by the Committee on the Rights of the Child (hereinafter CRC), the Committee on Enforced Disappearances (hereinafter CED), the Special Rapporteur on the Promotion of Truth, Justice, Reparation and Guarantees of Non-recurrence, the Special Rapporteur on the Sale and Sexual Exploitation of Children, the Special Rapporteur on Trafficking in Persons, and the Working Group on Enforced or Involuntary Disappearances.[25] The Joint Statement specified that both the rights of the child and 'the right of family to protection' are violated by 'illegal intercountry adoptions'.[26]

The rights of family to protection, and allied rights and responsibilities of parents in relationship to their children, are recognized in a variety of modern human rights instruments. Thus, the UNCRC, while, of course, focused on children's rights, acknowledges that "... both parents have common responsibilities for the upbringing and development of the child. Parents ... have the primary responsibility for the upbringing and development of the child" (Art. 18). Further, states are obligated to "render appropriate assistance to parents ... in the performance of their child-rearing responsibilities" (Art. 18(2)).

Indeed, the modern human rights tradition from the beginning focused on the family and, thus, explicitly or implicitly, the rights and responsibilities of parents. The Universal Declaration of Human Rights (hereinafter UDHR)[27] provided that "[n]o one shall be subjected to arbitrary interference with his privacy, family, home [...]" (Art. 12). Further, 'men and women of full age' have 'the right to marry and to found a family' (Art. 16(1) UDHR). "Motherhood and childhood are entitled to special care and assistance" (Art. 25(2) UDHR). These rights are founded in the recognition that "[t]he family is the natural and fundamental group unit of society and is entitled to protection by society and the State" (Art. 16(3) UDHR). While developments as to

24 UN Human Rights Treaty Bodies, 29 September 2022.
25 Ibid., para. 1.
26 Ibid., para. 3.
27 UN General Assembly, Universal Declaration of Human Rights, 10 December 1948, G.A. Res. 217 A (III), https://www.ohchr.org/en/human-rights/universal-declaration/translations/english.

gender and sexual orientation may make some of this language controversial today, the basic direction and meaning is still foundational. Further, if the other rights recognized in the UDHR were successfully implemented – rights as to the standard of living "including food, clothing, housing, and medical care" (Art. 25), employment, just remuneration and just working conditions (Art. 23), and "reasonable limitation of working hours" (Art. 25), the capacity of parents and families to care for and raise their children would be much improved.

The protection of the family is echoed in very similar language in the International Covenant on Civil and Political Rights (hereinafter ICCPR) (see Art. 23) and in the International Covenant on Economic, Social, and Cultural Rights (hereinafter ICESCR) (see Art. 10), which both restate the foundational view of the family as the "natural and fundamental group unit of society".[28] The ICCPR restates the language as to the right to marry and found a family (Art. 23), while the ICESCR confirms the obligation of special protections to mothers (Art. 10).

Regional human rights instruments also focus on the protection of the family. The European Convention on Human Rights requires respect for 'private and family life' (Art. 8) and also protects the right to marry and found a family (Art. 12).[29] The American Convention on Human Rights echoes the UDHR language on the family as the "natural and fundamental group unit of society" and protects the right to 'marry and to raise a family'[30] (Art. 17). The African Charter on Human and People's Rights states in Article 18:

> 1. The family shall be the natural unit and basis of society. It shall be protected by the State which shall take care of its physical health and moral.
> 2. The State shall have the duty to assist the family which is the custodian of morals and traditional values recognized by the community.[31]

---

28 International Covenant on Civil and Political Rights, adopted 16 December 1966, entered into force 23 March 1976, 999 UNTS 171 (ICCPR), https://www.ohchr.org/en/instruments-mechanisms/instruments/international-covenant-civil-and-political-rights; International Convention on Economic, Social, and Cultural Rights, 16 December 1966, resolution 2200A (XXI), https://www.ohchr.org/en/instruments-mechanisms/instruments/international-covenant-economic-social-and-cultural-rights.

29 Council of Europe, European Convention for the Protection of Human Rights and Fundamental Freedoms, as amended by Protocols Nos. 11 and 14, 15, 4 November 1950, https://www.echr.coe.int/documents/d/echr/convention_ENG.

30 AOS, American Convention on Human Rights "Pact of San Jose, Costa Rica" (B-32), 22 January 1969, https://www.oas.org/dil/treaties_b-32_american_convention_on_human_rights.pdf.

31 African Charter on Human and Peoples' Rights, adopted 27 June 1981, entered into force 21 October 1986, (1982) 21 ILM 58 (African Charter), https://au.int/sites/default/files/treaties/36390-treaty-0011_-_african_charter_on_human_and_peoples_rights_e.pdf.

The Lack of State-Granted Remedies to First Families

It should be obvious that parents and families have rights and responsibilities in relationship to their children. Similarly, it should be obvious that the loss of children to parents and the family is a serious loss which can constitute a substantial deprivation of fundamental rights deserving of substantial remedies. Yet what is obvious becomes obscure to many in the context of adoption.

Hence, so far as I can tell, very few states have ever offered state assistance and remedies to original families that have lost their children to illegal intercountry adoption. The primary exception occurs outside the context of the conventional intercountry adoption system. Thus, the activism of the Mothers of the Plaza de Mayo, and later Grandmothers of the Plaza de Mayo, organized in response to the estimated 30,000 disappeared persons during the Dirty War in Argentina between 1976 and 1982, did lead to some state-assisted national remedies. Many of the disappeared were murdered, but remedies regarding illegal adoptions or placements of children are encompassed within these remedial efforts (see Chapter 3). This is an important model of first family activism leading to cooperation between activist organizations and states, in the context of a national trauma. It does not appear that remedial efforts in other Latin American countries, addressing abuses within intercountry adoption systems, have advanced as far as Argentina's response to disappeared persons in the context of the Dirty War (see Chapter 3). The lack of state-provided remedies for first families regarding illegal adoptions from conventional intercountry adoption systems is notable.

Further, in the entire modern history of intercountry adoption I can only identify a handful of cases in which original family members were successful in obtaining remedies from states, and these required the original family to pursue litigation in the courts of the receiving state, something beyond the capacity of most families of origin. These few cases are discussed later in the sections on remedies. For now, it is sufficient to lament the scarcity of state-provided remedies for first families.

If you lost your child...

Imagine that you sent your child to summer camp. The day comes to pick up your child, but you are told that your child is gone. Imagine that a few days after birth your child disappears from the hospital nursery. Imagine that your child signed up for an international exchange programme, living with a host family in another country while studying abroad. When the time comes for your child to return, you are notified that the host family has adopted your child, who is now no longer a part of your family.

In all of these instances, the normal expectation of parents would be that state and society treat such instances as kidnappings or missing children cases requiring immediate emergency response. Yet such response is almost unknown in the context of intercountry adoption. It is characteristic of intercountry adoption that the class of parents and families who lose their children are typically unable to elicit much response to the loss of their children even before the case is linked to adoption. If the case does become linked to intercountry adoption, the chances of any kind of assistance or investigation decline even further. Adoption legitimizes the separation in a context of state-enforced secrecy that creates a dead end as to investigations or remedies.

Even more discouraging is that recent state plans to respond to illegal intercountry adoption apparently lack remedies and responses for the original family, unless such are provided in the context of responding to requests and remedies for adoptees (see Chapter 3). Adoptees, however, are commonly unaware of the circumstance which separated them from their original family and commonly do not initiate requests for birth/roots searches until well into adult life. If remedies for illegal separations of children from families wait for adoptees to initiate an investigation or roots search, such will often never occur, and the vast majority will not start until decades after that separation. Given the legal understanding of illegal separations and illegal adoptions as continuing wrongs,[32] the failure to provide mechanisms by which original families may initiate investigations and receive assistance is a fatal flaw in intercountry adoption systems.

Illegal Separations of Children from Families and Intercountry Adoption Systems

The separation of a child from the child's original family is only legal, under the UNCRC, where either 1. It was not possible for the child to remain or be returned to the original family (Art. 7(1)) or 2. Owing to circumstances such as abuse, neglect, maltreatment or sexual abuse, the child cannot remain, according to the best interests of the child (Art. 3(1), 19, 20(1), 34, 36).

Given years of research on illicit adoption practices, combined with the reported results of recent investigations, my conclusion is that "[t]he majority of the estimated one million intercountry adoptions completed over the last seventy years … occurred in contexts of chronic violations of basic ethical principles as now codified in international instruments".[33] The basic ethical violation in view is that of wrongfully building

32 UN Human Rights Treaty Bodies, 29 September, para. 12 ("States shall prohibit illegal intercountry adoptions as a continuing offense under criminal law.").

33 See, e.g., D.M. Smolin, 'The Case for Moratoria on Intercountry Adoption', *Southern California Interdisciplinary Law Journal*, Vol. 30, No. 2, 2021, pp. 501, 506.

adoptions on a foundation of unnecessary separations of children from their original families.

I have previously identified the following circumstances by which children have commonly been separated from their families, which all violate current international children's rights standards:[34]

Child Laundering
Child laundering is the use of force (i.e., kidnapping), fraud (misinforming the original family as to the significance of consents or the consequences of placements) or funds (the buying of children and/or consents, usually from desperately poor original families) to illicitly obtain children and separate them from the original family. The term child laundering captures as well the following stages, by which children illicitly separated from their families are then given paperwork identifying them as adoptable orphans and then processed for adoption.[35] Such illegal behaviour has been identified in adoptions from South Asia, East Asia, Southeast Asia, Latin America and Africa.[36]

Poverty
Adoptions due primarily to poverty have been an often accepted and central part of intercountry adoption systems from Latin America, South Asia, Southeast Asia, East Asia, Africa and Europe. To this day, too many perceive intercountry adoption as an appropriate response to poverty. To the contrary, current ethical and legal standards prohibit intercountry adoption or child separations due primarily to poverty. Given contemporary human rights standards, taking the children of the poor is a form of exploitation rather than compassion. There is cruelty and irony in spending far more on an intercountry adoption, including the expensive international travel involved, than would have been necessary to assist the family in staying together.[37]

When adoption is understood as a set of relationships and interactions between the first family, child and adoptive family, the problem becomes clearer. Imagine a circumstance where a comparatively wealthy family from Europe, Australia, the United States or Canada is travelling in a developing country, where they meet a desperately poor family struggling to provide the basics of food, shelter, clothing and education for their children. As the families interact, the wealthy foreign family is faced with a

34 Ibid., pp. 504-511; Smolin, 2006; Smolin, 2023.
35 Smolin, 2006; Smolin, 2021, pp. 506-507; Smolin, 2023.
36 Ibid.
37 UN Guidelines for the Alternative Care of Children, 24 February 2010, G.A. Res. 64/142, Art. 10, 15, 32; Smolin, 2021, p. 308; D.M. Smolin, 'Intercountry Adoption and Poverty: A Human Rights Analysis', *Capitol University Law Review*, Vol. 36, No. 2, 2007, pp. 413-454.

choice. They could easily afford to provide some forms of assistance that would enable the poor family to stay together and provide sufficiently for the children. But since the foreign family wants children for themselves, they instead spend far more money on an intercountry adoption than would be necessary to keep the first family intact, and take one or more of the children away forever from the original family, leaving the remaining family members destitute. Or perhaps the wealthy family even provides assistance to the poor family, but conditions that assistance on relinquishing some of their children. Or perhaps the wealthy family allows the poor family to relinquish their children based on the false premise that in sending their children abroad to another family they are expanding their family overseas, rather than subtracting some of their children from their family – the false hope that their children will still be a part of their family, will stay in contact while growing up, and will be in a position to assist them as adults.

Conceived as a set of interactions, such a choice is indefensible, and clearly exploits the vulnerabilities created by poverty. Clarity may come when the adoptee grows up and asks the adoptive parents: 'Why didn't you help me stay with my original parents and family?' If the truthful answer is 'we wanted you for ourselves', the ethical and legal breach should be painfully obvious.

Of course, in intercountry adoption practice such an interchange usually does not happen directly as intermediaries navigate all stages and the first and adoptive families do not meet at all, or only do so after the adoption has been arranged. But creating systems that scale up and depersonalize an illegal and unethical set of interactions makes the situation worse rather than better. Hence, adoption systems which systemically permit adoptions based primarily on poverty, without systemically offering unconditional aid for the family to stay together as an alternative to adoption, are systemically illegal and unethical.

Unmarried Mothers

Much of the modern history of adoption law and practice was shaped by systemically using adoption as a response to the situation of unmarried parents and the single mother. For example, the secrecy and closed records so central to many modern domestic systems arose because adoption laws were aimed primarily at single mothers in times of extreme stigma for mother and child. After all, the practices of secrecy and closed records make little sense for adoptions of literal orphans whose parents are both deceased. The baby-scoop era of systemically coercive domestic adoptions from single mothers occurred from around 1945 until around 1980 in many nations, including

Australia, Belgium, Canada, the United States and the UK.[38] Related mistreatment of single mothers and their children in Ireland are a major national scandal.[39] Domestic adoption systems were organized around exploiting societal and professional stigmas against single mothers and their children. Unfortunately, the same practice of building adoption systems in significant part around coercing stigmatized unmarried mothers to relinquish their children has also been a significant part of some intercountry adoption systems, particularly in adoptions from South Korea,[40] and also from other nations such as Greece[41] and India.[42]

Like adoptions based on poverty, this is another example of adoption systems of the past that were self-consciously based on criteria which are today understood to constitute serious ethical and legal violations.[43] Like adoptions based on poverty, this is a kind of unethical and illegal adoption that persists to an embarrassing degree in some intercountry adoption systems.

Exploiting Cultural Contrasts on the Meaning of Adoption

In many cultures and nations that have served as sending countries, family life is comparatively 'additive', allowing for the addition or acceptance of family members beyond the nuclear family – additional fathers, mothers, uncles and aunts. Similarly,

38 See, e.g., A. Fessler, *The Girls Who Went Away: The Hidden History of Women Who Surrendered Children for Adoption in the Decades Before Roe v. Wade*, London, Penguin Books, 2007; Baglietto et al., 2016, pp. 35-39 and 187-188; Senate Community Affairs References Committee, Parliament Australia, Commonwealth Contribution to Former Forced Adoption Policies and Practices, 29 February 2012, https://www.aph.gov.au/parliamentary_business/committees/senate/community_affairs/completed_inquiries/2010-13/commcontribformerforcedadoption/report/index; Who Are We?, Origins Australia, Forced Adoption Support Network, https://www.originsnsw.com/#:~:text=Origins%20was%20formed%20to%20research,care%3B%20and%20Aboriginal%20child%20removal; 'Flemish Bishops Apologize for Forced Adoptions', *Catholic Culture*, 25 November 2015, https://www.catholicculture.org/news/headlines/index.cfm?storyid=26798.

39 See, e.g., Government of Ireland, Department of Children, Equality, Disability, Integration and Youth, *Final Report of the Commission of Investigation into Mother and Baby Homes*, 12 January 2021, last updated on 22 November 2021, https://www.gov.ie/en/publication/d4b3d-final-report-of-the-commission-of-investigation-into-mother-and-baby-homes/#; CLANN: Ireland's Unmarried Mothers and their Children: Gathering the Data, 17 December 2021, http://clannproject.org/.

40 See, e.g., T. Hubinette, 'Korean Adoption History', *in* E. Kim (ed.), *Community 2004. Guide to Korea for overseas adopted Koreans*, Overseas Koreans Foundation, 2004, p. 10, http://www.tobiashubinette.se/adoption_history.pdf; C. Sang-Hun, 'Group Resists Stigma for Unwed Mothers', *New York Times*, 7 October 2009, https://www.nytimes.com/2009/10/08/world/asia/08mothers.html.

41 See, e.g., G. Van Steen, *Adoption, Memory, and Cold War Greece: Kid Pro Quo?*, Ann Arbor, University of Michigan Press, 2019; R. Bonner, 'Tales of Stolen Babies And Lost Identities; A Greek Scandal Echoes in New York', *New York Times*, 13 April 1996, https://www.nytimes.com/1996/04/13/nyregion/tales-of-stolen-babies-and-lost-identities-a-greek-scandal-echoes-in-new-york.html.

42 See, e.g., P. Bos, *Once a Mother: Relinquishment and Adoption from the Perspective of Unmarried Mothers in South India*, PhD Thesis, University of Amsterdam, 2007.

43 UN General Assembly, 'Guidelines for the Alternative Care of Children: Resolution/Adopted by the General Assembly', 24 February 2010, Art. 10, A/RES/64/142.

the extended family and broader categories of kinship have more day-to-day centrality and authority than may be common in some contemporary Western cultures. In such contexts, children may commonly circulate among trusted adults.[44] In addition, in some nations that have served as sending countries, 'orphanages' or 'hostels' serve as a kind of social safety net or boarding school for the poor, which poor families rely on in times of stress for the provision of food and education, while maintaining parental responsibility and status. In many cultures the concept that a parent can sever parental rights and responsibilities by signing a document is unfamiliar and appears absurd.[45]

These widespread cultural contexts in many nations that have served as countries of origin for intercountry adoption make purported 'consents to adoption' problematic. Families are likely to understand adoption as an opportunity to extend their family and create opportunities for their children and family, without in any way relinquishing the child's status in the original family. Families are unlikely to understand themselves as severing their relationship with their children. Even if the families understand that the child will be travelling overseas, they are likely to understand adoption as a kind of long-term sponsorship, or study abroad programme, and to perceive the 'adoptive' parents as additions to and extensions of the original family, rather than replacements for the birth family. If the term 'adoption' exists in the culture, it may refer to practices similar to simple adoption or guardianship that do not sever the link between the child and the original family. Indeed, even judges or government officials may not always fully understand the implications of full adoption in contexts where simple adoption or guardianship is also the prevalent legal practice and where the concept of full adoption involving a full severance of the parent-child relationship is not present in domestic law or practice.[46]

These cultural contrasts have been exploited as a part of child laundering schemes to fraudulently obtain consents. Intermediaries obtain consents to 'adoption' while making false promises of continued contact and relationship. Indeed, intermediaries do not necessarily have to lie but can instead simply allow first families to apply their own cultural understandings to the arrangement. Even if intermediaries are more ethical and attempt to explain the true meaning of a consent to an international adoption to a

---

44 C. Fonseca, D. Marre and B. San Román, 'Child Circulation in a Globalized Era: Anthropological Reflections', *in* R.L. Ballard, N.H. Goodno, R.F. Cochran, Jr. and J.A. Milbrandt (eds.), *The Intercountry Adoption Debate: Dialogues Across Disciplines*, Newcastle upon Tyne: Cambridge Scholars Publishing, 2015, pp. 157-192; C. Fonseca, 'Patterns of Shared Parenthood Among the Brazilian Poor', *Social Text*, Vol. 21, No. 1, 2003, pp. 111, 113-115; R.R. Högbacka, *Global Families, Inequality and Transnational Adoption: The De-kinning of First Mothers*, London, Springer, 2017; Loibl, 2019, pp. 67-68, 91-93.

45 Ibid.

46 Ibid.

first family, it may be difficult or nearly impossible to achieve actual understanding on behalf of the family.[47]

Recent developments in receiving states, like the United States, towards 'open adoption' as a prevalent practice within domestic full adoption systems traditionally practising full severance, closed records and secrecy, as well as the increased acceptance of birth searches in both domestic and intercountry adoptions, suggests that perhaps the 'additive' views common in non-Western cultures are more realistic views of the concept of 'adoption'.[48] Building adoption on the legal fiction that children are not related to those who brought them into this world, despite ties of genetics, gestation and varying periods of family life, was in my view never compatible with human dignity and human nature. This is an issue for adoption reform in general. But for present purposes, it is clearly illegal and unethical to fraudulently obtain consents to adoption by exploiting the cultural and legal disjunctions in the meaning of 'adoption'.

Adoptions from China

China has been the leading country of origin since taking over that position from South Korea in the mid-1990s. China maintained that position until its numbers were sharply reduced during Covid-19. China has sent over 140,000 children to other nations for intercountry adoption.[49]

The Chinese adoption system has several distinctive features that complicate discussion of both illegal adoptions and also remedies. First, unlike many other nations, the Chinese system is state controlled, including the participating 'orphanages' or social welfare institutions. The Chinese government arranges and controls all aspects of China's side of intercountry adoption; matches between children and prospective adoptive parents are determined by China's central authority.[50] China thus avoids the situation of private orphanages dealing directly with foreign agencies or intermediaries. To the extent that private Chinese intermediaries are involved, it occurs in illegal procedures in which private individuals have obtained children and then sold them to orphanages.

47 Ibid.

48 M.L. Seymore, 'Openness in International Adoption', *Columbia Human Rights Law Review*, Vo. 46, No. 3, 2015, pp. 163, 164, 168-183 (describing movement towards openness in domestic adoptions in the United States).

49 P. Selman, *Twenty Years of Hague Convention: A Statistical Review*, HCCH, 2015, https://www.hcch.net/en/instruments/conventions/publications1/?dtid=32&cid=69; P. Selman, *Global Statistics for Intercountry Adoption: Receiving States and States of Origin 2004-2021*, HCCH, 2023, https://www.hcch.net/en/publications-and-studies/details4/?pid=5891&dtid=32.

50 HCCH, Country Profile: China, 17 May, 2022, https://assets.hcch.net/docs/7c03cfbb-288f-4260-a58f-397585e12728.pdf; United States Department of State, How to Adopt, China, https://travel.state.gov/content/travel/en/Intercountry-Adoption/Intercountry-Adoption-Country-Information/China.html; L. Meng and Z. Kai, 'Orphan Care in China', *Social Work & Society*, Vol. 7, No. 1, 2009, pp. 46-47.

Unfortunately, government officials reportedly have abused their coercive authority to obtain children and then also sold the children to government orphanages.[51]

Second, unlike many other nations, China does not provide a legal means for parents to relinquish their children for state care or place their children for adoption. Thus, first families secretly 'abandon' their children while trying to avoid getting detected or caught, a process that also creates risks as the child must simply be left somewhere in the expectation of being quickly found.[52] This use of abandonment limits the information available as to origins, because there are no official documents identifying or describing the original parents. Abandonment as the official pathway for adoption also makes it even easier to hide illicit practices, as officials may follow the procedures for an abandoned child even where the child has been purchased or coercively taken.[53]

Third, the modern history of Chinese intercountry adoption developed in the context of China's population control policies, which provide a highly coercive context for decisions by first families. Given that coercive context, the concept of giving consents "freely" (Art. 4(c)(2), Hague Adoption Convention) is problematic.[54]

Fourth, in order to protect against evasions of their population control policies, China during certain periods had stricter rules for domestic prospective adoptive parents than for foreign prospective adoptive parents, a systemic violation of the subsidiarity principle requiring preference for domestic adoption over intercountry adoption.[55]

Fifth, during the peak years of China's role as a sending nation, girls overwhelmingly outnumbered boys. For example, as reported by China to the Hague Conference on Private International Law (HCCH) for 2005, one of China's peak years, China sent 18 boys and 1,626 girls under one year old, and 596 boys and 11,785 girls aged one to four.[56] This confirms the narrative that China's internationally adopted children were relinquished due to a combination of the coercive impacts of China's population

---

51 B. Demick, 'Chinese Babies Stolen by Officials for Foreign Adoptions', *L.A. Times*, 20 September 2009, https://www.latimes.com/archives/la-xpm-2009-sep-20-fg-china-adopt20-story.html; B.H. Stuy, 'Open Secret: Cash and Coercion in China's International Adoption Program', *Cumberland Law Review*, Vol. 44, No. 3, 2014, pp. 355-422.

52 K.A. Johnson, *Wanting a Daughter, Needing a Son: Abandonment, Adoption, and Orphanage Care in China*, St. Paul, Minnesota, Yeong & Yeong, 2004; K.A. Johnson, *China's Hidden Children: Abandonment, Adoption, and the Human Costs of the One-Child Policy*, University of Chicago Press, 2016.

53 See sources cited in footnote 51.

54 See sources cited in footnote 52.

55 Johnson, 2004, pp. 118-119, 155-182.

56 HCCH, China Adoption Statistics, https://assets.hcch.net/docs/f206acda-7dd4-4971-bca4-876a29dad958.pdf.

control policies and a culturally felt need to have at least one son.[57] Thus, probably most of the children sent for intercountry adoption in China, particularly during the peak years when most were healthy young girls, were separated from their families due in significant part to China's coercive population control policies.[58]

The numbers and characteristics of children being sent for adoption from China changed significantly in recent years. As it became clearer that there were very few healthy infants or toddlers of either sex in the orphanages, and as domestic adoptions were allowed more room to flourish, it became clear that there was no need to send healthy infants or toddlers for foreign adoption. Chinese citizens were willing to adopt healthy infants and toddlers of both sexes in sufficient numbers to negate any need for foreign adopters of such children. Further, as China has progressed from a one-child to a two-child to three-child policy,[59] and from concerns with overpopulation to concerns with an ageing and gender imbalanced population, sending healthy young girls abroad became an absurdity. In more recent years almost all of the children made available for adoption from China have been children with very serious disabilities, and/or much older children. Even with these changes, the numbers declined significantly.[60]

This analysis suggests that the modern programme of intercountry adoption from China was built on systemic government pressures in pursuit of population control that had the unintended but systemic impact of producing large numbers of abandonments of baby girls.[61] Building an adoption programme on such coercive policies violates human rights norms.[62] Nonetheless, in the early years, when reports indicated that the Chinese orphanages were overwhelmed by the large numbers of abandoned baby girls, and that children were sometimes receiving catastrophically poor care, there were sympathetic reasons to adopt from China. The numbers of adoptions from China increased dramatically and China seemed to have unlimited numbers of infant and toddler girls available for adoption. Chinese orphanages participating in sending children for intercountry adoption received thousands of dollars per intercountry adoption directly from the adoptive parents, and adoptive parents formed non-profit organizations to funnel additional funds to those orphanages for the children left behind. Scaling up Chinese adoptions to meet these felt needs, however, helped create financial incentives. Those financial incentives may not have been harmful in the early

57 Johnson, 2004, 2016.

58 Ibid.

59 BBC, 'China Allows Three Children in Major Policy Shift', *BBC News*, 31 May 2021, https://www.bbc.com/news/world-asia-china-57303592.

60 Selman, 2023.

61 Johnson, 2004, pp. 1-23, 43-48, 49-64, 76.

62 See, e.g., Art. 16(e) CEDAW: right to "decide freely and responsibly on the number and spacing of their children".

years when China's orphanages were overwhelmed with abandoned baby girls; indeed, perhaps those incentives caused some to pick up abandoned babies and take them to the orphanages. However, by the time the numbers were peaking, around 2005, the numbers of abandoned baby girls had sharply declined. It appears that sex-selective abortion significantly replaced sex-selective abandonment when ultrasound machines became widely used in China. China made it illegal to tell pregnant women the sex of their foetus and tried to make sex-selective abortion illegal in a context where abortion itself was widely available and legal. These prohibitions were difficult to enforce, however, and it appears that sex-selective abortion became common. Orphanages that had grown used to the benefits of sending children for intercountry adoption now had a shortage instead of an overabundance of healthy young baby and toddler girls. In order to continue the revenue stream of orphanage 'donations', the orphanages that had once been overwhelmed with abandoned baby girls were buying children. A market in adoptable young infants had been created with the orphanages as buyers in order to secure children to send abroad. This led to other abuses as population control officials sometimes took children from first families for the purpose of selling the children to orphanages. Private intermediaries were also selling children to orphanages. What had begun to fill a need was now incentivizing a market in children.[63]

This is, of course, a compressed and simplified narrative of the Chinese adoption system. It sets the context, however, for trying to define when, in the context of China, children were illegally separated from their families, and also indicates the difficulties of creating remedies for Chinese adoptions.

This narrative regarding adoptions from China is a reminder that each country of origin has its own specific narrative that impacts the kinds of illegal practices and the availability of remedies. Most of this chapter does not focus on individual nations, but instead describes categories of illegal adoptions and issues as to remedies that are common across multiple nations. Some of the chapters that follow focus more specifically on a single nation or a specific group of nations.

In the end, however, remedies for illegal intercountry adoptions must be remedies for individual adoptions that occurred between a specific country of origin and a

---

63 I describe and analyse these events at greater length in D.M. Smolin, 'The Missing Girls of China: Population, Policy, Culture, Gender, Abortion, Abandonment, and Adoption in East-Asian Perspective', *Cumberland Law Review*, Vol. 41, No. 1, 2010, https://works.bepress.com/david_smolin/9/; see also HCCH, China Adoption Statistics, https://assets.hcch.net/docs/f206acda-7dd4-4971-bca4-876a29dad958.pdf; Demick, 2009; Stuy, 2014; American World Adoption, China Adoption Travel Overview, p. 7 (adoptive families required to bring $7,700 in cash to China, including $7,500 in $100 bills, which includes 'orphanage donation' of $5,000 to $5,500), http://legacy.awaa.org/downloads/Travel/China_NonHague_Travel_Packet.pdf.

specific receiving state. Hence, in the end there will be no unified system of remedies, as expertise as to each state involved is needed to effectively provide remedies, and remedies must ultimately be local. One question, then, is how one creates systemic remedies in this complex multinational context.

Creating Systemic Remedies for Systemic Abuses

Seventy years of systemic abuses in intercountry adoption systems require systemic remedies. The remedies should match the gravity of the wrongs. Hundreds of thousands of adoptees were directly impacted. Often overlooked, however, is that such systemic abuses also deeply harmed many millions who comprise the original parents, siblings and family members of those who lost children to unethical and illegal intercountry adoptions. Adoptive families may appear to be the beneficiaries of such a system, but, in fact, those families relied on governments, intermediaries, agencies and intercountry adoption systems to ensure that the children they adopted came to them legally and ethically and were truly in need of a family – rather than having been wrongly separated from a family. The breaking of that implicit promise means that in many instances the adoptive families are also victims of these systems. It is a tragedy to make the extraordinary commitment and effort to adopt a child in need of a family, when the truth is that the child was, in fact, wrongfully taken from the first family.

The systemic nature of the abuses means that, in principle, most intercountry adoptions require a remedy. The majority of adoptions occurred in times and places where at least one of the kinds of unethical and illegal separations of children from parents was endemic – child laundering, exploitation of poverty, coercive pressures on single mothers or exploitation of cultural disparities. The first needed remedy is a determination of whether the adoptee was unethically and illegally separated from the original family. The only way to know whether an individual adoptee was illegally separated from the original family is to conduct an investigation that includes a birth search. Reviewing records and interviewing intermediaries is relevant but not sufficient, because records are so often unreliable and intermediaries not always truthful or accurate in their accounts.

This creates several dilemmas. In principle, most of the intercountry adoptions over the last seventy years should be investigated to determine whether the adoptees were improperly separated from their families. Such investigations would require a birth search in addition to a review of records and interviews of intermediaries and others. Who is going to initiate such investigations? Who is going to conduct them? Who is going to pay for them? Who is going to help adoption triad members navigate the relational and emotional complexities and traumas?

Thus far, governments have generally not provided remedies or assistance and indeed have sometimes impeded remedies by refusing to make records available. There is no system for remedies but rather adoption triad members (adoptees, adoptive families or original family members) working to self-remedy by initiating their own investigations and searches. Adoption triad members are often assisted by a variety of non-governmental actors. Some non-profit organizations have been formed to assist adoption triad members. Some individuals may assist without charging anything or only request reimbursement of expenses. Some offer their services for pay, with widely varying levels of expertise and empathy; the fees and expenses charged can be quite high, with the costs typically borne by adult adoptees. The rates of success with searches vary widely from country to country, the years since separation from the original family and the information available. The current situation of self-remedying illegal intercountry adoption necessarily produces haphazard results that supply remedies only to a very small proportion of those impacted (see Chapters 2 to 7 and 9).

A few nations (e.g. the Netherlands and Colombia) have proposed or initiated systems to provide remedies, or at least post-adoption services, for adoptees. No nation, so far as I know, has created a system for original family members that does not depend on adoptees first initiating a search, with the possible exception of Argentina, which is a response to the national trauma of the Dirty War and does not involve the conventional intercountry adoption system (see Chapters 3, 7, 9).

Could a system be created for systemically providing remedies for illegal intercountry adoptions? The following obstacles would have to be overcome.

Obstacles to Remedies

To the degree that remedies are not sought until the adoptee is an adult, full remedies are literally impossible. The adoptee was raised in a different family, culture and nation than would have occurred had the wrongful separation and subsequent adoption never occurred. The adoptee has become in many ways a different person than they would have been had the wrongful separation and subsequent adoption never occurred. No one can give back to the adoptee the childhood that would have been and the person they would have become. Similarly, no one can give back to the family of origin the experience of raising their child to adulthood and the bonding that would have occurred. Childhood is a developmental stage of life that cannot be restored, and its consequences for the child and the child's family are permanent.

The impossibility of full remedies for adult adoptees and their original families highlights the even higher stakes for remedies when adoptees are still children. Remedies for adoptee children may obviously still impact the childhood of the adoptee. Remedies for child adoptees raise the controversial issue of possibly returning the adoptee to the original family. Once the adoptee is an adult, the adoptee has the choice of where to live and with whom to relate; during childhood, however, while the child should participate in such decisions,[64] adults must take the responsibility to make difficult decisions.

Before addressing the difficult remedial issues related to child adoptees, this section reviews the barriers to remedies applicable regardless of the age of the adoptee.

1. First families are typically too powerless and poor to effectively seek remedies. First families may have been enlisted in their own victimization, for example, signing documents they did not understand or making decisions under the coercive impacts of poverty and/or stigmatized single parenthood. Being manipulated into participating in one's own victimization (and that of one's child) can create a crippling sense of guilt and self-blame that inhibits victims from seeking remedies. First families may face abuse and threats from the intermediaries in their own country that profited from the intercountry adoption and are unlikely to be in a social or economic position to defend themselves or challenge the power and connections of those intermediaries. Government officials in their own country that participated in the adoption will most likely be completely unsympathetic and non-cooperative and also may subject the original family to threats of negative consequences if they pursue remedies.

2. Adoptees most often are not aware of their own history, as they were too young to understand or even remember the circumstances under which they were separated from their original families. Even those separated at older ages may not understand the adult interactions and decisions that led to their losing their original families. Providing investigations and remedies for victims who do not know the stories of their own victimization is particularly difficult.

3. Adoptees have been recruited into their adoptive identity at ages at which this identity is constitutive of their development, family relations, personality and character. This recruitment and formation into their adoptive identity delays, changes and can limit the extent to which adoptees actually want remedies. Although some adoptees crave more information about their origins at a young age, most adoptees are not interested in investigating their pre-adoptive history until at least the teen years, and many not until well into adulthood. Some adoptees would prefer never to confront the intense emotions and questions intrinsic to a birth search. Adoptees may experience investigations and birth searches as profoundly unsettling and threatening

64 Art. 12 UNCRC.

as they can disrupt the adoptee's sense of self as formed in the adoptive family. While many, perhaps most, adoptees do eventually wish – sometimes intensely – for more information about their origins, they often lack the cultural and linguistic knowledge and skills to fully understand the stories of their origins once discovered. This lack of cultural and linguistic knowledge and skills also creates substantial barriers to positive post-reunion relationships. Adoptees may wish to stop the process of remedies, temporarily or permanently, at any stage of the process – investigation, document search, birth search, reunion or post-reunion relationships. Providing remedies for a group of victims that have been socialized in such a way as to limit their interest and desire for remedies, and for whom remedies can be sometimes intensely desired and sometimes rejected or delayed, is extremely difficult.

4. Remedies for illegal adoptions contradict the legal regime for intercountry adoption, which have strongly favoured full severance adoption and are thus based on the legal destruction of the original identity of the adoptee and the legal destruction of relationships between the adoptee and the first family. The same states which legally destroyed the original legal identity of the child and the original parent-child relationship are now expected to investigate and attempt to at least partially restore what those states had destroyed. Adoptees who were often raised in their adoptive families based on a unitary adoptive identity are now exploring or asked to explore a completely new identity which includes both original and adoptive identity. The process of exploring, seeking and providing remedies radically alters and places into flux the expectations to which adoptees, adoptive parents and first families are subject.

5. Adoptive parents usually were not involved in and were unaware of the illegal conduct involved in the adoption of their children. The information that adoptive parents were given about the adoption are often inaccurate or lack critically important details. Adoptive parents have generally trusted the often false information they have been given and thus presume their adoptions were legal and ethical. Having been promised full severance adoptions, many adoptive parents perceive the original family as a threat to their relationship with their adopted children. Even if adoptive parents have been more comfortable with the concept of openness in adoption, the possibility of illegal adoption raises the fear of literally losing the child forever if the child is returned to the first family. Adoptive parents who feel bonded to the adoptee and understand that they made a permanent commitment to the adoptee understandably have trouble pivoting to the possibilities for altering those relationships and commitments. All of these circumstances often result in adoptive families being highly resistant to investigations or birth searches or reunions, and often lead adoptive families to minimize any wrongdoing that is discovered.

6. The legal and cultural practices of full severance secret adoption in many states are weakening in recent years, but nonetheless create obstacles to remedies. Agencies, courts, hospitals, orphanages and governments may refuse to turn over documents or information based on the premise of full severance secrecy. Wrongdoing is particularly easy to hide in adoption systems that maintain secrecy, rather than transparency, as their ethical code. Adoptive parents and adoptees may experience information about origins, investigations, searches and reunions as destabilizing to adoptive relationships. Interest in the original family may be perceived as disloyalty to the adoptive family. Full severance adoption creates expectations that the past will not be examined or reopened and that no family relationship exists between adoptees and original families; these expectations then serve to hinder the investigations, searches and reunions necessary to remedy illegal adoptions.

7. The common situation of not seeking or providing remedies until adoptees are well into adulthood, decades after separation of the child from the original family, creates numerous obstacles. Original family members may have died, moved or remarried. The intermediaries involved may also have died, changed jobs or moved, or may be difficult to locate. Memories may become increasingly unreliable. Records may have been discarded, lost or destroyed. Investigations, searches and reunions decades after the separation can still be highly productive and healing, especially given the intergenerational and broader familial impacts of adoption. But the difficulties do increase over time.

8. The expectations and wishes of adoption triad members often conflict. Sometimes original family members resist reunion entirely, reject adopted-out family members, or only want to meet in secret, while adoptees are seeking reunions and restored relationships. On the other hand, adoptees sometimes want information but not reunion, or after reunion adoptees may refuse to engage in ongoing contact, while first families wish to restore familial relationships and make up for lost time. Given the full spectrum of responses by adoption triad members, there is often going to be a mismatch between the wishes of adoption triad members. These conflicts arise as traumas are reopened in a context of conflicting cultural understandings of family life. Communication is often hindered in addressing these sensitive issues by the lack of a common language.

9. Many intercountry adoptions took the children from the poor of developing countries and sent them to middle class to wealthy families in developed nations. This means that there is often a very large economic disparity between the first family and the adoptive family, and also between the first family and the adoptee. In the context of such a large disparity, what the adoptive family or adoptee perceives as the normal cost of a casual evening out for a meal and/or entertainment may constitute more than

the monthly income of the first family. Family relationships across such stark economic disparities pose severe difficulties. It is natural for first families to ask for money from family members perceived to be quite wealthy, in cultural contexts where relatives are commonly expected to help one another financially. It is also natural for adoptees to experience requests for money, in the midst of or after reunions, as an indication that their first family cares more about money than about them. First families are unlikely to understand the monetary pressures that adoptees and adoptive families experience in their own contexts and are unlikely to understand cultural contexts which discourage constant sharing of financial resources within extended families. Requests for assistance are likely to be a chronic feature of restored family relationships, rather than a mere one-time request. Thus, economic disparities and cultural differences as to how money is or is not shared within extended families are a severe obstacle to a fully restored relationship between the adoptee and the first family.

10. There is a distinct lack of political will on behalf of both receiving states and states of origin to provide remedies for illegal intercountry adoption. Intercountry adoption is a low-priority governmental service impacting comparatively few children and families, as compared with either the entire population or, more specifically, as compared with the numbers of vulnerable children or the numbers of children in some form of alternative care (i.e. foster care, institutional care, etc.) To the degree that intercountry adoption has been prioritized in ways disproportionate to its actual impacts, it stems from the monetary inducements providing disproportionate financial benefits for intermediaries, the demand for children within receiving states, and the historical reputation of intercountry adoption as a humanitarian intervention and an opportunity for positive international relations. Whatever priority intercountry adoption may have had dissipates when the subject turns to providing remedies for illegal intercountry adoption. Most of the empowered stakeholders in intercountry adoption – the governmental agencies, private and governmental intermediaries, adoptive parents and prospective adoptive parents – are highly resistant to accepting the evidence regarding a high prevalence of illegal and unethical practices, and are also resistant to providing resources or assisting remedies. Remedies for illegal intercountry adoption require states to acknowledge serious failures, which many states are quite unwilling to do. Thus far, activist adoptees and child rights institutions and organizations have been the primary voices urging investigations and remedies. Those voices, however, are usually only enough to create temporary and symbolic action regarding illegal adoptions that fall far short of any kind of systemic response to systemic abuses.

11. Remedies for illegal intercountry adoptions require actions to be carried out in both the receiving state and the state of origin. The adoptee and adoptive family reside in the receiving state, while the first family resides in the state of origin. In addition, there are important records and documents in both the receiving state and the state of

origin, and intermediaries are located in both the receiving state and the state of origin. Places of birth and of temporary care are located in the state of origin. The necessity of actions in both states substantially raises the cost and complexities of undertaking investigations, searches and reunions.

12. The necessity of investigations and actions in both states exacerbates the problem of a lack of political will. Even if one state has the political will, this is often not enough, as help is needed from both. Further, even states that might be willing to attempt to remedy illegal adoptions may hesitate or refuse to do so if it risks poisoning relationships with the other state. Intercountry adoption is a low priority compared with the strategic, military, trade, cultural and economic priorities in international relationships, and states are unlikely to be willing to unsettle these more important goals of international relationships for the sake of addressing wrongdoing in intercountry adoption.

13. Intercountry adoption as a practice is built on the cooperation of receiving states and states of origin. The Hague Adoption Convention sought to formalize this cooperation into a "system of co-operation" (see Art. 1(b) The Hague Adoption Convention), but, of course, it is basic to any intercountry adoption, as a child is transferred from one family and nation to another family and nation. Given the necessity for investigations of illegal practices to be conducted in both states, it would be logical for states to cooperate in these investigations. The Hague Adoption Convention provides the possibility of a formal procedure by which the central authorities of one state may communicate with the central authority of another state, both as to "general evaluation reports" (Art. 9(d)) or as to "a particular adoption situation" (Art. 9(e)). Unfortunately, that procedure of cooperation has been either unused or abused as to remedies for illegal intercountry adoptions. Typically, there have been no governmental investigations of illegal intercountry adoptions, but when they have occurred, usually only one of the two states has been willing to take the investigation seriously. All too often, when one state has made inquiries of another, the second state has offered false reassurances that nothing significant was amiss. The problem, of course, is that governments have self-protective motivations to minimize or deny wrongdoing, since investigations into illegal intercountry adoption inevitably include investigation into intentional, knowing, and/or negligent wrongdoing by the government. Thus, one of the obstacles to remedies is that the same 'system of co-operation' used to facilitate intercountry adoption has not been, and cannot be expected to be, effective to investigate and create remedies for illegal intercountry adoption.

14. Appropriate remedies for illegal intercountry adoptions would be expensive. Conducting record and document searches and reviews, interviews of intermediaries and others with significant knowledge, and birth search and reunions, in addition to appropriate counselling services for adoption triad members, could cost tens of

thousands of dollars per adoption. The travel costs alone could be quite substantial. Ongoing travel costs for additional trips after an initial reunion occurs is another significant expense. Rough estimates suggest that total remedial costs, if provided systemically, would require billions of dollars. For example, a remedial cost of $10,000 per adoption across half of the one million adoptions in the modern era of intercountry adoption would cost five billion dollars. While such costs, of course, could be shared among many countries, it seems unlikely in the extreme that governments would be willing to provide these remedies on the scale necessary to address the systemic nature of the illegal and unethical conduct – that is to say, to provide investigations of the majority of intercountry adoptions completed in systems where at least one form of illegal separation was endemic.

15. A possible mitigating factor regarding costs is that most victims will not come forward. Upon examination, however, this lack of large numbers of victims coming forward is itself a significant barrier to the provision of remedies. As noted previously, most adoptees have been recruited into their adoptive identity in a way that makes confronting the possibility of an illegal adoption difficult. Most original family members are far too powerless economically and socially to come forward, and many have been induced to participate in their own victimization in a way that tends to impede them from self-identifying as victims. Adoptive parents are usually unaware of the wrongdoing, and have been socialized to expect full severance adoption, and thus may not be supportive of investigations and other remedies. Some may wrongly perceive a lack of victims coming forward as a reason that remedies are not necessary – if victims do not come forward, what is the problem? Of course, the same problem occurs with many other kinds of crimes; for example, most adult and child victims of rape, sexual assault or sexual abuse do not report the crimes to the police or authorities.[65] The fact that certain kinds of victimization tend to dissuade victims from coming forward is not a victory but, of course, a profound defeat from human rights and justice perspectives. Rape victims are still victims even if they are too traumatized and mistrustful of the authorities to come forward. The lack of large numbers of victims of intercountry adoption coming forward, despite the evidence of systemic illegal and unethical adoptions, is another major obstacle to providing remedies.

---

65 See, e.g., World Health Organization, *Sexual Violence*, WHO/RHR/12.37, 2012, https://apps.who.int/iris/bitstream/handle/10665/77434/WHO_RHR_12.37_eng.pdf; D. Lievore, *Non-Reporting and Hidden Recording of Sexual Assault: An International Literature Review*, Commonwealth of Australia, 2003, https://www.aic.gov.au/sites/default/files/2020-05/non-reporting-and-hidden-recording-of-sexual-assault-an-international-literature-review.pdf; L. Sardinha, M. Maheu-Giroux, H. Stöckl, S.R. Meyer and C. García-Moreno, 'Global, Regional, and National Prevalence Estimates of Physical or Sexual, or Both, Intimate Partner Violence Against Women in 2018', *The Lancet*, Vol. 399, No. 10327, pp. 803-813; National Sexual Violence Resource Center, Statistics about Sexual Violence, https://www.nsvrc.org/sites/default/files/publications_nsvrc_factsheet_media-packet_statistics-about-sexual-violence_0.pdf.

16. Although the best interests of children should be "the paramount consideration" (Art. 21 UNCRC) in systems of adoption, intercountry adoption systems have, in practice, been driven instead by the adult demand for children in receiving states. This political dominance of prospective adoptive parents and their allies is a major reason why intercountry adoption systems have remained open or been reopened, despite repeated scandals and indications of illegal and abusive practices. The political dominance of this demand for children also presents a serious obstacle to the provision of remedies for past illegal adoptions. This overwhelming wish for children tends to blind prospective adoptive parents and their allies to the realities of seriously illegal and unethical practices, and hence severely lessens support for investigating and remedying illegal adoptions. While some adoptive parents are quite active in attempting to self-remedy illegal intercountry adoption, and in advocating for investigations and remedies, the predominant and heard voice of adoptive parents as a whole remains a serious obstacle to the provision of remedies (see Chapter 9).

17. The amount of expertise required to provide remedies for illegal adoption is daunting. Receiving states have generally worked with multiple states of origin, and states of origin have typically worked with multiple receiving states. Remedies for investigating individual adoptions require expertise into the laws and actual practices of each state involved, an understanding of the cultures involved, competency in the relevant languages, and an understanding of the relevant bureaucracies involved. Expertise about a nation's law and practices is not always sufficient, as sometimes the regional cultural differences will matter, the local languages used may differ in different parts of a nation, and some of the relevant legal rules may be local rather than national, requiring more localized expertise as well. Assisting reunions requires expertise into the psychological issues of adoption triad members and an understanding of cultural understandings and family practices relevant to both the adoptive and the first family. Creating systems for remedies includes expertise related to the creation and management of DNA match services and data services, as well as data privacy considerations. If remedies were scaled up there would likely be a shortage of those with relevant expertise; even now, with only sporadic self-help remedies available for most, it is often very difficult to find individuals to assist with relevant expertise.

18. The perception that victims have benefitted is another obstacle to the provision of remedies. Both in receiving states and in states of origin, there are broadly held perceptions that adoptees have benefitted from their adoptions, and that this benefit outweighs any illegal or unethical conduct, including being stolen from their original families. Many intermediaries in states of origin are middle-class persons or higher in their society that may perceive being able to immigrate to developed, wealthier states and societies, and to attain citizenship there, as a huge benefit that they or their family members would want. Some intermediaries in states of origin may have very negative

views of the social and economic classes from which most adoptees come, and may not perceive being removed from those families or communities as a significant loss. Those in receiving states often have stereotyped views of the greater benefits of their own society, especially as compared with developing nations.

Most adoptees indeed do live much more privileged lives, as to standard of living and education, than they would have lived if they had remained with their original family. The wounds of being torn illegally from one's original family, community, culture and nation are much more invisible than the tangible benefits of growing up in a middle-class or wealthy family in the United States, Europe or other developed economy. The sorrow and loss of original families is also invisible since their voices and faces remain unheard and unseen. This perception and even reality of significant benefit, accompanied by a minimization of the harms involved, makes it very difficult to mobilize support for investing significantly in remedies.

This set of perceptions is corrosive and harmful, as it diminishes the significance of family and community connections for the hundreds of millions of people who live in relative poverty in developing nations. Stealing children from the poor is implicitly viewed as a humanitarian rather than a criminal act. This set of attitudes also undercuts the much more central projects of improving the lives and living standards of the poor in developing nations, which remains one of the most important and unfinished projects of this century. Such attitudes, of course, also facilitate the wrongful taking of children from the poor, which, unfortunately, can too often be done with impunity, whether it is done for adoption trafficking, sex trafficking or labour trafficking.

The Cumulative Impact of the Barriers to Remedies

Given the cumulative impacts of the many barriers to remedies for illegal intercountry adoptions, systemic remedies for illegal intercountry adoptions of the past seventy-plus years will not be made available in the foreseeable future. To the degree that governments do provide remedies, it will be primarily due to the advocacy of adult adoptees and their allies, as well as child rights and human rights groups. Such governmental remedies will be quite incomplete, and focused primarily on offering limited remedies to adoptees who come forward asking for assistance. Most remedies will continue to be self-help by adoption triad members assisted by a variety of non-governmental actors. Original families will continue to be usually outside the scope of remedial efforts, except to the degree that assisting them is a part of the remedy for adoptees. There are currently a small number of non-profit groups focused on assisting original families who are victims of illegal intercountry adoption in a particular country; hopefully, they can create positive models that will find much greater support in the years to come. But realistically, the vast majority of original families victimized by the illegal loss of their children will never receive remedies, except to the degree that adoptees receiving or creating remedies include them.

Present Predictions in Light of Past Events

I hope I am wrong about these pessimistic predictions regarding provision of remedies for illegal intercountry adoptions. For what it is worth, my past pessimistic predictions have turned out to be mostly accurate. Indeed, it is helpful to put our present dilemmas in the context of past decades.

My early published analyses of the intercountry adoption system were written around 2004 to 2006[66] at what turned out to be the statistical high point of intercountry adoptions - about 45,000 in 2004.[67] Intercountry adoption had tripled in numbers from the early 1990s,[68] the Hague Adoption Convention was being increasingly implemented,[69] and proponents of intercountry adoption were optimistic. Reports of abuses were usually ignored or dismissed as rare aberrations within a safe, already over-regulated system[70] or as historical, pre-UNCRC/Hague Adoption Convention cases with little relevance to the present. Amidst this optimism regarding intercountry adoption, I was among the dissenters voicing significant concerns related to illicit practices prior to 2010, including, among many others, Trish Maskew,[71] Gita

66 Smolin, 2005, 2006; D.M. Smolin, 'Intercountry Adoption as Child Trafficking', *Valparaiso University Law Review*, Vol. 39, No. 2, 2004, pp. 281-326.

67 Selman, 2023.

68 P. Selman, 'The Rise and Fall of Intercountry Adoption in the 21st Century', *International Social Work*, Vol. 52, No. 5, 2009, pp. 575-594; D.M. Smolin, 'Child Laundering and the Hague Convention on Intercountry Adoption: The Future and Past of Intercountry Adoption', *Louisville Law Review*, Vol. 48, 2009, pp. 441-498.

69 See HCCH, Status Table, https://www.hcch.net/en/instruments/conventions/status-table/?cid=69.

70 See, e.g., E. Bartholet, 'International Adoption: The Child's Story', *Georgia State Law Review*, Vol. 24, 2007, pp. 333-371.

71 T. Maskew, 'Child Trafficking and Intercountry Adoption: The Cambodian Experience', *Cumberland Law Review*, Vol. 35, 2004, pp. 619-638; T. Maskew, 'The Failure of Promise: The U.S. Regulations on Intercountry Adoption Under the Hague Convention', *Administrative Law Review*, Vol. 60, 2008, pp. 487-512. Maskew later served for several years as chief of the Adoption Division in the Office of Children's Issues, U.S. Department of State.

Ramaswamy,[72] Desiree Smolin,[73] Jane Jeong Trenka,[74] Benyam Mezmur,[75] E.J. Graff,[76] Tobias Hübinette[77] and Claudia Fonseca.[78] By 2010, significant organizations were expressing concern with serious illicit practices in intercountry adoption, including Terre des Hommes (hereinafter TDH)[79] and International Social Services (hereinafter ISS).[80] The HCCH added a very significant focus on illicit practices at the 2010[81] and 2015[82] Special Commissions, under the brave leadership of Jennifer Degeling (2010) and

72 G. Ramaswamy and B. Bhukya, *The Lambadas: A Community Besieged: A Study on the Relinquishment of Lambada Girl Babies in South Telangana*, Women Development & Child Welfare, Government of Andhra Pradesh, Hyderabad, 2001, https://www.scribd.com/document/70681194/Unicef-A-Study-on-the-Relinquishment-of-Lambada-Girl-Babies-2001; R. Bonner, 'A Challenge in India Snarls Foreign Adoptions', *New York Times*, 23 June 2003, https://www.nytimes.com/2003/06/23/world/a-challenge-in-india-snarls-foreign-adoptions.html (discussing work of a group, led by Gita Ramaswamy, seeking a moratorium based on the view that "foreign adoption system in India is riddled with corruption and encourages trafficking in baby girls"). As can be seen from these dates, Gita Ramaswamy's work on adoption started a few years prior to 2004. Gita Ramaswamy recently published a well-received memoir of her life as an activist: G. Ramaswamy, *Land, Guns, Caste, Woman: The Memoir of a Lapsed Revolutionary*, New Delhi, Navayana, 2022.

73 Founder of adoption blog which tracked abusive practices: http://fleasbiting.blogspot.com/; my own work was done significantly in partnership with Desiree.

74 See, e.g., J.J. Trenka, *The Language of Blood: A Memoir*, Minnesota, Minnesota Historical Society Press, 2003; C. San-Hung, 'An Adoptee returns to South Korea and Changes Follow', *New York Times*, 28 June 2013, https://www.nytimes.com/2013/06/29/world/asia/an-adoptee-returns-to-south-korea-and-changes-follow.html.

75 B. Mezmur, 'From Angelina (To Madonna) to Zoe's Ark: What Are the 'A–Z' Lessons for Intercountry Adoptions in Africa?', *International Journal of Law, Policy and the Family*, Vol. 23, No. 2, 2009, pp. 145-173; Mezmur went on to become a leading global expert in children's rights, see bio at https://hrp.law.harvard.edu/faculty/benyam-dawit-mezmur/.

76 See, e.g., E.J. Graff, 'The Lie We Love', *Foreign Policy Magazine*, 12 January 2008. Graff was also primarily responsible for initiating and overseeing the valuable website, since archived, on illicit intercountry adoption practices, at Brandeis University's Schuster Institute for Investigative Journalism. For many years the Schuster Institute usefully collected link materials while also creating summaries, which were available for free on the website.

77 T. Hübinette, 'Comforting an Orphaned Nation: Representations of International Adoption and Adopted Koreans in Korean Popular Culture', Seoul: Jimoonda Publishing Company, 2006.

78 C. Fonseca, 'Inequality Near and Far: Adoption as Seen from the Brazilian Favelas', *Law & Society Review*, Vol. 36, No. 2, 2002, pp. 397-432 (36 pages).

79 I. Lammerant and M. Hofstetter, *Adoption: At What Cost? For An Ethical Responsibility of Receiving Countries in Intercountry Adoption*, Terre Des Hommes, 2007, https://resourcecentre.savethechildren.net/pdf/1650.pdf/; UNICEF, Terre Des Hommes, *Adopting the Rights of the Child: A Study on Intercountry Adoption and Its Influence on Child Protection in Nepal*, 2008, https://bettercarenetwork.org/sites/default/files/attachments/Adopting%20the%20Rights%20of%20the%20Child.pdf.

80 See, e.g., H. Boéchat, N. Cantwell and M. Dambach, *Adoption from Viet Nam Findings and Recommendations of An Assessment*, ISS, November 2009, https://resourcecentre.savethechildren.net/pdf/5366.pdf/.

81 HCCH, Special Commission of June 2010, https://www.hcch.net/en/publications-and-studies/details4/?pid=6162&dtid=57.

82 HCCH, Special Commission of June 2015, https://www.hcch.net/en/publications-and-studies/details4/?pid=6161&dtid=57.

Laura Martinez-Mora (2015), while institutionalizing that concern with ongoing work between Special Commissions.[83]

The critical voices of that time were echoing many of the concerns of a prior generation, who had been involved in the processes that created the UNCRC adoption provisions and the 1993 Hague Adoption Convention.[84] Indeed, those foundational instruments, including the brilliant analysis of Hans van Loon, reflected the concerns of that time with illicit adoption practices.[85] Some of those active from that earlier work, prominently including Nigel Cantwell, remained active not only in their own work but also in generously training the next generation of experts.[86] It seemed that in every decade and in every generation, throughout much of the modern history of intercountry adoption, it has been necessary to relearn the risks and realities of illicit practices, in a context where thus far the problems have been systemically intractable.

There have been two main lines of response to realization of the systemic nature of illicit intercountry adoption practices: reform through regulation or ceasing the systemic practice of intercountry adoption. The UNCRC allows either choice since neither adoption nor intercountry adoption are mandatory practices for states (see Art. 20(3) and 21); even the Hague Adoption Convention does not require contracting states to participate in intercountry adoption,[87] but, of course, the Convention is designed primarily as a regulatory solution to allow intercountry adoption to continue.[88]

Experts and activists have been divided along this spectrum of reform to abolition of intercountry adoption. My own response was to work with the HCCH and others on the reform agenda, while predicting in my writings that it would fail. I described the structural features and practices of intercountry adoption that incentivized illicit conduct.[89] I warned that mere ratification of the 1993 Hague Adoption Convention

83 See, e.g., HCCH, *Working Group on Preventing and Addressing Illicit Practices in Intercountry Adoption*, https://www.hcch.net/en/publications-and-studies/details4/?pid=6309&dtid=62.

84 J.H.A. van Loon, *Report on Intercountry Adoption*, Preliminary Document No. 1 of April 1990, in Preliminary Work, Proceedings of the Seventh Session 101, 10-29 May 1993, https://www.hcch.net/en/publications-and-studies/details4/?pid=918; Smolin, 2010 (analysing text and preparatory materials of the 1993 Hague Adoption Convention evidencing a primary concern with illicit practices such as child trafficking and the sale of children).

85 Ibid.

86 See, e.g., Cantwell, 2014. I am personally grateful to Nigel Cantwell for informally helping to train me in my own work on adoption and the rights of the child.

87 HCCH, *The Implementation and Operation of the 1993 Hague Intercountry Adoption Convention: Guide to Good Practice No. 1*, Bristol, Jordan Publishing, 2008, section 8.2.1, paras. 448, pp. 100-101.

88 See, e.g., H. van Loon, 'Statement on the Occasion of the Deposit of Ratification of the Hague Convention of 29 May 1993 on Protection of Children and Co-operation in Respect of Intercountry Adoption, by the United States of America (12 December 2007)', quoted in Smolin, 2010, pp. 452-453.

89 Smolin, 2004, 2006.

would not be sufficient to avoid child laundering, given a lack of political will and poor implementation by states.[90] I proposed specific reforms that could address the flaws of intercountry adoption systems and practice,[91] while also predicting those reforms would not be adopted or implemented, with the longer term result of the fall of intercountry adoption.[92] The Permanent Bureau of the HCCH and many others devoted to the reform agenda were and are, in my view, extraordinarily committed and competent but structurally quite limited to what they may do. What I was predicting,[93] therefore, was ultimately the unwillingness of states and the 'adoption-community' – especially the majority of adoptive parents and prospective adoptive parents and agencies and intermediaries – to regulate with sufficient strictness to overcome the structural pressures producing illicit practices.[94] It was not until 2021 that I finally called for moratoria on intercountry adoption[95] and then, finally, in 2022 advocated for ending the modern system of intercountry adoption.[96]

However, I had warned almost two decades ago:

> Without such systems of accountability, one can virtually never know, when holding an adopted child, whether the child was an orphan needing a home, or a beloved daughter or son illicitly taken from a home.[97]
>
> [A]lthough these reforms may be rational, it is not clear that there is a rational reason to hope for their adoption.[98]
>
> Intercountry adoption is a conditional good; intercountry adoption as child trafficking is an evil. Only when the law, society, and intercountry adoption system are reformed will the conditions under which intercountry adoption can flourish as a good be established. Unfortunately, the prospects for such reform are poor because there are few within the current intercountry adoption system with the motivation to demand it. Hence, the recurrent cycle of scandal, excuse, and ineffective "reform" will probably continue until

90 Ibid.
91 Smolin, 2004, pp. 475-493, 2006, pp. 171-200.
92 Smolin, 2006, p. 200.
93 Ibid.
94 Ibid.
95 Smolin, 2021.
96 Smolin, 2023.
97 Smolin, 2004, p. 493.
98 Smolin, 2006, p. 200.

> intercountry adoption is finally abolished, with history labeling the entire enterprise as a neocolonialist mistake.[99]

The Dutch report of February 2021,[100] in combination with the UN Joint Statement of September 2022,[101] appear to represent a pivotal point as to recognition of the systemic nature of illegal and unethical practices in intercountry adoption, both before and after the implementation of the 1993 Hague Adoption Convention. Of course, most people globally would not have heard of either, but for those involved in the international discourse on intercountry adoption it has become increasingly difficult to maintain the illusion of a safe system of intercountry adoption with only very occasional abuses.

The most irrefutable fact of intercountry adoption has been statistical decline: according to Professor Selman's statistics on intercountry adoption, as published on the HCCH website, a reduction of more than 85% from the 2004 high of 45,482 adoptions to 6,527 adoptions in 2019, the last pre-Covid-19 year.[102] The Covid-19 occasioned further decline, to 3,730 adoptions in 2020 and 3,983 adoptions in 2021.[103] Thus, intercountry adoption has declined by more than 90% and appears to be stabilizing at this much lower level.

I may have been wrong in predicting the complete abolition of intercountry adoption; such a prediction underestimates the continuing political impact of the demand side of intercountry adoption in receiving states. At the present time, for example, the United States and Italy continue to be significant receiving states, even if numbers are reduced internationally. But my predictions of substantial decline due to a continuing cycle of abusive practices leading to scandals leading to moratoria or slowdowns has generally been proven true. My predictions of a lack of political will to implement sufficient reforms has been accurate in at least most of the most active receiving states and in most of the active states of origin. Of course, in many instances the primary form of reform has been simply to withdraw from participating in intercountry adoptions or slow the numbers to a mere trickle, which are responses I anticipated. My scepticism concerned the capacity of states to implement reforms while still being quite active in intercountry adoption as to the numbers of children sent or received.

However, there may be some exceptions regarding a lack of reform within active nations that I did not anticipate. Although I am not in a position to verify it, there are

99 Ibid., p. 325.
100 Committee Investigating Intercountry Adoption, 2021.
101 UN Human Rights Treaty Bodies, 29 September 2022.
102 Selman, 2023.
103 Ibid.

indications that some of the most active states of origin today – for example, Colombia and the Philippines – have implemented Hague Adoption Convention norms with some degree of success. Colombia, as described in Chapter 3, is one of many Latin American countries that suffered with systemic illegal adoption practices prior to Hague Adoption Convention implementation, and so a marked improvement in Colombia's practice, while still sending large numbers of children, would be significant. These possible exceptions to the general failure to implement reforms are suggestive. Certainly, if some states did reform successfully, it heightens the responsibility of the majority that did not, for it proves that it was and is possible to implement real reforms and changes in intercountry adoption systems.

My pessimistic predictions of a lack of state-provided systemic remedies should not be taken as a rationale for fatalistic inaction but, on the contrary, serve as a mandate for activism. Whatever remedies are provided will occur only through activism driven by adoption triad members, allies and NGOs. Most remedies will be self-remedies by adoption triad members assisted by NGOs and informal networks of assistance, apart from state assistance, but activists in some circumstances may be able to spur some state-assisted remedies. Activism can and already has achieved some partial successes. Nothing will be given that is not first demanded.

Remedies When Adoptees Are Still Children

What should be done when possible or confirmed illegal separation of a child from the original family is discovered after the child has travelled overseas and is living with the adoptive family? There are clearly different approaches.

One approach sends the child back to the original family, and in some instances annuls or voids the adoption. The situation, in other words, is treated in a way analogous to a kidnapping – when the victim is found they are reunited and returned to their family. So far as this author can tell, there are perhaps only about fifteen such instances in the modern history of intercountry adoption, including both instances where the adoptive family voluntarily returned the child to the first family and also cases in which a court ordered such return. In the publicized case of the Ugandan child, Namata, adopted by the Davis family in the United States, the adoptive family in 2016 returned the child to the original family with the assistance of the small NGO Reunite.[104] A related Ugandan

104 J. Davis, 'The "Orphan" I Adopted from Uganda Already Had a Family', *CNN*, 13 October, 2017, https://www.cnn.com/2017/10/13/opinions/adoption-uganda-opinion-davis/index.html; see 'Kids for Sale', *CNN*, https://www.cnn.com/specials/kids-for-sale; Reunite, https://reunite.live/.

case had the same result.[105] Decades ago the Israeli courts returned a child to Brazil in the rare instance where the original family, with assistance, brought a lawsuit in Israel.[106] After a criminal prosecution related to the illegal adoption of about 80 children from Samoa, at least one of the families returned the child to the first family.[107] The chaotic mass evacuation of children from South Vietnam in Operation Babylift in 1975 at the close of the Vietnam War led to litigation when original family members who had made their way to the United States sought the return of their children through civil litigation, leading to a reported twelve children being returned to their original family. Of course, the Babylift children had left Vietnam under chaotic circumstances at the end of the Vietnam War.[108]

The opposite approach, which is what most often occurs, is that the child remains with the adoptive family without any contact with the original family, as the adoptive family successfully resists any remedies.[109] While most of these cases go unreported, there has been substantial reporting on the case of Karen/Anyeli, a child who was reportedly abducted at age two from her middle-class family in Guatemala. The parents, Dayner Orlando Hernández and Loyda Rodríguez immediately filed multiple complaints with various authorities, stating that two women had seized Anyeli and fled in a taxi. The authorities reportedly did nothing. Eventually, Anyeli was adopted by an American couple, Timothy and Jennifer Monahan. The details of the adoption process are available in a much fuller form than is typically the case owing to extensive investigation by the authorities in Guatemala and extensive journalistic reporting, and describe a classic case of child laundering. After the abduction a fake birth mother was paid to consent to the adoption, but the consent was voided when a DNA test (as then required in Guatemalan adoptions) showed the assigned birth mother was unrelated to the child. The adoption then stalled, until, in a workaround, the child was falsely labelled as abandoned, which facilitated the adoption. Loyda later found her daughter's

105 Ibid.; see also 'Violah Is Reunited With her Family', *CNN*, 13 October 2017, https://www.cnn.com/2017/10/12/africa/gallery/uganda-adoptions-violah-reunion/index.html.

106 See Chapter 4, at p. 133, citing M. Goldfeder, 'Adoption in Judaism and in Israel', *in* R.L. Ballard, N.H. Goodno, R.F. Cochran, Jr. and J.A. Milbrandt (eds.), *The Intercountry Adoption Debate: Dialogues Across Disciplines*, Newcastle upon Tyne, Cambridge Scholars Publishing, 2015, pp. 493-525, 520.

107 NZPA, 'Four Sentenced in Samoan Adoption Scam', *New Zealand Herald*, 28 February 2009, https://www.nzherald.co.nz/world/four-sentenced-in-samoan-adoption-scam/N5GNQF6LKNO5GL2JDZFYA4PD4I/; U.S. Department of State, 'Defendants In "Focus On Children" Case Sentenced In Federal Court', 25 February 2009, https://2009-2017.state.gov/m/ds/rls/127131.htm; B. Adams, 'Samoan Adoption Scheme Payments to be Cut', *Salt Lake Tribune*, 1 June 2011, https://archive.sltrib.com/article.php?id=51885509&itype=CMSID.

108 PBS, 'Operation Babylift (1975)', https://www.pbs.org/wgbh/americanexperience/features/daughter-operation-babylift-1975/; A. Varzally, 'Vietnamese Adoptions: A Question of Parenthood', *Boom California*, 30 March 2018, https://boomcalifornia.org/2018/03/30/vietnamese-adoptions/.

109 See, e.g., E.S. McIntyre, 'The Limits of Jurisdiction', *Guernica*, 1 December 2014, https://www.guernicamag.com/the-limits-of-jurisdiction/.

photo in the adoption file and validated her status as natural mother through a DNA match using a sample of the child's DNA that had been preserved. The Guatemalan government treated the adoption as a trafficking case and criminally prosecuted a number of individuals involved in the adoption; the Guatemalan government sought a second confirming DNA test and then the return of the child, but the US government refused to assist with either.[110] It appears that Loyda was unable to find or afford legal counsel to carry out her wish to file a case in the locality of the adoptive family. So far as can be determined, the child grew up in the United States with the adoptive family, apparently without any contact with the first family. This case is unusual in the degree of detail that is publicly available and in the legal activism of the country of origin on behalf of the first family; the case is typical in the capacity of the adoptive family to refuse all remedies during the childhood of the adoptee.

A third approach has sometimes been initiated by adoptive parents, which is to establish contact and reunions, after which a kind of de facto open adoption is practised with continuing contacts and, possibly, visits. This approach includes the participation and input of the adoptee and depends on the interest and cooperation of the original family. Since this has been a form of self-remedy, the high costs of international travel make the approach only accessible when the adoptive family can afford it. I know of various instances of this approach but none in which governments have contributed financially to the remedy.[111]

One creative approach was attempted in the prosecution mentioned previously of a set of illegal adoptions from Samoa involving around 80 children. The sentencing agreement required the former operators of the American adoption agency to contribute to a trust fund designed to facilitate contact between the adoptees, adoptive families and first families. The trust fund was overseen by an expert, Professor Jini Roby (herself an international adoptee and Professor of Social Work). Although a married couple and two other defendants were ordered to pay into the trust fund, the amounts paid and sought were around $85,000, with an ultimate goal of $100,000. The amount of money involved, however, amounted to only about $1,200 per child living in the United States, which was far too little to provide for travel; hence, the remedy focused on covering costs associated with communicating long distance, including translation services and language lessons. This remedy was innovative but fell far short of providing an adequate remedy for such a large group, illustrating the problem with inadequately funded remedies. The remedy also allowed adoptive parents control over the amount

---

110 Ibid.

111 See, e.g., J. Rollings, *Love Our Way: A Courageous Mother's Story that Gives New Meaning to the World Family*, London, Harper Collins, 2008.

of contact, making it irrelevant where the adoptive parents preferred to avoid any kind of contact. The remedy was also criticized because the perpetrators were subjected only to a probationary period with no time served in prison, despite the seriousness of their actions which had impacted so many families. Theoretically, probation rather than prison enabled the perpetrators to be in a better position to contribute to the trust fund, but this benefit was ultimately minimal because the perpetrators were required to provide only minimal contributions. Indeed, one wonders why the perpetrators, who reportedly would have earned over a million dollars over at least three years from the scheme, were as a group only required to contribute less than $100,000. While allowing the perpetrators to be on probation would, theoretically, have allowed them to continue to earn funds to contribute to the trust fund, it appeared that the subsequent contributions were very small – at most $15,000.[112] The married couple convicted in the case were reportedly allowed to complete the adoption of a child from China after being convicted, having previously adopted two infants from Romania who were then reportedly sent to Samoa to live around ten years later.[113]

Given these very different approaches, what are the best approaches to remedies for illegal adoptions discovered while the adoptee is still a child? I would suggest the following principles:

1. Remedies, in principle, should be available to all members of the adoption triad – adoptees, the first family, and the adoptive family. The first family and adoptive family include, of course, not only parents but also siblings, grandparents, and so on, as the intergenerational nuclear and extended families are all impacted.

2. Investigation and truth-finding and truth-telling are essential.[114]

3. Depending on the particular circumstances, it can be helpful that adoption triad members have multiple opportunities to tell their stories, from their own perspectives, to one another.

112 See P. Manson and S. Gehrke, 'Focus on Children Scam: No Jail Time in Adoption-Fraud Case', *Salt Lake City Tribute*, 25 February 2009, https://archive.sltrib.com/story.php?ref=/ci_11782689; B. Adams, 'Samoan Adoption Scheme Payments to Be Cut', *Salt Lake City Tribute*, 1 June 2011, https://archive.sltrib.com/article.php?id=51885509&itype=CMSID.

113 P. Manson, 'Couple on Probation in Samoan Adoption Case Adopt Child', *Salt Lake City Tribune*, 3 March 2010, https://archive.sltrib.com/story.php?ref=/news/ci_14507609.

114 UN Human Rights Treaty Bodies, 29 September 2022, paras. 13, 15, 17-18; E.C. Loibl, 'The Aftermath of Transnational Illegal Adoptions: Redressing Human Rights Violations in the Intercountry Adoption System with Instruments of Transitional Justice', *Childhood*, 2021, Vol. 28, No. 4, pp. 477, 484-485, 487.

4. Remedies should respect all of the adoptee's family ties and lived experience of family. Thus, so long as such relationships have been and would be positive, remedies should, wherever possible, be both/and or additive rather than subtractive, allowing for the adoptee to have continuing relationships with both the first and the adoptive family.[115]

5. It is appropriate in some cases to return the child to the first family, possibly annul the adoption, and restore the parent-child relationship of the first family.[116] But such a remedy does not necessarily require excluding continuing contact with the adoptive family. It is appropriate in some cases for the child to remain primarily with the adoptive family, while reopening the relationship of the child to the first family in a way analogous to an open adoption. In instances where the child has been illegally taken from the first family, the approach of allowing the adoptive family to simply prevent remedies is not appropriate, unless it can be demonstrated that the first family would be abusive to the child.

6. Remedies should be attempted even if child adoptees initially do not want to know about or have contact with the first family, unless that wish is based on a history of abuse or similar circumstances. It must be remembered that many adoptees have few memories of the first family and have been recruited into their adoptive identity and may not feel ready to confront difficult facts or have their lives be unsettled. Other adoptees may have had many memories of the first family but have been through the difficult process of adapting to a new identity, language, culture and family, thereby likely forgetting much of their first language (subtractive bilingualism or second first language acquisition).[117] The initial reluctance and reticence of young adoptees is understandable but should not be determinative. Some actions which are in the best interests of a child may go against the wishes of the child, which is why children have participation rather than autonomy rights as to many decisions (Art. 12 UNCRC). Moreover, where the child was illegally taken from the first family, the separation constitutes a continuing wrong and should, in principle, be remedied.[118] By analogy, if

115 Loibl, 2021, pp. 482-484 (discussing complexities of determining the child's best interests as to remedies for an illegally adopted child).

116 UN Human Rights Treaty Bodies, 29 September 2022, paras. 12, 15-18; Loibl, 2021, pp. 482-484; L. Long (ed.), *ICAV Perspective Paper, Illicit Intercountry Adoptions: Lived Experience Views on How Authorities and Bodies Could Respond*, July 2020, p. 10, https://www.academia.edu/43560775/Illicit_Intercountry_Adoptions_Lived_Experience_Views_on_How_Authorities_and_Bodies_Could_Respond_Perspective_Paper_2020.

117 See J. Price, K. Pollock and D. Oller, 'Speech and Language Development in Six Infants Adopted from China', *Journal of Multilingual Communication Disorders*, Vol. 4, No. 2, 2006, pp. 108-127; P. Silva, *Speech and Language Development for Children Adopted Internationally After Age 3: Two Clinical Case Studies*, MA Thesis, University of Texas, May 2015, https://repositories.lib.utexas.edu/bitstream/handle/2152/32239/SILVA-MASTERSREPORT-2015.pdf?sequence=1.

118 UN Human Rights Treaty Bodies, 29 September 2022, paras. 12, 15-17.

a child were stolen from a hospital nursery and raised by the kidnapper, the child would be returned to the first family regardless of the wishes of the child. In most cases, the adoptive parents were not responsible for or aware of the illegal separation, and thus as to the adoptive parent-child relationship the issue is somewhat different. But as to the loss of the child by the original family, the situation is the same as a kidnapping. Hence, the child adoptee should be guided by adults to understand the situation and to gradually process the facts of their life and the reality of their first family.

7. Where possible, adoption triad members should be supported by competent counselling.[119] However, in practice there are often not enough counsellors available. There are severe shortages of counsellors who are competent in adoption and even fewer who would be sensitive to the difficulties of remedying illegal adoption.[120] The high cost of counselling is an additional barrier, unless the state provides very significant resources.[121] Hence, in practice, culturally appropriate ways may have to be found to support adoption triad members even if professional counselling is not available.

8. Where possible, the adoption triad should be guided through a set of processes and interactions to mediated understandings as to the nature of future relationships and living arrangements. In some ways, the potential conflict between the adoptive and the first family can be viewed as analogous to a blended family created when divorced parents with children find new partners, providing the children with multiple parental households.[122] At best, the life of each child may be enriched by having supportive relationships and family in both households. However, as in divorce, there is, instead, a risk of the children being caught between conflicting adults who disparage one another to the children. As to adoption, the ultimate goal is that all of the adults who have played positive parental roles in the life of the child (including those who are genetic and/or gestational parents) are able to contribute positively to the growth and development of the child over time, while at the same time providing sufficient stability and clarity to the child. Even with ideal relationships among the adults, the specifics of living arrangements, means of contacts, visits, and so on will need to be worked out and adjusted over time.

---

119 Ibid., para. 17.

120 L. Long, *Intercountry Adoptee Voices, Consultation on the Intercountry Adoption Family Support Service*, February 2020, https://engage.dss.gov.au/consultation_ica_family_support_service_feb2020-submissions/1584003537/; Australian Psychological Association, Understanding Forced Adoption: Training for Psychologists, https://psychology.org.au/event/23364; B. Purrington, 'Adoption-Competent Therapy – What It Is, Why It Matters, and How to Find It', Boston Post Adoption Resources, 23 June 2022, https://bpar.org/adoption-competent-therapy-what-it-is-why-it-matters-and-how-to-find-it/.

121 Long, 2020.

122 V. King, L. Boyd and M. Thorsen, 'Adolescents' Perceptions of Family Belonging in Stepfamilies', *Journal of Marriage and Family*, Vol. 77, No. 3, 2015, pp. 761-774.

9. Ideally, where an intercountry adoption may have been built on the illegal separation of the child from the child's original family, one or both states, and the private intermediaries, if any, should pay the costs of the remedy. This means paying for investigations, birth searches, travel, translators, counsellors, language study, means of long-distance communication, and so on.[123] However, while the government or original intermediaries may justly be charged the costs, most often the services should be provided and guided by experts or NGOs independent of the government and of the original intermediaries who arranged the adoption. The government and original intermediaries have conflicts of interests and often a lack of expertise and should not be permitted to control or provide the critical services basic to remedies.

Remedies When Adoptees Are Adults

Some principles regarding remedies are similar regardless of whether the adoptee is a child or an adult. In both instances, if adoptions were processed in times and places where the wrongful separation of children from families was systemic, a complete investigation is necessary, including document disclosure and review, interviews with intermediaries and others with information, and birth searches. In both instances, the expenses for such should, in principle, be paid for by the responsible states and intermediaries, including paying for investigations, birth searches and counselling during the search stage. If the search is successful, the responsible states and intermediaries should pay for services related to reunions and restored relationships, including travel, translators, counsellors, language study, means of long-distance communication, and so on.[124] In both instances, investigations, searches, counselling services and reunion and restored relationship assistance services should be provided by NGOs and other non-governmental actors who were not involved in the original adoption, because governments and intermediaries who were involved have a conflict of interest. The role of states is to pay the costs and to use governmental authority to ensure access to information and documents.

However, the responsibility and power dynamics change significantly when adoptees are adults, which substantially changes the context for remedies. There can no longer be a dispute between the first and adoptive families concerning the custody or living arrangements of the adoptee. The power of adoptive parents and family is much reduced when adoptees are adults, as they no longer have the authority to control access to the adoptee. The adult adoptee cannot be prevented from relating to the first family, and the adoptee cannot be forced to relate to either adoptive or first family.

123 UN Human Rights Treaty Bodies, 29 September 2022, para. 17.
124 Ibid., paras. 15-18.

The financial situations of adoptees, of course, vary significantly, but some adoptees who have achieved financial independence would also have practical power to impact remedial possibilities.

Of course, as noted previously, the remedies for adult adoptees are different because childhood is over, and hence remedies cannot restore relationships with the first family during that critical stage of life. No one can give back to the adult adoptee or the first family the childhood together that was wrongly taken from them. No one can give back to the adult adoptee the person they would have been had they been raised to adulthood by their first family. In that sense, it is impossible to achieve "restitution to the original situation of the victim before the illegal intercountry adoption …"[125] for most illegal adoptions, since remedies are not attempted until childhood is over. This fundamental fact impacts those remedies that are available, in profoundly impacting the dynamics of reunions and restored relationships.

Given the formative nature of childhood, reunions are necessarily complicated by the adoptee having been formed, as to identity, language, culture, personality, character and religion, by a different family than their first family. The exact situation varies as to the age at which the adoptee left the first family, and came into the adoptive family, and also what occurred during any periods of temporary care. Nonetheless, reunions are an odd combination of the familiar and the foreign, the familial and the stranger. The process is stressful, and with adult adoptees completely dependent on the interest and choice of the adoptee to travel down this pathway. Either first family or adoptee may withdraw or limit involvement at any point in time. Remedies for adult adoptees can be revelatory and healing, but they are also immensely challenging.[126]

The Paradox of Remedies for First Families

Paradoxically, if remedies for original families were systematized, it would create an unsustainable model that could incentivize future abusive practices – at least if intercountry adoption continued. This problem would not occur if intercountry adoption as a systemic practice were ended. Hence, remedies being effective without incentivizing further abusive practices requires the ending or at least sharp limitation of intercountry adoption.

125 UN Human Rights Treaty Bodies, 29 September 2022, para. 17.

126 See, e.g., ICAV, Key Messages: Reunion and Beyond in Intercountry Adoption, August 2023, https://intercountryadopteevoices.com/wp-content/uploads/2023/08/Reunion-and-Beyond-Key-Messages.pdf; L. Long (ed.), *ICAV, Search and Reunion: Impacts and Outcomes*, July 2016, https://intercountryadopteevoices.com/wp-content/uploads/2016/07/search-and-reunion-icav-perspectives-july-2016-v12.pdf.

The problem is this: the proper remedy for first families would typically be restoration of relationship and regular contact with their children.[127] Whether done in childhood or adulthood, this would in many cases create the equivalent of an open adoption in which first families were connected to both their child (often by then an adult) living in a developed nation, and often to the adoptive family as well; in addition, their child would have citizenship in a developed economy. If these restored relationships were successful, there would, in course of time, be substantial financial benefits to the first family. Being related to family in the United States, Europe or other developed economies would in time bring the kind of remittances and assistance that relatives commonly send back to family still living in developing nations.[128]

This practice would in many instances fulfil the implicit promises that some first families had explicitly or implicitly received – that their child would go to a developed country and receive an education and other benefits there while supported by a host family – and over time would benefit the rest of the family remaining in the country. As indicated previously, it is one common form of child laundering to trick first families into believing that their children will in effect have a host family experience in another country, while remaining a part of their own family. Of course, in the typical child laundering scenario, those were false promises: the first family instead loses contact with their child, does not even know where or with whom their child is living, and legally is fully severed from a parental relationship with their child.

The remedial practice of restored relationship is just and necessary in a context of illegal separation. This result also practices adoption in a way more compatible with human dignity, as full severance adoption is based on a legal fiction of no relationship with the original family that fails to honour and respect our full humanity. Even if the original separation of the child from the original family was legal and ethical at the time, absent serious abuse or other such circumstances, open adoption, and continuation or restoration of relationship between the adoptee and the birth family, is usually the best adoption practice.[129]

However, connecting family members from middle class to wealthy circumstances in developed countries, with poor to lower middle-class family members in developing countries, creates expectations and often the practice of financial support. Apart from adoption, family members living in developed economies commonly send funds regularly to their relatives living in developing or transition economies. Remittances to

127 UN Human Rights Treaty Bodies, 29 September 2022.

128 World Bank Group, *Remittances Brave Global Headwinds*, November 2022, https://www.knomad.org/publication/migration-and-development-brief-37.

129 Seymore, 2015.

low and middle income countries total more than six hundred billion dollars annually, with India, China, Mexico and the Philippines being top recipients.[130] Remittances are a systematized and expected practice when families live in very different economic circumstances. Staying connected across international borders and sending remittances are far easier than in decades past, given technological advances available even among many of the poor in developing nations like India. Hence, when family relationships are restored, financial benefit will be expected and often practised.

If the equivalent of open intercountry adoption with accompanying lifeline financial family benefits were available to the poor of developing countries, it would likely be irresistible for large numbers of families of origin to agree to such circumstances. This would be seen as an alternative form of intergenerational migration and immigration to countries of greater opportunity. If instead of using this promise as a fraudulent inducement to full severance relinquishments, the offer of continued relationship was real and fulfilled on a regular basis, the temptation to turn children over for the benefit of the whole extended family would be difficult to resist. Indeed, many of the middle class in developing nations might be eager to send their older children to 'host families' in developed economies if this was practised as a form of family addition, immigration, citizenship in a developed nation and economic opportunity. Intercountry adoption would be transformed essentially into a massive hosting programme with citizenship, immigration and remittance benefits.

This is *not* an argument against supplying remedies to families of origin, who are owed such as a matter of remedying severe loss and injustice. Rather, this is an argument against continuing intercountry adoption. On the one hand, the only just way to continue intercountry adoption would be transform it into a system of systemically open intercountry adoption, which would provide a transparency and set of continued relationships that would guard against many of the abuses and harms of intercountry adoption practice. Yet, as soon as the actuality or perception of such a practice of intercountry adoption were systematized and scaled up, it would be perceived in developing nations as a kind of hosting, foster family programme with citizen and remittance benefits. This would create another set of injustices: adoptees as sacrificial lambs, sent away in childhood for the economic benefit of the entire extended family with expectations of lifelong assistance.

Full severance intercountry adoption is filled with hidden abuses, suppressed traumas and blatant injustices; correcting such programmes into more humane and transparent open intercountry adoptions would trade those harms for a different set of injustices.

130 World Bank Group, 2022.

Sending babies, young children or even teenagers away from their families with a mission and responsibility to succeed in a competitive developed economy and help support the entire nuclear and extended family back home is also a scenario highly incompatible with children's rights. The intercountry adoption system should not become an inducement to send children away. That inducement could be magnified to an unprecedented degree if the remedial approach to intercountry adoption became a model for future intercountry adoptions.

The modern intercountry adoption system grew and continued over seventy-plus years in environments of false promises, traumatic lifelong separations, hidden abuses and exploitation of severe economic and social disparities within and between nations. The remedies of truth-telling, reunion, openness and restoration of relations are required by justice but are not a bridge to a restored intercountry adoption system. Creating a new intercountry adoption based on remedying the flaws of the past would simply set the stage for a new and different set of injustices.

The Significance of Apologies

It is easy to be cynical about apologies. In themselves apologies do not provide the benefits of investigations, birth searches, reunions or counselling. Given that wrongful separations of children from families constitute continuing wrongs (and thus are not mere 'historical cases'),[131] apologies without remedies can add insult to injury; it would be like apologizing while simultaneously continuing to commit the crime. Apologies should thus not be a substitute for other remedies.

But apologies in conjunction with remedies can be a particularly meaningful addition in the context of illegal intercountry adoption. Done well, apologies are a way of communicating, to the adoption triad victims, to their broader families and communities, and to society, that something seriously wrong has occurred.[132] Apologies can thus counter the deeply entrenched tendencies to minimize the harms of illegal adoptions – a tendency that exists even among many of the direct victims, adoption triad members. Adoptees have been recruited into adoptive identities that, usually unknown to the adoptee, are often built on illegal separations from the first family. This recruitment may make it difficult for adoptees to conceptualize themselves as victims, even when investigation reveals that they were taken wrongfully from their original family. First families are typically ignored and sometimes have been tricked, coerced

131 UN Human Rights Treaty Bodies, 29 September 2022, para. 12.
132 Loibl 2021, pp. 486-487.

or tempted into participating in their own victimization in ways that may accentuate self-blame. Adoptive parents were usually unaware of the illegal conduct and may have difficulty even conceptualizing the idea that their beloved child was wrongfully taken from another family. Apologies would be a critical validation of adoption triad members as victims of illegal adoptions.[133]

This validation is also necessary in a context in which many in society do not recognize illegal intercountry adoption as a serious wrong and continue to see the adoptee as primarily a beneficiary of the adoption even when they were stolen or bought. Official apologies could communicate a necessary message that children being wrongfully taken from their first families is a real harm for which recompense and reparation are due.[134]

There are at least two kinds of apologies, both of which could be helpful in this context.

First, there are apologies to a group of victims, such as those that have been made regarding mistreatment of single mothers and regarding the forcible removal of indigenous children into boarding schools or for adoption. Such apologies are often national in scope and may come from the state, religious leaders or others. Typically, they do not occur until decades after most of the relevant wrongs were first committed.[135] Obtaining these kinds of national or even international apologies to the victims of illegal intercountry adoption would be a significant step forward, since to this point of time they have been mostly absent, the first such official apology occurring in the Netherlands in 2021.[136]

Second, apologies can be made to those impacted by a particular illegal adoption. Apologizing to each particular impacted family and individual would take an enormous amount of work, as it would require verification of the facts of each particular case and, of course, creating and delivering each individualized apology. Sometimes such apologies are avoided out of fear of opening the door to legal liability. Nonetheless, individual apologies can be particularly powerful precisely because they are so personalized. Unfortunately, the main circumstance where such apologies might occur is in the context of victims suing for civil remedies; apologies in that context may feel forced, lessening their impact.

133 Ibid.
134 Ibid.
135 Ibid.; D.M. Smolin, 'Beyond Apologies: Children, Mothers, Religious Liberty, and the Mission of the Catholic Church', *Cumberland Law Review*, Vol. 53, 2023, pp. 101-171.
136 Loibl, 2021, pp. 486-487.

Criminal Prosecutions

There are numerous examples of criminal prosecutions related to intercountry adoption. For example, criminal prosecutions have been pursued by Brazil, China, Chile, Colombia, Guatemala and India as countries of origin.[137] In the United States criminal prosecutions have been brought against American intermediaries in relation to adoptions from Cambodia, Poland, Samoa and Uganda.[138] The Zoe's Ark case concerning an attempt to smuggle over a hundred children from Chad to France resulted in prosecutions in both Chad and France.[139]

Despite these and other examples, the proportion of illegal adoptions that have been subjected to criminal prosecution is quite tiny, prosecutions have not always been successful, and statutes of limitations pose barriers in older cases, all of which significantly lessen the deterrent effect, as those involved in illegal adoptions may operate with virtual impunity, at least as to the risks of criminal prosecution. As a practical matter, those involved in illegal intercountry adoption have a very low risk of being criminally prosecuted, and even more so if they take a few precautions against exposing their behaviour.[140]

There are three other difficulties. First, criminal prosecutions in themselves do not provide remedies for victims, such as birth searches and reunions. Punishing criminals and deterring crimes is a different function from providing remedies to victims, and in some systems the needs of victims can be ignored during the prosecutorial process.[141] Second, states may sometimes prosecute less significant wrongdoers as sacrificial lambs while protecting higher status wrongdoers.[142] Third, states may use criminal

137 Smolin, 2004, pp. 456-474; McIntyre, 2014; Stuy, 2014; W. Hoge, 'Ring in Colombia Kidnaps Children for Sale Abroad', *New York Times*, 16 August 1981, https://www.nytimes.com/1981/08/16/world/ring-in-columbia-kidnaps-children-for-sale-abroad.html; see Chapters 4 and 5.

138 U.S. Department of Justice, Texas Woman Pleads Guilty to Schemes to Procure Adoptions from Uganda and Poland through Bribery and Fraud, 11 November 2021, https://www.justice.gov/opa/pr/texas-woman-pleads-guilty-schemes-procure-adoptions-uganda-and-poland-through-bribery-and; U.S. Department of Justice, Former Executive Director of International Adoption Agency Pleads Guilty to Fraudulent Adoption Scheme, 2 February, 2022, https://www.justice.gov/opa/pr/former-executive-director-international-adoption-agency-pleads-guilty-fraudulent-adoption; NZPA, 2009; U.S. Department of Justice, Hawaii Resident Pleads Guilty in Cambodian Adoption Conspiracy, 23 June 2004, https://www.justice.gov/archive/opa/pr/2004/June/04_crm_434.htm; Smolin, 2006, pp. 135-146.

139 B.D. Mezmur, 2009; 'French Charity Workers Jailed in Children-Smuggling Case', *France24*, 2 December 2013, https://www.france24.com/en/20130212-france-charity-workers-jail-sentences-children-smuggling-case.

140 Loibl, 2021, p. 480.

141 Ibid., p. 481.

142 Stuy, 2014.

prosecutions to create the appearance of a response to scandal, while generally doing very little as to remedies or reform.[143]

For all of these reasons, criminal prosecutions, while a significant form of response to illegal adoptions, are only one form of response and not necessarily the most important.

Conclusion

Progress has been made in recent years in recognizing that illegal, abusive and exploitative practices have been systemic and pervasive in the entire modern era of intercountry adoption. This chapter has suggested framing illegal intercountry adoption as usually involving the illegal separation of children from families. This reframing is factually accurate, as most forms of illegal intercountry adoptions do involve illegal separations of children from their first families. This reframing is also a helpful predicate to the task of providing systemic remedies for the systemic abuses in the modern intercountry adoption system, as it identifies the fundamental harms at the centre of illegal, abusive and exploitative intercountry adoptions.

Responses, remedies and reparations for illegal intercountry adoption have been rare and sporadic during the modern era of intercountry adoption. Yet in recent years the question of remedies has received increased attention, and now is thus a particularly opportune time to address the issue. This chapter, and indeed this book, is designed to assist in these recent efforts to provide remedies for the many victims of the modern era of intercountry adoption. The task is not easy, and, in the nature of things, some harms cannot be undone. It will be a struggle to achieve even very partial remedies and responses. Yet the effort must be made, as remedying illegal intercountry adoption is an obligation under international law. Indeed, every appropriate response and remedy that is provided has the potential to positively impact the lives of many across generations.

These remedial efforts are also necessary to strip away the blinders that prevent us from really seeing the harms done in the name of intercountry adoption. We cannot fully perceive the harms and costs of illegal intercountry adoption until we are fully engaged in the task of providing remedies and reparations. This eye-opening work, hopefully, can then guide decisions about the future of intercountry adoption.

The potential benefits of intercountry adoption have been obvious to many; we need to see just as clearly the very real harms and costs. Only then can we be equipped to make

143 Ibid.

balanced decisions about the future of intercountry adoption and whether, and in what form, it should continue.

PART 2: CHAPTER SUMMARIES

The chapters in this volume stand on their own as individual works reflecting the significant experiences and expertise of the authors. Here, however, I want to primarily comment on each chapter as related to the themes of this introduction. I am not using the actual chapter titles in the following summaries but rather highlighting each chapter's content.

CHAPTER 2: LESSONS FROM SOUTH KOREA ABOUT THE GLOBAL INTERCOUNTRY ADOPTION SYSTEM

Chapter two, by Kyung-eun Lee, focuses on adoptions from South Korea. Given the important role of South Korea over seventy years in influencing the global history of intercountry adoption, it is helpful to begin with an expert on South Korean adoptions. Lee describes the history of human rights violations related to Korean adoption and South Korea's history of evading state responsibility. She notes the prominent role of private agencies or intermediaries. She focuses on adoptees' rights to origins and notes the lack of protection of such rights. She states that the various treaties designed to curtail intercountry adoption abuses "failed to achieve a fundamental change due to the absence of state accountability and the exclusion of an effective mechanism to assure state parties abided by the conventions" (p. 95). She notes remedial efforts in South Korea, including the use of civil litigation and the acceptance of submissions related to intercountry adoption to the 2020 Second Truth and Reconciliation Commission (pp. 100-102).

Lee's chapter relates to my own scepticism about whether systemic remedies will be provided for the long history of systemic abuses. Lee correctly (from my standpoint) notes the necessity of investigations being done "in both sending and receiving countries" (p. 97). She argues that remedies should not depend on and be limited to responding to individual requests from adoptees but should instead take a "systemic approach" (p. 97). She notes that with "over 100 states engaged in intercountry adoption, whether as sending or receiving countries, a handful of investigations restricted to several receiving countries will, at best, uncover a fragment of the true scale of abuse" (pp. 97-98). She usefully emphasizes, from the 1993 Hague Adoption Convention, the principle of "co-responsibility" or "shared responsibility" as one of the "pillar principles" of the Convention (p. 98). Thus, Lee advocates leveraging the same cooperative ties that constituted the intercountry adoption system to "internationally standardize and conduct investigations", noting that investigative efforts should "operate within a multilateral system" (p. 102). At the same time, she anticipates the reactions (including mine) that this is "wishful thinking, considering that these same relationships constitute the global orphan adoption system" (p. 102). I can only hope that Lee is right and that I am wrong about the prospects for truly effective systemic multilateral cooperation in investigating and providing remedies for illegal intercountry adoption.

CHAPTER 3: COLOMBIAN AND LATIN AMERICAN ADOPTIONS: NEW PATHWAYS FOR REMEDIES?

Chapter three is authored by Susan F. Branco, a licensed professional counsellor and professor, who identifies herself as an adoptee from Colombia who "reunited with her birth family after a 25-year search" (p. 105 *note). Branco focuses directly on Colombian adoptions during a period of "dubious adoption practices during the 1970s through the 1990s" (p. 105). Her chapter also addresses Latin American adoptions more broadly, examining reparations models as well from Argentina and Chile. Branco provides a very useful chart comparing the different reparations models (pp. 124-125). Branco helpfully reviews principles related to reparations or remedies from the UN, HCCH Guide to Good Practice No. 1, a Model Procedure created by an HCCH Working Group, an adoptee survey conducted by Intercountry Adoptee Voices (ICAV), and the Conclusion to the multi-author ISS Professional Handbook on Responding to Illegal Adoptions (pp. 116-118).

Illegal intercountry adoptions from Latin America played a pivotal role in the creation and early implementations of the 1993 Hague Adoption Convention. Ten Latin American nations, including both member and non-member nations, participated in the HCCH proceedings to prepare the Convention. Provision was made to allow the Latin American representatives to speak in Spanish and have their remarks translated into the official working languages of French and English. Concern with child trafficking in Latin American adoptions was central to the broader purpose of the Convention to "prevent the abduction, the sale of, or traffic in children". Later, as Latin American countries ratified the Convention, the region has become a test case for evaluating how the Convention is implemented.

Branco's chapter is a reminder of the long, intergenerational process of uncovering and responding to illegal intercountry adoption. Most of the illegal conduct Branco specifically identifies as occurring from twenty to fifty years ago, with much of it at least thirty years old. Yet in reviewing Branco's chapter it seems the harms have grown rather than dissipated, like an untreated wound.

Chapter 4: Brazilian-Israelis Adopted Through Child Trafficking

Andrea Cardarello provides a history of illegal adoptions of Brazilian children to Israel and then focuses on obstacles for the impacted adoptees as to their rights of origins and identity. As in some of the other chapters, this focus on older cases allows fuller consideration of the long-term harms of illegal intercountry adoption and consideration of the considerable obstacles and resistance encountered by adoptees seeking remedies. The chapter includes interview data from a project the author conducted, along with Carol A. Kidron, of Haifa University, involving semi-structured interviews with five Brazilian-Israeli adoptees, and also reflects prior work by the author working with Brazilian families of origin who had lost their children in the 1990s to illegal domestic and intercountry adoption.

Brazil is, of course, distinctive from most Latin American countries linguistically, since Portuguese, rather than Spanish, is the dominant language. Nonetheless, Brazil's intercountry adoption narrative has some common features with Latin American adoptions generally, including a history of illegally separating children from families for the purpose of adoption, followed by increasing scandals and eventually a tightening of rules, based in part on ratification and implementation of the 1993 HAC.

Adoptions between Brazil and Israel were impacted by the highly publicized 1988 Israeli Supreme Court decision requiring Brazilian baby girl Bruna to be returned to her first parents. This is perhaps the only case where the court of a receiving state ordered an adopted child to be returned to the first family in the country of origin. The Court ordered the return of the toddler even though the adoptive parents had apparently not known that the child had been kidnapped from the first family and despite the lapse of two years in which the child had grown attached to the adoptive parents. As Cardarello recounts, a British TV producer who had been investigating illegal adoptions from Brazil assisted the first family in coming to Israel and filing the lawsuit. The case is an important precedent for remedies when an illegal separation of the child from the first family is discovered when the adoptee is still a child. Cardarello supplies important information for understanding the significance of the case. For example, she indicates a large-scale network of criminal gangs, judges, court officials, notaries, and federal police involved in illegally taking large numbers of children from their families; yet only three intermediaries were imprisoned, and, of course, only one child was returned. Thus, even this landmark, internationally publicized case involving the return of a kidnapped child to her family, understood in its context, is also a reminder of the usual lack of remedies for victims of illegal adoption. In the broader context, the lack of remedies for adult adoptees and first families described by Cardarello throughout her chapter suggests that achieving remedies usually requires overcoming resistance by the state and intermediaries, rather than actually receiving assistance from state authorities. The baby Bruna case is a unicorn, not a norm; a possibility, not an expectation.

Several of Cardarello's conclusions are similar to those in this introduction: First, she emphasizes the significance of the class differences between adult adoptees and their first families, in which the adoptees "can hardly be defined as subaltern" (p. 147). Cardarello notes this problem regarding Argentina and Chile, as well as Brazil. The 'multilayered' identities of adoptees include their complex relationship to their first nation, which in regard to Brazil, Cardarello, quoting Ribke & Bourdon, describes as follows:

> Brazil is both a former Third World nation with a long-standing heritage of poverty and exploitation, which are painful elements of their own particular life-stories, and a new global power, with a widely recognized and embraced vibrant popular culture, and is thus a place they are eager to identify with.

A part of the difficulty Cardarello identifies is how to make remedies for seemingly wealthy and empowered adult adoptees benefit the much less accessible, impoverished, first families that often come from the "lower class" of society (p. 147).

Second, Cardarello thinks that progress will only come from activism by impacted persons, including 'adoptees trafficked abroad', who must move beyond 'being only a support-group' to 'becoming more political' through the concept of "'collective responsibility' in the countries involved".

Chapter 5: Remedies for Cold War Greek Adoptions

The beginnings of Greek adoptions preceded those of South Korean adoptions. This largely forgotten chapter of intercountry adoption has in recent years been brought into view through the efforts of Gonda Van Steen, author of this chapter and of the 2019 work, 'Adoption, Memory, and Cold War Greece: Kid pro quo?' and through adoptee activism, including that of Mary Cardaras, editor of the 2023 adoptee collection, 'Voices of the Lost Children of Greece'.

The Greek precursor story of illegal international adoption, as told by Gonda Van Steen in this chapter and elsewhere, echoes many of the same themes seen throughout this volume. First, we see in this origin story of international adoption the same pattern of separating children unnecessarily from their original families. In Greek adoptions this occurred through exploiting the vulnerabilities of single mothers and the poor. In addition, first families were also tricked through exploitation of the gap between the pre-existing Greek law and practice of simple adoption that left intact some degree of family relationship between first families and adoptees, and an international practice that favoured full severance adoption, permanently separating the adoptee from the original family. Second, in Greek adoptions we see intermediaries learn to manipulate complex procedures to their own ends. Third, in Greek adoptions we see the significance of scandals in creating openings to tighten regulation and alter public perceptions.

Van Steen's chapter focuses on three specific adoptee 'demands' pertaining to remedies (or 'redress' as she terms it): records, restoration of citizenship (as a form of dual citizenship) and research.

Records: The chapter recounts the constant obstacles, delays and refusals faced by adult adoptees in seeking their own records, despite a 1996 law purporting to provide adoptees with rights to their records. Van Steen notes how these practices 'infantilize' adoptees by denying them adult agency and access to origins.

Restoration of Citizenship: Van Steen states that 700 of the 4,000 Greek adoptees seek restored Greek citizenship as a form of dual citizenship. Van Steen goes beyond the formalities of restored citizenship to discuss the relationship of the sent-away children to their Greek heritage and laments the lack of "a warm welcome home" (p. 164). By comparison with South Korea, which offers adoptees opportunities "to participate in 'motherland tours' or in similar programs of trans-culturalization or re-culturation", there are no similar practices for Greek adoptees (p. 167). While Van Steen notes that South Korean adoptees have critiqued offers of certain forms of assistance as still showing a "lack of understanding" (p. 169), Greek adoptees suffer from an even starker lack of remedies, coupled with an exclusion even from programmes directed to the Greek diaspora (fn. 35).

Research: As perhaps the pre-eminent academic researcher of Greek international adoptions, Van Steen notes that her own 2019 book "can only be a limited first step" (p. 172). The fundamental wish behind the demand for more research is that Greek's adoption history "should simply be better known" (p. 172). International Greek adoptees face the difficulties of being a part of a broader history that has been simply unknown, in part due to a state focus on "the avoidance of scandal and on damage control" (p. 176).

Van Steen expresses the urgency of these demands for redress since "time is running out" (p. 151), as the first parents have been dying and even most of the adoptees are more than sixty years old. Van Steen describes the tragedy of justice delayed as a fundamental denial of justice.

CHAPTER 6: SWITZERLAND RESPONDS TO ILLEGAL ADOPTIONS

Chapter 6, on Switzerland, transitions the chapters to a focus on receiving states. Sabine Bitter describes the "lifting of a decades-long silence surrounding abusive intercountry adoption in Switzerland" (p. 183) which has occurred in the last five years. A combination of investigative journalism, actions of certain politicians, and an interest group called Back to the Roots, "about half of whom are adoptees", has enabled Switzerland to take "first steps to deal with illegal intercountry adoptions" (title). "Almost all" of the activist adoptees in Back to the Roots "came to Switzerland as babies from Sri Lanka or India in the 1980s and 1990s". Once again we have an example of a long-delayed focus on decades-old illegal adoptions.

This delay, Bitter points out, was not inevitable, as concerns were voiced from legal academic perspectives from the mid-1970s onwards (pp. 187-188). In addition, "alarming" (p. 190) and prominent media reports from the 1980s onwards made concerns with illegal adoptions evident to society. Yet "the authorities remained largely inactive" (p. 190).

Bitter carefully reviews the partial progress made over the last five years:

Investigations: As to investigation, Bitter herself co-authored an independent, government-commissioned study of adoptions from Sri Lanka released in 2020, and is currently working with colleagues on another independent, government-commissioned study of adoptions from India to Switzerland.

Regret but no apology? Beyond the commissioning of independent investigations, the Swiss government expressed its 'regret' that "neither the federal government nor the cantons had fulfilled their duty to protect the children". Bitter describes the controversy over the failure of the government to use the language of apology in the context of illegal intercountry adoption, even though "the government had apologized more than once in the past for other abuses in connection with the placement of children" (p. 198).

State assistance for adoptees researching their origins: The government stated it would provide 'greater support' to adoptees placed from Sri Lanka during certain periods of time (p. 197). Yet Bitter reports that "[s]earching their origins has proven very time-consuming and expensive for adoptees" (p. 199). Bitter describes the complicated division of responsibilities across multiple governmental authorities which makes it difficult for adoptees to locate records. This complexity "implies a Kafkaesque journey through various offices, archives and institutions to gather fragments of their past". Bitter notes the governments' release of a "list of contacts and advisory services in the various cantons" as helpful but sometimes failing to promise to provide a "neutral contact point for adopted persons", given the self-interest of offices implicated in possible wrongdoing. Bitter therefore suggests the "establishment of a centralised service, unencumbered by previous misconduct and shortcomings and apt to assume the important task on behalf of the adoptees..."

Coordination Between Receiving and Sending State: Bitter describes meetings between several European states and the "central government authority in Sri Lanka responsible for adoptions" (p. 201). Bitter disagrees with the decision of Sri Lanka not to involve the Office for Missing Persons recently set up to assist with enforced disappearances during the civil war. Bitter considers intercountry adoption from Sri Lanka sufficiently related to the subject of enforced disappearances to be taken up within those mechanisms regardless of whether or not they are connected to the civil war (pp. 201-202), a topic considered in detail in Chapters 10 and 11 of this volume. In the absence of more active assistance from the government of Sri Lanka, the birth searches to date are "not likely to be of much use to use to adoptees seeking their origins" (p. 202). Bitter reports that none of the fourteen applications going through the cooperation protocol had yet found biological parents, although one person "managed to find her biological mother by herself" (p. 202).

Work of Back to the Roots (Adoptee Association): Bitter highlights the work of the voluntary association Back to the Roots, which advertises itself as an 'Association for Adopted People from Sri Lanka in Switzerland'.[144] As in other countries, some of the most important work assisting adoptees or first families is done by an NGO or voluntary association dedicated to that purpose. Bitter highlights the origins, purpose and work of Back to the Roots, including the provision of free DNA testing, which has so far produced twelve matches between Sri Lankan mothers and adoptees in Switzerland (p. 204). Bitter also notes the expansion of the organization's work to assist adoptees from India, which is particularly significant since adoptions from India were much more numerous than those from Sri Lanka, India being "the main country of origin of adopted children for Switzerland in the last three decades of the twentieth century" (p. 204). A review of the association website indicates plans to assist international adoptees from all countries[145] and the possibility of private organizations that 'close the gaps', such as Back to the Roots, receiving government funding.[146] Bitter seems to consider the best hope for remedies to be Back to the Roots continuing its work "with funding from the federal government and cantons" (p. 208) and with the involvement

144 See https://backtotheroots.net/.

145 See https://backtotheroots.net/eine-premiere-treffen-fuer-alle-international-adoptierten-personen-in-der-schweiz/.

146 https://backtotheroots.net/eine-premiere-treffen-fuer-alle-international-adoptierten-personen-in-der-schweiz/.

of the CED. Bitter is hopeful that "this civil service organization could … serve as a best-practice example to other countries".

Chapter 7: Financial Compensation for Intercountry Adoptees in the Netherlands

Dewi Deijle, an attorney and Dutch adoptee born in Jakarta, Indonesia, argues that the state should provide financial compensation for individual adoptee roots searches. Indeed, Deijle argues that the Dutch state is legally liable regarding illegal adoptions owing to a failure to protect the adoptees, as children, from deprivations of their rights, including the rights to private and family life. Adoptees were deprived of their right to "grow up with their birth parents as much as possible, while it had not been established that adoption was necessary and in the child's best interests" (p. 217). Thus, according to Deijle, compensation to carry out individual roots searches is a legal responsibility, not an act of charity.

Deijle describes the rejection of these claims by the Dutch state, despite the now famous 2021 Report and despite an apology by the state. The Netherlands is one of the most advanced receiving states as to recognizing the systemic nature of illegal intercountry adoption and in admitting the fault of the Dutch state for those systemic abuses. Yet, as a legal matter, the Dutch government has denied legal liability and appealed rulings finding liability (p. 225).

Deijle critiques the governmental exploration of a group search grant scheme as making "it clear that there is (still) no recognition of the root cause of the problem and that the minister has no idea of what an investigation into parentage information actually looks like" (p. 227).

Deijle's arguments are important to the question of remedies for illegal intercountry adoption. As a foundation for remedies, a legal obligation is much stronger than a request for assistance. At a moment when some states are commissioning investigations of illegal intercountry adoption and starting to acknowledge the findings of systemic abuses over decades, the question of remedies has become more urgent. It is frustrating to see how far the Dutch state has gone in acknowledging fault without acknowledging liability and in contemplating assisting adoptees apparently without comprehending what adoptees need.

Chapter 8: History and Genealogy of Intercountry Adoption

Elisabeth (Lies) Wesseling provides a summary and then a critique of historical narratives of intercountry adoption, focusing especially on the question of precursors – what past practices form the best lens for understanding intercountry adoption. Wesseling reviews the works of historians of intercountry adoption (ICA) from the United States, France and the Netherlands, as well as reviewing other European literature. Wesseling credits adoptees for some of the first publications "to confront the colonial antecedents of ICA in depth" (p. 242). Wesseling reviews practices of transnational and transracial child circulation throughout the 19th and early 20th centuries "as an integral part of empire" (p. 243). She then cites studies which "reveal unambiguously that the first ICA networks developed directly out of the child separation projects in the colonies" (p. 149). Wesseling thus argues that

> the idea of ICA as the successor project to domestic adoption is historically flawed. Rather, ICA is the continuation of the last chapter in colonial history which was written in the key of white saviorism, a potent cocktail of 'uplifting' the newer generations of colonized nations and subjecting them in the same process. (p. 249)

Wesseling's use of a colonial and postcolonial lens to view intercountry adoption has three similarities to what I propose in this introduction. First, Wesseling "reinsert[s] adoption into the whole gamut of child separation practices" (p. 250), which is consistent with my suggestion that illegal intercountry adoption be conceptualized as the illegal and unethical separation of children from families. Second, Wesseling's view of "transracial adoption … as a 'stratified form of assisted reproduction'" (fn 58), in which Western prospective adoptive parents feel entitled to a non-Western child (p. 250), is consistent with concerns with the demand side of intercountry adoption, which can sometimes masquerade as humanitarianism. Finally, as Wesseling notes, the humanitarian narrative "is conducive to the tenacious under-estimation of the systemic nature of adoptive malpractices". I opened this introduction with a concern that naively positive views of intercountry adoption make it difficult for both adoption triad members and the general society to appreciate the systemic nature of illegal adoption.

Although Wesseling does not state this directly, the colonial and postcolonial perspective on intercountry adoption provides an excellent foundation for establishing the necessity of systemic remedies, especially for first families and adoptees. Hence, Wesseling's chapter provides an excellent foundation for evaluating the justifications for providing systemic remedies for historical patterns of systemic abuse.

Despite my own sympathy for colonial and postcolonial narratives, they create complexities for the project of demanding systemic remedies for illegal intercountry adoption. First, colonial and postcolonial narratives may tend to blur the lines between legal and illegal intercountry adoption, by implicitly tainting all intercountry adoption. At that point debate may turn towards what some may view as ideological or political evaluations of intercountry adoption as a whole. While that is a useful debate, it may cause those who reject colonial and postcolonial perspectives as the most appropriate one for evaluating intercountry adoption to also reject the conclusion of systemic abuses. Ultimately, claims for remedies for illegal intercountry adoption require demonstration of illegal and unethical actions, regardless of broader historical narratives or precursor practices. Second, even assuming Wesseling is correct about precursor narratives, a colonial and postcolonial narrative may obscure the responsibility of countries of origin in more recent years and may fit some countries of origin more easily than others. Intercountry adoption, statistically, has been dominated by a relatively small number of countries of origin in each period of time, and the decisions and practices of those countries involve far more than postcolonial domination or exploitation. For example, the tripling of intercountry adoption that occurred from the early 1990s to 2005, when it peaked, occurred primarily through large numbers of adoptions from China, Russia and, to a lesser degree, Guatemala, nations with very different relationships to a colonial or postcolonial analysis. Third, accessibility is an issue. Many adoptees have been raised in adoptive families unfamiliar with the concept of postcolonialism. Some may be assisted in understanding the nature of systemic abuse by postcolonial narratives; for others, postcolonialism is simply too foreign to their own belief system or political identity or simply too distant from their own lived experience, as they understand it, to be helpful.

None of this is meant to detract at all from the significance of colonial and postcolonial historical narratives. Wesseling presents a potentially potent corrective to scholarly and popular historical narratives on the precursors and practices of intercountry adoption. She also presents a history that is often neglected, as to the history of child separation practices. For those who have ears to hear, let them hear.

Chapter 9: Resisting Adoption Reform (and Remedies)

Sophie Withaeckx's contribution focuses on resistance to adoption reform after the publication, in 2021, of reports in the Netherlands and Belgium documenting substantial abuses and recommending suspensions or pauses of intercountry adoption. Withaeckx attributes this resistance to the role of adoption as "an expression of a nation's 'humaneness,' solidarity, cosmopolitanism and generosity" (p. 262). For individuals who have constituted their identities through a discourse of adoption as humanitarian, such reports of adoption abuses "can become an experience of attack on the self" (p. 263). For adoptive parents and prospective adoptive parents, such reports and accompanying suspensions present as "an undesired intrusion into their personal … family projects …" (p. 267). For all those involved in the adoption system, there are the "suggestions that they could somehow be (co)responsible for abuses, an allegation that does not align with their understanding of their investment in adoption as solely arising from good intentions" (p. 268). Withaeckx thus situates this resistance in the context of "a humanitarian-compassionate narrative on adoption [which] relies on the constitution of two central figures: the humanitarian saviour and the helpless waif".

Withaeckx conducted a "discourse analysis of Belgian and Dutch newspaper articles" published "between 1 February 2021 and 31 July 2022" to further document the sources of resistance to adoption reform (p. 256). This analysis further documents how the resistance to reform is rooted in the humanitarian understanding of adoption.

Withaeckx notices that intercountry adoption had already decreased significantly in both countries and impacts "a relatively small number of children worldwide" (p. 256). Further, even before these reports there had been "re-occurring reports of systemic abuses throughout the history of modern adoptions". Yet, paradoxically, there "seems to be so much reluctance to properly address" the abuses or "to resort to alternatives". This observation reaffirms that resistance to adoption reform is rooted in the symbolic meanings of intercountry adoption that transcend the practical importance of the practice in assisting vulnerable children.

Withaeckx notes that this humanitarian discourse focusing on the humanitarian saviour and helpless waif or orphan "works to erase the figure of the adult adoptee …" (p. 270). In response, a social justice perspective focuses on "pressing problems in the here-and-now of adoptees' lived experiences" (p. 273):

> Many adoptees feel puzzled by the neglect of a government that is quick to come to the rescue of helpless children, but refrains from properly responding when these same, now adult children, express their changing needs: financial assistance for family searches, psychological support for distressed adoptees and adoptive families, the right to identity and access to information about their background. (p. 273)

The chapter thus focuses on the lack of remedies for adult adoptees and documents that adoptees are left to create and fund their own remedies (pp. 274-275). As Withaeckx expresses it, "[T]he now adult adoptees' emotional pleas for reparations, care and support are met with cold rejections" (p. 275).

Withaeckx also notes that neither adoptee nor adoptive parent discourses enable:

> the hearing of the voices of first parents ... as they are completely elided from the compassionate saviour/child relation, and simply unable to make their claims heard in a social justice perspective. (p. 276)

Finally, Withaeckx confirms the precursor point made by Elisabeth Wesseling in Chapter 8, as to continuities between the origins of intercountry and prior colonial child separation practices, stating:

> Present-day adoption agencies operate in narrow institutional continuities with these colonial [child removal] practices, as the same persons, organisations, practices and financial circuits often became involved in the newly rebranded humanitarian adoption agencies. (quote p. 261 around fn 32).

This precursor point fits Withaeckx's theme that the humanitarian-compassionate narrative on intercountry adoption is deeply rooted in the identity of many Western European nations as it reflects an attempt to replicate a positive self-understanding and identity in the new, postcolonial context. The defence and continued practice of intercountry adoption appears as a kind of national psychological defence mechanism against realization of decades of exploitative practices. If Withaeckx is correct about this, the realizations necessary to move forward with appropriate remedies for illegal intercountry adoption will be emotionally and psychologically difficult to attain and retain.

Chapter 10: Illegal Intercountry Adoption as Enforced Disappearances

Chapters 10 and 11 both concern the legal concept of enforced disappearances in the context of illegal intercountry adoption. Chapter 10 focuses on the obligations of receiving states as a remedial matter in the aftermath of illegal intercountry adoptions that constitute a violation of human rights norms against enforced disappearances. Chapter 11, described further on, will focus on individual criminal responsibility.

In Chapter 10, Elvira Loibl provides a clear legal analysis of when illegal intercountry adoption does and does not constitute a violation of the norm against enforced disappearances. As Loibl explains, the issue has gained prominence in part through the work of the CED, including their concluding observations to Switzerland in 2021, which addressed illegal adoptions of Sri Lankan children; earlier in 2021 Back to the Roots, an adoptee association, had approached the CED requesting they address the issue (p. 279).

Further, the CED and the Working Group on Enforced or Involuntary Disappearances joined three UN Special Rapporteurs in issuing a joint report on illegal intercountry adoption in September 2022, which noted that illegal intercountry adoption in "certain conditions" may violate "the prohibition of enforced disappearances" (p. 282).

The possible application, to intercountry adoption, of the International Convention for the Protection of All Persons from Enforced Disappearances (ICPPED) has, as Loibl explains, potential for furthering remedies for victims of illegal adoption:

> The ICPPED obliges State Parties to carry out a prompt, impartial and thorough investigation without delay once a possible enforced disappearance has come to their attention and to ensure that victims of enforced disappearance have the right to obtain reparation and prompt, fair and adequate compensation. (page 281, fn 13 and 14)

Loibl further stresses that "considering illegal intercountry adoptions as enforced disappearances" may further the recognition that "illegally obtaining children in intercountry adoption" is a serious crime and human rights violation (p. 281).

Loibl carefully analyses illegal intercountry adoption to see if and when it would qualify under the ICPPED three-part definition of enforced disappearances. As to the first element, deprivation of liberty, Loibl describes a number of typical illegal adoption scenarios in which either the child or the mother is deprived of liberty, including literal abductions and circumstances where 'means of deception or persuasion' would also constitute a form of abduction. Loibl, however, concludes that other forms of illegal adoption would not come within the Convention, including "purchasing children from their parents, falsifying the child's paperwork or bribing government officials to expedite an adoption or to subvert the subsidiarity principle..." (p. 286).

The third element involves a "refusal to acknowledge the deprivation of liberty or concealment of the fate of the disappeared person" (p. 286). Loibl notes that "numerous cases of illegal intercountry adoption that involve the abduction of a child" would 'probably' meet this element, due to the laundering process common in illegal adoptions. "Just as crime proceeds and 'dirty money' need to be laundered, illegally obtained children must be purified to be profitable" to make them appear to be "an abandoned or relinquished child that is in true need of a family" (p. 287). Hence, "birth certificates and adoption related documents ... are falsified or fabricated ..." (p. 287). This laundering process

> erases the true identity of the abducted child, essentially severing any link between them and their biological parents ... [s]ince their biological identity

> is not protected, their own personality is not recognized before the law. (pp. 287-288)

Indeed, "the adoptee is placed outside of the protection of the law" (p. 287). Hence, the laundering process commonly meets the element of a "concealment of the fate of the disappeared person".

The second element requires that the deprivation of liberty be carried out with the direct or indirect involvement of state agents, meaning that it was carried out either by 'agents of the state' or by non-state actors "acting with the authorization, support or acquiescence of the State" (p. 290). Loibl here reviews several documented situations of systemic illegal adoption, including from Guatemala, and the practices revealed by the recent Dutch and Swiss reports. Once again, the child laundering process is key to the analysis, since illegally obtained children

> are passed through the same legal channels as children that are actually eligible for intercountry adoption. Illegal adoptions are ... embedded within a legitimate system and rely on its official procedures: the children's birth needs to be registered, they need to be declared relinquished or abandoned and eligible for adoption, an official adoption decision needs to be rendered and a visa or passport application needs to be approved.... All these bureaucratic steps are commonly carried out or monitored by state actors, i.e., government officials, judges, diplomats etc. whose approvals and services are necessary for an adoption to be able to take place. (p. 293)

Loibl concludes that "in incidents where adoption abuses took place on a large scale, there is much to presume the involvement of state officials ..." (p. 294). As indicated in the chapter, investigations of Guatemalan adoptions indicate this was the case as to Guatemalan state authorities, at a minimum as to acquiescence, and the Dutch and Swiss reports indicated that their respective state officials were aware of illegal and abusive practices but nonetheless allowed the adoptions to continue.

Loibl also considers the temporal limitations of the ICPPED, which was only concluded in 2010. However, because "enforced disappearance has a continuous nature that does not cease to exist until the victim's fate or whereabouts are established" (p. 298), "receiving states can be considered responsible for enforced disappearances that commenced" decades before the Convention (p. 298). While the Committee on Enforced Disappearances (CED) "is precluded from examining individual cases ... that commenced before the entry into force of the Convention for the State concerned", the capacity to question states on "present compliance ... even in relation to past disappearances" remains. Hence, state obligations for older, pre-Convention cases remain applicable.

Finally, Loibl considers in some detail the obligations of states as to investigation and reparation, the latter including restitution, rehabilitation, satisfaction (including restoration of dignity and reputation), and guarantees of non-repetition. Loibl concludes that the Dutch and Swiss governments

> so far ... have done little to investigate the specific circumstances of illegal intercountry adoptions and to search for and identify the family members of those adoptees.... It seems that the governments want to close this chapter of the past and move on. However, the findings of the inquiries only mark the beginning of a reappraisal.... Enforced disappearances are continuous crimes that do not cease to exist until the victim's fate or whereabouts are established. Hence, the state obligation to investigate continues to apply until the specific circumstances of a possible illegal intercountry adoption are clarified and the true identity of the adoptee is established. (p. 306)

Chapter 11: Individual Criminal Responsibility for Illegal Intercountry Adoptions Following the Crime of Enforced Disappearance

André Klip's analysis of individual criminal responsibility for illegal intercountry adoption creates an interesting contrast to Elvira Loibl's prior chapter on receiving state's obligations. Both pertain to the recent interest in applying the law of enforced disappearances to illegal intercountry adoptions. But the conclusions are starkly different. Loibl perceives the human rights norms against enforced disappearances as often applicable to illegal intercountry adoption, and as providing significant norms of state responsibility for the provision of remedies. Klip, by contrast, perceives the applicable criminal law pertaining to enforced disappearances as lacking utility and largely counterproductive to efforts to bring perpetrators to justice. This contrast does not imply disagreement, as Loibl and Klip are addressing different applications. Standards for criminal prosecution are necessarily more rigorous since they implicate the rights of defendants to due process of law and focus on the conflict between the state and the alleged perpetrator, while human rights standards tend to focus more on the relationship between the state and the victim.

Klip's pessimism about the utility of individual criminal responsibility in this area has several sources, as follows: First, according to Klip, "there is not a single case reported in which a crime under the Convention has been prosecuted" (p. 308). Further,

> [the] very few references to judgements in which enforced disappearances play a role come from international criminal tribunals who decided these on the definition of enforced disappearance as a crime against humanity under their Statute and in which the attack on the civilian population resulted in many casualties. (p. 308)

Thus, the criminal law of enforced disappearance is an underdeveloped area, even apart from its attempted innovative application to intercountry adoption.

Second, Klip appears to agree with the critiques by some governments about the lack of utility of creating specialized criminal law around the norm against enforced disappearance. From this perspective the conduct prohibited by this norm

> is already covered by various existing penal provisions and therefore the added value of the crime of enforced disappearance is merely symbolic. The crime of enforced disappearance is not an easy crime to prove as it has many elements and there is not a sufficient state practice yet on its prosecution. (p. 321)

Hence, those who follow the CED's recommendations for a new and specialized crime, following the definitions in the Convention, "will automatically reduce the possibilities for prosecution", producing "an offense which only in rare cases can be proven in criminal proceedings" (p. 330).

Third, there is the related problem that states have demonstrated little enthusiasm 'at all stages of the Convention', including 'investigating and prosecuting' (p. 330). Again, this critique goes beyond the application to intercountry adoption, to a general lack of enthusiasm as to criminal enforcement of laws specifically targeting a crime of enforced disappearance, at least outside crimes against humanity involving large-scale civilian casualties, which anyway pre-exist the Convention.

Fourth, this lack of enthusiasm is partially expressed through state parties not implementing appropriate state legislation, for without national legislation there is no criminal responsibility (p. 320). The Committee recommends that "the offense of enforced disappearance be defined" both as a separate offence and also as a crime against humanity "in line with Article 25 of the Convention and the two separate offenses of Article 25". Yet Klip "did not encounter a single state party" that had followed these recommendations (p. 321), apparently in part owing to the view that existing national penal law adequately covered the conduct.

Fifth, the temporal aspects are accentuated in the area of criminal law, because of the requirement that a criminal law predate the conduct of the crime. As to state responsibility, Loibl used the continuing nature of the wrong of enforced disappearance to alleviate the difficulty that the Convention is rather recent. As to criminal law, it is unclear whether the continuing nature of the crime avoids the problem that, in so many intercountry adoption cases, the 'moment of abduction' of the child occurred decades prior to the creation of the Convention and implementing national laws (pp. 325-326).

Sixth, there are particular jurisdictional complexities in applying the convention and implementing national legislation to intercountry adoption, owing to the involvement of two states, the state of origin and the receiving state (pp. 323-324). These complexities create further obstacles.

Klip usefully describes the four different criminal offences defined by the convention, including enforced disappearance; enforced disappearance as a crime against humanity; wrongful removal of a child subjected to enforced disappearance or whose parents were so subject, or born during the captivity of a mother so subjected; identity concealment or substitution. Klip's analysis goes beyond the question of when illegal intercountry adoption meets the definition of one or more of these crimes as defined by the convention. Rather, Klip's analysis focuses on practical obstacles to criminal prosecution that, in total, appear in most cases insurmountable, at least at present.

Again, there is no inconsistency in the contrasting views of Loibl and Klip. The law of enforced disappearances, as to the question of state responsibility to provide remedies to victims, and as to the prospects of successful individual criminal prosecutions against individual defendants, are, in practice, quite different questions. Klip's chapter is a useful reminder of the importance of strategic evaluations of different avenues as to remedies for illegal intercountry adoption.

Part I
Sending Countries

2 Pursuing Truth, Justice and Rectification of the Global Orphan Adoption System: the Legacy of South Korea's Case

Kyung-eun Lee

Introduction

Human rights violations and crimes committed in intercountry adoption have attracted international attention. Incidents that were once isolated to local news reports have attained global media prominence, as well as closer scrutiny by international organizations and governments engaged in intercountry adoption. The shift in coverage and concern may be partially attributed to the pattern of serious child rights infringement and widespread child abuse that can no longer be dismissed as isolated or random. A growing body of research from a variety of disciplines has supported the claims of systematic abuses throughout intercountry adoption programmes.[1]

This chapter aims to contribute to the current discourse by assessing the global orphan adoption system, a set of legal frameworks and practices established by governments to grant a network of agencies and intermediaries the authority to engage in the large-scale movement of children from the Global South to the Global North. The chapter particularly focuses on South Korea since it pioneered this system with the U.S. in the 1950s and eventually served as a prototype for other sending countries.

A key element sustaining the global orphan adoption system is orphanization, which this chapter will explore. Since orphans were eligible for intercountry adoption, the process of orphanization, which entailed issuing an orphan certificate to classify a child as an orphan, acted as a linchpin to secure children to place abroad. A further

---

1 D.M. Smolin, 'The Corrupting Influence of the United States on a Vulnerable Intercountry Adoption System: A Guide for Stakeholders, Hague and Non-Hague Nations, NGOs, and Concerned Parties', *Journal of Law and Family Studies*, Vol. 15, 2013, pp. 81-151; K. Jeon, K. Lee and J. Trenka, *Baby Selling Country*, Seoul, Mayspring, 2019; Committee Investigating Intercountry Adoption, *Consideration, Analysis, Conclusions, Recommendations, and Summary*, February 2021, https://www.government.nl/documents/reports/2021/02/08/summary-consideration-analysis-conclusions-recommendations.

factor that facilitated this system involves the privatization of adoption processes and the involvement of private actors – the institutions, agencies and intermediaries.

The privatization of intercountry adoption and the process of orphanization not only subjected children to serious human rights violations but also represented direct transgressions of core international treaties, including the 1989 UN Convention on the Rights of the Child (hereinafter UNCRC) and the 1993 The Hague Convention on Protection of Children and Co-operation in Respect of Intercountry Adoption (hereinafter the Hague Adoption Convention), which implicates questions of state accountability. For this reason, the primary purpose of this chapter is to expose the state's responsibility for violating the rights of adoptees. Furthermore, the author seeks to contribute to discussions on the adoption system and policy reform while also foregrounding the state's obligation to restore the rights of adoptees to know their true origin and identity. The chapter concludes by proposing several strategies, some of which have already begun, such as investigations into past abuses of intercountry adoption in some receiving countries and adoptee lawsuits against states of origin.

THE LEGACY AND IMPACT OF 'ORPHAN' ADOPTION

The Origin of the Second Wave of Intercountry Adoption[2]

South Korea has played a leading role in sculpting the global landscape of intercountry adoption. In the aftermath of the Korean War, the country's intercountry adoption programme ushered in the second wave of intercountry and transracial adoption of Asian children by Western couples. In the first wave, intercountry adoption was a provisional measure to find homes for World War II orphans, and the procedure and practices reflected its temporary nature. However, South Korea institutionalized intercountry adoption to such an extent that its system extended beyond private adoption actors to include an industry of intermediaries to secure children and legislation to facilitate the efficient placement of these children abroad. Accordingly, the embedded nature of this system reinforced its expansion into a sustainable business that operated according to a market mechanism.[3]

2 A. Young, 'Development in Intercountry Adoption: From Humanitarian Aid to Market-Driven Policy and Beyond', *Adoption and Fostering*, Vol. 36, 2012, pp. 67-78.

3 Key features distinguish the first and second waves of intercountry adoption. Like the first wave, the second wave started as a provisional humanitarian response but transformed into an entrenched system populated by private agencies that placed children from the Global South in the homes of predominately white couples in the Global North. This trend reflected the socioeconomic disparities between sending and receiving countries and the racial difference between adoptee and adoptive parents. See K. Lee, *The Global Orphan Adoption System: South Korea's Impact on Its Origin and Development*, Seoul, Koroot, 2021, pp. 52-66.

Since the introduction of the South Korean intercountry adoption programme in 1953, adoptions from South Korea have continued uninterrupted. As of 2019, the official total number of children placed for adoption abroad is 167,864; however, the actual number is much larger at over 200,000 due to thousands of unaccounted clandestine adoptions. Receiving countries of South Korean children include the U.S., France, Sweden, Denmark, Norway, the Netherlands, Belgium, Germany, Switzerland, Italy, Luxemburg, Great Britain, Australia and Canada. This figure earns South Korea the legacy of having sent the most children overseas for adoption (Figure 1).[4]

Figure 1. Number of intercountry adoptions from South Korea (1953-2019)[5]

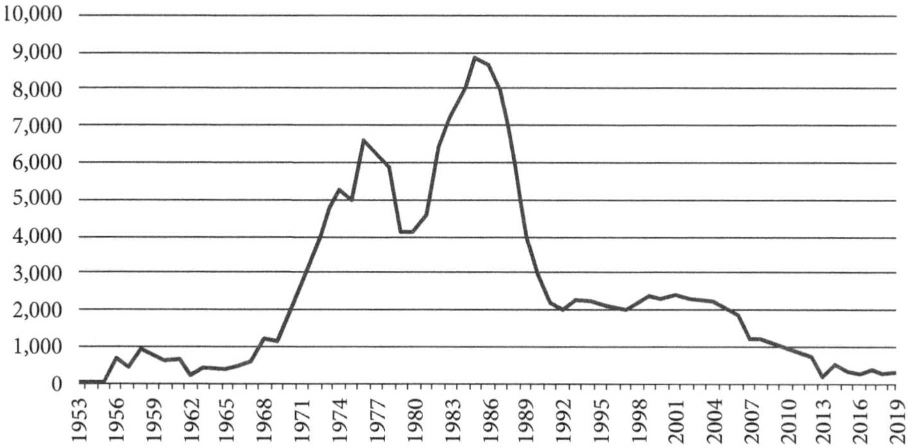

From 1961 to 1992, an authoritarian military regime ruled South Korea. Throughout the 1970s and 1980s, thousands of children left the country annually, peaking in 1985 at almost 9,000 (or over 1% of the total number of births in South Korea). The trajectory of this trend would have most likely proceeded uninterrupted if not for the 1988 Olympics. The South Korean military dictatorship sought to enhance its international reputation by hosting the world's largest sporting event. However, the country's excessive number of intercountry adoptions prompted international scrutiny and criticism with some

4 Intercountry adoption statistics have generally been collected from the immigration authorities of the receiving countries, and these numbers were then disaggregated according to the states of origin. As a sending country, South Korea is unique in that it collects, records and publishes the number of children it exports annually.

5 The numbers are collected from the adoption statistics of the annual Adoption Day Press Release by Ministry of Health and Welfare, https://www.mohw.go.kr/react/al/sal0301ls.jsp?PAR_MENU_ID=04&MENU_ID=0403. Korean intercountry adoption statistics are also available at https://kosis.kr/statHtml/statHtml.do?orgId=117&tblId=DT_11770N001.

media outlets dubbing South Korea a baby exporter.[6] In response, the military regime reduced the scale of the programme. As the numbers fell, international attention on the issue receded, but abuses and injustice persisted unabated.

During the 1990s, South Korea sent over 2,000 children annually for intercountry adoption. Around this time, the Korean government expressed concerns over the rapidly falling birth rate, which would eventually rank the lowest in the world by the 2000s. Although South Korea frets over solving its persistently plummeting birth rate, it has continued sending over hundreds of children overseas for adoption each year. Although these rates are significantly lower than in previous decades, human rights bodies have consistently criticized South Korea for maintaining an exceptionally high rate of intercountry adoption, given the country's economic and development status.

Presently the tenth largest economy, the country has earned a reputation for shedding its authoritarian regime in 1993 to become a vibrant democracy. This political transition and economic success represent a sense of national pride as it strives to promote itself among the global community. However, its protracted use of intercountry adoption denotes the presence of wider human rights violations and failures to provide adequate social protection for vulnerable families. As the intercountry adoption programme became more entrenched in the social and political system and laws of the country, it led to a deterioration of the national child protection system and stifled progress in family law. The government saw little need to invest in these areas as long as intercountry adoption could remove vulnerable children who would otherwise require government welfare expenditure.

Can a Country Overcome Its Legacy and History of Exporting Children?

Even though this country would prefer to regard intercountry adoptions as a vestige of its post-war past, the truth is South Korea has never been able to stop sending children away for adoption. Nowhere has this been more apparent than during the COVID-19 pandemic. As countries scrambled to slow the spread by introducing quarantine measures that brought global travel to a standstill, intercountry adoptions reflected a similar disruption. International Social Service (ISS) released a list of the major sending countries and their respective intercountry adoption rates for 2020 (Figure 2).

---

6 M. Rothschild, 'Babies for Sale: South Korea Make Them, Americans Buy Them', *The Progressive*, Vol. 52, No. 1, 1988, pp. 18-23.

Figure 2. Major sending countries in 2020[7]

State of origin	2012	2013	2014	2015	2016	2017	2018	2019	2020
Colombia	901	562	355	359	314	542	559	597	**387**
Ukraine	713	674	560	339	339	270	280	366	**277**
South Korea	797	206	494	406	362	396	303	254	**266**
India	362	298	242	233	323	518	456	503	**263**
China	3,998	3,316	2,734	2,817	2,475	2,189	1,773	1,059	**250**
Haiti	262	460	551	236	324	398	325	257	**209**

As depicted, all but one country reduced their intercountry adoptions. China and India in particular experienced dramatic declines, but South Korea appears to be an outlier. Besides ranking third in terms of children placed, it was the only country to increase its number of intercountry adoptions during the pandemic. This rise may be interpreted as a demonstration of South Korea's intercountry adoption programme's durability to withstand and even overcome external shocks. On the other hand, we should not lose sight of the fact that despite its status as one of the largest economies in the world, the country failed to afford enough protection for 266 children that it needed to seek homes abroad in 2020. If Denmark, Sweden, or the Netherlands engaged in similar practices as South Korea, then wouldn't they endure criticism? Then why doesn't South Korea suffer such rebuke? Do people just assume intercountry adoption is an inherent part of South Korean society? Does South Korean society believe that abandonment is a common occurrence? The question of why Korea continues intercountry adoption has been posed repeatedly, but people rarely ask why South Korea has not suffered greater reproach. Instead of asking only 'why', we must also enquire as to 'what'. What happens to a country that has exported its children for so long? What does that do to society? What does that do to those adopted from this country as children, and what does it do to the children raised here?

Much of the literature attributes the causes of intercountry adoption to conflict, disasters, poverty, high birth rate or discrimination,[8] but an analysis of the causal relationship between these supposed factors and the sending away of children is lacking in detail and objectivity. On the contrary, most studies have accepted these causes as *fait accompli*. However, on a deeper examination of South Korea's case, one will discover that none of these conditions serve as the true source. This is not to exclude conflict, poverty and discrimination acting as catalysts but rather to emphasize that the expansion of

7 International Social Service, Monthly Review No. 257, December 2021, https://extranet.iss-ssi.org/wp-content/uploads/2023/04/2021_257_MonthlyReview_ENG_.pdf.

8 S. Kane, 'The Movement of Children for International Adoption: and Epidemic Perspective', *The Social Science Journal*, Vol. 30, 1993, pp. 323-339; A. Young, 'Development in Intercountry Adoption: From Humanitarian Aid to Market-driven Policy and Beyond', *Adoption & Fostering*, Vol. 36, 2012, pp. 67-78.

intercountry adoption from South Korea from the 1950s to the 1970s transpired from the deliberate and methodical approach applied by the South Korean and U.S. governments to systematize the permanent placement of children from Korea to U.S. families.

Why Does the Intercountry Adoption System Need 'Orphans'?

The concept of 'legal orphan' originated from the process of classifying displaced or refugee children as those who lost their parents due to war and placing them in adoption as an interim measure with a humanitarian purpose.[9] This practice saw widespread use in the 1940s and 1950s. Just as in post-World War II Europe, intercountry adoption from Korea began at the outset as a means to find homes for children who had lost their parents during the Korean War. However, rather than drawing the programme to a close as the population of available orphans dwindled, the Korean government accelerated and expanded its intercountry adoption capabilities by coordinating with its receiving partners, specifically the U.S., to erect a legal and policy infrastructure that would permit Korean children to leave the country and enter the U.S.

The formation of this legal framework started in 1961. Under the Immigration and Nationality Act, the U.S. established that a foreign child designated as an 'orphan' could enter the country for adoption by U.S. citizens. The legislated definition of orphan recognized a wide range of children as adoptable, including those abandoned and those whose parents were unknown.[10] In the same year, South Korea passed the Orphan Adoption Special Act to introduce an official procedure for public authorities to issue orphan certificates to declare children as abandoned.[11] These corresponding pieces of legislation came to shape the fundamental structure of intercountry adoption from South Korea. This development had two significant impacts that transformed Korea into the world's oldest and largest sending country.

First, this arrangement relieved authorities in the state of origin from the burden of having to prove the birth parents' consent to adopt and validate the birth parents' whereabouts to establish the adoptability of the child. The issuance of an orphan certificate effectively erased the existence of the birth parents. Due to gaps between the

---

9 Displaced Persons Act, Pub. L. No. 774, 62 Stat. 1009 (1948) of the U.S. stipulated that "'Eligible displaced orphan' means a displaced person (1) who is under the age of 16 years, and ... (3) who is an orphan because of the death or disappearance of both parents,...".

10 INA, Pub. L. No. 87-301, §§ 1-4, 75 Stat. 650.

11 Orphan Adoption Special Act, Law No, 731, enacted on September 30, 1961, https://www.law.go.kr/lsSc.do?menuId=1&subMenuId=17&tabMenuId=93&query=%EC%9E%85%EC%96%91%ED%8A%B9%EB%A1%80%EB%B2%95#undefined.

family laws of the sending and receiving countries on adoption matters, establishing a child as adoptable in a family court presented the greatest challenge for adoption agencies in intercountry adoption. Therefore, the U.S. and South Korea devised a solution. The former allowed orphans to enter for adoption and the latter created a procedure to declare children as orphans regardless of whether they were or were not without parents.[12]

Second, the legal framework paved a path for agencies in Korea to secure visas to send children to the U.S. By acquiring an orphan certificate from the Korean government, the agency obtained a legal immigration status for the child. Because the steps involved in this process were administrative and without any verification of the child's family relations or care arrangements, agencies could essentially create 'paper' orphans by fabricating orphan documents to secure orphan certificates for adoption abroad.

How could such negligence exist? Before the 1950s, only the traditional '*yangja*' (literally meaning nurturing son) system existed. This centuries-old arrangement is often recognized by Korean and foreign scholars as an adoption system, but its purpose and usage differ from the modern concept of child adoption. Koreans have used the *yangja* arrangement solely for securing a male heir. It was not until the 1950s that child adoption was introduced in the form of intercountry adoption to the U.S. by foreign charities and individuals. Under the 1961 Act of Special Procedure for Orphan Adoption, intercountry adoption was treated separately from the general practice of the *yangja* system, which falls under Civil Act which is the general family law.

Although adoption legislation underwent successive amendments, it was not until 2012 that the law reserved a role for public authorities by stipulating that the family court must finalize an adoption of a child. Before this revision, adoptions occurred outside of the courts in South Korea. In intercountry adoptions, the receiving country's court issued the final decision.[13] Despite the involvement of the courts in the final decision of adoption in South Korea, the adoptions remain private since private agencies still assume control over the rest of the process, including decisions on adoptability, selection of adoptive families and choosing where to send the child.

---

12 C. Kim and T. Carroll, 'Intercountry Adoption of South Korean Orphans: A Lawyers' Guide', *Journal of Family Law*, Vol. 14, No. 2, 1975, pp. 223-252; R. Carlson, 'Transnational Adoption of Children', *Tulsa Law Review*, Vol. 23, 1988, pp. 317-377; R. Winslow, 'Immigration Law and Improvised Policy in Making of Intercountry Adoption 1948-1961', *Journal of Policy History*, Vol. 24, 2012, pp. 319-349 for more information on U.S. undertaking: Lee, 2021; Chapter 2 provides an explanation of the Korean government's efforts.

13 In most domestic adoption cases, false birth registration replaced the adoption report. By which, serious flaws in South Korea's birth registration system allowed adoptive parents to register their adopted child as their biological child. For more details, please refer to Lee, 2021, part 4.

Human Rights Violation Caused by the 'Orphan' Adoption System

Currently, several European countries have undertaken investigations into past intercountry adoption cases but have excluded South Korea in their inquiry. Despite being the largest state of origin in terms of children sent abroad, the omission of South Korea reflects major receiving countries' illusion that the country maintains a safe and transparent adoption programme.[14] Furthermore, the European investigative agencies and department must do more to examine the systematic nature of intercountry adoption programmes and the power that such agencies wield within this structure.

Orphanization and Identity Laundering

Figure 3. The process of orphan adoption[15]

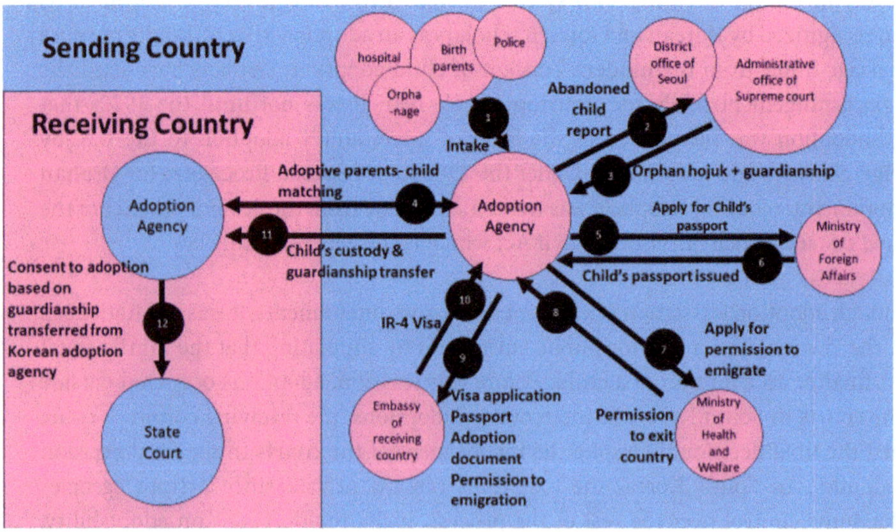

14 As of 2019, the number of Korean adoptees in each receiving country are as follows: 112,933 in the U.S.; 11,213 in France; 9,749 in Sweden; 8,808 in Denmark; 6,548 in Norway; 4,099 in the Netherlands; 3,697 in Belgium; 3,516 in Australia; 2,352 in Germany; 2,578 in Canada; 1,111 in Switzerland; 648 in Luxemburg; 476 in Italy; and 72 in the U.K. Since these are officially reported figures provided to the Ministry of Health and Welfare by the four intercountry adoption agencies in Korea, the adoptee community has suggested that these figures underreport the actual number of adoptees.

15 This figure is developed and used as an understanding tool for the Dialogues with Adoptees lecture by Dr Kyung-eun Lee. For more information, please visit www.hrbb.org.

The chart above depicts the manner in which orphan documents from the public authorities were used in the receiving countries' immigration procedures and adoption court processes.[16] As illustrated, adoption agencies in the sending and receiving countries serve as central actors in the system, with government bodies playing a supporting role for those private agencies. In the case of Korea, the Administration Office of the Supreme Court acted as the birth registration authority by issuing an orphan birth record (known as an orphan *hojuk*). The record lacks any trace of the child's background, providing only a name and birthdate, but this information is based on whatever the adoption agency reported. Even the child's birthplace is listed as the agency's address (see Figure 3).

The wide-scale claims of record fraud by adoptees against agencies and a recent announcement by the South Korean Truth and Reconciliation Commission to launch an investigation into the wrongful removal of children from their families indicate that the agencies engaged in deliberate and systematic efforts to manipulate information to make it appear that children were orphans in order to obtain orphan registration documents.

The following table reveals the efficiency with which this orphanization process operated. It compares the number of children reported as abandoned against the number of children adopted overseas. The former figures are reported to the Supreme Court Administrative Office to apply for an orphan registration document, while the latter numbers are submitted by the adoption agencies to the Ministry of Health and Welfare. To obtain a visa for intercountry adoption, one must submit an orphan registration document. The similarity in these numbers demonstrates how the child abandonment reporting system functioned as a means to facilitate intercountry adoption (see Table 1).

---

16 Up to 2012, this chart is applicable to South Korea-to-U.S. adoption procedures and, to some degree, also applies to adoptions between South Korea and Europe. Even after 2012, many of the steps depicted remain relevant and applicable between Korea and its receiving partners.

Table 1. Official Statistics of South Korea on the Annual Figures of Children Abandoned and Those Sent Overseas[17]

Year	Number of Children Found Abandoned	Number of Intercountry Adoptions	Year	Number of Children Found Abandoned	Number of Intercountry Adoptions
1976	6,585	6,597	1996	2,819	2,080
1977	6,326	6,159	1997	3,151	2,057
1978	5,248	5,917	1998	3,517	2,443
1979	4,836	4,148	1999	3,755	2,409
1980	4,769	4,144	2000	2,809	2,360
1981	4,741	4,628	2001	2,869	2,436
1982	6,661	6,434	2002	2,704	2,365
1983	9,658	7,263	2003	3,285	2,287
1984	8,703	7,924	2004	2,556	2,258
1985	9,287	8,837	2005	2,591	2,101
1986	8,562	8,680	2006	1,900	1,899
1987	6,405	7,947	2007	1,636	1,264
1988	6,192	6,463	2008	1,493	1,250
1989	2,187	4,191	2009	1,618	1,125
1990	2,916	2,962	2010	1,451	1,013
1991	2,429	2,197	2011	1,011	916
1992	2,636	2,045	2012	1,006	755
1993	3,001	2,290	2013	394	236
1994	1,835	2,262	2014	247	535
1995	1,621	2,180	Total	**104,598**	**103,268**

17 This table was created by the author for her PhD dissertation 'International Legal Protection of the Rights of the Child in Intercountry Adoption' of the Graduate School of Law of Seoul National University in 2017. See Lee, 2021, pp. 204-219. The Supreme Court's Administrative Office, which manages birth registration records, maintains records on child abandonment statistics. According to Korean law, the orphan document is issued as a form of birth registration. The statistics are listed in the *Annual Judicial Statistics* from 1976. Statistics since 2002 are available in electronic format at https://www.scourt.go.kr/portal/justicesta/JusticestaListAction.work?gubun=10.

South Korea's wilful deployment of unethical practices to supply children for intercountry adoption infringed on several specific human rights.[18] The disregard for children's best interests represents the most prominent violation. This fact is evident in the significance the UNCRC affords to this right. Nowhere else in the Convention is 'paramount' consideration for the child's best interests demanded except in adoption matters. Moreover, the Convention stipulates that competent authorities should perform an assessment and determination of a child's best interests. Second, the 1961 European Convention on the Adoption of the Child, the UNCRC and the Hague Adoption Convention ban private adoptions; however, South Korea maintains a private adoption system. Third, the Korean government deliberately prevents adoptees from knowing their origins by abandoning its duty to manage adoption records and failing to provide reliable birth search support. Lastly, since the start of intercountry adoption in Korea, the state has discriminated against adoptees and their birth families by sending them abroad rather than guaranteeing support to ensure that they may be raised in their families.

Privatization and Evasion of State's Responsibility for Child Protection

By privatizing the adoption system, private entities assume control over critical steps of the adoption process, such as determining the adoptability of a child, legal guardianship and obtaining consent. At the same time, the public authorities waive their responsibility to protect children by leaving essential procedures to private agencies, who receive fees from adoptive parents.[19] According to the UNCRC and international child rights norms,[20] this type of arrangement allows the state to evade its human rights obligations.[21]

The word 'intercountry' conjures notions of adoption having a bidirectional nature among two countries, but, in nearly all cases, children from countries in the Global South move to the more affluent West. Countries in North America, Western Europe and Australia have consistently remained the major receiving countries, and their numbers have remained constant at around 24. On the other hand, sending countries have numbered more than 80 and vary across continents. From the 1980s, the rate of

18 Most notably, the right to preserve and know one's origin and true identity as stipulated in Art. 8 UNCRC.

19 From the start of intercountry adoption in South Korea in the 1950s, adoption agencies should receive government authorization to engage in intercountry adoption. The government restricted authorization to only a few agencies and their number never exceeded five. Today, three major agencies – Holt Children's Service Inc., Eastern Social Welfare Society and Social Welfare Society – operate in Korea.

20 E.g., international legal documents dealing with the adoption of children such as Art. 21(a) UNCRC and Art. 4 European Convention on the Adoption of Children declares that adoption of children should be decided by public authorities.

21 UNICEF International Child Development, *Intercountry adoption*, Innocenti Digest no. 4, Florence, 1998.

sending countries surged, starting in Asia, then Latin America and Eastern Europe, and finally Africa.[22] The period in which the sources for children rapidly expanded corresponded with South Korea's campaign to curb its number of intercountry adoptions.

The key players among the diverse body of countries are the adoption agencies. They have commanded global connections and forged a division of roles between the partner agencies in the receiving and sending countries. In addition to the infrastructure, they also have the capacity to receive and care for infants and possess the knowledge and expertise to craft complex legal procedures to send those children transnationally. The fact that the practices of orphan adoption have been similar to such an extent as being nearly standardized globally hints at the close interaction and collaboration among members of the global network. In some cases, there are parallels in the laws and legal structure among countries. For example, in the 1990s, China's key law to implement its intercountry adoption programme bore close similarities to South Korea's Special Procedure Law for adoption, which serves a vital role as the primary legal basis for the orphan adoption system and the dominating role of private adoption agencies.

The ties between different countries and actors in intercountry adoption do not flow only horizontally but also vertically. Money flows from adoptive parents to adoption agencies and intermediaries in the receiving countries. A portion of the funds also often finds its way to the agencies in the sending countries under the excuse of 'child protection costs'. Critics have questioned the large sums charged by agencies, especially the fees in sending countries, considering that those expenses often exceed what is reasonable for the local living standard. Agencies have largely avoided these criticisms by concealing the fees under obscure or overly general labels such as donations or child protection expenses.

As early as the 1960s, international norms emerged to emphasize bans on private adoptions, and this prohibition has come to form a primary principle of the modern

22 S. Kane, 'The Movement of Children for International Adoption: And Epidemic Perspective', *The Social Science Journal*, Vol. 30, 1993, pp. 323-339; P. Selman, *Twenty Years of Hague Convention: A Statistical Review*, HCCH, 2015, https://www.hcch.net/en/instruments/conventions/publications1/?dtid=32&cid=69.

adoption system for the protection of children.[23] There are specific references in international human rights law that convert this principle into a right. Article 21(a) UNCRC stipulates that a competent authority, which is the court in most countries, shall decide on the adoption of a child. Because the practice of adoption is far from universal, the application of Article 21 is limited to States Parties that recognize and/or permit the system of adoption. For those countries engaged in intercountry adoption, Article 21 has been regarded as an essential obligation to protect children's rights; however, for decades, South Korea had remained the only country in the world that recognized and permitted adoption but maintained its reservation on this article.

While other countries had made reservations to Article 21 when they ratified the UNCRC, these States Parties were primarily restricted to Islamic countries in which the judiciary partially or fully applies Sharia law, which does not recognize the adoption system. As Article 21(a) only applies to those countries recognizing and/or permitting adoption, it already excluded Islamic countries; hence, when these countries still applied the reservation, Western countries heavily condemned and criticized them, claiming such actions weakened the Convention. On the other hand, no such condemnation has been levelled at South Korea despite the country still clinging to private adoption and refusing to fulfil its obligations under the Convention.[24]

In 2017, South Korea finally lifted its reservation to Article 21(a). In spite of the Committee on the Rights of the Child having regularly expressed concern over South Korea's reservation,[25] the country seemed unmoved by the pressure and only resorted to removing the reservation on its own accord. In general, reservations to human rights conventions undermine the spirit of those instruments, and it has been said that any reservation to a core principle should be prohibited since such exclusion would impede the effective implementation of the treaty. Article 21, while not a general principle

23 By the 1960s, European states gathered to discuss drafting a legal instrument to protect children in intercountry adoption. This includes determining a competent local authority, thereby removing the possibilities of private adoptions, and ensuring that the state plays a central role in ensuring that adoptions are carried out for the good of children. See Yves Denéchère. Regulating a particular form of migration at the European level: the Council of Europe and intercountry adoptions (1950-1967). Peoples and borders: movement of persons in Europe, to Europe, from Europe (1945-2015), November 2014, Padova, Italy. Also see the European Convention on Adoption of Children 1967 – one of the three main principles being that 'adoption must be ordered by an administrative or legal authority', thereby implying that independent adoptions be forbidden.

24 See the declarations and reservations submitted by States Parties of the UNCRC in the annex of the convention in the UN Treaty Collection System for specific comments made by States Parties, https://treaties.un.org/Pages/ViewDetails.aspx?src=TREATY&mtdsg_no=IV-11&chapter=4&clang=_en.

25 UNCRC, *Consideration on Reports Submitted by States Parties under Article 44 of the Convention Concluding Observations of the Committee on the Rights of the Child: Republic of Korea* (CRC/C/15/Add.51), 1996, (CRC/C/15/Add.197), 2003, (CRC/C/KOR/CO/3-4), 2011.

of the UNCRC, is so closely tied to the general principle of the best interests of the child that it is the only article in the Convention to refer to the best interests as 'the' paramount consideration, rather than 'a' primary consideration. The fact that South Korea was allowed to retain a reservation to an article crucial to protecting children's best interests in adoption while playing a leading role in intercountry adoption and largely avoiding censure or criticism raises questions about the effectiveness of the human rights community and the Convention.

Consequences of Orphan Adoption

Consent to adoption is a fundamental step in adoption. It legally severs the parents' authority and ties to the child. As a testament to its significance, the adoption legislation of many receiving countries dedicates specific provisions to this agreement. However, notable discrepancies emerge between these laws and the adoption apparatus of sending and receiving countries. In the post-World War II Western world, consent to adoption served as a cornerstone of the modern adoption system for the protection of children. Terms such as 'free and informed consent' and 'voluntary relinquishment', which were essential elements in receiving countries for an ethical adoption, lack corresponding meaning or translations in sending countries.[26] We must also be aware that these concepts in Western countries operated within a specific context that was not necessarily reflected in other countries. In Western countries, a set of rules and regulations to verify and regulate consent to adoption emerged, and this system developed to involve the public authorities. By contrast, in many sending countries, consent to adoption was a matter left to private parties, and if it was stipulated in law, it was often vague. The aim of describing these incongruencies is not to criticize one group as undeveloped but rather to emphasize that certain concepts, although seemingly identical, are embedded in different contexts, which ultimately changes the originally intended meaning of those concepts. In Western countries, consent to adoption constitutes a process within the child protection system. It is not only a question of whether to consent but also a series of subsidiary questions; for example, 'Who has the legal capacity to consent?' 'What are the conditions under which consent may be accepted?' 'What welfare and procedural justice measures are available to provide protection for the family and child while verifying the validity of consent?' Since consent represents an integrated part of the child protection

---

26 See N. Cantwell, *The Best Interests of the Child in Intercountry Adoption*, UNICEF, 2014, https://www.unicef-irc.org/publications/712-the-best-interests-of-the-child-in-intercountry-adoption.html for the implementation of the best-interests principle in case of intercountry adoption.

system, mechanisms exist to support vulnerable families and protect their rights, and this, in turn, reduces the need to rely on adoption.[27]

In contrast, sending countries have followed a vastly different trajectory surrounding the development of adoption laws and systems. In many Asian and Latin American countries, termination of parental rights, full adoption effects and public intervention in family matters were foreign concepts to traditional family law.[28] Accordingly, as intercountry adoption operations arose, it became apparent these countries were lacking a legal foundation for a modern adoption system for child protection. As a result, private entities exploited this legal vacuum, sometimes with the approval and even the support of the local and national governments. For the sending country, this presents long-term repercussions. The longer it engages in intercountry adoption, the more entrenched that system becomes, thus eroding motivation to establish a robust child protection system. In the absence of a child protection system or legal framework, obtaining consent to an adoption in the sending countries poses a challenge, especially if the receiving countries require evidence of the birth parents' agreement. Even where an agency may secure consent, other issues can arise, such as whether the birth parents understand the effects of their consent. To circumvent the quagmire of hurdles around consent, adoption agencies and intermediaries in sending countries often relied on the notion of an orphan by abandonment. Declaring a child an abandoned orphan was designed to act as a substitute for voluntary relinquishment, which the immigration authorities and the court in the receiving countries accepted in lieu of consent.[29]

The general approach of applying this concept entails the sending country's government declaring a child found abandoned regardless of whether the child is truly abandoned. Upon this declaration, the adoption agency determines the child as adoptable for intercountry adoption. South Korea built its intercountry adoption procedures on this

27 Lee, 2021, provides an explanation of the different developments of the adoption system as it pertains to family law in parts 1 and 2.

28 In 1988, in preparation for a new convention about intercountry adoption at The Hague Conference on Private International Law (HCCH), the then Secretary General published a report on the different countries' adoption systems. Refer to Van Loon JHA, *Report on Intercountry Adoption* (Prel. Doc. No. 1 of April 1990). The United Nations Department of Economics and Social Affairs, *Child Adoption: Trends and Policies*, 2009, (ST/ESA/SER.A/292) also undertakes research on the different practices of adoption around the world.

29 Many people understand that most Korean adoptees were relinquished by unwed mothers. However, South Korea's family law does not allow voluntary relinquishment of parental rights, and it lacks any judicial procedure to do so. Rather, this act of relinquishment was a practice used by Western adoption agencies and then repeated by Korean agencies. It has been said that more than 90% of adoptees come from unwed mothers, but since there has never been an official investigation to verify this figure, it is impossible to discern whether it is the truth or a fiction crafted by adoption agencies without proper evidence.

process. Since it lacked a judicial or official procedure to make a final adoption decision, the receiving country's court had to finalize the adoption procedure. In the receiving country, the court was required to consent to adoption to initiate a trial. An alternative means to proceed consisted of submitting the government-issued orphan document. South Korea resolved issues around guardianship by granting this authority to their adoption agencies. Therefore, theoretically, adoptees from South Korea have never been state wards under the guardianship of a public authority by judicial decision. This critical means of child protection was treated as an instrument to facilitate adoption court procedures in the receiving countries.[30]

Where intercountry adoption programmes dominate as heavily rooted systems supported by the government and facilitated by the law, international norms will wield limited influence.[31] Intergovernmental bodies and their members can applaud themselves for crafting human rights norms, but the conception of such obligations does not equate to enforcement. South Korea serves as a characteristic example of a country that employs every advantage available to skirt its duties without incurring condemnation from the human rights community.

A Way Forward to Face the Past

The following section provides recommendations on system reform, addressing current injustices and restoring adoptees' right to know their origins and identity.[32]

Two Goals

First, the laws and intercountry adoption systems of the states of origin remain weak, unjust and inadequate to protect children's rights and must undergo major reform. Second, adoptees have little recourse to address any infringements of their right to origins; therefore, states must institute new legal procedures and tools to allow adoptees to reclaim the truth surrounding their identity. The roots from which these two goals emerge, while connected, remain hard to separate. International norms developed to

30 E. Epstein, 'International Adoption: The Need for a Guardianship Provisions', *Boston University International Law Journ*al, Vol. 1, 1982, pp. 225-248, has noted this practice as a factor in making adoption from South Korea convenient to American adoptive parents.

31 Since the 1960s, multiple organizations, such as the European Council, the United Nations, the Hague Conference on Private International Law, and the Organization of American States, have established important international human rights instruments on intercountry adoption.

32 The right to origin encompasses more than just access to birth records. It is a holistic right stipulated in Art. 8 UNCRC.

achieve the former goal while the latter aim continues to linger on the periphery of human rights discussions. As adoptees come into adulthood, more and more speak out, but for a long time, many of these conversations centred on personal journeys rather than demands for rights. This lack of rights discourse, coupled with a dearth of academic research exploring adult adoptees' right to origins and a dominant narrative of intercountry adoption as a gift, has led to a narrow interpretation of damages and rights violations.

We must also remember that the injustice inflicted by intercountry adoption abuses extends beyond any individual to encompass collective wrongdoings that threaten all children in a sending country, not just those sent away. A country's involvement in intercountry adoption often undermines, if not impairs, other areas of the legal system, affecting birth registration and child protection. Thus, while those children placed in intercountry adoption may suffer direct rights violations, the consequence of the overall abuse can pose an imminent collective threat to the safeguards and rights of children within the country.

Furthermore, past illegal and unethical adoptions constitute the present injustice that adoptees endure. Although these adoptees are now adults, we speak about children's rights when referring to intercountry adoption abuses since these violations occurred during the early years of adoptees' lives. Despite this distinction in the name, children's rights are human rights that apply to everyone. Every person experiences childhood – that early stage of life marked by such vulnerability that one must completely rely on another for survival. Rights infringements during this period are challenging, if not impossible in some cases, to address later in life. The right of intercountry adoptees to know their origins exemplifies this problem, especially since the burden of proving any rights abuse in a lawsuit rests on the adoptee.

Four Strategies

To achieve adoptees' right to know their origins, four strategies are presented. First, concentrate attention on adoptees as rights-holders. This prioritization is not intended to discount or deny others affected by adoption. Much of the intercountry adoption research and literature has dealt with the adoption triangle, which includes birth parents, adoptees and adoptive parents. Birth-family search unquestionably constitutes an essential part of pursuing the true identity and origin of adoptees. However, the notion of the 'origin' of a human being should go beyond direct family lineage. According to the UNCRC, it can be extended to the name, nationality, ethnic group, religion and culture in which a person is born.[33] Many adoptees argue that language should be included as an essential element of origin.

Therefore, for the sake of practically applying a rights-based approach, this chapter advocates placing adoptees as the primary subjects since it is them whose right to identity has been violated. The author does not aim to devalue the injustice inflicted upon others affected by adoption by championing this stance. Rather, the aim is to underscore that the right to know one's origin and to know one's identity, as enshrined in international human rights instruments, applies to adoptees as rights-holders.

Where human rights violations occurred by the government's wrongdoings, remedies should be provided through an official procedure. However, adoptees searching for the truth surrounding their birth and adoption must knock on the doors of private adoption agencies. Whether or not they are given answers largely depends on the vague, arbitrary and inconsistent decisions of the agencies' case workers. If adoptees wish to challenge the answers, then they have little recourse without any public complaint mechanism. Likewise, birth-family searches are subject to the same problems since the same agencies conduct adoptions privately. Public authorities must intervene to establish procedures to address these concerns to cease the vicious cycle and provide a proper means for adoptees to demand their rights, especially in cases where they suspect wrongdoing. This is neither a recommendation nor a suggestion for best practices; rather, this is the government's human rights obligation.

Second, efforts must focus on the states' accountability on the protection of children in accordance with applicable international treaties and domestic laws. Intercountry adoption encompasses a complex web of rules and procedures that intersect the private realm of family relations and the public sphere of competent authorities, whose involvement is necessary for upholding children's rights. Placing a child across national borders concerns more than the family welfare and child protection laws of two countries. It also involves the emigration system of the sending country, as well as the immigration system and naturalization and nationality laws of the receiving country. Most notably, the subject of immigration is persistently absent from conversations about intercountry adoption to such a degree that one wonders if it were an intentionally neglected matter. Such an omission deprives us of fully understanding the key role that immigration authorities in receiving countries play in intercountry adoption. It also hinders us from recognizing the responsibility that these countries have for abuses. We only need to look at the orphan adoption programme that emerged after the Korean

33 UN Committee on the Rights of the Child, *General Comment No. 14: On the rights of the Child to Have His or Her Best Interests Taken as a Primary Consideration*, 29 May 2013, CRC/C/GC/14.

War between South Korea and the U.S. Lost in the often-repeated narrative of adoption arising as a solution to Korea's war-torn poverty is the fact that changes in the receiving countries' immigration laws enabled intercountry adoption.

Since the early 1960s, intergovernmental organizations have grappled with curtailing intercountry adoption abuses by establishing multiple treaties.[34] These efforts failed to achieve a fundamental change due to the absence of state accountability and the exclusion of an effective mechanism to assure that States Parties abided by the conventions. The governments of both sending and receiving countries confined their activities to monitoring or guiding private agencies or intermediaries involved in performing intercountry adoptions. Since private entities within the sending country engaged in the actual operations of securing and sending children, the receiving countries could assume a relatively detached role. This passivity permitted discrepancies to exist in the receiving countries' level of protection afforded to adopted children. Whereas those who were domestically adopted fell under the national protection system, the same degree of care and protection was not extended to those adopted abroad. This discrepancy is often disregarded and, instead, being accepted as if such a gap was an inherent outcome of the economic disparity between the sending and receiving countries. Without a careful examination of the discriminatory approach that receiving countries took towards children adopted abroad, discussions around illegal intercountry adoption risk overlooking the culpability of these countries.[35]

Third, a rights-based approach must prevail. Rather than complying with the best interests as enshrined in international law, charity organizations and sending countries, notably in South Korea, have co-opted this right as a propaganda tool to justify their abusive practices. Instead of public authorities applying a best-interests determination procedure to ensure the protection of the child's rights and well-being, private entities employed best interests as a self-justifying rationalization to assume full power when making crucial decisions about the welfare and fate of children under their care. To address this perversion of best interests and restore the rights of adoptees, a potential

34 United Nations Declaration on Social and Legal Principles to the Protection and Welfare of Children with Special Reference to Foster Placement and Adoption Nationally and Internationally (1986) (A/RES/41/85), Convention on the Rights of the Child (1989); Council of Europe, European Convention on the Adoption of Children (1967); Organization of American States, Inter-American Convention on Conflict of Laws Concerning the Adoption of Minors (1988); Hague Conference on Private International Law, Convention on the Protection of Children and Co-operation on Respect of Intercountry Adoption (1993).

35 Art. 21(a) UNCRC clearly states the responsibility of the receiving country to provide intercountry adoptees safeguards equivalent to those found in national adoption. However, since intercountry adoptions have been handled by private agencies, public welfare systems of receiving countries fail to afford intercountry-adopted children the same standards of monitoring and protection as those adopted domestically.

path forward is employing a rights-based approach, which entails holding the state accountable to fulfil its duties to the rights-holders.[36]

Furthermore, this chapter proposes truth, justice and rectification as the guiding principles to seek solutions for the massive human rights violations perpetrated by the state as it is affirmed by the UN General Assembly as the basic principles and guidelines on the Right to a Remedy and Reparation for Victims of Gross Violations of International Human Rights Law and Serious Violations of International Humanitarian Law.[37] To uncover the truth, a public committee consisting of relevant experts and granted with sufficient authority should conduct a thorough investigation into the system, actors and entities involved in past intercountry adoption practices. From the results of this body, we must then determine those parties accountable for illegal and unethical practices. This truth-seeking process functions as a critical element in reaching truth and justice because, without such a tangible step, any apology or attempts at rectification become mere gestures that evade accountability.

In 1998, Kim Dae-Jung, then President of the Republic of Korea, who garnered respect for his role in the democratization of the country, issued what some have dubbed an 'apology' to adoptees for the wrongdoings they suffered in the past and promised to reform and enhance relevant policies. On the contrary, neither laws nor policies were amended to rectify any systematic injustices. Instead, the Korean government provided funds for adoption agencies to promote homeland tours, Korean language learning programmes and other cultural activities. In other words, rather than address institutionalized abuses, the government did the antithesis by funnelling money into adoption agencies, who then used those resources to expand their own narrative of intercountry adoption and to further strengthen their influence. The new democratic government, instead of curbing poor adoption practices, cooperated with adoption agencies to serve as purveyors of the 'successful adoptee' myth. Unsurprisingly, this choice escalated adoption policy problems, and adoption agencies seized this opportunity to reimagine themselves as protectors of children's rights in Korea. These developments represent a fundamental reason for South Korea's continuous exportation of its children despite its outstanding economic growth. The orphan myth has served as

36 See N. Cantwell, *The Best Interests of the Child in Intercountry Adoption*, UNICEF, 2014, https://www.unicef-irc.org/publications/712-the-best-interests-of-the-child-in-intercountry-adoption.html.

37 UN General Assembly, *Basic Principles and Guidelines on the Right to a Remedy and Reparation for Victims of Gross Violations of International Human Rights Law and Serious Violations of International Humanitarian Law*, 21 March 2006, A/RES/60/147.

the seed of the country's intercountry adoption business, while the 'successful adoptee' myth acts as the fertilizer to sustain these operations.[38]

Fourth, special attention should be given to the current investigative efforts undertaken in major receiving countries in Western Europe.[39] The extent of these efforts and their results have varied, but, regardless of this aspect, they represent a collective trend of questioning the narrative that abuses were 'irregular'. In June 2022, to promote my book and research, I specifically chose those countries to visit as they represent the only place to take the first steps in redressing the legacy of intercountry adoption officially. I was fortunate to meet a variety of adoptee groups, experts, government officials and journalists, many of whom sought my views as I come from a sending country. I emphasized two points that I will reiterate here.

First, intercountry adoption constitutes a cross-border activity; therefore, for any investigation to be truly impactful, it must be done in both sending and receiving countries. Fact-finding on only one side, whether receiving or sending, uncovers only half the truth. Second, refrain from individualizing intercountry adoption abuses by requesting adoptees to file cases suspected of illicit activity; instead, assume a systematic approach by examining injustices in the laws and structure of intercountry adoption programmes. Asking adoptees to submit their own petitions places an extraordinary burden on them to collect their documents, which often entails traveling to their countries of origin, then trying to obtain information on events that happened decades ago in a foreign land. Even in Korea, many of the handwritten documents in adoption files are indecipherable, even for native Korean speakers.

With over 100 states engaged in intercountry adoption, whether as sending or receiving countries, a handful of investigations restricted to several receiving countries will, at

38 Political democratization in South Korea did not have a meaningful impact in addressing the injustices prevalent in the country's intercountry adoption programme. As part of President Kim Dae-Jung's apology, the Ministry of Health and Welfare assisted by seeking to promote a reconciliatory mood. However, rather than confront the hard truth, adoption agencies exploited this opportunity. They invited adoptees with notable achievements in their respective careers and publicized their stories as 'successful' cases that would not have happened without adoption.
In 2005, South Korea revised the Special Procedure Act on Adoption and established a National Adoption Day to promote domestic adoption. Every year on this day, the government awards official commendations to those it deems as 'people of merit'. During the first few years of this ceremony, the heads of adoption agencies received the highest award. Consequently, this recognition further promoted the idea within Korean society that adoption was a charitable act rather than a process to strictly regulate for the best interests and rights of the child.

39 The Netherlands, Belgium and Switzerland have conducted their own investigations. Sweden has formed an investigative committee for past adoption cases while France has announced an inquiry into past intercountry adoption cases.

best, uncover a fragment of the true scale of abuses. We must also recognize the elaborate network forged between the different countries. South Korea alone has exported its children to more than dozen countries. This fact demonstrates the challenge that public authorities must confront when attempting to carry out investigations in both sending and receiving countries. However, such complexity should not discourage investigative initiatives. On the contrary, international bodies, such as the United Nations or the European Union, should assume a more proactive approach, and human rights defenders should advocate for the inclusion of sending countries in the scope of investigations.

The Principle of Co-responsibility of the State of Origin and the Receiving Country in Regard to Article 4 of the Hague Adoption Convention

Among the core principles of the Hague Adoption Convention, one deserves greater attention than it has historically received – the principle of shared responsibility. Article 4 demands that the adoptability of a child should be established by the competent authority. While Article 21 UNCRC concerns decisions about adoption and encompasses a wide range of practices, the scope of Article 4 of the Hague Adoption Convention especially focuses on the determination of adoptability. This decision represents a critical step as it marks the severance of the child's familial ties and the beginning of the adoption process. Consequently, since this procedure usually takes place in the state of origin, Article 4 obligations have been interpreted as duties reserved for the sending countries, leaving receiving countries to stand passively aside to accept those decisions made beyond their borders.

However, when we recall the full title and the contents of the preamble of the Hague Adoption Convention, shared responsibility has an implicit presence and is considered as one of the pillar principles.[40] One could argue that one of the primary aims of the spirit of the Convention was to unify a sense of accountability among the disparate parties involved in intercountry adoption. When scandals erupt or allegations of adoption abuses arise in sending countries, the receiving countries react as if they were unaware of such violations and, therefore, not culpable. Therefore, greater effort must be applied to ensure all parties understand that shared responsibility pertains to the entire convention, including Article 4. As such, receiving countries should be

40 HCCH, *Accreditation and Adoption accredited bodies: Guide to Good Practice No. 2*, Bristol, Jordan Publishing, 2012, https://www.hcch.net/en/publications-and-studies/details4/?pid=5504, specifically mentions the principle of co-responsibility in para. 511.

held accountable for verifying whether decisions made under this article comply with international human rights standards.

Impelling the receiving and sending countries to undertake appropriate action is the most critical but also the most challenging task. On the one hand, without countries taking a comprehensive examination of their past adoption abuses, we lack good practices and models and must instead pave our own way forward. On the other hand, governments continue to resist admitting their responsibility and still avoid intervening to resolve these issues.

REQUIRING STATES TO IMPLEMENT THE RIGHT TO ORIGINS

Adoptee Activism in South Korea[41]

Starting in the 1970s, intercountry adoptions from South Korea surged. Those adopted during this era would reach young adulthood by the 1990s. As these adoptees came of age, they began to engage in activism in their receiving countries. This activism soon spread to South Korea in the late 1990s and early 2000s as adoptees began returning and forming activist groups and NGOs. Part of this new wave of adoptee activism in Korea reconstituted intercountry adoption abuses as human rights violations. By employing rights language, adoptee activists ushered in a fresh collective voice into Korean civil society. Whereas adoptees who had previously criticized intercountry adoption were dismissed as 'ungrateful' or 'angry', the use of rights discourse brought such a degree of legitimacy to their claims that South Korea could no longer ignore their grievances. This rights-focused activism brought together a constellation of parties affected by intercountry adoption, from birth mothers and single mothers to Korean NGOs that worked with adoptees. These disparate groups would eventually form a coalition, and their collective effort culminated in the revision of the Special Adoption Procedure Act in 2012.

In a few short years, they managed to do what the Korean government had failed to do for over half a century – pass a law to introduce a public authority into the adoption process. The amended adoption law granted the family court the authority to decide on adoptions, a minimum international standard to protect the rights of children. Around the same time, the coalition sought to validate their grievances as legitimate human

41 This part is based on the comprehensive experience of Ross Oke, the general manager of Human Rights Beyond Borders, as the co-founder and leader of a representative adoptee activist group and member of the UN Universal Birth Registration Working Group.

rights abuses by submitting their complaints to UN human rights mechanisms, which recognized their claims as rights violations.

However, despite the initial success of such activism, a variety of factors hampered the sustainability of this movement. Besides language and cultural barriers within Korea that hindered campaigning efforts, adoptee activism was driven by a small group of core activists. The transient nature of adoptees' stay in Korea meant that the movement struggled to maintain its ranks as people eventually left or pursued other endeavours. As the activism gradually faded, the momentum dissolved and fell short of achieving institutional solidarity with society and local human rights groups. However, this is not to say that adoptees did not attempt to mainstream their issues in society and among other civil society groups. On the contrary, despite adoptee activists' efforts, the public and human rights groups hardly saw intercountry adoption abuses as a Korean human rights issue.

Internationally, social media, such as Facebook, has helped adoptees forge international networks and share their private and personal stories and materials. Essentially, these online forums and networks have cultivated collective knowledge among adoptee communities, and an often-discussed topic is a possibility of filing lawsuits against the Korean government. However, the statute of limitations presented a major obstacle for most cases.

A Lawsuit and Official Investigative Committee

In January 2019, Shin Song-hyuk, whose American name is Adam Crapser and who had been adopted from Korea to the U.S., filed a civil suit in the Korean courts to pursue compensation against the Korean government and Holt Children's Services Inc. for damages and rights violations inflicted on him during his adoption process. Shin was born in South Korea in the 1970s and adopted to the U.S. in 1979. After 37 years of living, he suddenly found himself deported to South Korea. Everything he had come to know quickly dissolved as he found himself cast aside in a foreign land. He came to find that he had never acquired American citizenship. Although intercountry adoption is most closely associated with changes in family relations, Shin's case illustrates that naturalization and immigration procedures play an equally crucial role.[42]

42 The case name is '2019 GA-HAP 502520'. Since Korea does not include the names of the parties involved in legal cases, one could interpret the name of the case as 'Adam Crapser vs. Republic of Korea et al.'. It is estimated that the citizenship and adoption finalization status of tens of thousands of Korean adoptees in the U.S. remains unknown.

The litigation issues brought against the state of Korea in this case include negligence in its duty to protect in the process of intercountry adoption, unconstitutional use of proxy adoption, failure to monitor and verify the citizenship acquisition of adoptees, and failure to prevent financial gain by allowing unethical practices. Holt, the adoption agency, has been accused of negligence in the conduct of its duty to serve as a guardian by illegally transferring guardianship to the agencies of receiving countries and by providing fraudulent information to the registry office to register the plaintiff as an abandoned orphan despite knowing about the existence of his mother. These legal issues, far from unique, are common in most adoptions from South Korea.

The statute of limitations is a major hurdle for adoptees to raise a lawsuit in South Korea. Although Shin's adoption occurred decades ago, his lawyers claim that since he was deported in 2016, the damages inflicted upon him are within the statute of limitations. Despite the difficulties, the first trial remains ongoing as of February 2023 and represents a landmark attempt at bringing a civil suit against a state for violating children's rights by engaging in abusive intercountry adoption practices that contravened its domestic laws.

There is no denying that litigation can serve a pivotal role in restoring the rights of adoptees. On the other hand, adoptees must confront significant challenges in bringing their cases to court in the state of origin. Even when we overlook the statute of limitations, adoptees must still contend with language and cultural barriers while navigating a legal system that may be vastly different from their home country. For this reason, independent investigations by expert committees may offer an alternative method to rectify rights violations. The most prominent example of such a body is the Truth and Reconciliation Commission, South Africa, which addressed gross human rights violations committed by the state. These court-like bodies can play a crucial role in not only providing relief but also educating society to prevent similar wrongdoings from repeating in the future.

In 2005, South Korea launched its First Truth and Reconciliation Commission with a mandate to investigate atrocities committed from the Japanese colonial period to the end of the authoritarian regimes. Some adoptee activists took inspiration from the mission of this body and approached several experts on the country's truth commissions to explore the idea of campaigning to establish a similar committee dedicated to investigate into past human rights violations in intercountry adoption practices. While sympathetic, the experts explained that Korean society fails to recognize intercountry adoption abuses, with many Koreans seeing adoption abroad as a fortunate fate for adoptees. Moreover, unlike the Commission's scope of the investigation at that time, which remained limited to past abuses, the country continued to engage in intercountry adoption with powerful allied nations, who were uninterested in aiding any investigation into such matters. In 2020, the Korean government launched the Second Truth and Reconciliation Commission; some adoptees from South Korea have succeeded with submitting their cases to this Commission. Therefore, it is worth seeing where this may lead in the future.[43]

Bearing these cases in mind, we must recognize that intercountry adoption encompasses a series of cross-border procedures, and, consequently, the effectiveness of any investigation will transcend private and public laws. Accordingly, any truth-seeking endeavour into intercountry adoption matters demands a specialized body equipped with the necessary expertise and knowledge to handle such transnational issues. Given that South Korea has a history of using truth commissions, establishing a truth-finding body or enlisting a current truth commission to investigate intercountry adoption abuses would be a conceivable option.

During my discussions with several government officials and experts of receiving countries, they explained that each receiving country works with numerous sending countries through bilateral cooperation. Therefore, the crucial task would be to leverage these cooperative ties to engage in investigative work to accelerate efforts to uncover the truth. While some could dismiss this idea as naive or wishful thinking, considering that these relationships constitute the global orphan adoption system, the fact that this very apparatus exists demonstrates that establishing a similar scheme to internationally standardize and conduct investigations is not impossible. Just as intercountry adoption programmes operate within a multilateral system, so too should investigative efforts. The realization of truth, justice and rectification demands a variety of approaches, such as lawsuits in national and international courts, investigations by special committees and action by multilateral and international organizations.

The Most Urgent Task: Provide an Accessible Means for Adoptees to Know Their Identity

Ultimately, the most critical policy matter for most adoptees centres on finding a solution for birth searches and access to the materials and documents that will allow them to know their identity and fulfil their right to origins. Among the aim of achieving truth, justice and rectification, the lattermost remains the most urgent task. In spite of the multiple revisions of Korean adoption legislation, adoption agencies maintained their power over adoption and post-adoption services, including birth-family searches. As agencies are private entities, birth searches essentially remain a private matter, which

43 See https://www.jinsil.go.kr/en/ for the TRC's mandate and the cases being investigated.

leaves this activity vulnerable to being treated as a form of charity towards adoptees rather than a fulfilment of their rights.

If the state of South Korea genuinely strives to fulfil its duties to make the right to origins 'real' for adoptees, then it must establish a system and set of procedures accessible to adoptees. Rather than leaving matters about access to information with private agencies, the rules and procedures should be enshrined in law, and a competent authority should assume responsibility. In cases where an adoptee seeks to appeal a decision or action by such an authority, then they should be able to appeal to a complaint mechanism. This entails that the state ensures that adoptees understand their rights by providing translations of relevant information, including delivering services and support in the languages used by adoptees. Moreover, receiving countries have an obligation to investigate when potential cases of systematic abuse arise in states of origin. Where a state of origin has committed human rights violations, then the receiving state should seek the cooperation of the former to address such abuses. The very term *intercountry adoption* denotes the involvement of two or more countries; as such, responsibility for human rights violations does not stop at the border but implicates all states involved.

CONCLUSION

The year 2022 is the 70th year since South Korea started its intercountry adoption programme in 1953 in the aftermath of Korean War. The latest statistics shows that in 2021, 189 children left this country to be adopted to overseas families.[44] For many years, adoptees' grievances have been delivered to Korean society only as captivating individual narratives. When I framed this issue as systemized and collective human rights violations, I confronted the reality that this society does not want to cope with uncomfortable truth. Even some of the most renowned leaders of civil society groups scoffed, 'If this is really a human rights issue as you're insisting, then where are all of these 200,000 rights-holders? Why are they invisible and their voices silent?' This country never thought that adoptees who it sent away decades ago would ever return and start posing serious questions about their true identity and origins.

However, the inescapable obligation to face the truth is already at hand. During my 2022 book tour in European countries, I heard adoptees from diverse states of origin claim the right to know their origins and access the truth about their birth and family. It is good news that governments are making various efforts to find the truth and

44 See https://www.mohw.go.kr/react/al/sal0301vw.jsp?PAR_MENU_ID=04&MENU_ID=0403&page=55&CONT_SEQ=371450.

restore the rights of adoptees. I sincerely hope that such efforts do not end with treating symptoms and silencing complaints. It is what South Korea has been doing during the past seven decades. Authorities should be determined to get to the root of the problem; authorities should listen to adoptees, who were deprived of their voices years ago when they were severed from their families and the countries they were born in and sent to faraway lands.

3 'Quien Soy Yo?': The Right to Identity and Colombian Adoption Reparations

*Susan F. Branco**

Introduction

The transnational adoption industry in Latin America increasingly grew during the 1960s through the 2000s to provide children for families in Western countries.[1] During this span of time, the 1989 UN Convention on the Rights of the Child (hereinafter UNCRC) issued specific mandates surrounding one's right to identity to maintain biological, cultural and ethnic connections. While laws protecting children and birth families evolved during this time, the impact of corrupt practices on persons adopted during those eras are coming to light.[2] Subsequently, a new era of official recognition of the human right to access and know one's pre-adoptive identity serves as a lens by which global transnational adoption practices may be critiqued.

Colombia, a longstanding sending country, deserves such critique for dubious adoption practices during the 1970s through 1990s.[3] This chapter will offer an accounting of the historical processes and conditions connected to the Colombian adoption system

---

* The author (she/her/ella) is a 50-year-old cisgender woman and a transracial and transnational adoptee from Bogotá, Colombia, adopted by parents from the United States in the early 1970s. For most of her adult life, she did not have access to her pre-adoptive birth-family information despite multiple petitions and visits to her adoption house and *ICBF*. She became active in the Colombian adoptee specifically and transnational and transracial adoptee community in general in her early 30s. Through a combination of DNA testing and private investigators, she successfully reunited with her birth family after a 25-year search. Her lived experience and professional training as a Licensed Professional Counsellor and associate professor in a counsellor education programme support her research and advocacy efforts to expose problematic practices within the Colombian adoption system.

1 K. Lovelock, 'Intercounty Adoption as a Migratory Practice: A Comparative Analysis of Intercountry Adoption and Immigration Policy and Practice in the United States, Canada, and New Zealand, in the Post W.W period', *The International Migration Review*, Vol. 34, No. 3, 2000, pp. 907-949.

2 A. Molinaro and C. Clemente-Martinez, 'Irregularities in Transnational Adoptions and Child Appropriations: Challenges for Reparations Practices', *Childhood*, Vol. 28, No. 4, 2021, pp. 467-476; J. Palacios, D. Brodzinsky, D. Johnson, L. Martínez-Mora, J. Selwyn, S. Adroher, H. Grotevant, F. Juffer and R. Muhamedrahimov, 'Adoption in the Service of Child Protection: An International Interdisciplinary Perspective', *Psychology, Public Policy, and Law*, Vol. 25, No. 2, 2019, pp. 57-72.

3 D. Carreazo, 'Morir sin saber un origin: la realidad de miles de adoptados colombianos', *Vice News*, 10 October 2016, https://www.vice.com/es/article/ppnbz9/morir-sin-saber-un-origen-la-realidad-%20de-miles-de-adoptados-colombianos.

with focus on transnational adoption. An array of journalistic evidence documenting problematic and even corrupt circumstances in Colombian transnational adoption will be presented followed by a closer examination of the ground swell of adult Colombian adoptee activism in response to adoption-related injustice. Finally, as more evidence emerges of broad levels of unethical and illicit practices within Colombian transnational adoption, it is urgent for national reparative actions to be considered. Two other South American countries, Argentina and Chile, implemented reparations to address illegal adoption practices that impeded adoptees from the right to know their true identity. Both models will be explored to propose a reparative model for Colombia. For the purposes of this chapter the term 'illicit' will be used to describe illegal and unethical adoption practices.[4]

Colombian Adoption Programme

Colombia, the fourth largest South American nation, has endured economic and population growth, multiple civil wars and perhaps is most known for narco-trafficking and violence dominating several decades.[5] Colombia's historical context serves as a backdrop for its rise as a prominent South American sending country in international adoption. Maestranzi detailed the sociopolitical context that led to the creation of the National Adoption Programme in Colombia.[6] He argued that unlike other developing nations in South America, the primary factor for Colombian transnational adoption was not war but poverty paired with the concept of 'irresponsible parenthood'. Specifically, overpopulation during the 1960s led to duelling state and Catholic Church plans aimed to reduce such growth in an effort to slow increased poverty levels.[7] While the state sanctioned expansive birth control efforts, the Catholic Church found those plans immoral and encouraged adoption as a palatable solution to the increasingly widespread problem of child abandonment, illegitimacy, abortion and the phenomena of gamins, or children surviving on the streets.[8] Ultimately, poverty-based adoption, framed within the lens of middle- to upper-class Colombians attributing irresponsible parenthood to lower classes, became a popular solution to reduce poverty. In response, the *Instituto Colombiano de Bienestar Familiar* (hereinafter *ICBF*) was created in 1968 to oversee child

4 L. Long, 'ICAV Perspectives Paper', Intercountry Adoptee Voices, 2020, https://intercountryadopteevoices.com/wp-content/uploads/2020/07/Illicit-Adoptions-Responses-from-Lived-Experience.pdf.

5 D. Bushnell, *The Making of Modern Colombia: A Country in Spite of Itself*, Berkeley, University of California Press, 1993.

6 M. Maestranzi, *Politics of Colombian Adoption: State Formation, Church Authority, Population Control, and "The Best Interests of the Child"*, Unpublished master's thesis, 2013.

7 Ibid.

8 A. Simmons and R. Cardona, 'Colombia: Stages of Family Planning Adoption', *Studies in Family Planning*, Vol. 5, No. 2, 1972, pp. 42-49; Maestranzi, 2013.

welfare, including all adoption houses or *casas*, in Spanish, as they are commonly known, as a result.[9] Hoelgaard's seminal case study examining the Colombian adoption system reinforced similar rationales for the adoption programme based on class divides and delineated how the structure of the Colombian adoption system exacerbated conditions ripe for corruptive practices.[10]

Problematic Practices

Hoelgaard's 1998 comprehensive case study of the Colombian adoption system sheds light on several problematic practices related to legal policies, cultural beliefs in Western superiority, the role of privatized adoption houses, and the deleterious impact on the identity development of the adopted persons themselves. Adoption law in Colombia mandated that full adoption be enforced, whereas all ties to the child's first/birth families are broken entirely so that they may fully assimilate to the adoptive family.[11] Hoelgaard exposed how the Colombian 'clean break' policy ruptured the attachments of those children moving through adoption systems and created a confidential and secret system disabling those adopted persons from seeking their pre-adoptive identities.[12] Full adoption law in Colombia allowed for a child's original birth certificate holding the names and identifying information of their birth/first parents to be permanently replaced with an amended birth certificate with the names of their adoptive parents.[13]

Hoelgaard noted the rise in numbers of children eligible for adoption, mostly derived from poorer social classes, coupled with an increase in transnational adoption demand from Western countries like the United States and Europe, fit well with an overall sentiment that Colombian children would fare much better with 'socially and morally superior' Western adopters rather than remain in their birth county.[14] This overriding belief system limited, if not entirely prevented, Colombian foster families from legally adopting fostered children. In addition, the increased international demand for Colombian children also created opportunities for illicit practices, to be described later in this chapter, to secure children for financial gain.[15]

9 S. Hoelgaard, 'Cultural Determinants of Adoption Policy: A Colombian Case Study', *International Journal of Law, Policy, and the Family*, Vol. 12, 1998, pp. 202-241; Maestranzi, 2013.

10 Hoelgaard, 1998.

11 P. Monroy, 'Adoption Law in Colombia', *in* A. Bainhaim (ed.), *The International Survey of Family Law*, The Hague, Kluwer Law International, 1998, pp. 99-120,

12 Hoelgaard, 1998, p. 204.

13 Ibid., pp. 202-241.

14 Ibid., p. 218.

15 Ibid., pp. 202-241.

The *ICBF's* concerns about privatized adoption houses engaging in corrupt practices led to the cessation of the flow of *ICBF*-referred children to the adoption houses.[16] Many adoption houses were founded by family members of prominent and powerful politicians, which prevented close *ICBF* oversight. Subsequently, the lack of direct child referrals from *ICBF* created a scenario by which the houses relied on first mothers to voluntarily relinquish children, often setting up conditions where first mothers had few options other than terminating parental rights. For example, first mothers were told they had to pay a substantial sum, beyond the means of a single person from a low socioeconomic background, for medical care rendered while at the adoption house should they decide to parent rather than maintain an adoption plan. One institution director stated, "we don't want mothers to think they can use our facilities as a hotel."[17]

Hoelgaard also underscored the detrimental impact on the identity of the adopted Colombian child as the perfect storm of national policy, cultural beliefs and increased transnational adoption demanded erasing, in most cases, the child's pre adoptive identity. Since Hoelgaard's case study, many more studies have demonstrated the long-lasting and harmful effects created by closed adoption practices on the adopted person's identity.[18] A case study described how adult Colombian transnationally adopted persons discovered their original documentation was falsified and found dead ends when attempting to seek factual information despite Colombian Civil Code, Article 115, allowing for adopted adults to access their pre-adoptive records after a 30-year period of state-sanctioned secrecy.[19] Furthermore, in 2006, Law 1098, Article 76 of the Infant and Adolescent Code mandated that adoptees have the right to know their original families and indicated that the adoptive parents have the authority to decide

16 Ibid.

17 Ibid., p. 216.

18 A. Baden, J. Gibbons, S. Wilson and H. McGinnis, 'International Adoption: Counseling the Adoption Triad', *Adoption Quarterly*, Vol. 16, No. 3-4, 2013, pp. 218-237; D. Brodzinsky, 'A Need to Know: Enhancing Adoption Competence among Mental Health Professionals', https://njarch.org/wpress/wp-content/uploads/2015/11/2013_08_ANeedToKnow.pdf; D. Brodzinsky, 'Children's Understanding of Adoption: Developmental and Clinical Implications', *Professional Psychology: Research and Practice*, Vol. 42, No. 2, 2013, pp. 200-207; F. Darnell, A. Tavakoli and N. Brugnone, 'Adoption and Identity Experiences among Adult Transnational Adoptees: A Qualitative Study', *Adoption Quarterly*, Vol. 20, No. 2, 2017, pp. 155-166; H. Grotevant, A. Lo, L. Fiorenzo and N. Dunbar, 'Adoptive Identity and Adjustment from Adolescence to Early Adulthood: A Person Centered Approach', *Developmental Psychology*, Vol. 53, No. 11, 2017, pp. 2195-2204; S. Henz-Pedersen, 'Known and Unknown Identities: Openness and Identity as Experienced by Adult Adoptees', *Adoption Quarterly*, Vol. 22, No. 2, 2019, pp. 135-156; M. Koskinen and M. Böök, 'Searching for the Self: Adult International Adoptee Narratives of their Search and Reunion with their Birth Families', *Adoption Quarterly*, Vol. 22, No. 3, 2019, pp. 219-246.

19 S. Branco, 'The Colombian Adoption House: A Case Study', *Adoption Quarterly*, Vol. 24, No. 1, 2021, pp. 25-47; Monroy, 1998.

when the adopted child or adolescent may learn of their origins.[20] Most notably, in 2021, Colombia's transnational adoption practices from the 1960s to 1990s were examined by the Dutch government's Committee Investigating Intercountry Adoption.[21] The Committee determined that in Colombia, along with four other countries, "serious abuses surrounding intercountry adoption took place in the period of 1967 to 1998".[22] Examples of Colombian abusive adoption practices detailed in journalistic documentation are described next.

Journalistic Evidence

In 1981, a journalist for the *New York Times* described the arrests of several Colombian officials, lawyers, nurses and consulate members for trafficking 500 to 600 Colombian and Peruvian children to Western adopters in a multimillion-dollar business.[23] The article recounted the efforts undertaken to illegally secure children, including kidnapping, falsely telling birthmothers their babies were deceased and coercing impoverished women to sell their babies for a fee. The then director of *ICBF*, Juan Jacobo Muñoz, stated: "The lawyers prefer to give a child to a European couple who is willing to spend $10,000 rather than to a Colombian who offers much less and pays in pesos."[24] No efforts were undertaken to reunite the illegally adopted children with their first families. In 1986, *El Tiempo*, a Bogotá-based newspaper, reported further on the subject and clarified that 800 children were illegally trafficked in adoption and identified three notary registrars who falsified birth certificates to expedite the adoptions.[25]

In this decade, several journalistic exposés highlighted longstanding problematic and, in some instances, illegal, practices plaguing the Colombian adoption system. First, the news programme, *El Séptimo Día*, in April 2008 offered a four-part series, 'Niños: Made in Colombia', documenting the illicit adoption industry practices related to sending children to Western adopters as a result of high demand and financial gain for adoption

20 Organization of American States, *Ley 1098 de 2006: Por la cual se expide el Código de la Infancia y la Adolescencia, El Congreso de Colombia*, 2006, https://www.oas.org/dil/esp/codigo_de_la_infancia_y_la_adolescencia_colombia.pdf.

21 Committee Investigating Intercountry Adoption, *Considerations, Analysis, Conclusions, Recommendations, and Summary*, February 2021, https://www.government.nl/documents/reports/2021/02/08/summary-consideration-analysis-conclusions-recommendations.

22 Ibid., p. 15.

23 W. Hoge, 'Ring in Columbia Kidnaps Children for Sale Abroad', *New York Times*, 16 August 1981, https://www.nytimes.com/1981/08/16/world/ring-in-columbia-kidnaps-children-for-sale-abroad.html?smid=fb-share.

24 Ibid.

25 El tiempo, 'Prescribe acción penal por tràfico de niños', 27 November 1986, https://news.google.com/newspapers?id=nXEcAAAAIBAJ&sjid=NFkEAAAAIBAJ&pg=6982%2C4091093.

service providers.[26] The programme featured birth parents who lost their children to adoption and painfully sought information about their whereabouts to no avail; adults adopted to Western countries who returned seeking information about their birth families with no success; and Western adoptive parents who were unaware of the illicit adoption practices involved in their adoption process. Within days of the programme's airing on Colombian national television, the Colombian Inspector General announced that *ICBF* would be monitored because of kidnapping allegations.[27] Approximately one year later, in July 2013, *ICBF* announced the closure of its transnational adoption programme for children aged 6 and under to promote family preservation and domestic adoption.[28]

The abrupt changes to the transnational adoption programme did not cease the journalistic efforts to uncover illicit adoption practices. In 2016, Carreazo, a Vice news reporter, interviewed adult adoptees from around the world and within Colombia, *ICBF* officials, investigators assisting with adoptee searches, and adoption house staff members.[29] The exposé detailed the failed attempt of adoptees to obtain factual pre-adoption records, accountings of falsified birth registrations, and the void of records for those adopted during the 1970s through 1980s. Carreazo also linked a registrar arrested for child trafficking as being a longstanding lawyer for one of the prominent adoption houses.[30] Moreover, the exposé demonstrated the overall sentiment from adoption house staff continued to be one of surprise and even disdain for those returning adoptees for being 'disrespectful' for wanting to know their origins when they should be satisfied for the opportunity to grow up in Europe or the United States.[31] A 2018 feature article of a prominent television journalist and missing persons investigator, Alejandro Muñoz, described his decades-long search efforts to reunite adoptees with their birth families and his criticism of the transnational adoption programme as "part of a trans-national 'human-trafficking' problem".[32]

26 A.M. Cuevas, 'Ellos no son un negocio: Casos de adopción y el ICBF se defendien de acusasiones sobre irregularidades en los procesos de entrega de niños colombianos a padres extranjeros', *El Espectador*, 6 May 2012, https://www.elespectador.com/actualidad/ellos-no-son-un-negocio-article-344091/.

27 A. Daugherty, 'Colombia's Adoption Agency Monitored after "Kidnapping" Allegations', *Columbia Reports*, 6 April 2012, https://colombiareports.com/colombias-adoption-agency-monitored-after-kidnapping-allegations/.

28 C. Gonzalez, 'Colombian cerró la puerta a la adopción para extranjeros', *Radio Santa Fe*, 30 May 2013, http://www.radiosantafe.com/2013/05/30/colombia-cerro-la-puerta-a-la-adopcion-para-extranjeros/#more-244588; US Department of State Bureau of Consular Affairs; Country information: Colombia, https://travel.state.gov/content/travel/en/Intercountry-Adoption/Intercountry-Adoption-Country-Information/Colombia.html.

29 Carreazo, 2016.

30 El Tiempo, 1986.

31 Carreazo, 2016.

32 R. Emblin, 'Alejandro Muñoz: Investigator of Colombia's Missing Persons', 25 January 2018, https://thecitypaperbogota.com/features/alejandro-munoz-investigator-of-colombias-missing-persons/, para. 10.

In 2016, a historic peace accord was reached between the Colombian government and the Revolutionary Armed Forces (FARC), a leftist group. In 2017, Legislative Act 1, Decree 588, mandated the creation of the Colombian Commission for the Clarification of Truth, Coexistence, and Non-repetition (hereinafter CCCTCN). The CCCTCN aimed to provide a historical, fact-finding and transparent accounting of the various consequences of the longstanding armed conflict to avoid future replication. The final report (2022) noted that upwards of 50,000 Colombian children were exported for transnational adoption in the past 30 years. Furthermore, many transnational adoptees experienced stigma, discrimination and adoption-related trauma within a context of significant impediments to achieving birth family reunion and right to identity.[33] Notable to more recent accounts of illicit adoption practices are the advocacy efforts and voices of adult Colombian adoptees from around the world. Several of those efforts will be described in the following section.

Colombian Adoptee Advocacy

Transnationally adopted Colombian adult adoptees have reunited virtually and in person across the world. From e-mail listserv in the early 2000s to the proliferation of Facebook groups, adoptees united to share common experiences, including racial and ethnic identity development journeys, adoptive family relationships, and their search to find their birth family.[34] As more adoptees connected, advocacy groups emerged to collectively petition for social justice. One such group, Plan Angel, derived from a Dutch Colombian adoptee's quest to find her birth-family members. Marcia Engel, founder and director, stated,

> So much effort to find my own parents. For a right that every child has – the right to know who their parents are. I thought on the spot: this has to change, I'm going to help people. And this goes beyond looking for family members. I want to make people aware of their rights and responsibilities.[35]

Plan Angel staff paired with Family Tree DNA, a leading DNA collection and database service, to provide DNA testing to both Colombian adopted persons and birth/first families. Staff members travel to cities across Colombia to collect DNA samples and

33 Colombian Commission for the Clarification of Truth, Coexistence, and Non-repetition, '*Hay Futuro si Hay Verdad: Informe Final*', 2022 July, https://www.comisiondelaverdad.co/hay-futuro-si-hay-verdad.

34 Carreazo, 2016.

35 See Plan Angel on Facebook, 4 August 2022, https://www.facebook.com/planangel/posts/pfbid02M8EK6kzKWnU4CXAaTNfdGLfAQYGwQrgTNWMy5pjKgWqgtaVNYRgRjFECJDFxtPESl.

have aided over 300 families.[36] Additionally, Plan Angel offers search assistance to adoptees and has facilitated 40 birth-family reunifications.[37] In August 2022, Plan Angel partnered with a Colombian-based advocacy group and distributed and posted hundreds of flyers of adult transnational adoptees searching for their birth families in Medellin and Bogotá as part of their campaign to publicize adoptees as members of the displaced Colombian diaspora.[38]

Abby Forero-Hilty, a Colombian adoptee who reunited with her birth family, edited the book titled *Decoding Our Origins: The Lived Experience of Colombian Adoptees.*[39] The collection features seventeen transnationally adopted Colombian adults who described "the traumatic loss of their mothers, culture and identities; racism; and severe abuse".[40] All proceeds from the book's purchase go towards providing DNA testing for Colombian families searching for their children.

Another transnationally adopted Colombian adult, Nicole Culverhouse, established a Facebook group called Adopted from Colombia, as well as a fund to provide for DNA testing. Nicole's motivation to do so stemmed from her reunion experiences with her birth mother and the traumatic discovery that she was abducted as a child to be placed in the transnational adoption system.[41] She now travels to Colombia frequently to visit her birth family and distributes DNA tests to other searching adoptees and birth families.

Human Right to Identity

The right to one's identity is the framework supporting the rationale for Colombian adoption reparations in this chapter. Several international laws and policies address the child's right to identity to emphasize the gravity of this human right. The illegal adoption atrocities committed in Argentina, to be described later, paved the way for an

36 See https://www.familytreedna.com/groups/plan-angel/about.

37 R. McColl, 'Locating Colombia's Stolen Children', *Colombia Reports*, 21 June 2017, https://colombiareports.com/locating-colombias-stolen-children/.

38 Te Busco a Ti? Colombia on Facebook, 7 August 2022, https://www.facebook.com/tebuscoaticolombia/.

39 A. Forero-Hilty (ed.), *Decoding Our Origins: The Lived Experience of Colombian Adoptees*, 2017, CreateSpace Independent Publishing.

40 See https://decodingorigins.com/en/welcome/#book.

41 M. Begue, 'An Adoptee Who Found Her Biological Family in Colombia, Helps Others', *CGTN Newscast – America*, 1 November 2015, https://america.cgtn.com/2015/11/01/an-adoptee-who-found-her-biological-family-in-colombia-helps-others.

Argentinian, Dr Jaime Sergio Cerda, to sponsor the human right to identity, of Article 8 UNCRC, which reads as follows:[42]

> 1. States Parties undertake to respect the right of the child to preserve his or her identity, including nationality, name and family relations as recognized by law without unlawful interference.
> 2. Where a child is illegally deprived of some or all of the elements of his or her identity, States Parties shall provide appropriate assistance and protection, with a view to re-establishing speedily his or her identity.

Stewart attempted to further interpret Article 8 UNCRC by specifying four categories that constitute identity: family, tribal, biological and political.[43] They suggested family to include birth/first parents, ancestors and a family name; tribal to encompass racial, ethnic, cultural and religious identities; biological to include medical and genetic history as well as medical records related to one's birth; and political identity being the equivalent of nationality. Stewart highlighted how Article 8 UNCRC allows for the possibility of an adopted child to "assert their rights to know the facts of his [or her or their (sic)] true identity".[44] Furthermore, Article 25 of the 2006 UN International Convention for the Protection of All Persons from Enforced Disappearance outlines specific state responses to address illegal adoption classified as the forced disappearance of a minor child (see Chapters 10 and 11). Actions include criminal prosecution of those responsible for the concealment or falsification of the child's true identity and reestablishment of the child's original identity.[45]

McCombs and Gonzalez noted that "the right to identity protects an individual's significant and knowable personal attributes and social relationships".[46] To that end, Article 7 UNCRC states,

> 1. The child shall be registered immediately after birth and shall have the right from birth to a name, the right to acquire a nationality and, as far as possible, the right to know and be cared for by his or her parents.

42 G. Stewart, 'Interpreting the Child's Right to Identity in the UN Convention on the Rights of the Child', *Family Law Quarterly*, Vol. 26, No. 3, 1992, pp. 221-233.

43 Ibid.

44 Ibid., p. 227.

45 United Nations, '*Declaration of Basic Principles of Justice for Victims of Crime and Abuse of Power*', https://www.ohchr.org/en/professionalinterest/pages/victimsofcrimeandabuseofpower.aspx.

46 T. McCombs and J. González, *Right to Identity*, International Human Rights Law Clinic, University of California, Berkeley School of Law, 2017, p. 42, http://scm.oas.org/pdfs/2007/CP19277.PDF.

2. States Parties shall ensure the implementation of these rights in accordance with their national law and their obligations under the relevant international instruments in this field, in particular where the child would otherwise be stateless.

Both articles in the UNCRC aim to preserve and protect those identity markers delegated to a child upon their birth.

The 1993 The Hague Convention on Protection of Children and Co-operation in Respect of Intercountry Adoption (hereinafter the Hague Adoption Convention) was created to develop transnational adoption standards and principles protecting the best interests of the child. In 1993, the Hague Conference re-examined best practices related to state (i.e. country) post-adoption responsibilities.[47] Specifically, Article 16 of the Hague Adoption Convention, supporting the right to identity was highlighted, which reads as follows:

(1) If the Central Authority of the State of origin is satisfied that the child is adoptable, it shall –
  a) prepare a report including information about his or her identity, adoptability, background, social environment, family history, medical history including that of the child's family, and any special needs of the child;
  b) give due consideration to the child's upbringing and to his or her ethnic, religious and cultural background;
  c) ensure that consents have been obtained in accordance with Article 4; and
  d) determine, on the basis in particular of the reports relating to the child and the

  prospective adoptive parents, whether the envisaged placement is in the best interests of the child.

(2) It shall transmit to the Central Authority of the receiving State its report on the child, proof that the necessary consents have been obtained and the reasons for its determination on the placement, taking care not to reveal the identity of the mother and the father if, in the State of origin, these identities may not be disclosed.

47 HCCH, *The Implementation and Operation of the 1993 Hague Intercountry Adoption Convention: Guide to Good Practice No. 1*, Bristol, Jordan Publishing, 2008, https://www.hcch.net/en/publications-and-studies/details4/?pid=4388.

The Guide to Best Practices No. 1 suggests Article 16 of the Hague Adoption Convention be considered in tandem with Article 30 to capture the essence of the right-to-identity implementation.[48] Article 30 reads as follows:

> (1) The competent authorities of a Contracting State shall ensure that information held by them concerning the child's origin, in particular information concerning the identity of his or her parents, as well as the medical history, is preserved.
> (2) They shall ensure that the child or his or her representative has access to such information, under appropriate guidance, in so far as is permitted by the law of that State.

Both articles of the Hague Adoption Convention, however, include provisions suggesting efforts to support the child's right to identity must fall within the scope of the laws within the originating state, therefore opening the door for varied levels of implementation and interpretation.[49] Colombia ratified the Hague Convention in 1998.[50] An adoptee's right to identity is gravely violated when adoption practices are illicit. Colombia's transnational adoption policies maintained systemic problematic practices to include child trafficking, falsified or non-existent adoptee records, and overall state-sponsored secrecy; the sum of which prohibit adoptees from accessing accurate information about their original families. Leaving the question of the adoptee's right to identity entirely to the laws of the state of origin is particularly problematic in the context of illicit practices. In so doing, the sanctioned secrecy can be used to hide crimes and illicit practices which violate the rights of the child.

Reparations: Lessons Learned from Argentina and Chile

Individual and collective Colombian transnational adoptee advocacy efforts to reconnect adoptees with birth families are important; however, as more evidence of illicit practices are uncovered, a larger Colombian government-sponsored effort is urgently needed. A secondary analysis of adult Colombian transnational adoptees who have found their birth families revealed nearly half of the participants reported learning about an illicit practice impacting their adoption.[51] In the research, illicit practices were categorized as

48 Ibid.

49 Ibid.

50 HCCH, *Status Table: Convention of 29 May 1993 on Protection of Children and Co-operation in Respect of Intercountry Adoption*, last update on 14 November 2022, https://www.hcch.net/en/instruments/conventions/status-table/?cid=69.

51 S. Branco and V. Cloonan, 'False Narratives: Illicit Practices in Colombian Transnational Adoption', *Genealogy*, Vol. 6, No. 4, 2022, pp. 1-12.

sale in children, birth mother trafficking and abuse of practice. While the sample size of 17 participants is small in comparison to the total number of Colombian transnational adoptees, the study's findings sound the alarm for expedient review and response from the Colombian government, especially as decades have passed; information has been lost, destroyed or not documented; and birth-family members grow older or may no longer be alive. The following sections outline the definition of reparations as they apply to transnational adoption practices and provide summaries of adoption reparation practices in Argentina and Chile. A proposed reparations model for Colombia concludes the section.

The UN established five basic principles included in reparative practice for victims: (1) restitution of property, employment, citizenship as applicable; (2) compensation for financial losses; (3) legal, medical and psychological rehabilitation services; (4) public symbolic actions; and (5) systemic change to prevent reoccurrence.[52] Ottendoerfer recommended the concept of reparations broaden to include "measures that provide material and symbolic support for individuals or groups of victims".[53] The UN reparations framework is a helpful starting point to consider how compensatory practices can be applied to victims of international adoption illegalities.

To this end, International Social Service outlined four specific actions to begin the reparation process to address illicit transnational adoption practices specifically: (1) "Investigate individual adoptions and adoption systems as soon as possible whenever there are indications of illicit practices"; (2) "Mediate and balance the often conflicting needs and desires of adoption triad members, and the interests of justice, without recapitulating the inequalities and injustices involved in the original illicit practices"; (3) "Legitimise [and facilitate the work of activists]"; and (4) "Create sustained oversight and response by international organisations and NGOs [non-governmental organizations]."[54]

In 2019 and 2020, the Hague Conference on Private International Law (HCCH) convened a Working Group on Preventing and Addressing Illicit Practices in

52 United Nations, *Declaration of Basic Principles of Justice for Victims of Crime and Abuse of Power*, General Assembly resolution 40/34, 29 November 1985, https://www.ohchr.org/en/professionalinterest/pages/victimsofcrimeandabuseofpower.aspx.

53 E. Ottendoerfer, 'Translating Victims' "Right to Reparations" into Practice: A Framework for Assessing the Implementation of Reparations Programs from a Bottoms-up Perspective', *Human Rights Quarterly*, Vol. 40, No. 5, 2018, pp. 905-931, 911.

54 C. Baglietto, N. Cantwell and M. Dambach, 'Responding to Illegal Adoptions: A Professional Handbook', *International Social Services*, 2016, pp. 197, 198, 199 and 200, https://fiom.nl/sites/default/files/responding-to-illegal-adoptions-a-professional-handbook-iss-april-2016.pdf.

Intercountry Adoption.[55] Their Model Procedure to Respond to Suspected and Actual Cases of Illicit Practices included the following:

- disclosure and recording of suspected cases of illicit practices;
- considerations of temporary child protection measures;
- services to impacted persons;
- investigation;
- informing concerned authorities, bodies and persons;
- and possible actions following the investigation.[56]

The draft recommendations were approved by the general membership and included in the 'Toolkit for Preventing and Addressing Illicit Practices in Intercountry Adoption' released by the HCCH in 2023.[57]

Similarly, the advocacy group Inter Country Adoptee Voices (ICAV) sought responses from 60 adult adoptees representing 14 adoptive and 26 birth countries.[58] ICAV, an Observer to the HCCH Working Group on Preventing and Addressing Illicit Practices in Intercountry Adoption, collated and relayed responses to the HCCH working group with the stated goal to "break down the perception that illicit intercountry adoptions affect just a few".[59] Respondents answered two questions: (1) "What should authorities and bodies do to respond to specific cases of illicit practices?" (2) "What should authorities and bodies do to prevent and respond to patterns of illicit practices?"[60] The most popular responses will be shared here.

Regarding the first question, 24 respondents endorsed creating an independent Investigative Commission and 27 respondents endorsed funding for reparative services (trauma-informed counselling, DNA testing, legal services etc.) for impacted persons. For the second question regarding preventive measures, 15 respondents endorsed universal access to prenatal care and 12 supported increasing infrastructure for in-country family preservation. Two Colombian adult adoptees, impacted by illicit adoptions, participated in the ICAV working group. Both recommended legal consequences and sanctions for those persons who participated in illegal adoption practices, with no statute of limitations, as well as broad funding and support for

55 HCCH, *Special Commission Meetings*, 4-8 July 2022, https://www.hcch.net/en/publications-and-studies/details4/?pid=6668&dtid=57.

56 HCCH, *Report of the Working Group on Preventing and Addressing Illicit Practices in Intercountry Adoption*, Meetings of 8-10 July 2020, p. 3, https://assets.hcch.net/docs/24f5a339-2ae1-44fd-bbbc-2ba84fb80cf0.pdf.

57 HCCH, *Toolkit for Preventing and Addressing Illicit Practices in Intercountry Adoption*, The Hague, 2023, https://www.hcch.net/en/publications-and-studies/details4/?pid=8530&dtid=3.

58 Long, 2020.

59 Ibid., p. 2.

60 Ibid., p. 3.

victims seeking reparations to include mental health counselling, legal support and DNA testing.

Reparations offer those impacted by illicit adoption practices an opportunity for validation to acknowledge the harm incurred.[61] Argentina established reparative efforts to address illegal adoption practices while Chile more recently embarked on such endeavours. Both models are worth a closer examination to be discussed next.

Argentina

Argentina experienced a dark period of governance during its Dirty War from 1976 to 1982.[62] During this time, approximately 30,000 persons, designated as subversive, disappeared and/or were murdered by the ruling governmental military party.[63] Captured persons were held in secret detention centres where they were tortured and, in many cases, murdered. Those detainees who were pregnant were kept alive until after giving birth. To erase their identities, the babies were then illegally adopted using falsified birth certificates to members or allies of the in-power regime.[64] Similarly, young children detained with their parents were separated from them and illegally adopted using false documentation.[65]

In response to the governmental illegal activities during the Dirty War, in 1977 an advocacy group, Mothers of the Plaza de Mayo, galvanized to demand answers to the whereabouts of their disappeared sons, daughters and family members.[66] When the group became aware of the missing children born in captivity, they created the Grandmothers of the Plaza de Mayo in an effort to locate their grandchildren.[67] Their advocacy continued throughout the Dirty War and remained active after the dictatorial government was overthrown in 1983. Their activism influenced the newly elected democratic government to establish the National Commission on Disappeared

61 E.C. Loibl, 'The Aftermath of Transnational Illegal Adoptions: Redressing Human Rights Violations in the Intercountry Adoption System with Instruments of Transitional Justice', *Childhood*, Vol. 28, No. 4, 2021, pp. 477-491.

62 R. Arditti, '"Do You Know Who You Are?" the Grandmothers of the Plaza de Mayo', *The Women's Review of Books*, Vol. 24, No. 5, 2007, pp. 12-15.

63 Ibid.

64 Ibid.

65 Ibid.

66 Ibid.; V.B. Penchaszadeh, 'Ethical, Legal and Social Issues in Restoring Genetic Identity after Forced Disappearance and Suppression of Identity in Argentina', *Journal of Community Genet*, Vol. 6, 2015, pp. 207-213.

67 Penchaszadeh, 2015.

Persons.[68] The Grandmothers of the Plaza de Mayo, in collaboration with geneticists and forensic anthropologists, developed methods to prove biological relationship to their grandchildren.[69] Eventually, in 1987, a national genetic database was created to store donated relative genetic material to be used to identify disappeared and murdered victims and reunite grandchildren with family members.[70] In 1992, another commission was created to assist those individuals seeking clarity on their identity.[71] These efforts coincided with increased national outreach by the Mothers and Grandmothers of the Plaza de Mayo to educate the public on the right to identity for all persons, paving the way for the inclusion of this right in the UNCRC.[72] Gesteira et al. described the movement from the Mothers and Grandmothers advocacy for Right to Identity based on military repression to broaden and include

> other practices that have violated this right, such as the coercive separation of children from their family environment, the concealment of children's identity, false registration of parentage or stolen.[73]

Chile

During the Pinochet dictatorship of the 1970s through 1980s, Chile's transnational adoption programme flourished under lax adoption regulations that propelled the growth of child trafficking systems to support the demand for children.[74] Specifically, Agoglia and Alfaro described circumstances where birth mothers were coerced to relinquishing parental rights to children and/or were told their babies were deceased.[75] These children were then moved through the adoption process under laws allowing for de-identifying children via 'assumptions of birth' where a child was falsely registered to a person, not the birth mother, to allow for ease of deeming the child eligible for transnational adoption.[76] Such laws created conditions amenable for child trafficking and irregular adoption practices. One priest, Gerardo Joannon, was charged with illegal adoption practices involving many children to include identity theft of civil status and forgery of

---

68 Ibid.

69 Arditti, 2007.

70 Penchaszadeh, 2015.

71 Ibid.

72 Ibid.; Arditti, 2007.

73 S. Gesteira, I.R. Agoglia, C. Villalta and K.A. Monsalve, 'Child Appropriations and Irregular Adoptions: Activism for the "Right to Identity", Justice, and Reparation in Argentina and Chile', *Childhood*, Vol. 28, No. 4, 2021, pp. 585-599, 592.

74 I.S. Agoglia and K.A. Monsalve, '"Irregular Adoptions" in Chile: New Political Narratives about the Right to Know One's Origins', *Children & Society*, Vol. 33, 2019, pp. 201-212.

75 Ibid.

76 Pizarro as cited in Baglietto et al., 2016.

documents.[77] Joannon was accused of finding vulnerable birth mothers, reporting their children were stillborn and supplying those children to adoptive parents.[78] Because the time period for criminal responsibility expired, the case was eventually dismissed.[79]

In response to numerous investigative reports and complaints surrounding illicit adoptions, in November 2018, the Chilean Congress established a special commission to investigate the state's role in irregular adoptions.[80] In September 2019, the Investigations Police created a subdivision to examine reports of irregular adoptions during the Pinochet regime.[81] Additionally, two advocacy groups – (1) Chilean Adoptees Worldwide and (2) Children and Mothers of Silence – are actively attempting to reunite adopted persons with birth/first families through educational efforts and DNA testing.[82]

Chile's irregular adoptions differed in circumstances to Argentina as birth mothers were not forcibly disappeared by the military because of their ideological beliefs; rather, birth mothers were deceived and or coerced. Recent indictments, predominantly led by adult Chilean adoptees who learned of falsehood in their adoptions, demonstrated the widespread problem of child trafficking during a booming transnational adoption business during the 1970s through 1980s. In response, the Chilean Congress issued examinations into its role in the irregular adoptions as well as police investigation of all reported irregularities from the aforementioned era.[83] In January 2023, the Chilean parliament voted to establish a truth and reparations commission to address irregular adoption practices impacting both transnational Chilean adoptees and their first families.[84]

Argentina's reparative model is the most advanced and serves as an exemplar to other countries. In response to significant and sustained activism, the Argentinian government established a federal branch exclusively focused on re-establishing the right to identity of illegally adopted children, now adults, of the Dirty War era.[85] Legislation,

77 Agoglia and Monsalve, 2019; Pizarro as cited in Baglietto et al., 2016; A. Truesdale, '"Irregular Adoption" Investigations Underway-262 and Counting', *Chile Today*, 27 September 2019, https://chiletoday.cl/site/irregular-adoption-investigations-underway-262-and-counting/.

78 Agoglia and Monsalve, 2019.

79 Pizarro, 2016.

80 Agoglia and Monsalve, 2019.

81 Truesdale, 2019.

82 Ibid.; Gesteira et al., 2021, p. 592.

83 Agoglia and Monsalve, 2019; Truesdale, 2019.

84 Sweden Posts, 'Swedes Adopted in Chile Can Receive Compensation', 11 January 2023, https://sweden.postsen.com/news/amp/68098?fbclid=IwAR0afogDM2HsIljB0y3hF1v1eqX9en3uoBgCg8Bq5VThlbFTAEoM0qc8CWw.

85 Penchaszadeh, 2015.

public information campaigns and a DNA database, all serve to facilitate the right to identity. Chile is in the beginning stages of its reparative process, yet the establishment of a truth and reparations commission to investigate illegal adoption practices as well as adoptee advocacy efforts offer direction to other countries seeking reparative practice. These two country's models of reparation offer guidance for a model of Colombian reparations discussed next.

Proposed Colombian Reparative Model

Colombia's transnational adoption system was created in response to overpopulation and increased levels of poverty.[86] National sentiment that poor Colombian children would be better off with Western adoptive parents fuelled transnational adoption, and the Colombian adoption law mandating total secrecy of the adopted child's birth family created a systemic condition of illicit practices.[87] Adult Colombian adoptees seeking their birth-family information have discovered their records were falsified and/or non-existent and, hence, impeding their rights to identity.[88] While Colombia has ceased its transnational adoption programme for children aged 6 and under, a national reparative model has not been implemented. Table 1 compares Argentina, Chile and Colombia's reparative practices in response to illicit adoptions based on the International Social Services Guidelines and the HCCH Working Group on Preventing and Addressing Illicit Practices in Intercountry Adoption Model Procedure to Respond to Suspected and Actual Cases of Illicit Practices.[89]

Investigations

The proposed Colombian reparations model is templated from two other South American countries, Argentina and Chile, and follows the frameworks outlined by ISS and the HCCH Working Group on Illicit Adoption Practices.[90] Principally, the model calls for Colombia to establish an investigative office where reports of illicit adoptions may be received, catalogued and documented with the potential for retroactive investigations.

86 Maestranzi, 2013.

87 Hoelgaard, 1998; C. Kawan-Hemler, *From Orphan, to Citizen, to Transnational Adoptee: The Origins of the US-Colombian Adoption Industry and the Emergence of Adoptee Counternarratives*, Unpublished master's thesis, 2022; Monroy, 1998.

88 Branco, 2021; Carreazo, 2016.

89 HCCH, *Report of the Working Group on Preventing and Addressing Illicit Practices in Intercountry Adoption*, Meetings of 8-10 July 2020, p. 3; C. Baglietto, N. Cantwell and M. Dambach, *Responding to Illegal Adoptions: A Professional Handbook*, International Social Service, 2016.

90 Baglietto et al., 2016, pp. 197, 198, 199 and 200; Long, 2020.

The Child Identity Protection (CHIP), a Swiss independent organization, provides international standards for preservation, maintenance and accessibility to impacted parties of a child's pertinent identity information, to include birth-family data.[91] Both ISS and HCCH recommend countries to investigate all reports of possibly illicit or corrupt practices.[92]

Balancing Conflicting Needs

Second, the proposed model recommends Colombia follow Argentina's model where the needs of the adoptee and birth families are carefully balanced with appropriate services and judicial oversight. Argentina, for example, provides psychological aid to adoptees and birth families in reunion while also prosecuting adoptive parents who knowingly participated in illicit adoption.[93] It is important to note that no evidence exists suggesting Colombian transnational adoptive parents were aware of any illicit practices prior to their adoption proceedings. To support Article 76 of the Infant and Adolescent Code, ICBF established a search and reunion office to aid adoptees seeking their birth-family information; however, it exists in a vacuum of other supportive services such as psychological aid, judicial oversight and, perhaps most helpfully, a state-sponsored DNA database where both adoptees and birth families may register.[94]

State Legitimization and Oversight

The third proposed recommendation calls for state legitimization of advocacy and activist groups, as demonstrated with the Grandmothers and Mothers of the Plaza de Mayo in Argentina. Two Chilean advocacy groups, Chilean Adoptees Worldwide, and Children and Mothers of Silence, are at the forefront of their countries' reparations movement; however, they have not yet been officially recognized by the Chilean government.[95] Colombian advocacy groups like Plan Angel very recently were officially recognized by *ICBF* and will be able to offer support to adoptees and birth parents in

---

91 M. Dambach and C. Jeannin, 'Policy Brief 1: Respecting the Child's Right to Identity in Intercountry Adoption', Geneva, Switzerland, *Child Identity Protection*, 2021, https://child-identity.org/images/files/CHIP-Policy-Brief-Adoption-EN-V2.pdf.

92 Baglietto et al., 2016, pp. 197, 198, 199, 200; HCCH, *Report of the Working Group on Preventing and Addressing Illicit Practices in Intercountry Adoption*, Meetings of 8-10 July 2020, https://assets.hcch.net/docs/24f5a339-2ae1-44fd-bbbc-2ba84fb80cf0.pdf.

93 Arditti, 2007; Penchaszadeh, 2015.

94 Instituto Colombiano de Bienestar Familiar, 'Búsqueda de Orígines', https://www.icbf.gov.co/programas-y-estrategias/proteccion/subdireccion-de-adopciones/busqueda-de-origenes.

95 Truesdale, 2019.

reunion searches.[96] Such acknowledgement is crucial to include the voices of those most marginalized by illicit adoption practices – namely the adoptees and their birth families – in the reparations planning process.

The final recommendation calls for emulation of the Argentinian sustained oversight of illicit practice investigation, prosecution and response via legal enforcement.[97] Chile also enacted similar legal safeguards but did not consider barriers created by statutes of limitations, rendering investigation and prosecution null in some instances.[98] While, indeed, Colombia's cessation of transnational adoption practices for younger children is a worthwhile first step towards eliminating future problematic practices, its 2006 Law 1098, Article 76 of the Infant and Adolescent Code legitimizing adoptees' rights to know birth-family information does not have legal enforcement or oversight. Sustained legal enforcement supported by federal law and appropriate authorities to enact oversight (see the first recommendation) is crucial to support Colombian adoption reparations.[99]

96 Plan Angel on Facebook, 2022.

97 Rubja as cited in Baglietto et al., 2016.

98 Pizarro, 2016.

99 Organization of American States, *Ley 1098 de 2006: Por la cual se expide el Código de la Infancia y la Adolescencia, El Congreso de Colombia*, 2006, https://www.oas.org/dil/esp/codigo_de_la_infancia_y_la_adolescencia_colombia.pdf.

Table 1. Reparation Model Comparisons and Recommendations

ISS & HCCH Model	
	Argentina
(1) 'Investigate individual adoptions and adoption systems as soon as possible whenever there are indications of illicit practices' 'Disclosure and recording of suspected cases of illicit practices and investigation'	National Commission on Disappeared Persons and the DNA database. If a minor child was found to be a coerced displaced person because of irregular adoptions, a process was initiated to, in most cases, reunite the child with their biological family members. Suspected adult adoptees who declined voluntary DNA testing were ultimately required to submit to so doing as mandated by a 2008 Supreme Court ruling citing the interest of society and the state addressing crimes against humanity overriding an adult adoptee's individual right to privacy.[a]
(2) 'Mediate and balance the often conflicting needs and desires of adoption triad members, and the interests of justice, without recapitulating the inequalities and injustices involved in the original illicit practices' 'Services to impacted persons'	Judicial courts worked with psychologists to support the child as they returned to birth-family members, while at the same time carefully balanced the ethical dilemmas posed when young adult persons refused DNA testing when suspected of being a missing relative.[b] Adoptive parents connected to the Argentinian illegal adoptions faced prosecutorial measures for knowingly, in most instances, conspiring in the illegal adoption.
(3) 'Legitimise and facilitate the work of activists'	The Mothers and Grandmothers of the Plaza de Mayo were at the forefront of the advocacy movement both during and after the Dirty War. The Argentinian democratic government granted legitimacy to their advocacy efforts by sanctioning governmental reparative actions to identify the disappeared and victims of illegal adoptions.
(4) 'Create sustained oversight and response by international organisations and NGOs' 'Considerations of temporary child protection measures, informing concerned authorities, bodies, and persons; and possible actions following the investigation'	In order to ensure ongoing oversight, the Argentinian Supreme Court instituted case laws that addressed the right to identity and served to ensure the truth be made available to all parties involved.[c]

a. Penchaszadeh, 2015.
b. Arditti, 2007; Penchaszadeh, 2015.
c. Rubaja as cited in Baglietto et al., 2016, p. 199.

Country-Specific Responses	
Chile	**Colombia**
The special commission to examine the state role in facilitating irregular adoptions and the Investigations Police subdivision to pursue reports of irregular adoptions.	According to Hoge (1981) and El Tiempo (1986), several individuals were arrested and eventually indicted for child trafficking of approximately 800 Colombian children. Yet, the children who were trafficked internationally remained with their adoptive parents and no efforts were made to reunify them with their first/birth parents. **Recommendation:** Colombia should initiate a federal office charged with receiving reports of illicit and/or irregular adoptions to be retrospectively investigated.
While establishing judicial oversight and investigatory actions to address irregular adoptions is a promising starting point for Chile it remains to be seen how justice will be fully served to all parties involved: adopted person, birth/first parents and adoptive families.	No state-wide action has been undertaken to support the efforts for the reunification of adult internationally adopted Colombians with their birth/first families. Despite Art. 115 and 76 allowing Colombian adult adoptees to petition for and access their pre-adoptive information, many encounter impediments preventing full access and/or are told their records were lost, burnt in a fire or otherwise non-existent.[d] **Recommendation:** Similar to Argentinian and Chilean efforts, a national DNA database should be established where birth/first families and adoptees may submit DNA samples to determine biological connections.
Two advocacy groups, Chilean Adoptees Worldwide and Children and Mothers of Silence, exist to advance public awareness of the illicit adoption activities and to reunite adoptees and birth/first families; however, no official governmental collaborations or responses to these groups have been issued.[e]	Several advocacy efforts, including Plan Angel, were created in response to adult Colombian adoptees seeking their identities. **Recommendation:** Plan Angel and other adoptee-led advocacy efforts should be acknowledged and consulted with by *ICBF* and the national investigative commission (per the first recommendation) to ensure the voices of those parties most impacted are incorporated into the reparative practices.
A specific challenge in the Chilean legal system is the expiration of the statute of limitations holding those accountable by the time evidence of the crimes committed are brought to court. Such was the case with the priest Gerardo Joannon and may still be the situation for those charged with similar crimes whose legal cases are pending. Hence, Chilean legislation must be altered or created to holding persons accountable for crimes resultant in irregular adoptions with no time limits.[f]	Ceasing all transnational adoptions for children under the age of 6 is a promising first step towards rectifying a broken system; however, larger-scale investigations and oversight have not been implemented. **Recommendation:** Argentina and Chile instituted legal oversight to ensure the right to identity remained accessible to all parties involved in illegal adoptions.[g] Colombia needs to issue comparable legislation in order to permanently support and enforce the right to identity.

d. Monroy, 1998; Organization of American States, 2006; Branco, 2021; Carreazo, 2016.
e. Truesdale, 2019.
f. Pizarro as cited in Baglietto et al., 2016.
g. Rubaja as cited in Baglietto et al., 2016.

Limitations

Multiple limitations exist preventing the implementation of the proposed Colombian reparations model. An overarching limitation includes the Colombian adoption system or *ICBF's* public silence regarding past problematic practices. Such a starting point is necessary as the impetus to enact other legislative initiatives. While *ICBF* has created a small office, *Bùsqueda de Orígines* ([Search for Origins] *ICBFb*, n.d.), to support adoptees (regardless of whether adoption is suspected to be illicit or not) seeking their birth-family information, the application procedures are buried on the *ICBF* website.[100] Furthermore, search services are offered in isolation from other supplemental supports such as DNA collection and database services, psychological aid and counselling, and support for birth families. In fact, Colombian birth families are not eligible for the services to find their birth children according to the information page; however, they are encouraged to update their contact information in the state-sponsored Missionary Information System in the event the adoptee requests an *ICBF*-supported search.[101.] Another glaring obstacle is the absence of one unified and cohesive Colombian adoptee advocacy organization. While there are many individual and small collective groups supportive of reparations and justice for adoptees and birth families impacted by corrupt adoption practices, Plan Angel being the most notable, there is no unified entity like Argentina's Mothers and Grandmothers of the Plaza de Mayo or the Chilean Adoptees Worldwide group. A coalition of Colombian adoptee groups is ideal for advocacy and Colombian government acknowledgement.

Finally, it should be noted that although Argentina and Chile both are farther along than Colombia in terms of acknowledgement of illicit adoption practices, according to Gesteira et al.:

> Neither government has undertaken symbolic forms of reparation, such as public apologies in which these actions are recognized as they actually occurred, nor have material forms of reparation been implemented in either country, both of which exhibit a scarcity of state resources dedicated to address this issue.[102]

In comparison, the proposed Colombian reparations are up against longstanding policies of silence and inaction and will require significant dedication, effort and perseverance to enact.

---

100 Instituto Colombiano de Bienestar Familiar, 'Búsqueda de Orígines', https://www.icbf.gov.co/programas-y-estrategias/proteccion/subdireccion-de-adopciones/busqueda-de-origenes.

101 Ibid.

102 Gesteira et al., 2021, p. 594.

At the time of this writing, Colombian adoption reparations have not been initiated; however, demands for reparations are underway, principally led by adult Colombian adoptees via search and reunion advocacy efforts. The International Social Service Guidelines and the HCCH Working Group on Preventing and Addressing Illicit Practices in Intercountry Adoption aid in conceptualizing next steps in reparations.[103] Per the proposed model, a logical starting point would be for the Colombian state to issue a global admission of, and apology to, those victims of transnational adoption wrongdoing and to establish an investigative unit to address allegations of illicit adoption practices.

Conclusion

Problematic Colombian transnational adoption practices throughout the 1970s to1990s have been spotlighted as more evidence has accumulated. Widespread accounts of illicit practices, including child trafficking, falsified records and missing or non-existent pre-adoption documentation obstruct adult Colombian adoptees from accessing their right to identity, a UNCRC mandate. Two other South American countries, Argentina and Chile, established reparative actions to address prior illicit adoptions and serve as comparison points for a proposed Colombian reparation model. The HCCH is working to codify responsive actions to address illicit international adoption with the goal to establish universally recognized reparative practices.[104] In the case of Colombia, a vast advocacy network of adult Colombian adoptees continues to demand their right to identity be met and those responsible for corrupt adoption practices be held accountable. This chapter offered one proposed model of Colombian reparations to advocate for adult Colombian adoptees seeking their right to identity; this model could perhaps be adapted to other sending countries with problematic transnational adoption practices (i.e. Guatemala, Ethiopia, Vietnam etc.)

103 Baglietto et al., 2016; HCCH, *Report of the Working Group on Preventing and Addressing Illicit Practices in Intercountry Adoption*, Meetings of 8-10 July 2020, https://assets.hcch.net/docs/24f5a339-2ae1-44fd-bbbc-2ba84fb80cf0.pdf.

104 HCCH, *Special Commission Meetings*, 4-8 July 2022, https://www.hcch.net/en/publications-and-studies/details4/?pid=6668&dtid=57.

4 Obstacles in the Search for Origins and Identities of Brazilian-Israelis Adopted Through Child Trafficking

Andréa Cardarello

Introduction

Transnational adoption entails the global circulation of children from their biological parents or foster parents to adoptive parents where in most cases they no longer share a common sociocultural or ethnic and biological connection.[1] With roots in Western humanitarian practice, transnational adoption embeds a salvationist discourse, ideologically representing adoptee children as either abandoned or destitute, stranded in contexts of extreme poverty and/or conflict or post-conflict settings, with little or no mention of the fate of their family of origin in local communities.[2] 'Sending' countries have predominantly been developing countries in Asia, Africa, Eastern Europe and South America, while 'receiving' countries have been wealthy so-called first-world countries. Transnational adoption processes have often been morally questionable, with biological parents/foster parents ignorant of their rights and of the impending complete severance of ties with their children and, in many cases, an infraction of national and

---

1 I. Willing, P. Fronek and D. Cuthbert, 'Review of Sociological Literature on Intercountry Adoption', *Social Policy and Society*, Vol. 11, 2012, pp. 465-479.

2 See D. Cuthbert and K. Lothian, 'War Waifs and Warrior Women: Feminine Activism and the "Rescue" of Children in Operation Babylift, April 1975', *Paper Presented at the Vietnam Inheritance Symposium*, Monash University, Melbourne, 30 April 2010; L. Briggs, *Somebody's Children: The Politics of Transnational and Transracial Adoption*, Durham, Duke University Press, 2012.

international law.[3] In Brazil, during the 1980s and 1990s, judges, lawyers, notaries, police officers, social workers, psychologists, day care directors, NGOs, doctors and nurses, among others, were complicit in illegal adoptions in cases of stolen children, falsifying birth records, passports and death certificates, coercing, deceiving and threatening mothers and families to give up their children and sign documents.[4] Mothers who were usually very young, poor and poorly educated were easily deceived and induced to hand over their children, as they believed they were doing them good.[5] The dismissal of paternal authority without apparent reason granted by judges was another way of removing children from their families of origin. Families could have children kidnapped from their homes or maternity wards by nannies, social workers and people who were part of the family's circle of friends.[6]

3 A. Cardarello, 'The Movement of the Mothers of the Courthouse Square: 'Legal Child Trafficking', Adoption and Poverty in Brazil', *Journal of Latin American and Caribbean Anthropology*, Vol. 14, No. 1, 2009, pp. 140-161; A. Cardarello, 'The Right to Have a Family: 'Legal Child-Trafficking', Adoption, and Birth Control in Brazil, *in* S. De Zordo and M. Marchesi (eds.), *Reproduction and Biopolitics Ethnographies of Governance, "Irrationality" and Resistance*, New York, Routledge, 2015; D.M. Smolin, 'Child laundering: How the Intercountry Adoption System Legitimizes and Incentivizes the Practices of Buying, Trafficking, Kidnapping, and Stealing Children', *Wayne Law Review*, Vol. 52, 2006, pp. 113-200; C. Collard, 'Triste terrain de jeu : l'adoption internationale en Haïti', Gradhiva, No.1, 2005, n.s., pp. 209-224; E.C. Loibl, *The Transnational Illegal Adoption Market: A Criminological Study of the German and Dutch Intercountry Adoption Systems*, The Hague, Eleven International, 2019; S. Gesteira, I. Salvo Agoglia, C. Villalta, and K. Alfaro Monsalve, 'Child Appropriations and Irregular Adoptions: Activism for the "Right to Identity," Justice, and Reparation in Argentina and Chile', *Childhood*, Vol. 28, No. 4, 2021, pp. 585-599; C.K. Clemente Martínez, *Volver a los Orígenes – Una etnografía de la adopción transnacional*, Barcelona, Bellaterra edicions, 2022.

4 E. M. Leal, *A dúvida mais persistente: as formas de governo do desaparecimento de pessoas no Brasil*, Tese de doutoramento, Universidade Federal do Rio Grande do Sul, Porto Alegre, 2017, https://www.lume.ufrgs.br/handle/10183/173797, p. 290; A. Cardarello, *"Trafic legal" d'enfants: la formation d'un mouvement de familles pauvres contre les politiques de l'adoption au Brésil*, PhD dissertation, Department of Anthropology, Université de Montréal, Quebec, Canada, 2009; M.C. Soldheid da Costa, *Os "filhos do coração": adoção em camadas médias brasileiras*, Tese de Doutorado em Antropologia Social, Programa de Pós-Graduação em Antropologia Social, Museu Nacional da Universidade Federal do Rio de Janeiro, Rio de Janeiro, 1988; D. Abreu, *No Bico da Cegonha. Histórias de Adoção Internacional no Brasil*, Rio de Janeiro, Relume Dumara 2002; J.B. Foltran, 'O tráfico infantil nas sombras da adoção internacional', *in Brasil. Câmara de Coordenação e Revisão.* Ministério Público Federal (Org.), Tráfico de Pessoas: Coletâneas de artigos. Brasília, MPF, 2017, pp. 128-145.

5 Foltran, 2017, p. 129; see C. Villalta and S. Gesteira, *Prácticas de circulación coactiva de niños y niñas en la Argentina: Tramas institucionales, jerarquías sociales y derechos*, Runa, Universidad de Buenos Aires. Facultad de Filosofía y Letras, Instituto de Ciencias Antropológicas, 2019, pp. 149-167 for Argentina and I. Salvo Agoglia, and K. Alfaro Monsalve, 'Irregular Adoptions' in Chile: New Political Narratives About The Right To Know One's Origins', *Children & Society*, Vol. 33, 2019, 201-212 for Chile.

6 E.A. Mongim, 'Tráfico de seres humanos: o bem jurídico tutelado posto em risco e os aspectos sociais', *Athenas*. Vol. 2, No. 2, pp. 212-241, jul./dez. 2013 in Foltran, 2017. The literature also refers to cases where the parents receive some economic advantage and the child is resold to families abroad (Foltran, 2017, p. 138).

During the 1980s, Brazil was fourth among the countries providing children for adoption on a global scale, having placed approximately 7,500 children up for adoption.[7] From 1994 onwards, the number of international adoptions gradually decreased on the national level: from a high of approximately 1,850 international adoptions annually in 1993, the number dropped to under 400 in 2000.[8] As happened in other countries, the 'child trafficking scandals' heavily covered by the media and the series of subsequent regional investigations led to a steep drop in international adoption from Brazil.[9] Italy, France and the United States are the countries most implicated in the history of illegal adoption in Brazil in the 1980s and 1990s.[10] In the late 1980s, it was Israel's turn to receive media attention.

In this chapter, taking into account the research produced in Brazil and Israel, we turn to the past to try to explain why it is so difficult for Brazilian-Israelis adopted illegally to re-establish what is called their 'right to identity'. Then we discuss the implications of

7 S. Kane, 'The Movement of Children for International Adoption: An Epidemiological Perspective', *The Social Sciences Journal*, Vol. 30, No. 4, 1993, p. 329.

8 C. Fonseca, 'An Unexpected Reversal – Charting the Course of International Adoption in Brazil', *Adoption & Fostering*, Vol. 26, No. 3, 2002, pp. 28-39, 29. The decline in the number of international adoptions in Brazil since 1994 is a combination of internal and external factors and varies in each state: there is no unique explanation that is valid for the whole country. According to the data available, in the state of Sao Paulo, which alone was responsible for about 40 per cent of all intercountry adoptions in Brazil from 1992 to 2000 (reaching almost 53% in 1998), the number of intercountry adoptions only began to decrease in 1999, five years later (see Cardarello, 2006, pp. 296-305).

9 See P. Selman, 'The Demographic History of Intercountry Adoption', *in* P. Selman (ed.), *Intercountry Adoption: Developments, Trends and Perspectives*, London, British Agencies for Adoption & Fostering (BAAF), p. 24, and Cardarello, 2015, for a report by the Human Rights Commission of the Legislative Assembly of São Paulo and a parliamentary inquiry commissioned by the Federal Senate at the end of the 1990s, which had the effect of decreasing illegal and international adoptions in the state of São Paulo. A number of other Latin American countries such as Chile, Peru and El Salvador, which were important supply states for a number of years, have tightened their adoption procedures after reports of illegal adoption practices that occurred in the 1990s (P. Selman, 'The rise and fall of intercountry adoption in the 21st century', *International Social Work*, Vol. 52, No. 5, 2009, 575-594, pp. 582-583 in Loibl, 2019, p. 51; see also P. Selman, 'Intercountry Adoption Agencies and the HCIA', International Forum on Intercountry Adoption & Global Surrogacy, AFIN Research Group, Universitat Autonoma de Barcelona, no. 79, January 2016. The number of international adoptions has been on a constant decline since 2004 (see Loibl, 2019, p. 33). It is not sending countries alone that suspend international adoptions but also those that usually receive children. According to Loibl (E.C. Loibl, 'The Aftermath of Transnational Illegal Adoptions: Redressing Human Rights Violations in the Intercountry Adoption System with Instruments of Transitional Justice', *Childhood*, Vol. 28, No. 4, 2021, 477-491, p. 9), more and more Western countries have recently set up truth commissions to inquire into abusive practices in past international adoptions.

10 Leal, 2017, p. 37. Between 1994 and 1998, families from Italy adopted approximately 40% of the Brazilian children placed for international adoption (Commissione Adozioni, *Commissione per le Adozioni Internazionale e Italiana per l'adozione internazionale*, https://www.commissioneadozioni.it/; Fonseca, 2002, pp. 28-39). See Abreu, 2002 and Cardarello, 2015 on how, in the 1980s and 1990s, the term 'irregular adoption' was used in Brazil when Brazilians adopted children within an illegal but sometimes legitimized framework, while 'trafficking' was used when the children were adopted by foreigners.

their demands and the role that organized groups of adoptees can play transnationally and locally in advancing causes related to the search for origins.

This article uses ethnographic interview data from a pilot research project with Carol A. Kidron, Haifa University, Israel. The project explores the memory and identity work of Brazilian-Israeli adoptees who, through a process of transnational adoption of Brazilian children by Israelis, were trafficked to Israel in the 1980s and 1990s. From May to July 2019, we conducted semi-structured interviews with five adoptees, two men and three women, as well as the adoptive mother of one of them.[11] Data from other cases were collected from articles in the press and the academic literature. My analysis is also based on findings from a previous investigation that I carried out in 2000 and 2001 with Brazilian families of origin in the state of São Paulo who lost their children in the 1990s in cases of illegal domestic and intercountry adoptions.

The Case of Brazil-Israel

Brazilian children were adopted by Israelis from the end of 1970s until the 1990s. As in the case of other Western receiving countries, involuntary childless Israelis sought babies available for adoption in Brazil owing to a shortage of babies available for adoption in their home country.[12] Access to legal abortion, better social welfare and income maintenance programmes for single Israeli mothers made the option of keeping their babies more feasible, accounting for the decrease in the number of suitable infants available for domestic adoption.[13] There were also an increasing number of older single women choosing married biological fathers with whom to become pregnant, with the intent of raising the child alone. Most couples wanted to adopt infants, and there was no way to respond to this demand.

Eventually, and quietly, the kibbutz movement (intentional communal settlement – traditionally agricultural) began to assist kibbutz couples in locating and funding adoptions. This movement, over time, came to be over-represented in foreign adoptions, owing to the movement's ideological concern for the well-being of members, the importance placed on family life and national and communal continuity, access to

11 Oren Segal and Orli Yakoby collaborated as research assistants. Three of the adoptees interviewed had already travelled to Brazil on their own initiative, while one had never been to his country of birth but wished to do so in the future. Two adoptees were able to find members of their biological families.

12 See E.D. Jaffe, 'Foreign adoptions in Israel: Private paths to parenthood', *in* H. Altstein, and R.J. Simon (eds.), *Intercountry Adoption: A Multinational Perspective*, New York, Praeger, 1991, 161-181, p. 163.

13 Ibid., p. 164. See R. Högbacka, 'The Quest for a Child of One's Own: Parents, Markets and Transnational Adoption', *Journal of Comparative Family Studies*, Vol. 39, No. 3, 2008, pp. 311-330, 312 for similar factors in the USA, Scandinavia and the Netherlands.

information and resources as well as to organizational resources. According to Jaffe, this community took the plight of its childless couples into its own hands and actively helped them find children abroad.[14] For many Israelis, intercountry adoption was the answer to their prayers.

In 1987, Jaffe initiated a study of overseas adoption under the sponsorship of Hebrew University. The Israeli Ministry of Justice estimated that between 2,000 and 2,500 babies from Brazil were living in Israel in 1987.[15] Gangs charged up to $25,000 to mediate baby adoptions, and the police suspected that some of the babies may have been kidnapped.[16]

More than 30 years have passed since Jaffe's study. The Brazilian babies are now adults, and documentary films and popular media sources in Israel and Brazil have reported on the adoptee search for origins and return trips to Brazil, sometimes accompanied by their adoptive parents.

Exposure in the media, whether it be in films, on television programmes or in the press, is a characteristic of the case of Brazilian-Israeli babies trafficked in transnational adoption, in both countries and internationally.[17] The sensationalist treatment by TV programmes started in 1988, when the Israeli Supreme Court ordered the return of Brazilian Baby Bruna to her biological parents. The Court ruled that Bruna had been kidnapped two years earlier by a babysitter and was handed to a baby trafficking mob prior to being adopted by an Israeli couple.[18] The foreign adoption order and the birth certificate that were issued for the baby were forged. Bruna's biological mother went to Israel to claim her daughter with the help of a British TV producer who was

---

14 Jaffe, 1991, p. 173, who explores the centrality of children in Jewish cultural perceptions stating that "there is no way that childlessness will be accepted by Jewish couples anywhere as an acceptable norm" (p. 179).

15 Ibid., p.170. The Brazilian-Israeli adoptee activist Lior Vilk mentions 3,000 to 5,000 illegal adoptions to Israel (L. Vilk, 'Traficado Para Israel – A História De Lior Vilk – Parte 2', interview by Daniele de Aires, January, Rio de Janeiro, 2022a, https://www.youtube.com/watch?v=xrM2VZXhuDc).

16 See Repórter em Ação, 'Mulher líder da quadrilha de tráfico de bebês concede entrevista exclusiva', 14 November 2015, TV Record, https://www.youtube.com/watch?v=n1thGMjtBQM; Leal, 2017, pp. 135 and 219 mentions amounts between 7,000 and 12,000 U.S. dollars. Jaffe and his research team interviewed 56 couples and single persons all over Israel, 71% having adopted from Brazil, between 1983 and 1987.

17 See N. Ribke and J. Bourdon, 'Transnational Activism, New and Old Media: The Case of Israeli Adoptees from Brazil', *New Media & Society*, Vol. 18, No. 11, 2016, pp. 2649-2663.

18 M. Goldfeder, 'Adoption in Judaism and in Israel', *in* R.L. Ballard, N.H. Goodno, R.F. Cochran, Jr. and J.A. Milbrandt (eds.), *The Intercountry Adoption Debate: Dialogues Across Disciplines*, Newcastle upon Tyne, UK: Cambridge Scholars Publishing, 2015, pp. 493-525, 520; Ribke and Bourdon, 2016, p. 2654; Leal, 2017, p. 226.

investigating Brazilian baby exports.[19] The Bruna case shocked the Israeli public: for the first time, the issues of intercountry adoptions in which Israeli couples were taking the initiative by themselves in foreign countries became common knowledge and a shared national problem.[20]

Although criminal groups paid bribes to judges, court officials, notaries and federal police in this case, only three Brazilian intermediaries were imprisoned.[21] These included Arlete Hilo, who, according to articles in the Brazilian press, had an office in Israel and relied on other foreign intermediaries. She was responsible for the operational part of searching for children through her agents, then, through the judicial system, obtaining documents authorizing the adoptions (*escritura pública*), and distributing passports to the children. Her accomplice, Valdemar Reinert, was in charge of obtaining passports from the federal police. Hilo was convicted of abduction or robbery, the trafficking of minors and gang formation. Reinert was found guilty of falsifying documents and breaking Brazilian law by registering another person's child as his own. The third person arrested was Reinert's girlfriend, Regina Paulista Fernandes.

Hilo served two years in prison in 1986 and was incarcerated again in 1992.[22] In 1984, she told a Tel Aviv television network that she had brokered the adoption of 35 children in seven months for Israel, Italy, France and Sweden. Arrest was difficult because she used several names and false documents and travelled abroad (Israel and the USA) as well as through different Brazilian states. On the Brazilian television programme *Repórter em Ação*, on Record TV in 2016, she reported a case that year in which she had brokered an adoption for Israelis.

Another woman who was implicated in the gang of intermediaries was also arrested for child kidnapping. Police investigations into illegal adoptions in Brazil found blank birth certificates and passports in the possession of intermediaries. At that time, other cases of irregularity in international adoptions were investigated and reported by the press.[23]

---

19 For the price adoptees pay for exposure in sensationalistic and voyeuristic television and printed media, see Ribke and Bourdon, 2016, pp. 2653, 2659-2661. According to the authors, along with the ambivalent benefits of media exposure, the Brazilian-Israeli adoptees interviewed generally described their participation in such programmes as frustrating and even traumatic, giving them a feeling of loss of control.

20 Jaffe, 1991, p. 171.

21 Repórter, 2016; Leal, 2017, p. 220.

22 Repórter, 2016 and *Jornal do Brasil*, 03/04/1986, quoted by Leal, 2017, pp. 220-222.

23 For example, the adoption of 430 children in Feira de Santana, Bahia State, by Italian, American and other foreign couples, or the suspicion about the rise in the number of adoptions in the city of Fortaleza, Ceara State, in 1986 (Leal, 2017, pp. 221-222).

The Brazilian press's coverage of the cases of illegal adoption of Brazilian babies by Israelis, highlighting Arlete Hilo's involvement, made the role of intermediaries difficult in the State of Paraná from 1984 onwards. That year, the General Magistrate (*corregedor Geral de Justiça)* of Parana determined that all adoptions must be processed through the Court, requiring the adoptive parents to stay in the country during the period of family adaptation, as established in the Code of Minors of 1979.[24] However, according to an adviser to the Attorney General's Office of the Public Ministry (*Procuradoria Geral do Ministério Publico*) specialized in combating human trafficking, the difficulty in criminalizing the trafficking for purposes of illegal adoption that occurred in the 1980s lay in the fact that there were no criminal types to frame it at the time.[25]

The Challenging Search for Adult Adoptee Identity

Brazilian-Israeli adoptees, adopted in processes involving illegal intercountry adoption, who are seeking to discover their origins, face particular challenges. The search for their origins has encountered many barriers, one being language. Although they have attempted to discover their past and to follow a paper trail of documentation, these adoptees also face non-existent adoption records and/or have discovered that the documents relating to their origins have been destroyed. Another obstacle, the falsification of documents, has also sent them off on a path destined to fail, which has had a profound impact on them.

Costa's ethnography provides a depiction of the context in which adoptions were carried out in Brazil in that period, outlining practices that may account for the difficulties faced by adoptees seeking their origins.[26] The research was conducted between 1983 and 1986 in the cities of Curitiba and Rio de Janeiro with middle-class Brazilian adoptive parents and intermediaries, doctors, lawyers, psychologists, nurses and nuns, among others.

24 Leal, 2017, pp. 218, 225, 266.

25 Considering the criminal law background of this adviser to the Attorney General's Office of the Public Ministry, she does not believe in the effectiveness of human rights without their legal inscription (Leal, 2017, p. 266 and footnote 139). In her interview with Leal, she states that few causes of human trafficking are included in its definition in criminal law. This means that the definition does not cover criminalized conduct that could be framed in this criminal type – such as the subtraction of incapable (trafficking for the purpose of illegal adoption). Leal points out that, months after the interview, changes were introduced in the legislation. In October 2016, Law 13,344/2016 provides for the prevention and repression of internal and international trafficking in persons and for measures to care for victims, amending and revoking previous laws and provisions.

26 Costa, 1988.

What was termed at that time 'Brazilian-style adoption' (*adoção'a brasileira*) was a very common practice, a procedure that consisted of a notary registration of a child as one's biological child – the presence of two witnesses was enough to confirm the statements.[27] The information about the hospital, the address, the name of the midwife or the doctor responsible for the delivery was falsified. Costa's informants speak of the practice of shifting dates of birth by one day and even by months to obscure clues of origin. The data relating to the place of birth was also constantly being altered. Most importantly, Costa notes that the city of birth appearing in the child's final documentation was the city in which the adoptive parents lived when waiting to receive the child. To keep the location of the biological mother or the adoptee status secret, it was common among Brazilian adopters to seek a child in another state in Brazil or another city in the same state.[28]

Hospitals did not document information that might connect a child to a certain mother.[29] Even biological mothers searching for their adopted children do not have the information regarding their adoptive names; they only know the maternity hospital where their baby was born and the date of birth.[30] It should be noted that, in Brazil, it was common for many children to be officially registered a few months or even a few years after their birth. There were families who only registered children when a governmental institution required it, such as for enrolment in primary school. In research carried out in the early 2000s with families of origin who had lost their children to illegal adoptions in the state of São Paulo, I noted that many of these children had never been officially registered.[31]

---

27 Ibid., p. 188; D. Abreu, 'Baby-Bearing Storks: Brazilian Intermediaries in the Adoption Process', *in* D. Marre (ed.), *International Adoption: Global Inequalities and the Circulation of Children*, New York, New York University Press, pp. 135-153, 149-150; C. Fonseca, 'Family Belonging and Class Hierarchy: Secrecy, Rupture and Inequality as Seen Through the Narratives of Brazilian Adoptees', *The Journal of Latin American and Caribbean Anthropology*, Vol. 14, 2009, pp. 92-114. See Collard, 2004, p. 255 on the same phenomenon in Haiti, known as "Haitian-style adoption", Salvo Agoglia and Alfaro Monsalve, 2019 for Chile, and S. Gesteira, *"Legales pero ilegítimos": sentidos sobre la inscripción de la filiación y los documentos personales para quienes buscan sus orígenes en Argentina*, Etnográfica [En línea], 20, 1, Publicado el 03 marzo 2016, consultado el 09 febrero 2022 for Argentina.

28 Costa, 1988, pp. 174, 185, 187.

29 In research on Brazilian adoptees in domestic adoptions searching for their origins, Fonseca concludes that before the 1980s, hospitals were the major institutional source of adopted children (Fonseca, 2009, p. 98).

30 A. Boldeke, 'Tráfico de Bebês – Onde estão nossas mães?', Desaparecidos do Brasil, Parte 2, June 2011, last updated on 12 November 2014, http://www.desaparecidosdobrasil.org/procuro-minha-mae.

31 See A. Cardarello, *O interesse da criança e o interesse das elites: "Escândalos de tráfico de crianças", adoção e paternidade no Brasil*, Scripta Nova, Revista Electrónica de Geografía y Ciencias Sociales [En línea] Barcelona, Universidad de Barcelona, 15 de marzo de 2012, Vol. XVI, No. 395(10), http://www.ub.es/geocrit/sn/sn-395/sn-395-10.htm.

For those adopted by Israelis, there are many complaints attesting to the falsification of documents in Rio de Janeiro before they were sent abroad via Paraguay.[32] Despite birth certificates indicating that the children were born in Rio, this information is not reliable. One of the adoptees we interviewed in Israel, Elad, had such a birth certificate but had discovered that the number on his certificate belonged to another person, a woman.[33] His search of DNA banks led to the discovery that he was, in fact, born in one of Brazil's southern states. The Israeli television series *Avudim*, which recounts the search for missing people, described the desperate search by one Brazilian-Israeli adoptee for his true birth certificate. The adoptee was accompanied in this process by the journalist-anchor. The programme shows a terrified Brazilian woman in a police station, and it is later revealed that her identification number had been stolen and used for the adoptee's document. Another adoptee interviewed in our research believed he was born in Rio de Janeiro because of the information appearing on his passport.

Even babies' photographs in passports were falsified. Elad said he knew the photo on his passport was fake when another adopted woman in Israel showed him the same photo in her passport. The amount of false information documented has led adoptees to consider numerous hypotheses regarding their origins and the processes through which they were separated from their birth mothers. Elad explained:

> Given the false information related to my case, I think I was kidnapped. I was kidnapped or presumed dead.... There were mothers arriving at the hospital, where they had given birth, and they were told that the child had died.... Perhaps she (the biological mother) was someone who gave the baby up for adoption in the 1980s. Unless she lived with a family (*casa de familia,* as a maid), and the family did not accept her being pregnant again. Or I was a baby kidnapped from the hospital. Or (a consequence of) rape.[34]

As in other global cases of illegal adoptions, biological mothers were led to believe that their babies died during childbirth, with the complicit assistance of medical staff in the hospitals. In Brazil, birth certificates produced in different states in the country could create a problem of duplicate documentation in cases where there was

32 Leal 2017, p. 216.

33 See also Leal, 2017, p. 215 and Boldeke, 2011. The names of the adoptees used in this chapter are fictitious, unless they are public figures who have appeared in the media.

34 At the time, it was quite common for maids to live in the house of the family employing them (*casas de familia*). If the maid then became pregnant, she was often required to give up the baby for adoption if she wanted to keep her job (see Abreu, 2009, pp. 49, 99). For a mother who gave up her son under pressure from her employer, see Cardarello, 2006, pp. 256-257, and Fonseca, 2009, pp. 99-100 for another case. According to Fonseca, maids also played a major role as intermediaries in the choice of a child's adoptive family.

already some registration in the true city of birth.[35] Despite the fact that Brazilian-style adoption was a common practice at that time, there was already a law against the crime of adulterating or creating a certificate, contract or record, among other forms of documentation (*falsidade ideológica*) concerning an alleged childbirth.

Costa recounts the practice among judges of resolving this problem by making the child 'disappear' by producing a death certificate, or by destroying birth records, in this way assisting adoptive parents.[36] Among the cases of Brazilian-Israeli adoptees in Leal's study there are cases where doctors signed the death certificate without giving the biological parents access to see the bodies of the babies.[37]

SEARCH FOR ORIGINS AND ETHNO-RACIAL DILEMMAS

As mentioned previously, although their birth certificates may indicate Rio de Janeiro as their city of birth, many of those adopted in Israel – and, during the same period, in other countries as well – were actually born in the southern states of the country such as Paraná and Santa Catarina. These are states with a largely light-skinned and light-eyed population due to the widespread presence of descendants of European immigrants such as Germans, Poles, Dutch and Russians. For this reason, these states were preferred as adoption sources by both Brazilian and foreign adopters.[38]

Most of the Brazilian babies trafficked to Israel in Jaffe's study were converted to Judaism. This was the case for Michal, one of our interviewees. During her search for

35 Costa, 1988, p. 188.

36 Costa, 1988.

37 Leal, 2017; see also Foltran, 2017, p. 137. Jaffe, 1991, and Weiss, 2001 report similar methods in domestic adoptions in Israel, which were denounced by the Association of Yemenite Jewish Immigrants. The Association claims that Yemenite babies from large families who passed through Israeli hospitals in the early 1950s were secretly adopted by Ashkenazi Jewish couples, some of whom lived in the United States, and that false death certificates were issued to biological parents who lived in transitional camps. No tangible evidence of this arrangement has been discovered, but the Association insisted, and in 1995 the Israeli government opened an investigation into it (M. Weiss, 'The Immigrating Body and the Body Politic: The 'Yemenite Children Affair' and Body Commodification in Israel', *in* N. Schepper-Hughes and L. Wacquant (eds.), *Commodifying Bodies*, London, Sage Publications, 2001). A representative of the Yemenite community told the Commission that at that time it was thought that since Yemeni couples had so many children, why not give them to Holocaust survivors who didn't have children? (Weiss, 2001, p. 99). For similar cases in Chile see Salvo Agoglia and Alfaro Monsalve, 2019, and for Spain see M.A. De Lorenzi, A.G. Molinero and P.E.F. Moreno, 'Adopción y derechos. El acceso a los orígenes en Argentina, Chile y España', *América Latina Hoy*, Vol. 83, 2019, pp. 7-23, 15.

38 See Leal, 2017, p. 216; Costa, 1998, p. 111; A. Lucchese, *Vida de Adotivo*, Passo Fundo, Physalis Editora, 2020, p. 129 and J.M. Vieira, *Os filhos que escolhemos: discursos e práticas da adoção em camadas medias*, M.A. Thesis, Department of Anthropology, UNICAMP, Campinas/São Paulo, 2004.

her origins, she was concerned by the presence of descendants of Germans in the region where she was born, among whom were Nazis. Michal was haunted by the thought that she might have Nazi ancestors. She was relieved when, after finally meeting members of her biological family, they told her that she had indigenous ancestry, not German. In Michal's case, her 'indigenous' identity was one more layer to add to her already composite identity, which included Israeli, Jewish and Brazilian. She recounts:

> Since I was a little girl, I have sought out Indian things, something that people here in Israel did not understand because I am white. I always said I was Indian. And people said to me: 'No, you're white!' Here in Israel they asked me: Why do you like Indians so much? I did not know, but I used to say 'I am Indian.' I felt it (since I was little).[39]

Unlike Michal, not all Brazilian adoptees in Israel can "pass as white". On the one hand, the fact that Israel is a multi-ethnic country with dark-skinned Jewish-Israelis may make it a less challenging destination for adopted children from Brazil.[40] Like Brazilians, Israelis can have different phenotypes. According to Jaffe's study, however, although all of the adoptive parents in the late 1980s were satisfied with the adoption outcome, a third of the parents predicted that their children would suffer from some form of identity crisis because of what they or others might correctly or incorrectly perceive as racial, national or religious aspects related to their adoptions.[41]

Even though these ethno-racial dilemmas described previously are only beginning to be explored in the research, our data highlights the importance of demographics for communities in which adoptee children were raised, as well as the relative commonness of lighter or darker-skinned in these populations. Yoav, for example, recounted that, when he was 16 years old, he had a girlfriend who was also a Brazilian adoptee. She had darker skin and had grown up on a kibbutz. Yoav said it had been difficult for her to be the only dark-skinned person on the kibbutz. Being adopted by Sephardic Jews [of North-African origin, often darker-skinned than Israelis of European descent], Yoav looked like the other children in the urban neighbourhood where he lived. He reports

---

39 This indigenous identity encompasses groups from North America: Michal explained during the interview how a 'dreamcatcher' in her home worked before delving into the theme of her identity. It did not refer to a particular Brazilian indigenous group.

40 It is important to note that at the end of 2020 there were approximately 159, 500 Black Israelis of Ethiopian origin out of a total Israeli population of 9, 364 million in 2021. Ethiopian Jews have been in Israel for more than three decades, yet the vast majority continue to live on Israel's social periphery (Jewish Virtual Library Ethiopian Jewry, 'The Situation of Ethiopian Jews in Israel', https://www.jewishvirtuallibrary.org/the-situation-of-ethiopian-jews-in-israel.

41 Jaffe, 1991.

that he was shocked by his girlfriend's conflicts with her adoptive parents – in each fight, she would bring up the issue of her adoption.

Proof of Brazilian Citizenship and Impunity

Given so many false documents, it can be very difficult for adoptees to find all the necessary legal documents that establish their Brazilian citizenship. Locating these documents is one of the main goals of those who are searching for their origins. Some of our interlocutors asserted that they were considering living in Brazil in the future. For them, accessing documentation would be an important step towards their agenda. Those who have found records keep these documents in safe places, in light of the great emotional and, at times, financial cost of obtaining them.[42] They depict a complex pilgrimage to public institutions both in Israel – such as in the Brazilian embassy – and mainly in Brazil where they procured non-falsified birth certificates, 'CPFs' (a tax-related identification number generated once a person has been registered into the Brazilian Revenue system) and the 'RG' (official national identity document in Brazil), involving endless battles with public officials.[43] Adoptees also write to various bodies of the Brazilian government, such as the embassy, the Secretary of Human Rights and the Order of Attorneys of Brazil (National Bar Association of Brazil, *Ordem dos Advogados do Brasil*).[44] Eventually, they may receive help from volunteers and NGOs related to the search for missing persons, like *Desaparecidos do Brasil*.[45] One of the adoptees who had access to her records recounts the tale of her friends – other Brazilian adoptees – who went to the Brazilian embassy in Israel to be told there that there was no proof 'that they were real Brazilians':

> For me they didn't cause problems, but for others they did, I don't know why … 'We don't have proof that you are real Brazilians' (*brasileiros de verdade* – they said at the embassy).… Many friends went there (to the Brazilian embassy) and said: 'Help me, I don't know how' (to have access to documents). They

42 On the careful and delicate handling of the identity documents of those Argentinians who have 'legal but illegitimate' birth records, see Gesteira, 2016, pp. 11, 14.

43 CPF stands for '*Cadastro de Pessoas Físicas*' (Natural Persons Registry). The 'RG' (from *Registro Geral*, General Registry) or *carteira de identidade* is a card that contains the name of the person, affiliation, place of birth, date of birth, signature and thumbprint of the bearer.

44 Boldeke, 2011.

45 Some of these volunteers started their work with personal life stories. The volunteer Lindalva gave a daughter up for adoption when she was young and unmarried, out of fear of her father and because she was unable to raise the child. She ended up locating her daughter 12 years later (Leal, 2017, pp. 248-249, 255). Sandrinha promised her 14-year-old adopted daughter, who wanted to meet her birth mother, that she would find her, and she did. Amanda began her volunteer work by searching for her brother, who had been missing for 10 years.

> don't want to help. They know Portuguese and Hebrew and didn't want to help.

According to the data collected by Fonseca, in 2007, among Brazilian-born adoptees adopted in Brazil, the geographical proximity of birth families and legal registries do little to facilitate the adoptee's search.[46] Fonseca notes how these adoptees may also describe their search as a sort of pilgrimage. In addition to financial obstacles pertaining to the fees required for each file requested, adoptees must also confront reluctant, hostile or indifferent authorities when attempting to obtain information about their birth families.[47]

The names of the birth mothers that appear in forged documents are very common, with hundreds of homonyms existing in the country.[48] In addition, in the 1980s, when a baby was abandoned in a hospital, found on the streets or in the garbage, the baby was under the protection of the Juvenile Court, which would order that a birth certificate be issued.[49] If there was a couple interested in adopting the child, the register could include their names. Otherwise, the judges, not allowing in the register the term 'unknown parents', listed a 'mother of charity' (*mãe de caridade*) on the birth certificate, using a name that did not identify anyone specific, such as 'Maria da Silva'. This registration had, in principle, a provisional character, since the child had, ideally, to be placed in a family.[50] If this did not happen, the provisional 'mother Maria' would ultimately appear on the child's documentation.

The birth certificate with the name of a 'mother of charity' on it never mentioned any 'father of charity'. Government employees at the time were instructed not to request data on the father 'to avoid embarrassment' related to the question of the biological mother's and her family's honour.[51]

Finally, we must consider the impunity of all the authorities who participated in these many years of trafficking. According to a study by Leal on the search for missing persons in Brazil, a Brazilian woman who has dedicated her life to finding missing persons claims that the cases of missing children are the most difficult because, in addition to

---

46 Fonseca, 2009.

47 Ibid., pp. 95 and 109 and C. Fonseca, 'Direito às origens: segredo e desigualdade no controle de informações sobre a identidade pessoal', *Revista de Antropologia*, Vol. 53, Nr. 2, 2010, pp. 493-526, 504. See Gesteira, 2016, pp. 18-19 for similar complaints by Argentinians who are searching for origins.

48 Boldeke, 2011.

49 Costa, 1988, p. 186.

50 A. Cavallieri, Alyrio, *Direito do menor*, Rio de Janeiro, Ed. Forense (Série Direito: Perguntas e Respostas), 1986 in Costa, 1988, p. 187.

51 Costa, 1988, p. 187.

the falsification of documents, powerful and influential people are involved – people who were never brought to trial.[52]

The Struggle for the Implementation of DNA Banks

Between 2000 and 2008, an online forum for Israeli adoptees gradually developed.[53] The group started out as an online community, and through the internet, they organized a support group, which then became activist, with actual 'offline' encounters. In 2008, an Israeli English language Facebook page, titled 'Brazilian Adopted Young & Adults', was created.

Lior Vilk is a key figure in the history of Brazilian-Israeli adoptees and their search for their origins. After learning Portuguese, while he was in search of his own origin story in the early 2000s, he became actively involved in the case of other adoptees, helping as an interpreter for NGOs and volunteers in Brazil while also compiling information on adoptees and biological families. He participated in establishing more than one group of adoptees in Israel and internationally. His appearance in soap operas (*telenovela Salve Jorge*, 2012-2013) and in large-audience TV programmes in Brazil (live studio programme *Domingão do Faustão*, 2012) culminated in new contacts with biological families and adoptees.[54]

Vilk recommended that other adoptees who have false documents, as in his own case, enter their data in one of the DNA banks. He and others have since successfully traced relatives by this means. In Vilk's case, he discovered a paternal biological aunt and another biological uncle, although he does not yet know his origins on his maternal side. Vilk recounts in an interview, on January 2022, that a group of adoptees in Israel decided to publish an article requesting the assistance of authorities in DNA banks, specifically asking for free tests in order to discover whether they had biological

52 Leal, 2017, p. 252; Cardarello, 2015. According to Loibl (2021, p. 3), the failure to properly punish wrongdoers in illegal adoptions might encourage repetition: failing to hold those who were involved in abusive practices responsible is to invite other stakeholders within the adoption system to consider such practices as legitimate and acceptable.

53 Ribke and Bourdon, 2016, pp. 2652-2653, 2661.

54 See Ribke and Bourdon 2016, Boldeke 2011 and L. Vilk, 'Traficado Para Israel – A História De Lior Vilk – Parte 1', Interview by Daniele de Aires, January, Rio de Janeiro, 2022b, https://www.youtube.com/watch?v=7MEj70KF4Jg, and Vilk, 2022a. On the importance of autobiographical storytelling for international adoptees, which allows them to produce a collective identity, and thus provide the necessary unity for activism, education or for influencing policy, as well as for creating alternative pedagogical narratives to develop socially and politically informed adoptee stories, see N. Cherot, 'Transnational Adoptees: Global Biopolitical Orphans or An Activist Community?', *Culture Machine*, Vol. 8, 2009, pp. 11-12.

brothers or cousins.[55] Thanks to the intervention of the Israeli adoptee group, My Heritage contacted them and decided to distribute 15,000 free DNA kits to Brazilian biological families. Work then began, instructing families regarding the registration process.

According to Vilk, the activists' attempt to convince the Brazilian government to create a national DNA bank fell on deaf ears. Vilk reports how adoptees and volunteers associated with NGOs were invited to discuss the matter with government agencies, but the necessary investment was never made despite occasional initiatives by institutions like the Civil Police of the city of Curitiba. It was as if, according to Vilk, Brazil just wanted to "close the matter in a nice way". For this adoptee, investing in a national DNA database would be like "assuming the blame, because it's also their fault". In an article published online in 2014, the representative of the NGO *Desaparecidos do Brasil*, Amanda Boldeke, called on the Brazilian government to set up a free DNA database, which the government promised to do but has not yet done.

As most databases are inaccessible to citizens, it is clear that without an effective national DNA bank in Brazil, information depends on networks established by adoptees. Access to these databases and other related resources is available only for individuals who work in public institutions, but it also depends on partnerships or judicial authorization, which is not always possible and even when it is, it is extremely time-consuming.[56]

Conclusion: Demands Regarding the Aftermath of Illegal Adoptions

From the 1970s onwards, a consensus on the importance and the right of transnational adoptees to know their origins has grown in different countries, commonly termed the 'right to identity'.[57] In part, this was problematized socially, politically and legally as a result of the criminal appropriation of children during the dictatorship era in Latin America and, especially, the work of the Grandmothers of Plaza de Mayo in Argentina, which influenced articles of the 1989 UN Convention on the Rights of the Child. Articles 7, 8 and 11 of the Convention specify the right to identity as the child's right to have a name and a last name, a nationality, to know the identity of her or his parents, and to be cared for by them. Clemente points out that today, in the culture of adoption, the transparency of information is increasingly valued.[58] The language of human rights permeates that of

55 Vilk, 2022a.
56 Leal, 2017, p. 244; Fonseca, 2009, pp. 109-110.
57 Salvo Agoglia and Alfaro Monsalve, 2019; Gesteira, 2016.
58 Clemente, 2022, pp. 69-70.

adoption and provides a framework for reflection from which transnational adoption is debated.[59]

On 2 December 2021, the association Adotiva – Brazilian Association of Support for Adopted Persons – was created.[60] This association has a group that addresses origins and DNA and aims to inform adoptees about their rights to knowledge about origins and about the possibilities of searching for their biological families. The organization even founded a study group on these topics, with discussions of academic articles; the first discussion occurred in June 2022. Another goal of Adotiva is "fighting in favor of historical reparation for the violation of rights by the State".[61] According to Larissa Alves, co-founder of the association, Adotiva emerged as an outcome of convergence of Brazilian adoptees from different parts of the country to give visibility to their neglected demands and achieve improvements.[62]

In Brazil, the rupture of ties with the family of origin and the establishment of secrecy regarding adoption began to be questioned by adoptees at the end of the 20th century.[63] Since 2009, Law #12.010/09 has guaranteed that adoptees over the age of 18 had the right to know their biological origin as well as to obtain unrestricted access to the process in which the measure was applied. There is also the possibility of accessing the adoption files for minors (those who are still under 18 years of age), in addition to ensuring guidance as well as legal and psychological assistance. Brazil is also a signatory to the United Nations Convention on the Rights of the Child.

---

59 As Clemente Martínez (2022, p. 95) recalls, the search must be a possibility, an option, a right, but not an obligation. It is necessary to take into account that not all adoptees will want to know or search for information about their past nor that they have any intention of doing so in the near future, nor that they feel the need to achieve the final step in the search: contact and reunion. In fact, one of the adoptees we interviewed clearly mentioned that he does not need to know his origins. See Cherot, 2006 for an "adoptee community pedagogy" that creates narratives against establishing a unique Vietnamese adoptee identity in the United States.

60 L. Paludo, 'Primeira associação de filhos adotivos do Brasil será fundada em dezembro', *Gaúcha ZH*, 26 November 2021, https://gauchazh.clicrbs.com.br/comportamento/noticia/2021/11/primeira-associacao-de-filhos-adotivos-do-brasil-sera-fundada-em-dezembro-ckwgvwpyl005c016fbwktmro3.html.

61 M. Pichonelli, 'Filhos se reúnem para criar 1ª associação de pessoas adotadas do Brasil', 21 November 2021, UOL, https://tab.uol.com.br/colunas/matheus-pichonelli/2021/11/20/filhos-se-reunem-para-criar-1-associacao-de-pessoas-adotadas-do-brasil.htm.

62 L. Alves, Depoimento in Ata da audiência pública realizada pela Defensoria Pública do Estado de Santa Catarina, 3ª Defensoria Pública do núcleo regional de Blumenau, "Vulnerabilidade social X destituição do poder familiar", 31 de agosto de 2022, pp. 9-12, 12.

63 J. de Alencar Auler, 'Adoção e direito à verdade sobre a própria origem', *Jurisprudência Mineira*, Belo Horizonte, a. 61, nº 194, 2010, pp. 23-46, jul./set. 27-8.

However, for obstacles to the search for origins to be considered a social problem, more than changes in national and international legislation will be needed.[64] In August 2022, at a hearing before the Public Defender in Blumenau (Santa Catarina) regarding the cases of poor mothers whose children were forcibly removed from their custody and put up for adoption, the journalist and lawyer Larissa Alves of the organization Adotiva explained the demands put forth by Brazilian adoptees in the following way:

> The legislation states that adoptees have the right to a biography, to access the adoption files, but how many adoptees know how to do that? Are there national campaigns stimulating and educating people about this subject? … Does the State hold itself responsible for leaving adoptees on the sidelines of their own history for so long? For disregarding the importance of this process? Are we at the mercy of genetic testing and good luck? Do we know adoption reality in Brazil? How many adoptees are there, taking into consideration both legal and illegal adoptions? … Even when everything is going well and the adoptive family guarantees the right to a biography, it is important to reflect on the fact that the origin of the adoption itself is already an imprint (*marca)* in a personal history. It is simply not easy (*confortável*) to be the result of social inequality, of institutional violence, of this situation that forces you to go somewhere else. Being adopted means coexisting and dealing with many complex feelings: from love to pain.… Having in your biography the imprint of a compulsory withdrawal is not a simple thing. It is not easy to have in your story the imprint of a "lost time", because it was not a lack of affection, but neglect, social abandonment on the part of those who should have protected citizens.… Are there professionals specialised in mediating between adoptees and families of origin, especially in cases involving institutional violence? And who takes care of the biological family's traumas of this separation? … Seeing adoption as the only solution makes the process of enhancing pre-adoption public policies less important, as well as generating scenarios for violence and even crimes …. It is not the adoption that should "solve" complex social issues, but what causes them to begin with that needs to be resolved, prevented, fought.… When we think about collective responsibility, we expand the action … Today's adoptees need to grow up with references and have an adoption and post-adoption process with proper oversight, one that has been designed for them and by them, they need services, professionals and research done about them.[65]

64 See Cardarello, 2006.

65 Alves, 2022, pp. 10-11 (author's translation).

In Alves's testimony we see the demands of national campaigns about available information for adoptees searching for their origins, the need for research and the production of data about adoption in Brazil, for professionals specialized in mediation between adoptees and families of origin, and the strengthening of pre-adoption public policies. As noted previously, Alves also insists on collective responsibility as well as on adoption and post-adoption services that are designed, in collaboration with adoptees, to meet their needs.[66]

Based on the 2005 UN Basic Principles and Guidelines on the Right to Remedy and Reparation for Victims of Gross Violations of International Human Rights Law and Serious Violations of International Humanitarian Law, Loibl claims that a policy on remedies for illegal adoptions should provide for, among others, any expenses related to searches, reunions and DNA tests.[67] The author points out that an Australian truth commission, set up in 2012 by the government, made it possible to establish a reparation fund for searches and reunions as well as for counselling and support services offered to victims of forced adoptions. In the Netherlands, a reparation fund to compensate for abuses in illegal intercountry adoptions was also promised by the Dutch Minister of Justice and Security. In 2021, a governmental committee report found that Dutch adoption agencies, as well as several government officials, had, between 1967 and 1998, knowledge of systemic abuses in adoptions to the Netherlands from Brazil, Bangladesh, Colombia, Indonesia and Sri Lanka. This committee concluded that some government officials even facilitated illegal adoptions from abroad. It was following the committee's recommendations that the Dutch Minister recognized the harm caused by the adoption abuses, announced the suspension of intercountry adoptions and apologized to the victims.[68]

However, in Latin America, researchers in Argentina and Chile have noted how attempts to formulate the adoptees' demands within a human rights framework have been hindered in large measure by the class origins of the families of those children.[69] This is no different in Brazil, in that the women who continue to lose their children to

66 In her speech, Alves specifically mentions the forced removal of children from indigenous mothers in Brazil, the theft and illegal adoption of babies during the military dictatorship, the compulsory removals of children from homeless mothers and the "case of Arlete Hilu, who illegally took children from Brazil to Israel". In November 2022, with the support of a public defender, a group of mothers from the city of Blumenau, whose children were forcibly removed, managed to have the children of one of the families returned to them (T. Catie, 'Família de Blumenau consegue reaver guarda de crianças enviadas à adoção', *NSC Total*, 11 November 2019, https://www.nsctotal.com.br/noticias/familia-de-blumenau-consegue-reaver-guarda-de-criancas-enviadas-a-adocao).

67 Loibl, 2021, p. 11.

68 Ibid., pp. 9-10.

69 Gesteira et al., 2021, p. 596.

adoption are domestic workers, beggars, gypsies, sex workers, poor teenage mothers and women who have been incarcerated, among others, and who all have in common the fact that they belong to the lower class of Brazilian society.[70] Leal lists similar cases in his research on missing persons in Brazil: in addition to those illegally adopted, there are migrants, homeless people, victims of domestic violence and unidentified bodies.[71]

Demands by Brazilian adoptees in Brazil and abroad for national and free DNA banks, information campaigns, post-adoption support, support for reunifications, and services for adult adoptees and birth families will more likely be met with the participation of adopted adults with higher economic and social capital than their families of origin. We agree with Ribke & Bourdon that, like the adoptees we met in our research, the young, educated, middle-class Brazilian-Israeli adoptees they interviewed can hardly be defined as subaltern.[72] As the authors claim, their evolving identity is a multilayered construction emergent from the two countries they feel they belong to in some way:

> Israel is a nation that sees itself at the periphery of the Western world, but is also a rich, developed country by international standards. From the adoptees' point of view, Brazil is both a former Third World nation with a long-standing heritage of poverty and exploitation, which are painful elements of their own particular life stories, and a new global power, with a widely recognized and embraced vibrant popular culture, and is thus a place they are eager to identify with. (p. 2650)

The transnational social activism of Brazilian-Israeli and other adoptees trafficked abroad can undoubtedly make a contribution to better advancing this cause. This will depend on the existing adoptees' groups becoming more political. The spirit and practice of activism, rather than being only a support group, should predominate, focusing less on individual demands and more – as proposed by the Brazilian adoptee activist Larissa Alves – on disseminating the idea of 'collective responsibility' in the countries involved.

---

70 See Cardarello, 2006; S.S. Bastos, E.S. Barretto, R.V. Santana, A. Cardarello, A.C. do C. Nascimento and J. de S. Souza, 'Direito à convivência familiar e comunitária: interseccionalidades de classe social, raça e gênero na destituição do poder familiar', UFAL e UFBA, Anais do XVII Congresso Brasileiro de Assistentes Sociais 2022, and Fonseca, 2010.

71 Leal, 2017, p. 276.

72 Ribke and Bourdon, 2016.

5 Finish What You Start: The Cold War Greek Adoption Experience and Recommendations for Current Policy Reform

*Gonda Van Steen**

Introduction: Who Are We and What Do We Want?

It is not complicated: some 4,000 Greek-born adoptees want their adoption records, and about 700 of them want their Greek citizenship restored to them. This chapter advocates with them and for them, provides the historical and sociopolitical background information, and contrasts reasonable and legally grounded demands with unreasonable delays. I have captured the movement's demands under the three R's of *r*edress: *r*ecords, *r*estoration of citizenship and research. These three demands also provide the structural framework to this chapter.

When intercountry adoption was first conceived in the late 1940s, it was moulded in a historical, institutional and legal void. Any policy recommendations and practices of the post-World War II period addressed immigration needs, not long-term child welfare provisions benefiting children and their first families. Greece of the post-Civil War era (post-1949) was in the forefront of the rush towards mass adoptions of its children to the USA: the war-torn country was keen to solve an orphan problem that thinly disguised a lack of domestic services; it also masked an unwillingness to give leftist-communist, impoverished and/or 'illegitimate' offspring equal opportunities in the nation's dollar-fuelled 'decade of reconstruction' (1950s). Greek-to-American adoptions and, regrettably, also their transgressions, provided the model and 'manual' for the first large-scale international adoptions, well before these became a mass phenomenon typically associated with Asian children (and the Korean War). What began around

* I express my warm thanks to the editors, Elvira Loibl and David Smolin, who have lent their unstinting support through the process of researching and writing this chapter. My gratitude also goes out to Mary Cardaras, Gabrielle Glaser and Gregory Luce, who have helped me broaden my horizons on the subject of domestic as well as intercountry adoption. I am obliged, too, to Katerina Bakogianni, Nikos Konstandaras, Niki Lymberaki and Margarita Pournara, journalists of extraordinary sensitivity and resourcefulness.

1948 as an emergency response and semi-humanitarian mission of placing orphaned Greek children with better-established Greek American relatives deteriorated quickly into a money-making scheme in which any petitioning white American couple could be approved for parenthood in a Greek-to-American adoption. No attention was paid to the enduring consequences for the children and their first families. The label of 'orphan' continued to be used through the mid-1960s but became window-dressing covering for 'illegitimate' babies born to young unwed Greek mothers, whose motherhood was impeded or even pre-empted by rigid social and institutional stigmas. Greece went on to consider its intercountry adoption history, scandal-ridden by the late 1950s, as a minor one-off aberration, a war-induced taboo kept up for the greater good, or as a 'private' matter that left contemporary and subsequent governments unscathed. Mediators hardly cared to compile, let alone keep, the records. Post-adoption services were as superficial as the prior screenings of prospective adoptive parents had been. Investigation and study were non-existent. Most Greeks and Greek Americans forgot that this adoption history ever even happened and affected some 4,000 children (including 600 Greek children who were sent to the Netherlands). Ironically, the Greek state and its citizens are currently pressing the United Kingdom to return the Parthenon Marbles. But what about the repatriation, symbolic or otherwise, of more than 4,000 Greek-born adoptees? Some 4,000 Greek adoptees have been waiting since 1950 for the kind of Greek response that will mark recognition and reconciliation on the part of their home country and culture. Don't make them wait as long as the Parthenon Marbles.[1]

Sixty and seventy years later, the ageing Greek-born adoptees still seek access to their records, and they formulate demands to have their Greek citizenship restored (as a second citizenship).[2] They turn to activism to ask for recognition of their histories and experiences (and traumas) from the Greek state and from the then-intermediaries (some organizations are still active but deny involvement). Some adoptees have written

1 I develop the parallel further in M. Cardaras and G. Van Steen, 'Bring them Back!', *The Pappas Post*, 16 June 2021, https://pappaspost.com/opinion-bring-them-back/.

2 The former demand is, of course, similar to the request/recommendation that was most persuasively articulated by Sorosky, Baran and Pannor in 1978, mainly on behalf of US domestic adoptees. This similarity should make us question why so little progress was made in the span of 45 years, not only for Greek adoptees but also for Irish and many other adoptee groups. The pioneering authors of 1978 give us an answer that only gains more potency with the passing of time: "Opening the sealed records is merely the tip of the iceberg, under which lies a vast mosaic of contradictions that questions the entire institution of adoption as it has been practiced" (A.D. Sorosky, A. Baran and R. Pannor, *The Adoption Triangle: The Effects of the Sealed Record on Adoptees, Birth Parents, and Adoptive Parents*, Garden City, NY, Anchor Press/Doubleday, 1978, p. 219).

(and self-published) their own memoirs (but only since 2011);[3] others have contributed to press articles, online blogs and documentaries. Many have found their campaign voices through contact with other adoptees and with the first scholarly literature on the subject (since 2019). This activism driving one of the oldest intercountry adoptee groups is a new and exciting phenomenon that does, however, suffer from some leadership and trust issues. Nonetheless, the campaign has now raised awareness in Greece at the highest levels, leaving some ill-informed sensationalism of the mid-1990s behind at last.

The surviving Greek-born adoptees living in the United States (an estimated 2,000 of the original 4,000) are stating their demands, loudly and clearly. They want redress, and they are making a case for this redress from a human rights perspective.[4] The Greek-born adoptees drill down to identity rights as well: they specifically ask for their birth and adoption records and for the restoration of their Greek citizenship (as a second citizenship); they state the need for a full historic investigation that must turn up hitherto unknown documents. This chapter, then, delves into the details of our concrete policy recommendations (records, restoration of citizenship, research) with the aim of providing a blueprint for opinion- and policymakers to rectify a 70-year-old adoption history burdened by national as well as family and individual shame. But Cold War dependencies and personal vulnerabilities can hardly continue to impede progress and transparency in the 2020s. The time for redress and ultimately recognition and reconciliation is now. Why? Because time is running out, if not for the adoptees themselves, then surely for their first parents. Currently, however, the Greek legal and institutional system remains in a deficit, but I have the advantage of writing about legal and policy reform as these processes are unfolding (2020 through 2023). Together with the Greek adoptees, I argue from a position of social and restorative justice, of correcting a historic wrong. We do not accept post-war attitudes or the passing of time as valid excuses for inaction today. We represent a grass-roots movement that has gained momentum with the first publication in English (and subsequently in Greek) of

3 For a study of some of these recent memoirs, see G. Van Steen, 'Relief from Relief?: Greek-Born Adoptees "Talk Back"', *Ex-Centric Narratives: Journal of Anglophone Literature, Culture and Media*, Vol. 6, 2022, pp. 107-120.

4 The recent UN Human Rights Treaty Bodies, *Joint Statement on Illegal Intercountry Adoptions*, 29 September 2022 invokes a "human rights-based and gender sensitive approach to preventing and eradicating illegal intercountry … adoptions" (p. 1), https://www.ohchr.org/sites/default/files/documents/hrbodies/ced/2022-09-29/JointstatementICA_HR_28September2022.pdf. The Greek-born adoptees, with whom I align myself as 'we', invoke the emancipatory demands and the legitimate language of forcibly displaced groups worldwide (such as indigenous children placed in white institutions or families, Irish babies taken from their unwed mothers without consent, the 'appropriated' Argentinian children whose restitution their grandmothers seek, and so on).

the Cold War Greek adoption history: *Adoption, Memory and Cold War Greece.*[5] This movement is also attuned to global developments in the adoption world of the twenty-first century. The Greek adoptees' demands are twofold, and they could hardly be more straightforward, reasonable or timely:

1. Records: Give us adoptees proper access to our birth and adoption records, that is, eliminate the levels of bureaucratic gatekeeping that have been in place for far too long. Many countries still obstruct searches for one's roots. Obstruction and secrecy greet petitioners in Greece at every turn; bureaucrats continue to send them through revolving institutional doors. Greece does not want to be indifferent to international advocacy and conventions arguing for the unsealing of birth and adoption records, including medical histories. This gatekeeping on Greek records is particularly noxious given the hard-won 1996 law, which grants Greek adoptees statutory rights to their

5 G. Van Steen, *Adoption, Memory, and Cold War Greece: Kid pro quo?*, Ann Arbor, University of Michigan Press, 2019 (Greek translation by A. Loukakou, *Ζητούνται παιδιά από την Ελλάδα: Υιοθεσίες στην Αμερική του Ψυχρού Πολέμου*, Athens, Potamos, 2021). The book draws on ten years of research; it lays out the Greek post-war adoption history and presents indisputable evidence of episodes of undue pressure or actual wrongdoing. It establishes the numbers, the procedures, the channels used by the intermediaries, the actual costs and the profits involved, the lack of screening and follow-up, the inadequate audit trails, the psychological issues and the current activism. After I had made the first startling discoveries in 2013, my writing style grew deliberately multivocal, and my analysis became more concrete in its juxtaposition with real adoptee lives. These deliberate features of the book and also its section of practical guidelines for Greek adoptees who are searching for their roots have elicited a steady stream of adoptee questions and viewpoints, which have generated new, still raw research materials and data. Thus, this ongoing research project recalls circuitous physical and psychological journeys, and it touches people's lives even today. It also prompts political and ethical questions. It drives home policy points and the need for reform. My book further offers an extensive list of works cited. Here, however, I will keep bibliographical references to secondary sources to a minimum of very recent studies. For comparative data and further historical background, readers may consult E. Baughan, *Saving the Children: Humanitarianism, Internationalism, and Empire*, Oakland, CA, University of California Press, 2022; A. Casavantes Bradford, *Suffer the Little Children: Child Migration and the Geopolitics of Compassion in the United States*, Chapel Hill, NC, The University of North Carolina Press, 2022; S. Fieldston, *Raising the World: Child Welfare in the American Century*, Cambridge, MA and London, Harvard University Press, 2015; G. Lynch, *Remembering Child Migration: Faith, Nation-Building and the Wounds of Charity*, London and New York, Bloomsbury, 2016; C. McGettrick, K. O'Donnell, M. O'Rourke, J.M. Smith and M. Steed, *Ireland and the Magdalene Laundries: A Campaign for Justice*, London, I.B. Tauris, 2021; M. Neagu, *Voices from the Silent Cradles: Life Histories of Romania's Looked-After Children*, Bristol, Policy Press, Bristol University Press, 2021; and R.R. Winslow, *The Best Possible Immigrants: International Adoption and the American Family*, Philadelphia, PA, University of Pennsylvania Press, 2017; McGettrick et al., 2021, is particularly helpful for describing, in detail, how an adoptee campaign unfolded over the course of many years of committed activism.

early life files and adoption dossiers.[6] The old institutional habit of keeping adoptees from their records is nothing short of infantilizing. Moreover, it is antiquated given the increasing availability of commercial DNA testing – and all the instant revelations that biogenetic testing brings with it.

2. Restore Greek citizenship to us adoptees as a dual citizenship, if we so wish (and some 700 Greek-born adoptees would like to have their citizenship restored). Greek-to-American adoptees with the least early life data tend to come from the cities and surroundings of Patras and Athens. They were sent on their way abroad as Greeks, with Greek passports and occasionally even with Greek birth certificates, unless they were foundlings (έκθετα). Theirs is, therefore, a genetic and even a recorded citizenship or other form of initial political and legal inclusion, even as they suffered social exclusion.[7] Yet their lives were overhauled by way of biopolitical decisions or of adoptions stemming from economic hardship, social ostracism and family pressure. As children and teenagers, they lost their Greek citizenship through no fault of their own, as part of the adoption and US naturalization process. It is only right for Greece to take action to restore or reconfirm citizenship to this group of forgotten child-citizens and to do so proactively.

6 Since 1996, Greek adoptees have the right to their identity information based on Art. 1559 of Decree no. 2447, published in the 30 December 1996 issue of the *Government Gazette of the Greek Republic*. Greek open-records-activists, nearly all in-country adoptees themselves, fought hard to attain adoption law 2447/1996, which, on paper at least, supports the adult adoptees in their quest for their first family or for any other data concerning their adoption. The 1996 law draws strength also from the Greek Code of Administrative Procedure (Κώδικας Διοικητικής Διαδικασίας, Law 2690/1999), whose Art. 5 confirms the right of access to one's documents. However, the open-records struggle in support of searching Greek adoptees must continue, because the law's implementation has been far from consistent: many state employees do not know about the 1996 legislation or prefer not to act on it, or they hide behind the vague wording of the law. They make *ad hoc* decisions whether or not to share the data with the adoptee. Recourse against their decisions is very difficult to obtain, *a priori* for the intercountry Greek adoptees who cannot easily pursue costly legal action from abroad.

7 I have found the broader reflections of Dimitris Christopoulos to be very relevant to the Greek adoptees' demand of Greek citizenship (D. Christopoulos, 'Ποιος ήταν και ποιος είναι έλληνας πολίτης; Κράτος και ιθαγένεια από τον 19ο στον 21ο αιώνα.' 'Who Was and Who Is a Greek Citizen? State and Citizenship from the 19th to the 21st Century', Conversation with Kostis Karpozilos, for radio broadcast of 24 March 2019, published in the online series "2 Αιώνες σε 21 Εκπομπές," "2 Centuries in 21 Broadcasts," Athens, Contemporary Social History Archives (ASKI), No. 8, 2021, pp. 1-32, http://www.askiweb.eu/.../2_aion.../8EllinasPolitisSmall.pdf). Christopoulos's call for a birthright Greek citizenship adds poignancy to the request of those born in Greece but silenced for more than half a century.

Records, Identity and International Standards: 'Who Am I? I Have the Right to Know.'

Very often, the search process extends to a search for people with an equally honed sense of justice. Mary Cardaras, a spokesperson for the Greek-born adoptees, speaks to the right to know one's origins on behalf of adoptees worldwide, as in a compelling four-minute video titled 'Who Am I? I Have the Right to Know' – a title I have borrowed here.[8] In 2021, Cardaras and I joined Mia Dambach, Executive Director, at an international NGO called Child Identity Protection (CHIP), which was founded in Switzerland as recently as 1 December 2020. Drawing on a wide range of experiences and expertise, CHIP amplifies the adoptees' claims to their right to fully know their identity and to have identity information restored to them in case it was lost, overlooked or destroyed. CHIP dedicated a 2021 fact sheet to the right to identity of children in Greece, which includes refugee children.[9] The fact sheet delves into historical as well as current challenges to the preservation and restoration of children's identity and to the challenge of accessing origins in the case of adoptees. The fact sheet, which was submitted to the UN Committee on the Rights of the Child in advance of its 90th session in early 2022, makes explicit recommendations, which are worth quoting for their immediacy:

> [I]t is regrettable that neither public recognition of the history of these unfortunate adoptions nor public apologies were made by the [Greek]

8 M. Cardaras, 'Who Am I? I Have the Right to Know', 27 February 2022, https://youtu.be/ApPboMlswkA and also on the website of Child Identity Protection, under the section 'Voices Chip in: Adults with Lived Experience', https://child-identity.org/en/voices-chip-in/lived-experience.html?start=18.

9 Child Identity Protection (2021), 'Children's Right to Identity in Greece: Factsheet Submitted to the UN Committee on the Rights of the Child', Session 90 (17 January 2022 to 04 February 2022)/State Periodic Report CRC/C/GRC/4-6. The report and delegation of Greece were brought before the UN Committee on the Rights of the Child on 3-4 May 2022, as part of the Universal Periodic Review process, which operates on five-year cycles. For Greece's submission, see the 'National Report' prepared by the Ministry of Foreign Affairs, 11 August 2021, https://documents.un.org/doc/undoc/gen/g21/222/10/pdf/g2122210.pdf?token=fk4ImhFzZPNf0oAqVw&fe=true. While addressing adoption, page 19 of this recent report fails to mention the need to address the issues related to Greece's historic adoptions and the rights to identity of the Greek-born adoptees dispatched overseas during the post-war decades. The 4 May 2022 meeting summary/press release is highly critical but not about the issue of the adoptees' right to identity: "Experts of the Committee on the Rights of the Child Ask Greece about Roma Children and Push Backs of Refugees at the Border," https://www.ohchr.org/en/press-releases/2022/05/experts-committee-rights-child-ask-greece-about-roma-children-and-push-backs. The issue of the lack of proper identifying data pertains not only to adoptees but to all children whose circumstances might prevent them from having access to vital identity information (such as child refugees and unaccompanied minors and also children conceived and birthed by way of surrogacy arrangements). See further UNICEF and Child Identity Protection, "Key Considerations: Children's Rights & Surrogacy. Briefing Note," February 2022, https://www.unicef.org/media/115331/file on children's rights in the context of surrogacy. The latter source explains: "Having one's own identity is also a gateway to the enjoyment of the child's other fundamental rights, such as those related to protection, health, education, and the maintenance of family ties" (2022, p. 2).

> government – or have thus far been considered. This is so notwithstanding the fact that Greece and various money-making intermediaries bear responsibility for the overseas adoptions that occurred in the 50s and 60s. In order to correct this historic wrong, together with public recognition and apologies, it is recommended that their Greek citizenship be restored as an act of restorative justice. Indeed, their Greek citizenship was invalidated by these haphazard adoptions which left the adopted children with very few records.
> ...
> Action needs to be taken on behalf of the more than 3,000 Greek-born children who were adopted out roughly between 1950-1970, mainly to the USA, and who are now looking for their roots with very little acknowledgement or assistance.[10]

Our work with CHIP allows me to place the Greek demand for restoring identity in a broader, international perspective. CHIP also invokes the relevant sources, as in its recent briefing note related to EU data protection rules and compliance with children's rights as enshrined in international standards.[11] CHIP refers explicitly to the March 2016 Report of the Special Rapporteur para 95 (j), which makes the recommendation, at the national level, to:

> Ensure the right to information about one's origins and access to information about the rights of victims of illegal adoptions, and facilitate the work of

10 Child Identity Protection (2021), 'Children's Right to Identity in Greece: Factsheet Submitted to the UN Committee on the Rights of the Child', Session 90 (17 January 2022 to 04 February 2022)/State Periodic Report CRC/C/GRC/4-6, p. 3.

11 Child Identity Protection, "Briefing Note: Aligning Data Protection Rules with International Standards," 20 June 2022, https://www.child-identity.org/images/files/CHIP-BriefingNote-DataProtection-EN.pdf. In late June 2022, CHIP launched its signature publication C. Baglietto, L. Bordier, M. Dambach and C. Jeannin, *Preserving "Family Relations": An Essential Feature of the Child's Right to Identity*, Geneva, Switzerland, Child Identity Protection, 2022, https://child-identity.org/images/files/CHIP-Preserving-Family-Relations-EN.pdf. The strongest words, however, come from Mike Milotte, who, in 2012, reflected back on the impact of the publication of his first book (on the Irish adoption exports) in 1997, fifteen years prior to the appearance of the book's second edition (M. Milotte, *Banished Babies: The Secret History of Ireland's Baby Export Business* (2nd ed.) Dublin, New Island Books, 2012). His words apply, *mutatis mutandis*, to the predicament in which the Greek adoptees still find themselves, now some ten years later:

> [I]n continually prevaricating over access to information that might help reunite adult adopted people and their natural mothers, the State and the adoption societies are also protecting themselves. It is now clear that not everything in the past was done in a legal and above-board manner.... By keeping mothers and offspring apart, a multitude of past sins, errors and shoddy practices by all those involved can be kept from view.... And in the determination to keep the doors locked on the adoption files, how many male—and prominent male—reputations were still being protected? ... *[I]t seems to be the unstated intention of those who continue to think up excuses for keeping information under lock and key to deny till they die.* (2012, pp. 226-229; italics his)

> victims' organizations in that respect, including in terms of helping them to trace biological parents and children.[12]

In late June 2022, the UN Committee on the Rights of the Child issued 'Concluding Observations on the Combined Fourth to Sixth Periodic Reports of Greece' that demand unequivocally, under the subheading 'Right to identity':

> The Committee urges the State party to ensure the right of children to preserve their identity in cases of abandonment in institutions and to have access to information about their origin if born through assisted reproduction technologies, including surrogacy and donor arrangements, as well as in the case of adoption.[13]

In the subsection on adoption itself, the same document, 'Concluding Observations', recommends that Greece '[e]nsure post-adoption monitoring and services'.[14] The combined recommendations of the UN Committee on the Rights of the Child could hardly be clearer. Greece's record of compliance with the 1989 UN Convention on the Rights of the Child (hereinafter UNCRC) will be examined again in 2027. We hope that the reports and documentations that Greece will be submitting at that time, or already at the stage of a mid-term review, will be able to credibly describe the measures taken to preserve *and restore* adoptee identity rights. We are eager to contribute to that endeavour, to see it completed in a timely fashion.

Since 2016, I have given many online and in-person presentations explaining what the process of accessing one's records entails. In mid-July 2021, I also met with and answered the specific questions of the officers of the Greek Ministry of Labor and Social Affairs, walking them through the history and the processes of granting legitimate access to records. In a meeting with Ms A., the Head of the Department for Foster Care and Adoption, in the Directorate of the Protection of Children and Family, at Greece's Ministry of Labor and Social Affairs, I proposed new access policies to address the requests of the Greek-born adoptees seeking their personal and medical records. For this office, I also wrote a manual of some 13 pages of practical guidelines (including a list of suggested readings) to facilitate Greek adoptee searches. Ms A. and her colleagues gratefully accepted my offer and promised to centralize further efforts on their part.

12 United Nations General Assembly, Human Rights Council, *Report of the Special Rapporteur on the Sale of Children, Child Prostitution and Child Pornography*, A/HRC/34/55, March 2021, p. 22, https://documents.un.org/doc/undoc/gen/g16/440/24/pdf/g1644024.pdf?token=wbyFiqsOKyzDCuY4ek&fe=true.

13 United Nations Committee on the Rights of the Child, 'Concluding Observations on the Combined Fourth to Sixth Periodic Reports of Greece', CRC/C/GRC/CO/4-6, 28 June 2022, p. 6 (22).

14 Ibid., p. 10 (32.d).

Our plan is to send out this manual to all Greek consulates in the USA and in the Netherlands, where many Greek adoptees make contact but might not find adoption-related expertise. Ms A. and other ministry officers have since stayed in touch, and some of our common searches have generated better and faster results.

In the midst of this arduous process, we have wondered if the offices to which we turned were ready for the kind of upstream activism we brought on topics of the past and the personal. But we just did not let the issue go away. Tellingly, no Greek-born adoptees have received copies of their full adoption file for the past half a century from the state-sponsored institution called PIKPA (the Patriotic Institution for Social Welfare and Awareness), which resorts under the same Ministry of Labor and Social Affairs. Also, the slow responses to several recent requests were delayed even further because Greece has been reeling from its 'Watergate Scandal'.[15] The grim reality of government spying on political opponents, which recently raised a public outcry, is, of course, the most blatant violation of privacy protection enacted by the highest levels of the Greek government itself. The same conservative government has been obstructing adoptees' access to their very own files from the 1950s and 1960s, all while invoking (a misinterpretation of) Greece's personal data protection legislation. Historical ironies – and injustices – are seldom so poignant.[16]

The real question now is, how many Greek adoptees who have no recourse to guidance will be receiving their records, and what will it take? After all, the gatekeeper responded to one PIKPA adoptee that there was 'nothing of interest' in the adoption files.[17] Such preposterous value judgments are altogether unnecessary. They not only express but

15 See Anon., 'Greek Phonetap, Spyware Scandal Raises Worries of Surveillance', *The National Herald*, 12 August 2022, https://www.thenationalherald.com/greek-phonetap-spyware-scandal-raises-worries-of-surveillance/; J. Horowitz and N. Kitsantonis, 'A Greek Spying Scandal Reverberates as Eavesdropping Expands in Europe', *New York Times*, 12 August 2022, p. 8; H. Smith, 'Greek PM under Pressure over Tapping of Opponent's Phone', *The Guardian*, 7 August 2022, https://www.theguardian.com/world/2022/aug/07/greek-pm-kyriakos-mitsotakis-under-pressure-over-tapping-of-opponents-phone?fbclid=IwAR0vyNIXmqQyI72KdT446a2ryxMeDNpYaX3LbYmTzoqoTv6r0yyRb0weUt4.

16 Journalist Alexander Clapp did not mince words:

> It is … the unsustainable contradiction between the country Mr. Mitsotakis insists on pitching abroad – an unimpeachably democratic state whose respect for the rule of law and liberal bona fides ought to be rewarded with corporate investments and tourism dollars – and the one he actually presides over
>
> (A. Clapp, 'The Rot at the Heart of Greece Is Now Clear for Everyone to See', *New York Times*, 22 August 2022)

17 Sporadic e-mail communications of July 2021 through June 2022. Katerina Peripanou, on-site communication with Mary Cardaras, 30 June 2022. See also M. Cardaras, 'Our Stories and Our Records Belong to US', *Kathimerini*, 25 January 2023, https://www.ekathimerini.com/society/1203006/our-stories-and-our-records-belong-to-us/?fbclid=IwAR0HOaFX5TvRqVx1SwemLMIuCo8JfwVhr0t9gP2tCZEgXaPp9QmaLiYkMMo.

also perpetuate the legal discrimination against adoptees that has been part of the Greek system for far too long. A reminder that any response or act of redress should be based on the principle of 'do no further harm' is certainly in order. Or, in other words, we should now do better because we now know better – and cast the patronizing aside. Also, given how easy it was to adopt Greek children in the post-war Wild West era of intercountry adoption, adoptees should not now have to endure a protracted ordeal to simply obtain access to their first identity. Adoptees ought to be served by an ethical, professional and legally viable road map to their records and to redress at large.[18]

The Greek adoptees are asserting their 'right to know' and are striving to abolish the controlling of early life data and adoption files that is still occurring.[19] They now speak in their own strong voices, and they target just the right occasions, as Cardaras does in her article '4,000 Greek Adoptees Can't Celebrate National Genealogy Day on March 12.'[20] Many have found their activist voices through contact with other adoptees and with the first scholarly and then more popular literature on the subject. Fourteen of the Greek-born adoptees have joined together to publish a collective volume in which they speak and write in their own, empowered voices (edited by Cardaras, January 2023, see further on).

18 Here I note an encouraging development that was initiated by the International Social Service Hellenic Branch at the time when this chapter entered into the publication process. In response to the many requests that the now better informed adoptees started fielding, the ISS decided to digitize its vast collection of approximately 1,500 adoption-related files. Its aim is to then provide individual and protected access to the hundreds of adoptees whose cases it handled in the time span ranging from 1954 through the early 1980s, including some search and reunion cases. This is a pioneering initiative that implements a more enlightened archival policy and that honours a vision of decolonizing the archive. May this first step inspire the strictly Greek institutions that handled historic adoptions to do the same.

19 Van Wichelen discusses the adoptee's 'right to know' extensively, but with a somewhat exaggerated scepticism about how the answers might enhance identity and subjectivity formation (S. Van Wichelen, *Legitimating Life: Adoption in the Age of Globalization and Biotechnology*, New Brunswick, NJ and London, Rutgers University Press, 2019, p. 125, and her chapter 5, pp. 124-153). Adoptee foundlings, who have no identifying information whatsoever, find statements such as the following rather disrespectful of their lifelong quests: "The geneticization of human identity collapses identity and, by proxy, kinship, with biology and advances a discourse of determinism" (Van Wichelen, 2019, p. 128).

20 M. Cardaras, '4,000 Greek Adoptees Can't Celebrate National Genealogy Day on March 12', *The National Herald*, 11 March 2022, https://www.thenationalherald.com/4000-greek-adoptees-cant-celebrate-national-genealogy-day-on-march-12/. See also M. Cardaras, 'Demanding What Belongs to Us: Our Greek Identity', *The Pappas Post*, 7 June 2021, https://pappaspost.com/demanding-what-belongs-to-us-our-greek-identity/.

Like other adoptees, the Greek adoptees are backed by Articles 7 and 8 UNCRC. In force since September 1990, these Articles stipulate children's right to identity as a human and civil right, with emphasis on their biogenetic origins:[21]

> *Article 7*
> 1. The child shall be registered immediately after birth and shall have the right from birth to a name, the right to acquire a nationality and, as far as possible, the right to know and be cared for by his or her parents.
>
> *Article 8*
> 1. States Parties undertake to respect the right of the child to preserve his or her identity, including *nationality, name and family relations* as recognized by law without unlawful interference.
> 2. Where a child is illegally deprived of some or all of the elements of his or her identity, States Parties shall provide appropriate assistance and protection, with a view to re-establishing speedily his or her identity.
> (italics mine)

At stake is whether the right to identity – and to full identity information – is seen and respected as an integral part of the notion of protected private life. Verdicts in individual cases that have been informed by the foregoing directives have declared that all adopted persons have the right to know from which parents they stem and the right to their personal history, development and identity as unique human beings. This scope enabling people to establish the details of their biogenetic identity includes the right to learn of their origins and related identifying data, such as the circumstances in which they were born. Individuals are entitled to such information, because it is formative to their personality growth and their long-term personal well-being. In sum, the UNCRC

21 As of January 2022, 196 countries are state parties to the UNCRC, which makes the UNCRC the most widely ratified human rights treaty in the world. However, the current and former chairs of the UNCRC rightfully remain concerned about compliance. They have aided in the process of creating understanding and scrutiny by publishing an open-access volume issued in January 2022 (Z. Vaghri, J. Zermatten, G. Lansdown and R. Ruggiero (eds.), *Monitoring State Compliance with the UN Convention on the Rights of the Child: An Analysis of Attributes*, Cham, Switzerland, Springer, 2022). See also J. Tobin, *The UN Convention on the Rights of the Child: A Commentary*, Oxford, Oxford University Press, 2019 that provides comprehensive presentations of the various Articles of the UNCRC.

Articles guarantee a person's right to know the identity of his or her natural parents,[22] which is the question that most concerns the Greek adoptees. However, unlike Greece, the United States is not a signatory to the UNCRC. The cases of the Greek adoptees searching for their roots fall, nonetheless, within the ambit of international conventions, which protect their right to receive the information necessary to uncover the truth about vital aspects of their identity.

Invoking Article 8(2) UNCRC, legal expert David Smolin takes the consequences of the failure to adhere to the adoptee's identity rights a step further:

> an intercountry adoption is illegal if the State failed to "provide appropriate assistance and protection, with a view to re-establishing speedily his or her identity," where "a child is illegally deprived of some or all of the elements of his or her identity."[23]

The case of the Greek-born and other international adoptees is backed by another global instrument: the 1993 Hague Convention on Protection of Children and Co-operation in Respect of Intercountry Adoption (hereinafter the Hague Convention). This convention, too, imposes reporting requirements on its member states. Greece's laws implementing the Hague Convention entered into effect on 1 January 2010.[24] But what

22 E. Loibl, *The Transnational Illegal Adoption Market: A Criminological Study of the German and Dutch Intercountry Adoption Systems*, The Hague, Eleven International, 2019 (PhD dissertation, Maastricht University), p. 100. Loibl's chapters 3 and 4 offer some of the most recent studies of the legislative work pertaining to international adoption (2019, pp. 81-129 and 131-177, respectively). Admittedly, Art. 8 of the UNCRC, which intersects with the Art. 8 of the (older) European Convention on Human Rights (right to respect for private and family life), raises a host of complex issues, which may revert to becoming country-specific, despite the conventions' international remit. E. Steiner, 'Odièvre v France – Desperately Seeking Mother – Anonymous Births in the European Court of Human Rights', *Child and Family Law Quarterly*, Vol. 15, No. 4, 2003, pp. 425-448 has cogently explained these issues in the context of the notorious French case of *Odièvre v. France*, which went up to the European Court of Human Rights, only to be denied. The European Court has the power to assess whether *reasonable* measures have been taken by the member states to guarantee the petitioners' enjoyment of certain rights. In this case, the French state was granted a wider 'margin of appreciation' than expected (Steiner, 2003, p. 441). France has traditionally given the first mother more leverage than the adopted person. The Greek legal system has incorporated many French influences. The most controversial cases have stayed in the news and in the scholarly literature, where they have become points of reference. See, for instance, G. Mathieu, 'D'Odièvre à Godelli: La jurisprudence de la Cour Européenne des Droits de l'Homme en matière d'accouchement anonyme a-t-elle évolué?,' *Journal du droit des jeunes*, Vol. 325, 2013-2015, pp. 41-53. Mathieu refers to the case of Godelli v. Italy (2012), in which the European Court of Human Rights decided that there had been a violation of Art. 8 of the European Convention on Human Rights.

23 D.M. Smolin, 'The Legal Mandate for Ending the Modern Era of Intercountry Adoption', in N. Lowe and C. Fenton-Glynn (eds.), *Research Handbook on Adoption Law*, Cheltenham, Edward Elgar, 2023, pp. 384-407, p. 394.

24 See Law 3765/2009 of 1 July 2009, with which Greece formally signed on to the Hague Convention (*Efimeris tis Kyverniseos tis Ellinikis Dimokratias* N/3765/09).

does that reporting, let alone implementing, look like? In July 2020, Ms A., from the Greek Ministry of Labor and Social Affairs, returned a filled-out 'country profile' in the form of a detailed questionnaire to the central office of the Hague Convention. Ms A., as the Head of the Department for Foster Care and Adoption, and also Ms V. signed off for the Greek Ministry's Central Authority of Intercountry Adoptions. Question 26 c) of this public document could not be more explicit:

> Does your State permit the following persons to have access to information concerning the child's origins and / or information concerning the adoption of the child:
> (i) the adoptee and / or his / her representative(s);
> ...?
> If so, are there any criteria which must be met for access to be granted (e.g., age of the adopted child, consent of the birth family to the release of information concerning the child's origins, consent of the adoptive parents to the release of information concerning the adoption)?

To this question, the two respondents answer: (i) *Yes* – please explain any criteria: *18+ of age only.*[25] This is the only and ever so succinct response given under the heading of "Post-Adoption Matters" and, specifically, "Preservation of, and access to, information concerning the child's origins (Art. 30) and the adoption of the child". The reference is to Article 30 of the Hague Convention, which is, however, less straightforward on the subject of the child's right to identity than its predecessor, the UNCRC:

> *Article 30*
> (1) The competent authorities of a Contracting State shall ensure that information held by them concerning the child's origin, in particular information concerning the identity of his or her parents, as well as the medical history, is preserved.
> (2) They shall ensure that the child or his or her representative has access to such information, under appropriate guidance, in so far as is permitted by the law of that State.[26]

25 Ms A. and Ms V. as the Central Authority of Intercountry Adoptions for the Hellenic Republic, 'Country Profile: 1993 Hague Intercountry Adoption Convention. Receiving State, Country Name: Hellenic Republic', July 2020. 26-page questionnaire issued by the HCCH ('July 2014 version'). The italics are mine.

26 A. Diver, 'Conceptualizing the "Right" to Avoid Origin Deprivation: International Law and Domestic Implementation', *Adoption & Culture*, Vol. 3, 2012, 141-181, pp. 151-152 points to contradictory statements and promises within the text of the Hague Convention (especially the wording of its Arts 16 and 31). See also A. Diver, *A Law of Blood-ties – The 'Right' to Access Genetic Ancestry*, Cham, Switzerland, Springer, 2013.

The brief response given by the Greek Central Authority of Intercountry Adoptions complies with the Greek law of 1996 but does not reflect the current Greek practice, which is in violation of the applicable legal instrument on adoption. Notably, the respondents did not invoke any further criteria beyond the minimum age requirement that is set for any Greek adoptees who seek their identifying information. There is no mention of the intercountry Greek adoptee needing to hire a Greek lawyer (as is often required in practice, without any guaranteed results). There is no mention, either, of the counselling sessions, which many Greek gatekeepers present as mandatory, for the adoptee as well as for the first mother. Most Greek-born adoptees who have been faced with the latter requirement interpret it as an infantilizing measure that is also a convenient stalling technique. 'Waiting is for the weak', many Greeks say. No other groups of people are required to undergo mandatory counselling sessions as a precondition to accessing information; such a requirement restricts the individuals' exercise of fundamental information rights, which applies arbitrarily only to them. The gatekeepers' professed concern for the privacy of the birth parents fails to distinguish between two separate acts: that of accessing information and that of making contact with the birth family. One act does not necessarily imply the other and should not be curtailed because of the other. Also, public authorities should not be allowed to select which information can be disclosed and which cannot.[27] These baseless strategies of silencing and discouraging amount to practices of re-abuse. Meanwhile, some adoptees have lost their opportunity to meet a first parent because of the additional time needed to let such therapist sessions unfold. Also, some first mothers have felt intimidated by what they perceived to be an extraordinary and frightening process. Cardaras shares from her personal experience:

> When my mother was finally located, she was encouraged to see a psychologist, and I was encouraged to find one, too. Information about my own early life was kept from me. And I would be kept from my own mother because an agency that continues to place children across borders thought we couldn't handle it. Time ran out. I found out late last year that my mother died in 2020. I was a year too late. I was her only child.[28]

27 Making a disclosure dependent on a third party's death, for instance, is another common but ungrounded precondition that violates international standards. Some Greek adoptees are told that they can only learn their birth parents' names if it can be ascertained that the latter have passed away. Here and previously, I have liberally drawn from Maud De Boer-Buquicchio, who expressed her legal views on the Irish Birth Information and Tracing Bill 2022 in a statement of 23 April 2022 ("Legal Opinion on Irish Birth Information and Tracing Bill 2022," written on behalf of Child Identity Protection, https://www.child-identity.org/en/resources/advocacy-and-policy/580-legal-opinion-on-irish-birth-information-and-tracing-bill-2022.html).

28 Cardaras, 27 February 2022.

Restoring Citizenship: "I Was Born Greek"[29]

The topic of reconfirming Greek citizenship is critical: the Greek-born adoptees feel strongly that they lost their Greek citizenship through no fault of their own. After all, they were sent away as children whose fate was decided by adult parties. But the desire of some 700 of them to reconnect with their citizenship of birth, as with their family and culture of birth, is strong and leaves many outside observers surprised. Here are the facts: the adoptees left Greece as children on a one-way-out Greek passport issued by the Greek state that *at that time* acknowledged them as Greek, that is, in the very act of spiriting them away from their homeland. For the many foundlings among the Greek-born adoptees, the Greek citizenship that was validated by their exit visas and confirmed by their blue departure passports was the only fact known about them with any certainty. The American naturalization procedure overwrote that crucial piece of a precarious but still documented identity. In light of such deliberate state and bilateral actions, adoption issues are no longer private or familial issues; they are not victims' issues either. Time and again, the historical data and analysis attest to the responsibility of the state and of the go-betweens. Therefore, the matter of restoring citizenship should not be the adoptee's private struggle but should be a collective act of recognition on the part of the parties that need to be held accountable. Neither should the adoptees be made to feel as if they have to prove the integrity or innocence of their intentions in seeking to re-establish their Greek citizenship. The burden of proof is not on them. This is by no means a trial. This should not be trying, this should not be so difficult. The initiative to pursue Greek citizenship should not be weighed down by the guilt-ridden terms of negligence or by insinuations of lack of loyalty. Rather, it should be a celebratory reiteration of the open-mindedness of a state that is coming to grips with its past and that recognizes the rights of the most vulnerable in its society.

No doubt, the adoptees' push for the restoration of their Greek citizenship requires further interrogation. The dislocation associated with international adoption raises issues about political and ethical allegiance, about civic duty, about obligations as well as rights. Granting, restoring Greek citizenship posits the fundamental question of the individual's integration in society and, therefore, of collective as well as individual identity. The Greek-born adoptees have now made the transition from the initial, genealogical focus of Greek adoptee-hood (centred on their Greek parentage) to identifying as empowered adopted persons – no longer adopted children. The more vocal adoptees' activism has subverted linear conceptions of history and identity (via

29 Several Greek-born adoptees have adopted this famous statement by Melina Mercouri, the iconic Greek actress who protested her disenfranchisement by the Greek military dictatorship of 1967-1974. The declaration is also the title of Mercouri's protest memoir (M. Mercouri, *I Was Born Greek*, *Garden City*, New York, Doubleday, 1971).

lineage, preserved or interrupted); it has posited a more extrovert and circular notion of Greekness, in which adulthood and childhood intersect. Also, these adoptees are fully aware that their progress, or their creative revolving back to the collective past, comes with rights and responsibilities, moral as well as political.

Being restored to one's citizenship of origin would mean being granted formal acceptance and recognition; it would symbolize a warm welcome home, regardless of what the adoptee intends to make of that genetic, ethnic and cultural connection. Thus, citizenship becomes a powerful tool of restorative justice, social and political alike. The pursuit of Greek citizenship looms very large in diaspora debates, but the adoptees can justifiably claim a 'bloodline' citizenship, without the need to essentialize the *jus sanguinis*. In fact, the adoptee demands may help to relax, from without and from within, the grip of national heritage and 'birthright' in their narrow definitions. There is no need to think of birthright as the only criterion for granting citizenship to the adoptees. The adoptees can rightfully claim to *embody* a different kind of heritage: one of displacement, migration, silence and secrecy, and then reconnection and the relearning of language and culture. Thus, the adoptee diaspora's heritage may temper a carefully guarded national narrative of patrimony and lineage, which will no longer be defined in terms that are discursively, geographically or materially restricted. The adoptees could be the first recipients of an extrovert, affirming kind of citizenship and belonging that reconfigures family and country affiliation more creatively. At stake is not a confined but a redefined citizenship.

The topic of the Greek adoptees' desire to see their birth citizenship restored needs to be situated in recent conversations about civic identity, inclusive versus exclusive citizenship, and historical belonging in Greece and the diaspora. The activism of the adoptee diaspora and the diaspora scholarship on citizenship may meet each other in multiple productive ways. Notably, the demand for restored citizenship is a vivid desire shared with other post-war intercountry adoptee groups. The Korean-born adoptees seek similar forms of redress and reparation. So do the many adoptees from Romania, Russia, China or Chile, to name just a few groups. The right to access genetic ancestry information and the right to cultural and social/political belonging feed a type of adoptee activism that has become a global phenomenon, with the Korean-born adoptees taking the discursive lead. The parallel claims of other groups remind us that the demand for redress and recognition is not unique to Greece. What is unique in Greece, however, is that its adoption history is still too little known qualitatively as well as numerically, unlike, for instance, the painful Irish history of the disempowerment of unwed mothers and of adoptions abroad. Irish adoptees speak of the 'Philomena effect', the shift in popular opinion that resulted from the release and widespread acclaim of the 2013 movie *Philomena*. Does Greece still suffer from a 'Philomela effect', by which the violated female victim is still confined to silence? Greece has not yet experienced the birth of a movement in which the first mothers dare to unite and speak up – not only about unwed motherhood and adoption pressure but also about rape, as in the Greek myth of Philomela, who had her tongue cut out by the rapist to prevent her from denouncing the crime.[30] The chances of the Greek first mothers (or fathers, for that matter) creating a movement are exceedingly slim, given the advanced age of many of the first mothers who gave birth in the 1950s and 1960s – if they are still alive. But the Greek-born themselves are now more committed than ever to making their experiences known. They have moved beyond the feel-good reunion stories, which obscure the problematic nature of the adoption history and the number of people it adversely affected, especially among the members of the first family.

Since 2013, the diaspora of some 4,000 Greek children adopted out abroad has moved to the centre of a new, activist discourse that subverts the previous one, that of the intermediaries who left the adoptees voiceless and rendered their first parents invisible. I claim 2013 as a starting date, because the adoption topic required not only a multi-year research process but also the construction of an appropriate language and conceptual framework to communicate adoption-related topics relative to Greece. With the growing awareness of the issue and its appeal to civil society came the need for a legitimate vocabulary of activism in English. Prior engagements with the Greek adoption history, in 1995 and 1996, led, unfortunately, to breaches of confidentiality and search ethics, as well as to divisions among the various adoptee groups (some fuelled by the frenzy of the early internet).[31] The adoptee diaspora brings home the need for Greece and for Greek America to own their past. It also points to opportunities to create a different, more inclusive and more impactful diaspora history, a history that shows its willingness to revisit and revise the silences and untruths of the recent past.

In January 2023, Mary Cardaras published the seminal collection *Voices of the Lost Children of Greece*.[32] She collected the testimonies of thirteen fellow Greek adoptees and contributed her own, ever-evolving story. She framed these essays by pieces that explain the historical context – then and now. This is a pioneering initiative, given that no previous Greek collection existed in English. The fourteen stories bring home the experience of international adoption, whose impact is lifelong but is not properly measured, let alone acknowledged. The stories further bring home the need to name the

30 The mythical Philomela reveals the crime perpetrated by her brother-in-law, Tereus, by way of the woven word. Perhaps the adoption scholar who pays attention to the trauma of the silenced first mothers becomes a weaver of their words as well.

31 One organization that has weathered the past 25 years is the Roots Research Center (https://www.roots-research-center.gr/en/home/). Roots has productively expanded its mission beyond reunifications to advocate for better in-country child- and foster care solutions.

32 M. Cardaras (ed.), *Voices of the Lost Children of Greece: Oral Histories of Cold War International Adoption*, London and New York, Anthem Press, 2023.

experience before one can heal from it. Mary is also the author of *Ripped at the Root*, which is perhaps the best example of how one adoptee may assist another in bringing out a difficult story.[33] The work that the adoptees themselves have done, individually and collectively, merits full acknowledgement: they have turned the tide and debunked the clichés (Figure 1).

Figure 1. Greek adoptee essayists proudly displaying their collective volume, *Voices of the Lost Children of Greece*, 28 January 2023

Photo credit and permission: Robyn Zalewa.

An estimated 400 (of a total of some 4,000) Greek-born children went to American Jewish families. A documentary film called *The Greek Connection*, directed by the late Ronit Kertsner, will be brought to completion in the near future. This documentary will give the research questions and the budding life-writing projects a new impetus, for transcending linguistic, religious, national and ethnic boundaries. Interest in the Greek adoptions existed in Israel before it emerged in Greece: Kertsner's film was first shown as a work in progress at the Tel Aviv Cinematheque on 24 September 2021, and demand for further screenings of the film, once completed, remains high. On the occasions of its screening, the adoptees present will speak up for broader reformative impact and for policy change. They seek to raise consciousness and bring stakeholders to the table across Greek, Greek American, Greek Dutch, Greek Jewish and other fault lines. They point to more areas in need of coverage in this vast, uncharted domain, in

33 M. Cardaras, *Ripped at the Root: An Adoption Story Based on True Events*, New York, Spuyten Duyvil, 2021.

geographical and chronological terms but also in terms of policymaking, social and welfare studies, adoption histories and critical adoption studies. New research and informed dialogue aim to motivate formal apologies, shape intercountry adoption reform and help to revise the Hague Convention. They strive to underpin policymaking in the newer field of legislative work on international commercial surrogacy as well. The adoptees themselves inspire others to take charge of their story and history.

The South Korean intercountry adoption history is perhaps the best known: the numbers of Korean children sent overseas are much larger, and their members tend to be younger. This vast and very international group includes more scholar adoptees, filmmaker adoptees and superbly tech-savvy adoptees who know how to get the word out. Therefore, diaspora organizations, too, have before them an opportunity to engage with the transnational civic issues and potential of the adoptee demographic. Their shared activism can make a difference in real lives across the globe. South Korea has recognized its adoptee diaspora. Ireland has yet more work to do. Italy has left the lead to the Italian-to-American adoptees, as have Germany and Austria to their adoptee groups. Greece finds itself at the crossroads of various models and options, and it can only be hoped that it will choose the wisest and most satisfactory path forward, to the benefit of the adopted persons and of the first families.

Many of the South Korean adoptees have been able to participate in 'motherland tours' or in similar programmes of trans-culturalization or re-culturation, which are meant to reintroduce adoptees sent abroad to the culture of South Korea. Such programmes have not yet been initiated in Greece, and neither have any processes of memorialization of the country's adoption history and experience. When a South Korean adoptee friend registered for the November 2021 online conference organized by the Overseas Koreans Foundation (OKF), she received a 'Korea Culture Experience Box' in the mail ahead of the gathering's starting date. This box contained a traditional Korean stamp set, a Korean Hangul calligraphy set and a kit with which to assemble an eco-bag. It had me wonder, which objects would a 'Greek Culture Experience Box' contain? What would be presumed to make Greece's culture material and tangible to overseas adoptees – and fit in a box? The danger is, of course, that the hoped-for immersion in Greek culture stays on mere introductory or superficial levels, as when the emphasis is on or stays with food – the most favoured item in Greek gift exchanges or rituals of welcoming. Kimberly McKee addresses this limiting emphasis on food as a mode of 'consuming Koreanness' when she relates how South Korean adoptees seek to reconnect with their birth culture by way of food: "The overemphasis on food reveals a hyper focus on surface notions of culture that reduces Korean culture to edible bites."[34] The same

34 K.D. McKee, *Disrupting Kinship: Transnational Politics of Korean Adoption in the United States*, Urbana, IL, University of Illinois Press, 2019, p. 97.

applies, *mutatis mutandis*, to Greek culture and its ready consumability. How does one pass on native culture in an authentic way?

Again, Greece has no homecoming programmes in place of the kind that enable South Korean adoptees, for instance, to visit their homeland in organized groups. But such programmes could certainly be held within the framework of the formal restoration of Greek citizenship to the Greek-born adoptees. There is undoubtedly a need for some forms of re-acculturation, especially since many Greek adoptees dream of spending extended periods of time in their country of origin. Adoptees who grew up in American households that were not Greek American have had hardly any exposure to Greek culture. Those who did grow up in Greek America may at times be perceived as carriers of a Greekness that is not 'authentic'. Cultural repatriation of any kind is far from easy. However, Greek culture-keeping, or 'Greekness' of the – belatedly – acquired kind, is inevitably socially and ideologically constructed. Here I ask the AHEPA, the American Hellenic Educational Progressive Association, which was deeply involved in placing Greek children abroad for adoption, to help right the wrongs, to help create at least a sense of cultural citizenship, tenuous and complex though it may be.[35] I also encourage the Greeks themselves to welcome those in their midst who are Greek by origin but have not acquired any Greek social, and therefore cultural, capital. This path, too, is long and arduous. As South Korean adoptee Kara Bos explains:

> the Korean government's way of showing regret in sending thousands of kids around the world for adoption is to give adoptees 'free language courses,

35 On 26 September 2020, AHEPA Hellas Governor Efstathios Kefalidis extended an invitation to all Ahepans and to all Greek Americans to visit Greece on the occasion of the 200th anniversary of the Greek Revolution. But the call to travel 'home' in 2021 did not include an invitation to the Greek-born adopted persons who were sent abroad as children. Kefalidis's invitation—and not only his—marked a stark contrast with the AHEPA's approach to other strands of the Greek diaspora: 'recognized' Greek Americans are afforded access to their family histories through online resources and assistance from the various citizen services centres. The AHEPA has shown widespread support for Hellenic genealogy tourism, but it has yet to include the *nostos* of the Greek-born adoptees. See the online panel discussion hosted by Ilias Katsos on 26 July 2020, "200th Anniversary of the Hellenic Revolution of 1821 and Hellenic Genealogy Tourism," https://www.youtube.com/watch?v=l0J2pgZakAg. At about 35 minutes into the discussion, Kefalidis explains the details of a new and ambitious project called 'Live the Story of Your Origins' but, again, adoptee origins are not on the AHEPA's radar.
G. Van Steen, 'Of Foundlings and "Lostlings": When the Scopas Scandal Rocked the Unstable Foundations of the First 1950s Intercountry Adoptions', Annales de démographie historique, special issue on the history of adoption, "Formes adoptives (XVIe-XXe siècles)," Vol. 141, No. 1, 2021, pp. 123-155 is based on an in-depth study of the legal records associated with the Stephen Scopas case: PEOPLE v. SCOPAS (June 1959, June 1960, and March 1962, on appeal), People v. Scopas, 11 N.Y.2d 120, 181 N.E.2d 754 (1962). Printed record on appeal at the Pace Law Library, White Plains, NY. Online case briefs at www.leagle.com. The unambiguous archival record calls out for the AHEPA's urgent engagement with the issues that research projects and publications have now brought to light.

> an F4 visa, and a right to dual citizenship [, which] just shows the lack of understanding of what adoption means to us.'[36]

Another rallying cause is the lack of US citizenship that has afflicted many intercountry adoptees of the earlier generations. American adoptive parents of the post-war era were strongly encouraged to pursue naturalization and US citizenship for their foreign-born children. No intermediary or agency kept checking, however, or had the authority to enforce this recommendation. Some American parents failed to realize that foreign adoptees were not automatically granted US citizenship but had to formally apply for it. US legislation on this matter changed as late as 2000, when the Child Citizenship Act was issued, which still does not cover all incoming adoptees from abroad. Any adoptee who was not yet naturalized and over eighteen years old in 2000 went unprotected by the Act. If the American parents or the older Greek-born children themselves had neglected to pursue US citizen status, adoptees aged eighteen or older in 2000 were suddenly left without it – and also without Greek citizenship for that matter. Such drastic consequences deflate, of course, all illusions of permanence that the first intercountry adoptions tried hard to conjure up. Several cases are known of Greek-born and other, older foreign adoptees who have since found themselves in a situation of statelessness and in immigration limbo, especially after they had a brush with the law.[37] Legal citizenship standing, whether in Greece or in later life in the United States, has not come easy. Since November 2019 the National Alliance for Adoptee Equality has been championing reform, by way of the Adoptee Citizenship Act of 2019.[38] And yet legal citizenship pales in comparison with social belonging. Loving and caring familial relations are crucially important for the emotional well-being of adoptees, but they cannot substitute for respect and belonging in the public sphere.

Much will depend on the degree of adoptee mobilization around issues of archival access and citizenship rights. When, in July 2020, Greek Prime Minister Kyriakos Mitsotakis announced more transparent measures and faster procedures for Greek

---

36 Bos is quoted by J. Hicap, 'Korean-American Adoptee Files Landmark Paternity Suit against Her Biological Father in South Korea', *Manila Bulletin*, 24 May 2020, https://mb.com.ph/2020/05/23/korean-american-adoptee-files-landmark-paternity-suit-against-her-biological-father-in-south-korea/.

37 The issue has gained the international spotlight by way of the recent movie release of *Blue Bayou* (2021), directed by Justin Chon. The surprise factor is an important element in this movie. See further A.J. Perry, L. Donnella, D. Mohtasham and K. Grigsby Bates, 'Waiting in No Man's Land', *National Public Radio*, 29 June 2022, https://www.npr.org/2022/06/27/1107966562/waiting-in-no-mans-land.

38 On the National Alliance for Adoptee Equality and its advocacy, see https://sites.google.com/kagc.us/adoptee-equality/about. See also the Adoptee Rights Campaign, 2016, https://adopteerightscampaign.org/, and Adoptees for Justice, 2018, https://adopteesforjustice.org/. See further the US government website on the subject of 'Adult Adoptees and U.S. Citizenship', https://www.uscis.gov/adoption/adult-adoptees-and-us-citizenship#:~:text=Adoptees%20may%20become%20U.S.%20citizens,for%20naturalization%20after%20age%2018.

families to adopt children domestically,[39] the cameras followed him around facilities caring for healthy infants. The media coverage of adoption frequently overlooks the fact that older children and children with special needs are the ones who need families most but are at risk of being forgotten by prospective parents and by the system altogether. For its lack of attention to first family support, infant adoption thus continues to be "a treating of symptoms and not of disease".[40] Additionally, the new 2018 law did not resolve the pending issues of the older generations of Greek-born adoptees sent abroad. One of them responded in a Facebook post of 8 July 2020:

> If this [the implementation of better procedures] had only been the case when over 3,000 of us, Greek children, were sent for adoption to America in the scandal-ridden decades of the 1950s and 1960s. "The Lost Children of Cold War Greece" ... are seeking their roots and want to come home, Mr Prime Minister ... Where in your "modern and transparent adoption and fostering system" is the transparency for us? Where is the unfettered access to our records, access to an adoptee/birth family DNA database, and the pathway to reclaiming Greek citizenship?

The lack of dual citizenship was most poignantly felt by many Greek-born adoptees when, during the pandemic lockdown of summer through winter 2020, Greece allowed only Greek citizens to enter the country. Robyn's biological brother had been diagnosed with a terminal illness, and she was hurriedly trying to attain Greek citizenship but to no avail. Here is her reflection of 4 October 2020 (posted on Facebook):

> Like many who were adopted and raised by Americans who couldn't care less about their adopted child's birthright.... I struggled to support myself as soon as I was old enough to move out ... I am ... waiting now for the Consulate to contact me with an appointment to go and "fight" for my citizenship. I have been told ... by many ... that I have the one document needed to achieve it. My original Certificate of Birth and Baptism, in Greek of course. I also now have my Family Registry, in Greek, my preliminary and final adoption decree, in Greek. My birth parents' death certificates, in Greek. I have had my marriage license, naturalization certificate and divorce decree translated and apostilled, to show the name change (was not cheap). You tell me why this

39 Greek Law 4538/2018 (*Efimerida tis Kyverniseos tis Ellinikis Dimokratias* N/4538/18, or ΦΕΚ 85/Α/16-5-2018) was intended to lay the foundations on which new, efficient and equitable adoption procedures would be built. These procedures must address the domestic demand for in-country adoption and for the de-institutionalization of children. They also place online platforms and resources at the disposal of the petitioners. See https://www.anynet.gr.

40 I owe this insight to Daniel Drennan ElAwar, an intercountry adoptee from Lebanon and active blogger at https://danielibnzayd.wordpress.com/.

> is such a problem for ANY Greek-born adoptee to claim something that is rightfully theirs … Sorry, but this is a very difficult time for me, and I need so very much to be in Greece right now. I have only had 12 years with my birth family, scraping up the funds whenever I could just to go spend a couple of weeks at a time with them … Not near enough time to be able to handle a loss, such as the one that is imminent … It hurts so very much.

The group of Greek-born adoptees could legitimately ask for more than records, restored citizenship and research: it could ask for a professionally monitored DNA database to match Greek-born adoptees and Greek families' missing newborns, for post-adoption services provided by qualified psychologists and therapists, and for expert assistance with communication and reunification efforts, among other claims. With the adoptee activists, I have also made recommendations that are of a more general nature and could assist intercountry adoptees and domestic adoptees worldwide: they pertain to strengthening the legal provisions, the search infrastructure and the psychological support network available to adoptees. Each one of these propositions may take different forms in different countries. Some adoptees have expressed the wish to pursue further training or re-schooling in social work, psychology and adoption therapy. Adoption agencies and intermediaries in sending and receiving countries could set up several no-strings-attached scholarship funds for those who desire to gain professional training in these fields, to the benefit of other adoptees. Lastly, a lot can be changed in and through the use of appropriate language. Many adoptees choose to refer to their complex families in different terms. Rather than imposing (reductive) language such as 'birth mother', we would all gain by asking the adoptees themselves which language they prefer to use. Surprisingly, the older generations of intercountry adoptees still frequently use the term 'birth mother'. Lastly, narratives should be recast to again restore adoptee agency. How about starting adopter-driven news and other story coverage with the pertinent trigger warning that says:

> The making of one family almost inevitably means the loss of another. International adoption may trigger discomfort or pain among adoptees who realize the loss of family, culture, and identity.

Or, in the words of Alice Diver,

> To be deprived of origin … is to be so 'othered' as to be essentially rights-less in terms of one's family life, original identity, or indeed perhaps nationality.[41]

41 A. Diver, 'The Right to Identify One's Ancestors: Why the Notion of "Limping Parentage" Is Increasingly Relevant to Origin Deprivation', abstract and online lecture, Korean Adoptee Adoption Research Network, 27 January 2021, https://kaarn.org/events.

Lastly, adoptee voices have gone up in some countries (as in the UK) to demand the legal option to revoke an adoption, to reclaim one's birth identity or to select a different, chosen identity. This discharge from the adoption already exists in Australia, where activists are currently fighting to streamline no-fee procedures to discharge adoption orders.[42] Most national jurisprudences, however, are in deficit on this topic, as is Greece. But there are still plenty of Greek-born adoptees who would wish to be emancipated from the agentless status of being the adoptee with an assigned identity, whether or not abuse was part of their lived experiences. Some adoptees desire to pursue the option of revoking their adoption on a no-fault basis, as if it were a no-fault divorce, without having to undergo a process of argumentation or re-traumatization. The three R's, however, of records, restored citizenship and research rise to the top of the priority list of the Greek-born adoptees. The demands for three-fold redress best capture the sense of a diaspora once silenced and misrepresented but now finding its voice.

Research? A Long Overdue Greek Investigation

My role in the Greek adoptee activist movement is one of both following and leading. I have captured the movement's demands under the three R's of *r*edress: *r*ecords, *r*estoration of citizenship and also *r*esearch. I have explained, on multiple occasions: at stake is not an *ex gratia* redress; redress in this case should not be a gift but a right. I have publicized this demand for three-fold redress also before the President of the Hellenic Republic. My special request for further research, then, pushes the limits of our knowledge and is intertwined with my historical treatment of the topic: this Greek adoption history, which lays bare so many important issues for moral, social and political renegotiation, should simply be better known. My book of 2019 can only be a limited first step, and I welcome every form of constructive dialogue and study that will breach former limitations. Research, after all, validates voices. Ideally, however, this scholarly but also ethically and socially engaged research must lead to a full-scale, transparent and independent investigation of the Greek post-war adoption circuits. I recommend that such a Greek investigation be conducted on the Dutch model of the Joustra Committee (18 April 2019 to 8 February 2021), which has now inspired other Western European governments to initiate their own, long overdue investigations.[43] Worthy of emulation are also the

42 Parliament of Victoria, August 2021, pp. xxix, 172-182.

43 In the spring of 2019 and in response to the demands of its cross-border adoptees, the Netherlands set up the Joustra Committee, formally the Committee Investigating Intercountry Adoption in the Past, which was tasked with examining the Dutch government's knowledge of and involvement with possible abuses related to international adoption between 1967 and 1998, 'at a minimum'. In mid-June 1967, the Netherlands issued its formal guidelines for intercountry adoption, and in 1998 it ratified the Hague Convention.

documented writings and recommendations that were recently issued by the Legislative Assembly Legal and Social Issues Committee of the Parliament of Victoria, in the framework of its *Inquiry into Responses to Historical Forced Adoption in Victoria.*[44] These recent developments merit further explanation and follow-up. The Dutch investigation, in particular, bears relevance for an anticipated Greek study, but other authors in this book have provided the proper contextualization to it (see Chapters 7 and 9). What the various emerging historical studies do show, however, is that legal inertia only prompts a time bomb to keep on ticking. Meanwhile, the demand for reparation law or other reconciliation strategies will grow louder, as will the stipulation that no country take advantage of another country's times of crisis to enact adoption as emergency rescue. The ethics of child protection and family preservation ought to prevail.[45]

The summary language of the Dutch report is bold and transparent. The opening paragraph of the press release in English deserves to be quoted in full here:

> "The current system of intercountry adoption cannot be maintained," concludes the Committee investigating intercountry adoption after an extensive investigation. Not only have there been many abuses in the past, the system of intercountry adoption is still open to fraud and abuses continue to this day. The committee therefore recommends suspending intercountry adoptions. Moreover: "The committee has serious doubts about whether it is possible to design a realistic public-law system under which the abuses identified would no longer occur".[46]

---

44 Parliament of Victoria, Legislative Assembly Legal and Social Issues Committee, *Inquiry into Responses to Historical Forced Adoption in Victoria*, Victoria, Australia, Victorian Government Printer, August 2021, https://www.parliament.vic.gov.au/48fd29/contentassets/9cffb4b530044ffcaa1ddb864940ff85/lalsic_59-03_responses_to_historical_forced_adoption_in_vic.pdf. The important recommendations, 56 in total, appear on pp. xxvii-xxxv.

45 See P. Selman, 'Intercountry Adoption after the Haiti Earthquake: Rescue or Robbery?', *Adoption & Fostering*, Vol. 35, No. 4, 2011, pp. 41-49, reflecting on emergency responses after the Haiti earthquake of 2010. I support the statement issued by Child Identity Protection in early March of 2022, which ties the repercussions of old emergencies to the possible fallout of the developing crisis in Ukraine:

> Long-term decisions as to the extra-familial care of a child, such as adoption, must never be made during or in the immediate aftermath of the emergency, as this can cause, among other things, the arbitrary and unwarranted modification of a child's identity in violation of international law.
> (CHIP, 'Ukraine and Other Affected Countries: Protecting All Rights of Children, Including Their Right to Identity', March 2022)

46 Press release in English, 8 February 2021, 'Intercountry Adoption System Not Sustainable'. The recommendation to suspend intercountry adoption relates to David Smolin's influential article on moratoria (2021). The authors of the Dutch report followed up with an article recommending a strong moratorium but showing awareness of the danger of that moratorium being eroded over time, despite the government's acknowledgement and apology. See Y. Balk, G. Frerks and B. de Graaf, 'Investigating Historical Abuses: An Applied History Perspective on Intercountry Adoption in the Netherlands, 1950s-Present', *Journal of Applied History*, 2022, 1-28, p. 28.

The Dutch report sent shockwaves through the international adoption world, with its startling admission that "[f]rom the late 1960s, the Dutch government was aware of adoption abuses".[47] Notably, each of its seemingly local case studies has afforded an opportunity for comparison and reflection within a global framework. But we are still far removed from uniform responses to illegal adoptions. Significantly, the committee's research team has, since May 2020, also paid attention to the older adoptees who travelled from Greece to the Netherlands.[48] At that time, I was able to provide the Dutch investigators with information about the Greek-to-Dutch adoptions that covered the decade prior to 1967: thus, the Greek cases, which started to occur from 1956 onwards, brought forward not only the starting date but also the documented instances of unethical practices. The Dutch report identified Greece as one of the countries in which systemic abuses occurred. The Greek adoptions to the Netherlands were, for the Dutch, the first mass adoptions from abroad, after scandal and anti-Americanism had begun to slow down the Greek-to-American adoption traffic.

The Greek government and the then intermediaries have yet to conduct their own investigations. An in-depth review of the Greek adoptions abroad is both necessary and urgent, especially since various Greek governments have promised thorough investigations since 1959 but never saw them through. There has thus far been no state policy aimed at discovering the truth. There may be a lack of political will to do so: after all, these mass transports of Greek-born children to the United States counter and ultimately debunk the post-war reconstruction narrative in which the Greek American diaspora is heavily vested, given how much charitable aid it sent over to the war-torn homeland. US-bound adoption was and is not a sign of benign tutelage. Rather, it exposes a tremendous national precarity that cast doubts on the legitimacy of political parties and governments. The vulnerability of the nation's youngest and most helpless citizens, and their mass adoptions abroad, cannot but challenge the nation-building claims of leaders who failed to provide an infrastructure that would have allowed the nation to raise its own citizens, *all* its citizens. Here, I single out Prime Minister Konstantinos Karamanlis, who committed to Cold War defence spending before spending on child welfare structures. The pro-Americanism of his regime served as an ideological, even 'humanitarian' banner, celebrating these adoptions that involved hundreds of young lives. But liabilities remain and need to be addressed. These liabilities cannot be dismissed because more than half a century has passed – or because some agents remember to 'forget'. Leaving the sixty- to seventy-year-old Greek adoption history buried in the past, without acting on its painful remembrances, constitutes an act of

47 Press release, 8 February 2021.

48 Van Steen, 2021. Van Steen refers to the 600 Greek-to-Dutch adoptions that started being negotiated from 1956 on (2019, pp. 61-62, 79-80, 108, 130, 171, 225, 264 and 273).

injustice against the adopted children, now ageing adults, and also against the first parents, whose experiences, emotions and agency were erased.

It is my hope that the Greek state will conduct a thorough review, on the Dutch model, which will reach as far back as 1948. There are hopeful signs that we may be moving closer towards this goal of introspection that will break the silence. I have proactively issued calls to the Greek government to commission a proper investigation, led by an expert task force, that must also address the demands of the adoptees and resolve their concerns before it is too late. I have further proposed to assist with centralized efforts to re-establish the adoptees' original (political and social) identities. Further research, however, will broaden the evidence base on which policy responses must be built. My meetings with Greek government officials have been to the point. The meetings with the President, the Prime Minister's office and the Greek Ministry of Labor and Social Affairs have been particularly productive. President Sakellaropoulou granted me a private meeting on 2 March 2022. Given that she is careful not to be seen micromanaging political issues, this formal meeting and her incisive querying acknowledged that the Greek adoptee cause is no longer a party-political cause but a moral cause of truth and reconciliation. For her and for me, it will be a challenge to keep this deeply social issue on the Greek government's radar while the economic crisis and the acute military crisis in Ukraine keep setting the agenda, in addition to the imminent Greek general elections. Pathways are now open for the upper executive echelons to work either through executive order or via an amendment to the current legislation (and, hopefully, not by way of the courts). Indeed, more remains to be done to proceed from recommendations to concrete action, whether or not that will entail the issuance of a formal apology on the part of the Greek state and/or any go-betweens. By late November 2021, after the book launch of the Greek translation of *Adoption, Memory, and Cold War Greece* and the ensuing media attention, the case for uninhibited adoptee searches and for restoring original citizenship (as a dual citizenship) had been won in the court of Greek public opinion but not yet in legal or administrative terms. A political response must now follow the emotional or empathetic response. All along, my aim has not been to provoke by exposing a denied reality but to correct what can still be corrected.

The phenomenon of American and Dutch couples adopting from Greece stopped some fifty years ago. This passage of time leaves the history of the Greek adoptions of the 1950s and 1960s suspended behind a wall of disbelief, if not outright denial. "I have never heard of these adoptions of Greek children sent to the USA or to the Netherlands," is the most common polite objection I encounter. Clearly, we have more work to do to integrate this adoption history into the national narrative, to dispel the cognitive dissonance and to inspire restorative action. Those who have heard promptly start idealizing this historical practice. Both of these reactions express a deep scepticism about any critical study of this adoption movement. Moreover, this scepticism comes not only from Greek and Greek American audiences but also from leaders of organizations that were involved in placing Greek children abroad for adoption. Some aspects of the post-war international adoption history will continue to resist interpretation, let alone interpretation we can all agree upon. But we are certain that some children's lives were enriched by the overseas adoptions while others' lives and families were destroyed by it. Some post-Civil War adoptions delivered an adequate family life to true orphans in need of a home. Most adoptions of the late 1950s through the 1960s, however, favoured American couples in need of a child. This sought-after white child, preferably a 'blank-slate', healthy infant, was still called an 'orphan', which erased the single, unwed first mother whose parenthood was not supported. Irregularities took place as well, and they have cast a long shadow over those adoptees who have come to realize that their adoptions essentially broke the law.

"I am close to saying what I dread to say" (Sophocles, *Oedipus Tyrannus* 1169)

It needs to be stated in no unclear terms: Greece of the late 1940s through the mid-1960s had no laws on the books that prohibited the removal of Greek children from their country of origin by way of intercountry adoption. Even as the international adoptions were ongoing – and peaking – Greece hardly took measures to protect its children and their first families. As adoption scandals broke out in 1959 and again in 1962, the need for reform was finally being discussed, but the Greek state's focus was on the avoidance of scandal and on damage control. New Greek laws on adoption were at last issued in 1966 and 1970, but by that time, more than 3,500 children had been banished from their country as citizens without a say.[49] When the Greek government put better adoption criteria in place, it acted to protect mainly the child's religious and cultural identity, but it did not guarantee protection as far as the child's well-being was concerned.

Post-war Greek institutions, with the condoning of the state, sent out very high numbers of 'illegitimate' children for adoption overseas. The officials saw this kind of adoption as paramount to better nation-building: in their view, children born out of wedlock and poor single mothers did not make desirable citizens for a future and stronger Greece. Adoption abroad became intertwined with issues of public morality. Therefore, a moral and ethical solution is now called for to redress a biopolitically driven child export policy. Moreover, the post-war Greek state and court system saw adoption as a matter of private family law, even if it transcended borders. The United States, on the other hand, approached adoption from abroad as a topic of immigration law. Significantly,

49 Van Steen, 2019, pp. 40, 116-117, 260, and 2021.

it kept the related immigration files, which are today the adoptees' best source of archival information (once they, as individuals seeking private information, have filed a Freedom of Information Act or FOIA request). Greece needs to implement similar and more consistent information disclosure procedures. Gaining access to personal data should be a matter of public concern and public policy but not in the restrictive sense in which the Greek authorities have invoked the General Data Protection Regulation (GDPR) regulations since 2019.[50] Greece has been hiding behind the GDPR and behind the framing of adoption as a private problem. The GDPR offers rights to the adoptee and researcher as well as obligations; it is not meant to be a legal firewall preventing the adoptees from accessing their very own data. Greece needs to reframe the issue as a public and ethical cause that also acknowledges the psychological experience of adoption beyond the legal and political ramifications.

So much bold language … Are there risks and dangers along the road? Of course, there are, and not just those pertaining to frankness and potential censorship. In the past, international adoption was couched in a salvationist master narrative, and the child's upbringing in a foreign country and culture was presented as nothing short of a fairy tale. Conversely, stories of abuse may swing the pendulum in the opposite direction and may become sensationalized in the mass media. Now sixty and seventy years later, there should be no need any more for that kind of adoption allure or adoption voyeurism, for outsiders' casual references to experiences that were, far more often than not, *not* theirs. The danger that, even today, we, as the consuming audience of ongoing worldwide international adoption, become too enamoured with the stories of reunion – with the redemption narratives – is another important pitfall. We have all read the unreflective reunion stories that ignore the family complexities and perpetuate the noise without substance. Such rehashed stories lead to the misconstrued notion that a state-organized mass practice can be resolved at the individual or private level. If such a past practice could be corrected by private initiative alone, we might underestimate the enduring need for a centralized plan for redress, to repair a *man*-made crisis (and nearly all unscrupulous intermediaries were indeed men). Another risk lies in adoptee

50 In August 2019, the Greek Parliament passed a bill that incorporated the European Union's General Data Protection Regulation (GDPR of 2016, https://eur-lex.europa.eu/legal-content/EN/TXT/?uri=CELEX:02016R0679-20160504) into the body of Greek national law. Law 4624/2019 (ΦΕΚ 137/A/29-8-2019). See https://www.e-nomothesia.gr/kat-dedomena-prosopikou-kharaktera/nomos-4624-2019-phek-137a-29-8-2019.html and https://www.dpa.gr/sites/default/files/2019-10/celex_32016r0679_en_txt.pdf.

activism that loses its connection to research and fact or that plagiarizes the researcher's findings and demands while seasoning them with factual errors.[51]

The phenomenon of 'saviour blindness' has cast a long shadow over this sensitive realm, in which the Greek-born adoptees have gradually moved from disappearance to visibility. Saviour blindness today repeats the mistakes of the past – of the saviours who thought that they needed to place 'orphans' and eventually created paper orphans.[52] At work now is a new kind of white saviourism, not that of the adoptive parents, but that of loud and again white searchers or 'experts' who monetize content at the expense of the adoptees, who are once more reduced to orphan ornaments. Terms and titles such as 'paying it forward' and 'search angels' or claims that "finding birth mothers earns one a seat in heaven" should not have a place in any exchanges with adoptees, who would otherwise never be done 'owing'. Additionally, these privileged 'saviours' dismiss social work all over again and ignore the need for aftercare for the reunited family, and especially for the adoptee. Often, they flaunt the lack of circumspection that very private histories deserve, subjecting them to public displays of their do-goodership. After a roller-coaster reunification with the first family, rushed through by such 'heroes' and accompanied by Facebook blasts and fundraisers, many reunited adoptees feel once more used and exposed. International adoption has traditionally figured at the intersection of faith, philanthropy and the free-market economy. There is no need for the 'influencer', 'content-creating' business of the search praxis to go down the same sad path. Anything else would only indicate that 'doing good' is back again as a commodity in its own right, pursued in new, self-righteous ways for the public prestige it delivers – and the occasional economic benefits via 'suggested donations'. Adoptees have been brokered; they have been taken for costly rides when searching or trying to regain their citizenship. Now they are being tapped for 'annual memberships' or 'charitable donations'. Enough with the money-making on the back of adoptees!

Work in the public humanities that interfaces with the specific interests of the adoptee collective must still adhere to the highest academic standards, without

51 This unforeseen development, too, has unfortunately been part of my experience, even though I do not claim a monopoly in telling the story. So is the phenomenon of outsiders claiming victory in a battle, our battle that has yet to be won. The turn to social media has left us with the kind of casual venues where anyone can communicate unreliable 'facts'. Facebook and Twitter have created platforms for anyone to claim expertise and to do so without having to address informed criticism regarding the validity of those 'truths'. But that does not mean that extreme caution and discretion are no longer required. Equally important are the international standards of personal data protection and confidentiality. The role of the historian is not only truth-telling via concrete evidence but also the legal, ethical and professional management of records. Those whose aim is to expose the adoptees (breaching their privacy) and collect 'donations' based on loose promises of reunification efforts do not serve the adoptees. They merely repeat the patterns of exploitation that are now more than half a century old.

52 Van Steen, 2019, p. 42.

compromising on certain truths. This adoptee collective is both an existing and a new demographic, a network in the making as more adoptees come out of the woodwork to join the conversation. The adoptee movement of the Greek American diaspora has only been recognized belatedly in scholarship as well as in the media. It still has a long trajectory to cover to generate additional research and to achieve solidarity and closure, as it grapples with its own identity politics. If and when, however, work in the public humanities interfaces with the interests of this movement, it will help open up policy and also feminist studies: it will address silenced and 'forgotten' pasts, while empowering particular demographics, especially women and children.

Conclusion: Who Does Greece Want to Be?

> Our exchanges help to heal matters that are unfortunately so personal and private when they should be collective and public.
> – Dinos P., Greek adoptee, 20 April 2021

The adoptions of Greek children to the USA and to the Netherlands were among the oldest post-war mass international adoptions. The US-bound adoptions were being negotiated from 1948 onwards and eventually totalled more than 3,500 cases. Greece also sent 600 of its children to the Netherlands – and never kept a list of either. These people have organized themselves and have spoken for themselves, and some have written books, essays and blogs related to their adoption experiences. They have also been voicing their concerns and demands. Greece has taken note and needs to move towards corrective action. It is not too late yet. Greece has had a lot to celebrate recently: it just set out on its third century of independence after the hard-won revolutionary war of 1821. But the cause of adoptee records, restored citizenship and research remains pending, despite the alarming lack of alignment with international standards that characterizes the Greek policy and praxis – despite, also, the many rising voices of the adoptees, who have staged their own revolution. Adoption as a ground of contestation goes to the heart of Greek society. What and who does Greece want to be in its third century of independence? Is Greece ready to adopt its own wounded past? "One of the great failings in adoption culture," says Liz DeBetta, "is the inability to deal with truth."[53] How does Greece want to deal with its adoption truth? "[T]he existing block to the past may create a feeling that there is a block to the future as well," claimed Sorosky, Baran and Pannor in 1978, on the subject of the demand for open records spearheaded by US domestic adoptees. But I want to leave this ominous statement as a

53 L. DeBetta, 'Negotiating Space to Heal: Adult Adoptee Narratives as Autoethnography', *Adoption & Culture*, Vol. 10, No. 1, 2022, 116-134, p. 131.

subject to ponder for a nation that actually has the power *and* the obligation to remove the existing blocks, for the sake of its future.

The adoption mediators of the past who are still active and their successors could contribute in many ways to the meaningful and effective participation of adoption victims, to help these victims of reckless adoption schemes reclaim the Greek components of their identity, to bring closure to their first relatives, to deliver truth to the adoptive family members. They could also support the adoptee activist effort by joining the conversation about restoring the Greek citizenship of the Greek-born adoptees. They could reiterate the need for widespread education, training and legal aid pertaining to the issues at stake. Thus, they could model the kind of recognition that the USA and the Greek state owe to this forgotten diaspora group – a recognition that is, for some people, seventy years overdue. The Cold War Greek adoption history does not have to become a ground of contestation between the American or Greek establishment and the individual adoptees, who are united especially around the demand for a reconfirmed Greek citizenship. All parties to the adoption history have been seeking emancipatory and creative forms of belonging, all have questions to pose and stories to tell, and yet the master narrative has traditionally been shaped by the least affected parties: the intermediaries active then and silent now, who have missed the chances to get to know the children they placed, even when the opportunities presented or present themselves.

The best part of adoptee activism is that it keeps on inviting *other* voices in order to gain much-desired policy changes and responses. Thus, the ongoing campaign and research project have linked us to diverse groups of stakeholders, such as interracial international adoptees, Greek Roma-born adoptees, first mothers' self-help groups and NGOs, inquiring adoptive parents, inquisitive social workers, and other parties involved in the adoption process. Meanwhile, our search for truth, truth-telling and a formal apology continues unabated. We will continue to try to force the Greek government's hand to open the records, reaffirm first citizenship and commit to an investigation. We will continue to ask all governments involved to grant generous health and social care measures for the victims and to set up educational and memorialization activities for those who need to learn so as not to repeat. As the adoptee demands in this chapter underpin, the requests can be legitimate, the path straightforward, the company galvanized – all bonding together to pressure sending and receiving countries to finish what they started and then to finish intercountry adoption altogether.

Part II
Receiving Countries

6 Switzerland Takes First Steps to Deal with Illegal Intercountry Adoptions

Sabine Bitter

Introduction

This chapter describes the lifting of a decades-long silence surrounding abusive intercountry adoption in Switzerland. It explains how in the last five years, political and civil society initiatives by committed women, in particular, have galvanized a process supported by investigative journalism and academic research to deal with this aspect of Switzerland's recent history. The chapter starts by describing politicians' and adoptees' responses to the revelations of abusive adoptions and what the Swiss authorities have undertaken to date towards the historical reappraisal of abusive practices. It then employs case studies to illustrate illegal and abusive practices facilitated by Swiss adoption agencies acting with or without state authorization in the last third of the 20th century in Sri Lanka. The chapter goes on to discuss the Swiss authorities' comments with regard to the revelations, before listing what politicians and the authorities have done in practice to date by way of providing redress and assisting adoptees in their search for their origins. The last section explains the role of the civil society interest group Back to the Roots and describes what the association has achieved so far. The conclusion summarizes the reappraisal and reparation efforts to date in connection with the illegal intercountry adoptions and what remains to be done.

First Steps to Deal with Illegal Intercountry Adoptions

Women in Parliament Launch Political Initiatives

In autumn 2017, the Dutch public service broadcaster *BNNVARA* aired an episode of the TV documentary series *Zembla*, revealing how massive adoption fraud had taken place in the 1980s in Sri Lanka. The investigative report described how babies were brought to European countries under illegal and abusive circumstances.[1] It raised an alarm both in

1 See BNNVARA, Zembla, 'Adoptiebedrog Deel 2', 20 September 2017, https://www.bnnvara.nl/zembla/artikelen/adoptiebedrog-deel-2.

the Netherlands and in Switzerland, which had granted entry permits to 955 Sri Lankan children between 1970 and 1999 alone.[2]

In Switzerland, the report mobilized several politicians, including Rebecca Ruiz, a former Social Democratic Party member of the National Council from the canton of Vaud.[3] In December 2017, Ruiz submitted a procedural request to Parliament in the form of a postulate, which was referred to the National Council in 2018. She called on the Federal Council, Switzerland's executive government, to answer questions related to the adoptions from Sri Lanka in the 1980s and to investigate the practices of the placement agencies and competent authorities. The postulate demanded that the Federal Council submit a report shedding light on the misconduct and measures taken at the time. In addition, it asked the government to examine the existing legal provisions on international adoptions and issue recommendations regarding current practice. Finally, Ruiz asked the government how adoptees were being supported in the search for their origins.[4]

Member of the National Council Barbara Gysi,[5] a Social Democratic Party member from the canton of St Gallen, submitted another postulate, instructing the Federal Council to launch an investigation in every canton during the period 1960 to 2000 and a National Research Programme inquiring into intercountry adoptions from the ten most frequent countries of origin.[6] The programme, she requested, must examine the practices of the placement agencies and authorities as well as investigate the consequences of these practices for the development of the children and adolescents and whether any irregularities came to light. Gysi also asked the government to examine whether sufficient attention was paid to the best interests of the children in accordance with the UN Convention on the Rights of the Child and the Hague Convention on Protection of Children and Cooperation in Respect of Intercountry Adoption, which has been in force in Switzerland since 2003. The Federal Council took a preliminary position on the postulate in 2020, stating that it wanted to wait for the results of ongoing studies before determining the need for and scope of any new studies on the matter.[7]

2 Statistical Service, Central Aliens' Register, Federal Office for Migration: Entry permits issued to foreign foster children by citizenship, 1970-1979, 1980-1989, 1990-1999.

3 See https://www.parlament.ch/en/biografie/rebecca-ana-ruiz/4143.

4 See https://www.parlament.ch/de/ratsbetrieb/suche-curia-vista/geschaeft?AffairId=20174181.

5 See https://www.parlament.ch/en/biografie/barbara-gysi/4121.

6 A study with a first overview concerning several countries was published in December 2023, See: Ramsauer, Nadja, Bühler, Rahel und Girschik, Katja: Hinweise auf illegale Adoptionen von Kindern aus zehn Herkunftsländern in der Schweiz, 1970er- bis 1990er-Jahre: Bestandesaufnahme zu Unterlagen im Schweizerischen Bundesarchiv. Zürich 2023. https://doi.org/10.21256/zhaw-2426.

7 See https://www.parlament.ch/de/ratsbetrieb/suche-curia-vista/geschaeft?AffairId=20203722

Also, Social Democrat Flavia Wasserfallen, a member of the National Council from the canton Bern, put a series of questions to the Federal Council in August 2020.[8] She asked how adoptees could be better supported in their search for their origins and whether the government was prepared to set up a dedicated agency independent of the authorities to offer legal advice to adoptees. A final point in the interpellation concerned the safeguarding of documents. She requested that documents be transferred from private to public archives in order to facilitate access for those affected. In its response to this interpellation, the Federal Council stated that the board of the Conference of Cantonal Justice and Police Directors had issued recommendations to the cantons in January 2020 asking them to facilitate access to documents and information for adoptees. It had also recommended that they process such applications free of charge and, 'if possible', establish a neutral point of contact. It therefore planned to include Sri Lanka in efforts to improve access to the files.[9]

Finally, a politician at the cantonal level also became involved. In 2020, Yvonne Bürgin, a member of Zurich's Cantonal Council for the Party *Die Mitte*, put a question to the cantonal government asking whether the laws and practices in the canton today would guarantee that illegal intercountry adoptions could no longer take place and whether specific measures were in place to prevent illegal placement activities. The government replied that the legal basis and implementing procedures were adequate to prevent illegal activities. In recent years, the authorities had detected 'a small number' of suspicious cases. In these cases, either criminal charges had been brought or the prospective adoptive parents had decided not to adopt the child after all.[10]

Sri Lankan Adoptees Organize Themselves

At around the same time as the four political interventions and subsequent inquiries, and as authorities were making the first efforts to facilitate access to records for people tracing their origins, a civil society initiative was launched. The Dutch TV report on adoption fraud in 2017 had raised awareness of many of those who had come to Switzerland as babies from Sri Lanka in the 1980s and 1990s. Among them was Sarah Ramani Ineichen, a midwife from profession, who, in 2018, founded an interest group called Back to the Roots, together with other women who also had questions about their origins, how they came to be in Switzerland and their biological parents. Chaired by Sarah Ramani Ineichen, Back to the Roots aims to provide information about the

8 See https://www.parlament.ch/en/biografie/flavia-wasserfallen/4224.
9 See https://www.parlament.ch/de/ratsbetrieb/suche-curia-vista/geschaeft?AffairId=20203677.
10 See https://zh.die-mitte.ch/anfrage-gesetzliche-grundlagen-und-aktuelle-praxis-von-auslandsadoptionen/.

circumstances surrounding adoptions from Sri Lanka in order to support adoptees in search of their origins and to advocate for their concerns at the political level.[11] Today, the interest group has 600 members, about half of whom are adoptees. Almost all of them came to Switzerland as babies from Sri Lanka or India in the 1980s and 1990s.

Of the 300 adoptees known to the association, about 90 percent are female and 10 percent male.[12] Many of them have been in the dark about their own origins for years. Sarah Ramani Ineichen has still not found her biological mother. Her research has revealed that her adoption was abusive and illegal both in Sri Lanka and in Switzerland. According to her adoption records, her adoptive parents were only 29 and 32 years old and had only been married for 11 months. By law, both parents had to be older than 35 years or married for more than five years to adopt a child.[13] Moreover, the couple's suitability should have been assessed and authorization granted before the child was handed over to the couple in Sri Lanka.[14] In fact, permission to take in a child as foster parents with a view to later adoption was only granted to the couple retrospectively after they had already entered Switzerland with the baby. And this despite the involvement of an agency, recognized by the Swiss authorities, which was obliged to know the law and act legally. Sarah Ramani Ineichen's research in Sri Lanka revealed, furthermore, that she had been handed over to her adoptive parents not by her biological mother but by an 'acting mother' – a woman who had received 30 dollars to play the role of her biological mother in court.[15] Sarah Ramani Ineichen, therefore, knows what the adoptees who turn to Back to the Roots in the hope of clarifying their parentage are going through and what motivates them. On the website, she summarizes their common experience as follows:

> Those affected are very unsettled. Instead of finding answers, they face existential questions. Why do I have two different birth names in my adoption file? Key documents are missing from my adoption file. Was the adoption procedure carried out carefully at all? How will I cope if the investigations in Sri Lanka show that the story of my adoption was a lie? What will I build my identity on now?

Such questions pull the rug out from under the feet of many of those affected. Even for someone in a stable family environment with good friends, this pain is difficult to process. The adoptees find themselves alone and need help to exercise their right

11 See https://backtotheroots.net.
12 Recorded interview with S.R. Ineichen, Chair of the Association Back to the Roots, 27 April 2022.
13 Swiss Civil Code 1973, Art. 264a, para. 2.
14 Ordinance of 19 October 1977 on the Placement of Children in Foster Care, Art. 8, para. 1.
15 Recorded voice message from S.R. Ineichen to author, 23 May 2022.

to their own identity.[16] This right is enshrined in Article 8 of the UN Convention on the Rights of the Child, which came into force in Switzerland on 26 March 1997.[17] The revised adoption provisions under Swiss law, which came into force on 1 January 2018, also give adopted children the right to information both about their birth parents and about natural siblings and half-siblings who are of age and consent to this disclosure.[18]

Authorities Launch Investigations into Intercountry Adoptions from Sri Lanka

There was no widespread public or political debate about the circumstances surrounding the adoption of non-European children in Switzerland until a few years ago, despite the fact that such adoptions had been taking place since the 1960s. There are until today a lot of blind spots.

With the introduction of birth control pills, the number of unwanted pregnancies sank.[19] While demand from prospective parents remained stable, fewer children in Switzerland were given up for adoption. In the following decades, people turned to other countries – mainly non-European countries in the global South – to fulfil their desire to start a family. In these countries, there were still poor families and single mothers who were ostracized and often forced to give up their child. The intercountry adoption trend was encouraged by the fact that long-distance travel became increasingly affordable for middle-class couples, who were thus able to travel to another continent to choose a baby.

The first real examination of the circumstances surrounding international adoptions arose in Switzerland from the mid-1970s in legal academic circles. The lawyer Cyril Hegnauer began investigating the legal basis and gaps and criticized the cantons' inadequate supervision of the placement agencies.[20] In the mid-1980s Robert Zuegg began to study child welfare in connection with the placement of foreign adoptive children from a legal perspective. He continued to pursue this issue into the 1990s and advocated for preventive measures.[21] Finally, in 1991, the lawyer Marie-Françoise

16 See https://backtotheroots.net/jahresbericht-2018-2019/.

17 See https://www.fedlex.admin.ch/eli/cc/1998/2055_2055_2055/de.

18 See https://www.admin.ch/gov/de/start/dokumentation/medienmitteilungen.msg-id-67489.html.

19 See http://www.hoepflinger.com/fhtop/BevoelkerungswandelCH.pdf, p. 38.

20 C. Hegnauer, *Grundriss des Kindesrechts und des übrigen Verwandtschaftsrechts* (4th edition), Bern, Stämpfli, 1994; C. Hegnauer, *Berner Kommentar. Das Familienrecht. 2. Abteilung: Die Verwandtschaft, Sonderband: Die Adoption, Artikel 264-269c Schweizerisches Zivilgesetzbuch und 12a-12c*, Bern, Stämpfli, 1975.

21 R. Zuegg, *Die Vermittlung ausländischer Adoptivkinder als Problem des präventiven Kinderschutzes*, Zürich, Pro Juventute, 1986; R. Zuegg, *Adoptivkinder aus fernen Ländern. Studie zum präventiven Kinderschutz in der Schweiz*, Aachen, Shaker, 1996.

Lücker-Babel, who worked for the Geneva-based children's rights organization Defence for Children, drew attention to a specific problem: She had discovered that not all the children brought to Switzerland for this purpose ended up being adopted.[22] Some of them were placed in homes owing to difficult family circumstances, without anyone having sought to ensure that their adoption in Switzerland went through. Others stayed in the family that took them in with the status of foster child and hence in a situation of legal uncertainty in which, for example, they were not able to obtain Swiss citizenship and a part of them – like the Tibetan children – remained stateless.

The legal studies carried out at the time have only recently been followed up by the first investigations into international adoptions in Switzerland. In 2015, the historian Fàbio Macedo described how the organization *Terre des hommes* in Lausanne brought Algerian and Tunisian children to Switzerland in the 1960s, officially to recuperate but, in fact, to put them up for adoption.[23] In 2018, the author of this chapter, together with journalist Nathalie Nad-Abonji, traced the history of 160 Tibetan foster children who had come to Switzerland between 1960 and 1962 with the help of industrialist Charles Aeschimann in agreement with the Dalai Lama. The children were placed with foster families and in most cases were later adopted.[24] The broadcast of the Dutch investigative TV report 'Adoption Fraud', in autumn 2017, got a lot of publicity, including in Switzerland. The canton of St Gallen followed the report and launched a first scientific investigation into adoptions from Sri Lanka. It had an important reason for doing so: here, in the municipality of Jona in 1964, social worker Alice Honegger had opened the placement agency, which she ran until her death, in 1997.[25] The canton of St. Gallen commissioned the author of this chapter to conduct the research. The project aimed to give an overview of the activities of this adoption agent, who had arranged the placement of hundreds of babies from Sri Lanka and India in families throughout Switzerland. The study demonstrated that the Swiss authorities knew as

22 M.-F. Lücker-Babel, *Auslandadoption und Kinderrechte. Was geschieht mit den Verstossenen?* Freiburg i. Üe., Universtitätsverlag, 1991.

23 F. Macedo, 'Action humanitaire et adoption d'enfants étrangers en Suisse. Le cas de Terre des Hommes (1960-1969)', *Relations Internationales*, no. 161, 2/2015, pp. 81-94.

24 S. Bitter and N. Nad-Abonji, *Tibetische Kinder für Schweizer Familien. Die Aktion Aeschimann*, Zürich, Rotpunktverlag, 2018.

25 S. Bitter, A. Bangerter and N. Ramsauer, *Adoptionen von Kindern aus Sri Lanka in der Schweiz 1973-1997. Zur Praxis der privaten Vermittlungsstellen und der Behörden. Historische Analyse betreffend das Postulat Ruiz 17.4181, Zurich*, 2020, p. 57, https://digitalcollection.zhaw.ch/handle/11475/19562.

early as the 1980s that Alice Honegger was working in Sri Lanka with a lawyer who was involved in a commercial child trafficking network.[26]

The first findings pointed to serious irregularities, which, in 2020, prompted the canton of St. Gallen to commission a second study, focusing specifically on Sri Lankan adoptions. This research project, headed by Francesca Falk, lecturer in migration history at the University of Bern, examined all adoption procedures between 1973 and 2002, in which couples living in the canton of St. Gallen had taken in one or more children from Sri Lanka for adoption. There were 85 children who – with one exception – were only a few weeks or months old when they entered Switzerland. This study confirmed previous findings, concluding that Sri Lankan procedures were not solely to blame for the errors and shortcomings. Inadequate management of the procedures by the cantonal and communal authorities in St. Gallen also played a role. Based on sources available for the first time, the study confirmed that the Swiss adoption agent Alice Honegger must have been aware that she was involved in commercial adoptions.[27]

Prompted by the political initiative of parliamentarian Rebecca Ruiz, the Federal Council sought to develop a scientific basis on which to handle the matter of Sri Lankan adoptions. In 2019, the Federal Office of Justice within the Federal Department of Justice and Police commissioned Zurich University of Applied Sciences (*ZHAW*) to conduct an extended study on adoptions from Sri Lanka, followed by two Swiss National Science Foundation studies in the National Research Programme on 'Care and Coercion'. The 2020 *ZHAW* study should provide basic information on the activities of Swiss adoption placement agencies and the processes by which children from Sri Lanka were brought to Switzerland for adoption. Based on this study, the Federal Office of Justice should answer the questions raised in the Ruiz postulate.[28] The authors, including the author of this chapter, sorted through several thousand documents from competent authorities at the federal, cantonal, district and communal levels. These included entry permits, Interpol files, correspondence of the Swiss embassy in Colombo, files from the cantonal youth welfare offices, supervisory authorities, district court adoption orders and municipal guardianship files. They also included travel diaries kept by the adoptive parents and lists of expected gifts and tips for the helpers of the Swiss adoption agencies in Colombo. Numerous documents reveal a system of corruption, indicating how

26 S. Bitter, *Die Vermittlerin. Die Kinder-Adoptionen aus Sri Lanka von Alice Honegger und die Aufsicht der Behörden (1979 bis 1997). Bericht im Auftrag des Amts für Soziales des Departements des Innern des Kantons St. Gallen*, St. Gallen, 2019, p. 40, https://www.sg.ch/content/dam/sgch/gesundheit-soziales/soziales/familie/Adoptionen%20von%20Kindern%20aus%20Sri%20Lanka%20in%20den%20Jahren%201979%20bis%201997%20%E2%80%93%20Bericht%20von%20Sabine%20Bitter.pdf.

27 See https://www.hist.unibe.ch/unibe/portal/fak_historisch/dga/hist/content/e11168/e44569/e875636/e875637/pane875642/e1242049/Bericht_final_ger.pdf.

28 Bitter et al., 2020, pp. 7-11.

babies came to be transferred to Switzerland, how these processes were enmeshed in an international child trafficking network, and that several Swiss authorities were aware of what was going on. The research team also analysed a number of adoption rulings in the cantons of St. Gallen, Bern and Geneva to reveal massive legal violations. Children were given fictitious identities, changed hands in dubious procedures and were often brought to Switzerland without the necessary documentation, such as a declaration of consent from their birth parents. The study concluded that in many cases the adoptions from Sri Lanka were arranged under abusive and illegal circumstances.[29]

All of this happened even though pedagogical and legal experts at the time had criticized what was going on.[30] The authorities in Switzerland allowed the adoptions to take place despite alarming foreign media reports about the child trafficking in Sri Lanka and other countries of the global South. As early as 1982, the German weekly news magazine *Der Spiegel* described this 'baby transfer' as a 'variety of neo-colonialism' and aid for a single child as a "fig leaf for an inhumane world economic order". "When children are traded like coconuts or transistor radios, the self-confidence of the whole nation suffers," stated the newspaper, quoting the British news magazine *Asiaweek*. It also mentioned the UN delegate and Sri Lankan Foreign Minister Abdul Cader Shahul Hameed (1928-1999), who had already spoken of 'sugar-coated slavery' in 1977.[31] At that time, large swathes of the general public in Switzerland were also aware of the deplorable situation. A comprehensive investigation into child trafficking in Sri Lanka, entitled *Babys zu verkaufen* (Babies for Sale), had appeared in the widely circulating weekly *Schweizer Illustrierte*, which was available at practically every hairdresser's at the time.[32] Nevertheless, the authorities remained largely inactive, never undertaking a systematic examination of the adoption system and only interrupting the illegal practices once for a few months in the case of Alice Honegger.[33]

---

29 Ibid., pp. 136, 206.

30 J. Aebersold et al., *Adoption von aussereuropäischen Kindern im Kanton Bern. Eine Untersuchung bei Eltern, Fachstellen und Behörden über offene Fragen und auftretende Probleme*, Bern, 1984; Lücker-Babel, 1991; Zuegg, 1986; Zuegg, 1996.

31 See https://www.spiegel.de/politik/10-000-dollar-fuer-ein-baby-aus-kolumbien-a-5e9ea750-0002-0001-0000-000014348458?context=issue.

32 G. Zanetti, 'Babys zu verkaufen', *Schweizer Illustrierte*, 24 May 1982, p. 20.

33 Bitter, 2019, p. 10.

Case Studies

Illegal Adoptions through Accredited Adoption Agencies

The *ZHAW* study, co-written by the author of this chapter, is the most comprehensive analysis of Sri Lankan adoptions to date and relates to all of Switzerland. We sought both to reveal the structures of the adoption market in Colombo, in which Switzerland participated, mainly in the 1980s, and also to shed light on the origins of the people who came to be adopted illegally and are still suffering today.

P. N., for example, was born on 6 September 1982 in the North General Hospital in Ragama, a suburb of the capital city of Colombo.[34] She was one of 955 children brought to Switzerland from Sri Lanka between 1974 and 1999, most of them for adoption.[35] According to a document issued, the 38-year-old mother signed a declaration before a court notary on the day she gave birth, relinquishing her parental rights. This declaration, called an affidavit, was written in Latin script and in English. The mother's signature is in Sinhala script next to the passage that would change the lives of mother and child: "Read over, explained to and affirmed at Colombo on this 6th day of September 1982 by the affirmant."[36] Two weeks later, on 20 September, P. N. was handed over in a district court to a couple who had travelled from Switzerland. Who exactly handed the child over to her adoptive parents is not clear from the documents. Just four days later, on 24 September, the little girl landed in Switzerland.[37]

P. N. was placed for adoption by the Swiss social worker Alice Honegger (1915-1997). Honegger ran an adoption agency in Bollingen in the canton of St. Gallen – in the vicinity of Zurich, Switzerland's largest city. In Sri Lanka, she worked with Rukmani Thavanesan-Fernando, whom she called her 'trusted lawyer'.[38] Agencies had to obtain special accreditation from the supervisory authority for an intercountry adoption placement. The agent was also required to be well informed about conditions in the children's country of origin and to comply with international law.[39] Alice Honegger had the necessary accreditation from the cantonal authority and was officially recognized as adoption placement agent throughout Switzerland.

---

34 Birth register extract dated 9.9.1982, adoption file of P.N., disclosed to author, e-mail dated 3 May 2022.

35 Statistical Service, Central Aliens' Register, Federal Office for Migration: Entry permits issued to foreign foster children by citizenship, 1970 to 1979, 1980 to 1989, 1990 to 1999.

36 Affidavit dated 6 September 1982, adoption file of P. N., disclosed to author, e-mail dated 3 May 2022.

37 This is evident from a document issued two years later: Confirmation of residence dated 31 July 1984, Adoption file of P. N., disclosed to author, e-mail of 3 May 2022.

38 Bitter et al., 2020, p. 74.

39 Ordinance of 28 March 1973 on Placements with a view to Adoption, Art. 5, para. 1c, effective 16 April 1973.

When P. N. was placed by Alice Honegger with a couple from the canton of St. Gallen in 1982, provisions had long been in place under Swiss adoption law for the protection of mother and child. Under Swiss law, a mother had to wait at least six weeks before consenting to the adoption of her child. The law also provided for a further six weeks during which she had the right to revoke her decision.[40] It did not specify whether these rules also applied to mothers who had a child abroad and gave it up for adoption in Switzerland, and the question arose neither at the time P. N. was handed over nor when she entered Switzerland. This is an astonishing omission for two reasons. First, children had been brought to Switzerland for adoption from numerous non-European countries since the 1960s. Second, amendments to the legislation on adoption had come into force on 1 April 1973. There would have been time to address problematic gaps and grey areas in the law regarding international adoptions and regulate them appropriately. At the very least, a procedure could have been established to fill in the gaps in the legal provisions, which would have offered more protection to mothers and children in other countries.

Sri Lankan adoption rulings were not legally recognized in Switzerland. Children brought to Switzerland for adoption were initially placed in foster care with their future adoptive parents for a minimum of two years. In the case of P. N., in the summer of 1984, the competent district court in the canton of St. Gallen examined the Sri Lankan documents. The district court did not inquire about the fact that a mother had signed an affidavit giving up her child on the day she gave birth, or at least the date on this document received no mention or comment in the adoption file. If the date is correct, the mother must have signed the affidavit shortly before or after giving birth. If she signed it just before birth, there must have been some urgent reason. Was it a condition for receiving medical care? Would the child have to be taken away directly after the birth and if so, why? If the signing took place after birth, how was the mother able to sign a document in the presence of a notary on the same day in the wake of such a physically and emotionally demanding experience? Did the notary come to the delivery room, or was she taken to him just after giving birth? Either situation would have been terribly difficult for the mother – although apparently not worth enquiring about in Switzerland.

A complete examination of the documents in P. N.'s file shows that the authorities overlooked several serious irregularities. The documents show, for example, that the local authority whose responsibility it was to assess the foster parents' suitability before the child was placed in their care was biased. He was the employer of the prospective adoptive father. The prospective father was the secretary of the guardianship authority.

40 Swiss Civil Code of 1973, Art. 265b, paras. 1 and 2.

A critical assessment of the family situation of the future parents would therefore have entailed a conflict of interest. The guardian, who was legally obliged to represent the rights of the child, was also biased. He was a family relative.[41] A network of relationships thus formed the backdrop to P. N.'s placement. The decision maker and the person whose job it was to oversee the process were a work colleague and a relative – a relationship of mutual obligation existed between them. This means that the child may not have had anyone on her side to examine the fostering and adoption relationship in an independent, unbiased manner.

Especially scandalous was the fact that P. N. was handed over to her future adoptive parents in September 1982, at a moment when the social worker Alice Honegger was no longer authorized to act as an agent in bringing children from Sri Lanka to Switzerland. The cantonal supervisory authority, the St. Gallen Department of Justice and Police, had withdrawn her accreditation and explicitly ordered her to stop working with Rukmani Thavanesan-Fernando.[42] The authorities had been aware, since 1981, of the prevalence of child trafficking in the Sri Lankan adoption system. The Sri Lankan daily newspaper *The Sun* had reported that among the 800 or so children given up for adoption abroad every year, less than ten per cent of the placements occurred in legal circumstances.[43] Asoka Karunaratne (1916-1988), the Minister of Social Services at the time, admitted that the laws in Sri Lanka were inadequate and described himself as 'helpless' to stem the trafficking.[44] Given that 138 children entered Switzerland from Sri Lanka in 1981 alone, the Swiss authorities were aware that Switzerland was an important destination country and thus caught up in the trafficking.[45]

Claude Ochsenbein, chargé d'affaires at the Swiss embassy in Colombo, collected the newspaper reports on child trafficking that were being published in Sri Lanka and sent them to the Swiss Federal Aliens' Office (SFAO) in Bern. He also conducted his own investigation and recorded what he found in a report dated early May 1982. The report described for the Bern authorities how child trafficking was organized in Colombo and its links to Switzerland. At around the same time, several people in Switzerland who were interested in adopting a child in Sri Lanka complained about Alice Honegger's conduct and business practices in Colombo and demanded that the Swiss authorities investigate her and her activities.[46] It was only when a Zurich daily paper revealed Switzerland's

41 Statement by P. N., e-mail to author, 9 May 2022.

42 Bitter, 2019, p. 10.

43 Press campaign with various newspaper articles on child trafficking in Sri Lanka, in *The Sun*, 1-3 December 1981.

44 A. Karunaratne, quoted in *The Sun*, 3 December 1981.

45 Statistical Service, Central Aliens' Register, Federal Office for Migration: Entry permits issued to foreign foster children by citizenship, 1980 to 1989.

46 Bitter, 2019, p. 39.

direct involvement in international baby trafficking from Sri Lanka that the cantonal supervisory authority felt compelled to act. It was at this moment that the St. Gallen Department of Justice and Police withdrew Alice Honegger's accreditation as an agent authorized to arrange the placement in Switzerland of Sri Lankan children. Despite the legally binding order to stop, she continued under the nose of the cantonal supervisory authority to place Sri Lankan children with Swiss families.[47] On 24 September 1982, four days after the court hearing in Colombo, the prospective adoptive parents of P. N. were able to fly back to Switzerland with the illegally arranged baby.

In addition to Alice Honegger in the canton of St. Gallen, the Lausanne-based child welfare organization *Terre des hommes* in the canton of Vaud was also active in Sri Lanka for a time without authorization. *Terre des hommes* operated in Colombo without accreditation from the cantonal supervisory authority. Edmond Kaiser, the organization's founder and head spoke of wanting to bring 'orphans' and 'abandoned children' to Switzerland. His choice of words suggested that the Sri Lankan children had neither any parents nor anyone else who could take care of them. It was easy for couples seeking children to assume that these children had no one to claim them. The fact that *Terre des hommes* was operating in Sri Lanka without an official permit and, thus, in breach of the law was both sanctioned and legitimized by the cantonal supervisory authority, which retroactively issued the organization with the necessary accreditation.[48]

'Independent' Adoptions

Several people who had never been accredited in Switzerland were active in the placement of Sri Lankan children. They included Maria Elisabeth Cornelia Koran-Van der Hoorn aka Ries Koran. In 1977, it came to the attention of the Federal Aliens' Police that she had placed 18 children from Sri Lanka with families in the canton of Zurich. Ries Koran had never possessed the required accreditation from the competent authority, the Zurich Cantonal Youth Welfare Office. The Federal Office of Justice, which investigated the case, concluded that she was a Swiss extension of the Dutch placement agency Kasih Bunda,[49] an organization which had been involved in abusive and illegal activities.[50]

Another major figure in the transfer of babies from Sri Lanka to Switzerland was Dawn de Silva, who had been arranging the placement of Sri Lankan children in Swiss

47 Bitter et al., 2020, p. 225.
48 Ibid., pp. 84-92.
49 Ibid., pp. 106-109.
50 COIA, 'Rapport Commissie Onderzoek Interlandelijke Adoptie', The Hague, February 2021, pp. 86-88.

families since as early as 1974.[51] How many in total is not yet known. The author of this chapter has registered at least 40 cases in files in the Swiss Federal Archives and in different cantonal archives. Dawn de Silva ran both a travel agency in Sri Lanka and a guesthouse on the west coast in Wadduwa – the hotel *Strand Cabanas*. Attached to this was a building where women kept babies ready for interested hotel guests. De Silva was assisted by her husband. According to a report by the German Bundestag in 1990, he was a former dentist whom the police in the Federal Republic of Germany had been seeking without success:

> Weißgerber obviously had good connections with high-ranking public figures – and presumably the protection that came with this. In early 1987, his whereabouts remained unknown. For this reason, the competent German public prosecutor's office had not filed an extradition request for Weißgerber, who was wanted by Interpol for property and fraud offences. He was suspected to have absconded to Kenya (Nairobi) under his wife's name ('de Silva'), possibly with a Sri Lankan passport. Since then, the Embassy has heard nothing more of him – not even in newspaper reports.[52]

In Switzerland, in 1986, the couple was able to advertise freely although they were wanted by Interpol. They offered their placement services to the Cantonal Youth Welfare Office of the canton of Vaud. In his dealings with the authority, the German dentist used the slightly altered name 'Weissgärber'.[53] The *Strand Cabanas* and guests from Germany, the Netherlands and Switzerland were discovered in a raid by the Sri Lankan police in early 1987.[54] Dawn de Silva was arrested, while it seems her husband escaped. Twenty women, who had been staying with 22 babies in a separate building in the adjacent compound, were questioned. The police recorded their statements:

51 Bitter, 2019, p. 44, 45, 71.

52 Report of the German Bundestag, Response of the federal government to the major interpellation of Member of Parliament Schmidt (Hamburg), and The Greens parliamentary group, '*Zum Problem privater und kommerzieller Adoptionsvermittlung in der Bundesrepublik Deutschland (Kinderhandel)*', 7 July 1990, p. 35. See also several newspaper-articles: K. Somaratne, 'Interpol Report on German Dentist. Dutch Couples Take Custody of 4 Babies', *Daily News*, 3 February 1987, further AFP, 'Deutscher Zahnarzt als Hauptdrahtzieher', *Volksrecht*, 26 January 1987 and Reuters, 'Europäer an Babyhandel beteiligt', 26 January 1987. These reports blame 'German dentist Willy Weissgerber and his local wife Dawn de Silva' for the trafficking. These articles are part of a collection of newspaper articles in the Swiss federal Archive and are listed in: Bitter et al., 2020, p. 124 and 126.

53 Bitter et al., 2020, p. 105.

54 Ibid., p. 122.

> Several women who were arrested during the raid have told police they were forced to have sexual relations with foreigners who visited the guest house where the farm was operating.[55]

Dawn de Silva was released on bail, "presumably as a result of protection".[56]

In 1977, a number of civil servants had already raised the alarm about Swiss couples in Sri Lanka having been given or having had a child flown to Switzerland without the involvement of a Swiss placement agency accredited and supervised by a competent authority. The extent of the baby trafficking remained unknown, however. When, in 1984, adoption specialist and lawyer Cyril Hegnauer asked the SFAO how many children had arrived in Switzerland in this way so far, he was told that the authority had not kept any statistics.[57]

Adoptive mother Marie-Ines Suter-Widmer describes what an 'independent' adoption may have looked like in her autobiographical report *Ruwan – The Jewel: Adoption in the Tropical Paradise of Sri Lanka*. In the book, she recounts how, in 1996, she received a child through an aunt who ran a guesthouse on a beach in Sri Lanka. Recalling the message from her aunt that led to the adoption, she writes:

> Last night, a Sinhalese woman brought her newborn child to our house. She is looking for parents to give him a new home. Would you take the baby in? He's a lovely child.[58]

Marie-Ines Suter-Widmer immediately faxed her aunt and agreed to take in the baby. In another passage, she describes how a German couple in the neighbourhood of the guesthouse came to receive a child. The man had impregnated a young Sri Lankan girl so as to obtain as light-skinned a child as possible for himself and his wife. The author writes:

> Hämelate's daughter Rada was chosen as the surrogate mother. Of course, the child would not be conceived artificially but by natural insemination, he explained. A short time later, Rada was pregnant. After the birth, Hanne, the German woman, would raise the child as its mother, and Rada would be much

55 A. Tillekeratne and H. W. Abeypala, 'Officials Uncover Plans to Breed "superbabies"', *The Sun*, 22 January 1987, front page and p. 16.

56 Report of the German Bundestag, 1990, p. 35.

57 Bitter et al., 2020, p. 99.

58 M.-I. Suter-Widmer, *Ruwan – das Juwel. Adoption im Tropenparadies Sri Lanka*, Frankfurt a. M., R. G. Fischer, 2008, p. 13.

> richer. That was the plan of the two families. Plans for the future sometimes come together according to their own laws.[59]

A young woman is raped, and her body is exploited to produce a baby. She has to go through pregnancy and childbirth under these circumstances to give birth to a child so that it can be taken away from her and sold. The lack of critique and self-reflection with which the author describes such abuse is difficult to comprehend, as it appears to suggest that a violent assault and the theft of a baby were merely a matter of course. The 'own laws' that the author sees at work here are those of sexism, racism and social discrimination. Nevertheless, her book was published in Germany in 2008 and was well received in Switzerland.[60]

Authorities Comment on the Revelations

Government Expresses Regret

While the first academic research was under way, adoptees and journalists were carrying out their own investigations in Sri Lanka.[61] These revealed the cancer of an unscrupulous system characterized by profit-seeking, corruption and abuses of power. The Federal Council took a position on the matter in December 2020 in its response to the postulate of parliamentarian Rebecca Ruiz. It acknowledged the shortcomings revealed thus far, namely that the Swiss authorities had not prevented adoptions from Sri Lanka despite having been alerted to the problem early on and despite the clear indications of illegal practices prevailing there. It expressed regret that neither the federal government nor the cantons had fulfilled their duty to protect the children. For this reason, it stated, it was prepared to provide greater support to those who had been brought to Switzerland for adoption in this period and who were seeking information about their origins. A working group with representatives from the federal government, the cantons and private-sector organizations, in addition to adoptees, would look into possible measures. In addition, the scope of historical investigations into illegal adoptions in Switzerland was to be broadened in order to find out if there were any indications of systematic irregularities in adoptions from other countries. It would be advisable for a group of

---

59 Ibid., p. 159.

60 Radio programme 'Geschichte einer geglückten Adoption', *Siesta, Swiss Radio DRS 1*, 29 July 2008.

61 See https://www.srf.ch/news/international/adoptionsbetrug-in-sri-lanka-wir-hoffen-einfach-wirklich-unsere-familien-zu-finden and https://pages.rts.ch/emissions/temps-present/9787679-les-bebes-voles-du-sri-lanka-un-scan-%20dale-suisse.html. See also https://www.nzz.ch/schweiz/adoptionsbetrug-in-sri-lanka-die-babyluege-ld.1460678?reduced=true and https://www.srf.ch/play/tv/dok/video/illegal-adoptiert---der-handel-mit-adoptivkindern-aus-sri-lanka-und-dem-libanon?urn=urn:srf:video:f61a4aea-0a9a-412c-8394-12ca41fd7fd2.

experts to examine the current adoption system. Should this reveal any irregularities, the Federal Council would propose amendments to the law.[62]

Regret But No Apology

The fact that the Swiss government expressed its 'regret' but failed to offer an apology initially raised eyebrows, because the government had apologized more than once in the past for other abuses in connection with the placement of children. In 1986, for example, the Federal Council had apologized to those who had been harmed by the *Kinder der Landstrasse* (Children of the Road) project of the organization *Pro Juventute.* Families who lived as travellers and thus had no fixed abode were systematically torn apart by this organization between 1926 and 1973. In 586 documented cases, *Pro Juventute* removed children from their families and placed them in homes.[63] Fifty years ago, the magazine *Beobachter* had drawn attention to this discriminatory practice, which was supported by the welfare authorities. The revelations brought to light a great deal of violence and abuse, resulting in the dismantling of the organization.[64]

In 2013, the Federal Council, representatives of the authorities, churches, welfare institutions and the Swiss Farmers' Union collectively issued apologies to the victims of what was known as 'compulsory measures'.[65] These were children and adolescents identified as 'at risk' and having been taken away from their parents because they were poor, born into unconventional or difficult family circumstances, illegitimate, or who behaved in a way that was considered socially unacceptable.[66] Right up to 1981, they were sent to work on farms or forcibly placed in foster families or homes. Juveniles were sent to prison without having committed any offence. Women who became pregnant out of wedlock were forcibly sterilized, obliged to have an abortion or coerced into adopting their child. Children and adults alike were used for drug trials without their consent.[67] All this occurred in the context of a consolidating welfare state in the 20th century, in an effort to dissuade people from undesirable ways of life.

---

62 See 'Illegale Adoptionen von Kindern aus Sri Lanka: Historische Aufarbeitung, Herkunftssuche, Perspektiven', Report of the Federal Council in response to postulate 17.4181 Ruiz Rebecca of 14 December 2017, Bern, 11 December 2020. See: https://www.newsd.admin.ch/newsd/message/attachments/81430.pdf

63 See https://hls-dhs-dss.ch/de/articles/016627/2012-01-12/.

64 Ibid and https://www.beobachter.ch/administrativ-versorgte/kinder-der-landstrasse-die-kinderdiebe-der-pro-juventute.

65 See https://www.admin.ch/gov/de/start/dokumentation/medienmitteilungen.msg-id-48480.html.

66 B. Ziegler, G. Hauss and M. Lengwiler (eds.), *Zwischen Erinnerung und Aufarbeitung. Fürsorgerische Zwangsmassnahmen an Minderjährigen in der Schweiz im 20. Jahrhundert*, Zürich, Chronos, 2018, p. 19.

67 M. Meier, M. König and T. Magaly, *Testfall Münsterlingen. Klinische Versuche in der Psychiatrie, 1940-1980*, Zurich, Chronos, 2019.

The first investigations into these systematic abuses in the Swiss welfare system all follow a similar pattern: Pressure from victims and critical public debate instigated the historical reappraisal of the practices.[68] This triggered inquiries and debate on possible reparations. In the end, around 9,000 victims of the compulsory social measures and forcible removal of children from their families were able to claim a 'solidarity contribution' amounting to a maximum of CHF 25,000 per person.[69]

The research to date on the Sri Lankan adoptions has found that here, too, children were in many cases placed in foster families in illegal and abusive circumstances. Couples and families in Switzerland benefitted from this to fulfil their desire to have a child. All those adopted under such circumstances as children now have to deal with burdensome gaps in their biographies. Some of those affected criticize the fact that the Federal Council, then represented by the head of the Federal Department of Justice and Police, Federal Councillor Karin Keller-Sutter, used the word 'regret' with reference to the abusive adoptions and not 'apology'.[70] Back to the Roots, however, welcomes the fact that at the end of 2020, the country became the first state to officially admit to wrongdoing in connection with adoptions from Sri Lanka and to pledge support. For the adoptees in Switzerland, this is an important step at the start of a joint process to come to terms with what has happened.[71]

Authorities Support Individuals in the Search for their Origins

Publication of a List of Addresses and Advisory Services

Searching their origins has proven very time-consuming and expensive for adoptees. In Switzerland's federal system, it can be difficult even to find out which authority was involved in the placement and adoption process at which level. The competent municipal authority in the family's place of residence was responsible for assessing the social and financial circumstances of the prospective family, for example, whereas the adoption agency was under the purview of the cantonal authority. If a child arrived from Sri Lanka, the SFAO was responsible for issuing the entry permit, but it was the job of the cantonal immigration police to grant a residence permit. Before the child could even enter the

68 Ziegler et al., 2018, p. 19.

69 See https://www.bj.admin.ch/bj/de/home/gesellschaft/fszm.html.

70 See https://www.nzz.ch/schweiz/adoptionen-sri-lanka-bundesrat-bedauert-versagen-der-behoerden-ld.1591949?reduced=true.

71 Back to the Roots press release dated 14 December 2020, 'Schweiz anerkennt als erstes Land Verfehlungen bei Adoptionen aus Sri Lanka'.

country, however, the Swiss representation in Colombo had to issue a visa in consultation with the SFAO. And, finally, for the adoption to be officially recognized following a two-year compulsory foster care period, a judicial authority had to issue an adoption order. In the canton of St. Gallen, for example, a district court ruled in adoption cases. To make matters worse, the names of the competent authorities can vary from canton to canton, and the authority may have gone by a different name at the time of the adoption. For the inexperienced, it is therefore very difficult to gain an overview of who was responsible for what and who holds which records and thus to locate documents pertaining to one's origins within a reasonable time. For adoptees, it implies a Kafkaesque journey through various offices, archives and institutions to gather fragments of their past. The Federal Office of Justice responded to criticism of this situation by compiling a list of contacts and advisory services in the various cantons.[72]

This measure can be seen as another step by the Swiss authorities to deal with the past in respect of illegal intercountry adoptions. Providing a list of contacts may seem like a simple and practical step. However, some of the addresses and advisory services on the list are offices whose duty it was to supervise adoption agencies in their canton in the 1980s and 1990s. As evidenced in St. Gallen, some of them had failed to perform this duty adequately. Not all of the offices that appear on the list published by the Federal Office of Justice can therefore be described as 'neutral'. The design of this measure thus falls short of the Federal Council's initial promise to "designate, if possible, a neutral contact point for adopted persons", as it had stated in its response to the interpellation by parliamentarian Flavia Wasserfallen.[73] The establishment of a centralized service, unencumbered by previous misconduct and shortcomings and apt to assume this important task on behalf of the adoptees, would represent an important step.

Safeguarding of Records from Private Archives

Records pertaining to children brought to Switzerland for adoption are to be found not only in the archives of various authorities of the Swiss federal system but also in those of private placement agencies. There are specific provisions for the storage and retention of these records under Swiss law. A placement agency must create and keep a file of documents pertaining to each child it places with foster or prospective adoptive parents. It must hand over these documents to the cantonal supervisory authority, at the latest when it ceases operations. The agency must also disclose these documents to

---

72 The list is available at https://www.bj.admin.ch/dam/bj/de/data/gesellschaft/adoption/herkunftssuche/zustaendigkeiten.pdf.download.pdf/zustaendigkeiten.pdf.

73 See https://www.parlament.ch/de/ratsbetrieb/suche-curia-vista/geschaeft?AffairId=20203677.

the cantonal supervisory authority and to the Federal Office of Justice whenever it is ordered to do so.[74] Agencies often fail to fulfil this legal requirement in practice, however. The documents on the 160 Tibetan children that the entrepreneur Charles Aeschimann placed with adoptive parents in the 1960s remained in the family's archives for decades.[75] Only after long and tough negotiations with the cantonal authorities for the board of the Adoption Foundation, did the organization, which succeeded Alice Honegger's adoption agency, agree to hand over 253 dossiers on adoptive families so that they could be transferred to the state archives of the canton of St. Gallen.[76]

Collaboration with Sri Lanka

In 2018, in the aftermath of the initial shockwave unleashed by the Dutch TV documentary, Switzerland set up a group with members from several European states (the Flemish Community of Belgium, Denmark, France, Germany, the Netherlands, Norway and Sweden) to agree on a cooperation protocol with Sri Lanka, setting out the procedure to be followed by the authorities in the receiving countries and in Sri Lanka, so that the adoptees can rely on a recognized and transparent procedure in their search for origin.[77] The protocol would also apply to adoptions that had taken place before the Hague Convention came into force in Switzerland in 2003.[78] In order to draft a protocol on cooperation, the group met in January 2018 in Geneva with International Social Service Switzerland and representatives of the central government authority in Sri Lanka responsible for adoptions, the Department of Probation and Child Care Services. In July 2019, a delegation from the Federal Office of Justice also travelled to Sri Lanka for a working visit. With the Sri Lankan Department of Probation and Child Care Services it clarified the procedure for those searching for their origins and in the following months drew up the protocol.[79] The delegation also noted, however, that the meeting with the Office for Missing Persons in Sri Lanka did not "reveal any prospects for effective support by this office" since this authority was a newly created body whose remit was limited to 'enforced disappearances' during the civil war.[80] Although many

---

74 Ordinance of 29 June 2011 on Adoption, Art. 19, paras. 1-3 (see https://fedlex.data.admin.ch/filestore/fedlex.data.admin.ch/eli/cc/2011/505/20120101/de/pdf-a/fedlex-data-admin-ch-eli-cc-2011-505-20120101-de-pdf-a.pdf).

75 Bitter and Nad-Abonji, 2018, p. 15.

76 Press release of the Department of the Interior of the Canton of St. Gallen 'Files on Sri Lanka adoptions better available', 27 February 2020. See: https://www.sg.ch/news/sgch_allgemein/2020/02/akten-zu-sri-lanka-adoptionen-besser-verfuegbar.html

77 See Protocol: Search of origin process in Sri Lanka, in: https://www.bj.admin.ch/bj/en/home/gesellschaft/adoption/illegale-adoptionen.html.

78 See https://www.fedlex.admin.ch/eli/cc/2003/99/de.

79 See https://www.bj.admin.ch/bj/en/home/gesellschaft/adoption/illegale-adoptionen.html.

80 See Report of the Federal Council in response to postulate 17.4181 Ruiz Rebecca, 11 December 2020, p. 31.

of the adoptions from Sri Lanka took place during the armed conflict in Sri Lanka between 1983 and 2009, the research to date on the placement of Sri Lankan children in Switzerland has not identified a clear link between the civil war and the sending of babies – or war orphans – to Western countries. Why the removal of children from Sri Lanka in illegal circumstances without the knowledge of their biological parents should not be considered by the Office for Missing Persons as enforced disappearance is unclear.

Against this backdrop, the protocol for cooperation with Sri Lanka is not likely to be of much use to adoptees seeking their origins. Of the first 14 applications forwarded on the basis of the cooperation protocol to the Department of Probation and Child Care Services in Colombo, only three applications could be deemed 'closed' by the end of 2020. In no case were the biological parents found. In the meantime, one of the three persons has managed to find her biological mother by herself.[81]

Official Pilot Project

Searching for their origins is a psychologically difficult and stressful process for those affected. It is also expensive. Applicants seeking their origins incur processing fees and costs for the translation of documents, travelling, DNA tests and interpreting services. At the start of the process to deal with the issue of illegal adoptions, few cantons were willing to contribute financially to such expenses.[82]

In recent years, adoptees have expressed criticism of the fact that they have to bear the bulk of the costs themselves, and the authorities have also come to recognize this as unacceptable. The Conference of Cantonal Justice and Police Directors took a stance in December 2021 announcing it would provide funding to Back to the Roots to enable it to assist adoptees in their search for their origins. Funding from the cantons and the Confederation will enable Back to the Roots to expand its current support services over three years.[83] In May 2022, an agreement to this effect was signed in Bern by Federal Councillor and head of the Federal Department of Justice and Police, Karin Keller-Sutter, Cantonal Council member and President of the Conference of Cantonal Justice and Police Director, Fredy Fässler, and Sarah Ramani Ineichen, Chair of Back to the Roots. During the three-year pilot starting in 2022, the association will assume the task of helping people brought to Switzerland for adoption between the 1970s and

81 Ibid., p. 31.
82 Ibid., p. 31.
83 Press release '*Adoptionen aus Sri Lanka: Die KKJPD beschliesst erste konkrete Unterstützungsmassnahmen für adoptierte Personen aus Sri Lanka*' of the Conference of Cantonal Justice and Police Directors, 9 December 2021.

1990s to discover their origins. Specifically, it will explain the possibilities and limits of such a search and inform them of the procedures and responsibilities of the various authorities. Adoptees will also receive assistance in obtaining information and in locating and examining records, both in Switzerland and in Sri Lanka. The adoptees will also be supported in their efforts to locate people in Sri Lanka. They can request private tracing services, for instance, of the International Social Service or the Swiss Red Cross.[84] These services will be funded by the Confederation and the cantons to a maximum of CHF 250,000 per year based on the actual costs incurred.[85] Switzerland's funding of such a pilot project is an important step in providing redress for the abusive and illegal adoptions of Sri Lankan children. According to the chair of Back to the Roots, this support is a great achievement for the civil society initiative, which was established only in 2018:

> We are immensely proud of this great milestone and are delighted that so much trust has been placed in us. We will continue on this same path and will not stop asking the necessary questions.[86]

Committed Initiative Back to the Roots

Reuniting Mother and Child

From the start, one of the aims of Back to the Roots has been to give adoptees from Sri Lanka the support they need to research their origins so that they can clarify their ancestry and identity and probably find their biological mothers. To this end, the association launched a project in 2019 to enable mothers in Sri Lanka and children in Switzerland to provide DNA samples. To draw the attention of women in Sri Lanka to these efforts, Back to the Roots published advertisements in newspapers and online in the capital Colombo. Women who respond to an advertisement and are interested in taking a DNA test are informed about the procedure by a trustworthy person who speaks their language. If the woman wishes, this can lead to an in-depth exchange in a safe, quiet environment, such as the grounds of a temple. So far, 40 mothers searching for their children have taken advantage of this offer to talk. 'I want to see my child again before I die', says Chandrawathi Vithanage, for example.[87]

84 See *'Illegale Adoptionen von Kindern aus Sri Lanka: Historische Aufarbeitung, Herkunftssuche, Perspektiven'*, Report of the Federal Council in response to postulate 17.4181 Ruiz Rebecca of 14 December 2017, Bern, 11 December 2020, p. 25.

85 See https://www.ejpd.admin.ch/ejpd/en/home/latest-news/mm.msg-id-88825.html.

86 See https://backtotheroots.net/.

87 See https://backtotheroots.net/mother-and-child-reunion-in-sri-lanka/.

The association provides the DNA tests free of charge. So far, 70 mothers have made use of them. The samples are deposited in the Texas-based international database Family Tree. Several hundred DNA samples from women looking for their children are registered in this database. So far, there have been twelve DNA matches between Sri Lankan mothers and children in Switzerland.[88] Back to the Roots can now step up this project aiming to reunite mothers and children thanks to financial support from the Confederation and cantons for 2022 to 2024.

Inclusion of Adoptees from India

In the few years since its launch, Back to the Roots has made a great deal of progress on behalf of the adoptees from Sri Lanka, playing an active role in these early academic and political efforts to investigate and shed light on the story of irregular and illegal adoptions. It has successfully advocated for the interests of the adoptees, resulting in the three-year pilot to aid adoptees in the search for their origins.

Since 2021, the association has also advocated for adoptees from India. The reason is that adoptees brought to Switzerland from India have also contacted the association and asked for help in seeking their origins. A first meeting was held in spring 2022.[89] The inclusion of adoptees from India is likely to be important both for those seeking their origins and to further efforts to deal with the issue of intercountry adoptions. India was the main country of origin of adopted children for Switzerland in the last three decades of the 20th century. From 1970 to 1999, 2,799 children from India received an entry permit, most of them for the purpose of adoption. This means that almost three times more visas were issued for Indian children during this period than for the 955 registered children from Sri Lanka.[90] In Switzerland, Zurich was one of the main receiving cantons of Indian children in the last third of the 20th century. In July 2022, the cantons of Zurich and Thurgau commissioned a first study focusing on adoptions from India.[91]

---

88 Recorded interview with S. R. Ineichen, Chair of Back to the Roots, 27 April 2022.

89 See https://backtotheroots.net/adoptierten-treffen-fuer-adoptierte-personen-aus-indien-12-maerz-2022-2/.

90 See Bundesamt für Migration BFM, Zentrales Ausländerregister, Statistikdienst, Entry permits issued to foreign foster children by citizenship, admitted with a view to subsequent adoption or for other reasons, 1970 to 1979, 1980 to 1989, and 1990 to 1999.

91 See https://www.zh.ch/de/news-uebersicht/medientmitteilungen/2022/07/auslandadoptionen-in-den-kantonen-zuerich-und-thurgau-eltern-fuer-kinder-oder-kinder-fuer-eltern.html.

Complaint to the UN Committee on Enforced Disappearances

As well as extending its efforts to another country of origin, Back to the Roots took a further step towards addressing the issue of illegal intercountry adoption in February 2021, when it approached the UN Committee on Enforced and Forced Disappearances.[92] In view of the many coercive, abusive and violent circumstances, in which Sri Lankan children were taken abroad for adoption, Back to the Roots argues that adoptees who are taken from their families and who disappeared abroad under a false identity, without a trace, should be covered by the International Convention for the Protection of All Persons from Enforced Disappearance (see Chapters 10 and 11).[93] In Sri Lanka, birth mothers were pressured to sign an affidavit that they did not understand. Back to the Roots is aware of 12 cases in which women were made to believe their newborn baby had died, when in fact it had been placed in the care of prospective parents in Switzerland by an intermediary in the child trafficking network.[94] Lies, fraud, false identities, unidentifiable signatures and the label of 'abandoned child' severed any connection of these children to their parents, to the extent that parent and child were made to disappear entirely from each other's lives and retained nothing of each other's existence.

The International Convention for the Protection of All Persons from Enforced Disappearance has been in force in Switzerland since 2017. Switzerland thus recognizes the competence of the Committee on Enforced Disappearances to receive and consider both inter-state and individual communications.[95] Individuals or their relatives in Switzerland who believe their rights protected under the Convention to have been violated can thus submit their concerns to the committee for examination. The UN Committee examined the concerns communicated by Back to the Roots about the protection of the rights of persons in connection with enforced disappearance. The outcome of this review was a report published in May 2021. In some passages, the report comments specifically on adoptions from Sri Lanka. It notes that Switzerland has recognized that, in some cases, illegal adoptions could be the result of enforced disappearance. It also notes the Federal Council's acknowledgement of Switzerland's failings and the regret it has expressed towards the adoptees and their families. The UN Committee further acknowledged that the Federal Council plans to undertake a broader analysis of the situation regarding intercountry adoption in Switzerland.[96]

92 See https://backtotheroots.net/ein-weiterer-wichtiger-meilenstein/ and see https://backtotheroots.net/un-experten-nehmen-stellung-zu-den-illegalen-interstaatlichen-adoptionen/ and see https://backtotheroots.net/back-to-the-roots-und-die-un/.

93 See https://www.ohchr.org/sites/default/files/disappearance-convention.pdf.

94 Recorded voice message from S.R. Ineichen, 25 May 2022.

95 See https://www.fedlex.admin.ch/eli/cc/2016/757/de.

96 UN Committee on Enforced Disappearances: 'Concluding observations on the report submitted by Switzerland under article 29 (1) of the Convention', 21 May 2021.

The Committee expressed concern, however, about Switzerland's treatment of adoptees from Sri Lanka, who have encountered difficulties obtaining information about their origins. It also said it was concerned that Switzerland did not appear to be taking steps to prosecute the perpetrators of the offences and in this sense to recognize and fulfil the victims' right to reparation. It urged Switzerland to conduct thorough and impartial investigations to determine whether children adopted in Sri Lanka during the 1980s and 1990s were victims of enforced disappearance and whether other offences had been committed, with a view to identifying and punishing the perpetrators of such offences. It also urged Switzerland to identify the victims and provide them with the support needed to establish their identity and parentage and to guarantee their right to reparation. Finally, the UN Committee invited Switzerland to review the definition of 'enforced disappearance' in the Swiss Criminal Code to ensure that it is in full conformity with that contained in the Convention.[97] Back to the Roots followed up on the Committee's May 2021 report three months later in a letter to the Federal Office of Justice. It asked the Federal Office to specifically examine cases in which children were placed for adoption in uncertain circumstances with regard to the criminal offence of enforced disappearance.[98] A reply was still pending in May 2023.

Conclusion

The process to investigate and confront problematic and illegal adoption practices began in 2017 in the wake of the investigative report of the Dutch documentary series *Zembla*, which gave rise to several parliamentary questions at the federal and cantonal levels. Since then, the Swiss state has taken the first important steps to deal with the issue of illegal intercountry adoptions. In December 2020, in response to a report it commissioned, the Swiss government officially expressed its regret to the individuals brought to Switzerland from Sri Lanka in illegal circumstances. In view of the findings, the government acknowledged the need to examine both past and current adoption procedures and the practices of adoption agents also in the case of children from other countries of origin. Switzerland has not yet answered the fundamental question of whether it can guarantee today that children in intercountry adoption arrangements are no longer trafficked. There is little public debate on the issue. One reason for this could be the number of intercountry adoptions, which has fallen sharply from 246 children in 2011 to 41 in 2021.[99]

---

97 Ibid.

98 Letter '*Bericht des UNO-Ausschusses gegen das Verschwindenlassen vom 11. Mai 2021*' by S.R. Ineichen, Back to the Roots, to the Federal Office of Justice, 16 August 2021, disclosed to author.

99 Statistics on the entry of children to Switzerland in the context of an intercountry adoption procedure, available at https://www.bj.admin.ch/bj/de/home/suche.html#statistik%20internationale%20Adoption.

The first academic research into intercountry adoptions coincided with the start of the political movement to address the issue. In addition to the 2020 report by the Zurich University of Applied Sciences, two further studies were commissioned as part of a National Research Programme of the Swiss National Science Foundation. St. Gallen was the first canton to commission research to investigate adoptions from Sri Lanka. The canton also secured the transfer of pertinent records from the private archive of adoption agent Alice Honegger to the public archives (the State Archives of the Canton of St. Gallen). The cantons of Zurich and Thurgau followed suit and, in July 2022, took the first step towards addressing the issue by commissioning a research project on the adoption of children from India.

To date, political efforts to confront the issue of illegal adoptions in Switzerland have focused primarily on the victims of abusive and illegal intercountry adoptions from Sri Lanka. In many cases, the transfer of children between Colombo and Switzerland was linked to the criminal offence of child trafficking. The authorities have so far shown little intention of launching criminal investigations, although a number of the intermediaries who were involved in the trafficking in Sri Lanka (and also other countries) are still alive and have been known to the authorities in Switzerland and abroad for decades.[100] Adoptees, on the other hand, who were or have reason to believe that they were trafficked as a child, would like to know whether the authorities are doing anything to bring the perpetrators to justice. Whether it is still legally possible to prosecute offences in connection with adoptions in the 1980s and 1990s and whether the state could be held liable for neglecting its supervisory role are also questions that are apt to interest the public. Furthermore, a thorough investigation of the adoptions in question remains necessary to determine whether what has happened constitutes a violation of human rights and, if so, to identify appropriate measures,[101] since according to the rules of international human rights law, victims have a right to remedy and reparations. The clarification of such legal questions is another step in the political process to address the issue of illegal intercountry adoptions, which, with the convening of a legal expert group at federal level, has only just begun.

The bilateral diplomatic effort resulting in the protocol between Switzerland and Sri Lanka has not been very effective in aiding adoptees searching for their origins, especially since the Office for Missing Persons in Sri Lanka does not consider itself responsible for children who disappear without a trace in connection with adoptions.

100 Report of the German Bundestag, 1990, p. 35.

101 E. Loibl, 'The Aftermath of Transnational Illegal Adoptions: Redressing Human Rights Violations in the Intercountry Adoption System with Instruments of Transitional Justice', *Childhood*, Vol. 28, No. 4, 2021, pp. 477-491.

Since Back to the Roots is currently the Swiss organization with the most expertise in this area, it made sense for the federal government and the cantons to award it a contract and funding for a three-year pilot project (2022-2024). As part of the project, the civil society organization will accompany adoptees in their efforts to locate records in the various offices and archives and organize DNA tests for them if they wish. Provision has also been made for psychological support, knowing that it will not be possible to reunite parents with their children in every case.

On a more critical note, it could be argued that the federal government and cantons are making things easy for themselves. By commissioning an adoptee organization with this task, they have passed on part of the responsibility – a responsibility they would normally have to assume in view of the admissions of past misconduct on the part of the authorities – to those in search of their origins. They also minimize several risks. The funding cap of CHF 750,000 over three years keeps their costs in check. Furthermore, efforts to deal with Switzerland's past of illegal intercountry adoptions remain within a narrowly defined framework in that they are restricted to adoptees from Sri Lanka. This means that the creation of a neutral information service that would act as a nationwide hub to assist adoptees searching for their origins is probably off the table for the time being. The establishment of a dedicated interdisciplinary unit or task force comprising archivists, specialists in the tracing of missing persons, international private law experts, psychologists and historians would still be an important step – especially in view of the likelihood of illegal adoption cases regarding other countries of origin. People from the global South who were unlawfully taken from their biological parents should be able to count on dedicated efforts committed to human rights to find out what has happened in their past.

From the point of view of the adoptees from Sri Lanka and India, however, the most important thing now is for Back to the Roots to be able to continue its rigorous and extensive efforts on their behalf with funding from the federal government and the cantons. It is praiseworthy that this initiative, which arose out of the needs of the victims, has been able to position itself as a driving force in the nation's efforts to deal with the issue of illegal intercountry adoptions. By involving the UN Committee on Enforced Disappearances, the association has also succeeded in bringing its concerns to the attention of an international public. The highly professional and successful efforts of this civil society organization could thus also serve as a best-practice example to other countries.

7 The Struggle Towards Collective Justice Through Financial Compensation for Intercountry Adoptees in the Netherlands

Dewi Deijle

Prologue

It is January 1980 when a nine-year-old girl is playing in the streets of Semarang, Indonesia, close to where she lives. A woman unknown to her approaches the little girl, asking her to come with her. Not much later, the girl and a different woman are on a train. After hours of travelling, the girl is delivered to a shelter where children and other people unknown to her are present. The girl does not understand what is happening. She is anxious. She wants to run away and tries to do so, but when she manages to jump the fence, she does not recognize anything outside from where she was playing carefree before. She cannot find her way back home. Three months later, the little girl is put on a plane. When she has landed and gets off, she notices cold air. Where she comes from, it is always warm. She is taken to people she does not know but whom she needs to call 'mom' and 'dad'. This is how Yani's new life in the Netherlands begins. All alone.

She goes through life with the name Yanien. Unfortunately, her life with her new parents does not go well. She has to struggle in a completely different culture and in a new family that is unknown to her. It is a daily struggle for her. She is constantly in survival mode. She is sent to kindergarten. She has to learn to talk to Dutch children, whereas in Indonesia she could already read and write. Her new parents soon start to doubt that she is five years old. A dental analysis reveals that Yanien is actually several years older than indicated on her adoption documents. Yanien has tried to explain much earlier that she is older than assumed, but nobody has believed her, which is why she has suddenly had to behave like a toddler. Even now, no one is allowed to know her real age. Yanien hides what she has seen and felt when she was suddenly torn away from the safety and security of Indonesia and learns to adapt to an unfamiliar world over the years ahead.

For years, Yanien does not dare to search for her family in Indonesia, but she finally makes an attempt. Through a local television broadcast, a call with her photo is aired. And then a miracle happens. Her mother's new husband, a brother of Yanien's late father, recognizes her. And so it happens: a few weeks later, Yanien is reunited with her mother, brothers and other family members. Her mother, meanwhile, has moved elsewhere with her new husband. After Yanien disappeared, the mother had first been admitted to a psychiatric centre for a year. This was because she had gone mad with grief when she could no longer find Yanien. Her child had been kidnapped. She went looking in shady neighbourhoods with a knife in her pocket. Nobody helped her, the police couldn't do anything for her either, and she didn't have financial resources to investigate the whereabouts of her child. At some point she stopped, because where else was she supposed to look? After all, she was looking for her daughter whose identity had been erased. Her mother confirmed that Yanien was born in April 1970.[1] However, according to the adoption documents, she was born in 1974. So on paper, she was made five years younger. A complex and costly (legal) procedure follows, in which Yanien tries to change her true date of birth. This turns out to be quite a struggle, as she has to prove that the identity details she entered the Netherlands with are false. In doing so, Yanien finds it rather strange that no one, including the municipal office and the Dutch judge, questions how it is that she has been walking around with an incorrect date of birth all this time. There are three dates of birth noted in her adoption file. Apparently, no one found this remarkable.

Yanien now has a family with a partner and three children. She has survived her trauma. No one ever thought about the psychological and social consequences when she was adopted. Yanien constantly relived her abduction. She will remember this traumatic event for the rest of her life. She experienced a great deal of misunderstanding from those around her. In addition, she had to cope with an enormous culture shock. Yanien fought quite a battle on many fronts. Her adoptive parents told her to be grateful to be adopted as she now had a better life. She broke up with them and to this day does not have contact with them. The years moved on, without Yanien really being able to tell her story, until she got in touch with several adoptees from Indonesia, like me. She found out that she was not the only one who felt misunderstood by those around her because she felt something went wrong in her adoption. Finally, on 28 March 2018, Yanien told her story in a TV programme about illegal adoptions from Indonesia, after which a new era began not only for her but for many intercountry adoptees in the Netherlands: an era of struggle for recognition and restoration of justice.[2]

1 'Yanien from Apeldoorn was kidnapped for adoption as a child: I broke down with grief', 24 June 2018, de Stentor.

2 BNNVARA, Zembla, 'Adoptiebedrog Deel 3', 28 March 2018, https://www.bnnvara.nl/zembla/artikelen/adoptiebedrog-iii.

Yanien is grateful to have been able to find her family in Indonesia and therefore wishes that every adoptee have the opportunity to explore what happened around their adoption. It is a real miracle that Yanien found her biological family after a relatively short time; after all, she was abducted, transferred to the other side of the world, and adopted on the basis of falsified identity documents. Unfortunately, not every adoptee manages to reunify with their natural parents and to re-establish their real identity.

Yanien's story is not an isolated one. I myself was adopted from Indonesia in 1980. I can confidently say that, unlike Yanien, I ended up in a warm and loving family and had a happy childhood. I never consciously concerned myself with my adoption, except for a few questions I occasionally had about my origins. My adoptive parents always gave me enough space to ask questions about my adoption and to look for my birth parents. After the death of my adoptive father, in 2009, I began to wonder about my roots. While I thought it was only logical that I wanted to know more about my origins, I could not explain why it was only after this event that I explicitly felt the need to search.

In 2010, I embarked on a roots trip to Indonesia. However, while searching for the address of my birth mother indicated in my adoption documents, I heard many obscure stories about adoption procedures from Indonesia. For instance, I was visiting the children's home where I and many other adoptees from Indonesia came from. The current manager told me that he suspected that in about 90% of the adoptions of children from that children's home, the identity details or background information was false. As the son of the former owner of the children's home who died in 1994, he sometimes noticed strange things, such as women signing waivers in exchange for money and midwives and witnesses making false statements about the child's status, for example, that it was an orphan. The manager's mother was arrested in the early 1980s on charges of child abduction. Midwives and others involved in the adoptions, and with whom his mother had worked, were also arrested. In Indonesia, there was much unrest within the Muslim community as children were taken away and sold without the parents' consent. In the Muslim religion, adoption does not exist as the child is considered to always belong to the parents. However, this was not the case in practice: parents lost legal custody of the child, and ties were completely severed through adoption. Indonesian newspapers reported about baby gangs snatching babies and children from parents under false pretences.

The manager told me that when he took over the management of the children's home after his mother's death, adoptees regularly came by with questions about information in their adoption files. For an adoptee, he had once traced a mother, but after DNA testing, there was no match. This confirmed what he had heard and read about stories of child trafficking. In doing so, the son stated that his mother had the best interests of the children at heart. He, however, decided to stop helping adoptees find more information about their adoption, as the data in adoption files often turned out to be false. So he did not want to help me further either.

Although I found this news hard to grasp, I couldn't do anything with it at the time. I thought: all these shady practices took place in Indonesia, so what does the Netherlands have to do with it? Disappointed, I continued to search for my mother's address but soon reached a dead end and so decided to stop. However, what I had heard and experienced during my roots journey kept gnawing at the back of my mind.

It was only a few years later that I felt the need to continue my search for my birth mother. This was when I got in touch with Ana van Valen, one of the founders of *Mijn Roots*, a foundation which she set up together with Christine Verhaagen.[3] Both were adopted from Indonesia. Their mission is to reunite adoptees from Indonesia with their biological relatives by carrying out roots searches for adoptees. Ana told me what they experience during their searches for adoptees. She told me what they experience in their searches for adoptees: In their first case, they had found the woman that the adoption documents indicated as the mother of the adoptee but felt it was important to conduct a DNA test to examine whether it was actually the adoptee's mother. As it turned out, the woman and the adoptee were not at all related.[4] Ana also encountered all kinds of complications in the searches for adoptees. For instance, some biological mothers she managed to find told her that they had temporarily placed their child in a shelter because they had to work or because of their medical situation and suddenly did not get their child back. Some of them were told that the child had been adopted, but some other mothers never knew what had happened to their child. In other cases, mothers that had just given birth were told that their baby had died. Furthermore, Ana came across adoption files stating that the mother had not signed the waiver because she was illiterate. However, no fingerprint had been used. There have also been waivers with only a cross as the mother's signature. This is also how it happened with Ana. She was told the true story of her birth mother she had found. Because the mother had to work and could not take care of Ana, she had placed Ana with a foundation's shelter run by a Dutch board as a temporary solution. However, when she came back to pick up Ana, she had disappeared.

I found questionable information in my file too. My adoption file indicates two different dates of birth. Furthermore, it states that my mother had not received education, yet, the waiver showed a fully written out name as a signature. I was no longer sure that my

3 See https://www.mijn-roots.com/.

4 To date, the foundation has encountered many more such mismatches. If a relative is found in the country of origin, it is often advisable to use a DNA test to check for kinship, especially now that it is known that there have been illegalities in adoptions.

birth mother actually gave consent to my adoption, after listening to the stories of the manager of the children's home in Jakarta and later of Ana about what she experienced during the root searches in Indonesia.

Faced with this uncertainty, I felt the need to investigate whether it had been known in the past that when children from Indonesia were adopted, things were seemingly not so clean. First, I delved into the Dutch newspaper archives. I was greatly surprised to note that since the 1970s there were repeated media stories about alleged abuses in child adoption not only from Indonesia but also from other countries, such as Bangladesh, Colombia and Brazil.[5] After reading the newspaper articles on illegal adoption of children from various countries – and there are many – I concluded that there was a well-oiled machine for producing adoptable children. The foreign contacts made sure in all sorts of devious ways that there were enough children to export. The birth parents were either not properly or fully informed about the consequences of an adoption or they were unaware that their child, whom they had temporarily placed in a child care institution, was actually sent abroad for adoption. The children's paperwork was fabricated or falsified, wrongfully stating that their parents had died and that there were no other family members who could care for the child. Identity documents of babies and children and relinquishment statements were made up. The whole administration process naturally had to be paid for by the prospective adoptive parents, most of whom relied on the modus operandi of those involved in the adoption. In my opinion, this was cross-border organized crime. Babies and children were seen as profitable commodities.

Ana told me that a roots search costs money and that not all adoptees can afford such a search. Especially in cases where certain information in the adoption file is incorrect, there are more costs involved because more searches have to be done. I began to wonder how it was possible that children from abroad could enter the Netherlands, despite numerous newspaper reports about all these illegal practices that the Dutch authorities apparently already knew about. After an extensive search in all kinds of historical parliamentary documents to find out what rules applied when adopting foreign children in the 1970s and 1980s, I came to the shocking discovery that there were hardly any guidelines for adoption procedures from the Dutch government.

---

5 'Adoptieschandaal in Indonesië, Babyhandel opgerold: „Weesjes" duur verkocht', *De Volkskrant*, 8 August 1979; 'Handel in kinderen op Java', *De Waarheid*, 9 August 1979; 'Bende koopt baby's op voor adoptie, Nieuwsblad van het Noorden, 8 August 1979; 'Weer arrestaties Kinderhandel Indonesië', *Het Vrije Volk*, 20 November 1979; 'Gevonden op vliering van vroedvrouw Baby's in Jakarta, voor adoptieouders in Nederland bestemd', *Leeuwarder Courant*, 30 December 1980; 'Baby's ontvoerd in Indonesië voor adoptie', *Nieuwsblad van het Noorden*, 9 June 1981; 'Na ingrijpen Indonesische politie, Nederlandse ouders uit Jakarta zonder 'hun' baby's', *Nieuwsblad van het Noorden*, 13 July 1981; 'Indonesische baby's vooral in Nederland verkocht', *De Waarheid*, 30 December 1981.

Introduction

Both Yanien's and my stories are examples of intercountry adoptees' stories. In the past couple of years, I meet many Dutch adoptees who found that the information regarding their identity in the adoption documents is wrong or who suspect that they were adopted illegally as they come from countries in which abuses took place on a large scale and because the information in their adoption paperwork is inconsistent. There is a whole generation of adoptees who wonder where they come from and what actually happened to them between their birth date and their adoption. In this chapter, I explore the psychological need of adoptees to know and restore their identity and argue that the Dutch state is obliged to financially support adoptees who search for parentage information (both in the Netherlands and in the countries of origin and including DNA research) and, if necessary, to restore their identity based on the adoptees' rights to identity laid down in Article 8 ECHR. I clarify what exactly this right entails and explain how it helped adoptees in Dutch legal proceedings to successfully claim damages from the Dutch state. Finally, I argue that a group search grant scheme which the Dutch minister promised to set up does not properly meet the needs of individuals doing roots searches and explain how adoptees can best be supported in their root searches.

Recognition and Denial by the Dutch Government

The negative consequences of adoption have become more visible in recent years as adult adoptees and advocacy organizations for adoptees have spoken out more about, among other things, the complications they face in their search for parentage records. In this process, increasing attention was paid to abuses in adoption procedures both in politics and the media. In recent years, a number of advocacy organizations have increasingly held the government responsible for having failed to take appropriate measures to prevent illegal intercountry adoptions from occurring in the past. For example, on behalf of adoptees from Indonesia, *Mijn Roots* has brought legal actions against the Dutch state in 2017, demanding a public apology as well as financial support for roots searches of adoptees.[6]

Owing to the increasing pressure placed on the government, Dekker, then minister for legal protection, established the 'Committee Investigating Intercountry Adoption in the Past' on 18 April 2019, led by Tjibbe Joustra (hereinafter, Joustra Committee). The commission had the task to examine possible abuses in intercountry adoptions

6 BNNVARA, Zembla, 'Overheid aansprakelijk voor misstanden adopties', 28 March 2018, https://www.bnnvara.nl/zembla/artikelen/overheid-aansprakelijk-voor-misstanden-adopties.

during the period between 1967 (the year in which the first Directive on the adoption of foreign foster children went into force) and 1998 (which is when the Netherlands ratified the 1993 The Hague Convention on Protection of Children and Co-operation in Respect of Intercountry Adoption).[7] It thereby specifically focused on Bangladesh, Brazil, Colombia, Indonesia and Sri Lanka. The report of the Joustra Committee was released in 2021 and described systemic abuses in past intercountry adoptions from the mentioned countries, including abduction and purchase of children, bribery and document falsification. Notably, the Joustra Committee concluded that abuses were regularly reported even after 1998, when the Hague Convention went into force in the Netherlands. This was a reason for the Commission to also pay attention to the development of intercountry adoption after 1998. On the role and responsibility of the Dutch government in intercountry adoption procedures of foreign children, the Joustra Committee concluded in a nutshell:

> In intercountry adoptions, the government has been following and passive and has not acted. Both in the countries of origin and in the Netherlands, this created impunity around abuses in inter-country adoptions.[8]

On 8 February 2021, the minister accepted the Joustra Committee's report in a press conference, in which he acknowledged the abuses and officially apologized for them on behalf of the Dutch government:

> Adoption abuses came to light as early as the 1960s. But the Dutch government failed to fulfil its responsibilities and obligations. The government did not do what could be expected of it. It should have taken a more active role to prevent abuses. This is a painful observation. Apologies are in order for this, and I therefore apologise to the adoptees today on behalf of the government.[9]

The minister also announced a suspension of intercountry adoption procedures effective immediately. He went on to state that the Dutch government has a moral responsibility to support adoptees and thus announced the creation of a national expertise centre on intercountry adoption which intercountry adoptees can turn to for support and answers to questions regarding their adoption and origin.[10] Regarding root searches, adoptees

7 See Besluit van de Minister voor Rechtsbescherming van 18 april 2019, nr. 2569840, houdende instelling van de Commissie Onderzoek Interlandelijke Adoptie in het verleden (Instellingsbesluit Commissie Onderzoek Interlandelijke Adoptie in het verleden), Staatscourant 2019, 23086, https://zoek.officielebekendmakingen.nl/stcrt-2019-23086.html.

8 COIA, 'Rapport Commissie Onderzoek Interlandelijke Adoptie', The Hague, February 2021, p. 126.

9 COIA, 2021.

10 Rijksoverheid, 'Ontwikkeling Expertisecentrum Interlandelijke Adoptie', Vol. 2, No. 10, July 2022, https://www.rijksoverheid.nl/actueel/nieuwsbrieven/expertisecentrum-interlandelijke-adoptie/2022/nieuwsbrief-expertisecentrum-interlandelijke-adoptie-juli-2022.

were directed to existing organizations established (often by adoptees themselves) with the aim of helping adoptees reunify with their biological families.

Although many adoptees appreciated the official apology made on behalf of the government, they did not feel fully recognized. While apologies as a symbolic form of reparation are valuable in themselves, they must be combined with material forms of reparation, including restitution, compensation and rehabilitation, which affirm that the apologist (in this context, the Dutch state) is committed to recognizing the rights and dignity of victims and their well-being.[11] What adoptees need is financial assistance that enables them to know and, if necessary, re-establish their identity.

THE PSYCHOLOGICAL NEED TO KNOW AND RESTORE ONE'S IDENTITY

Many intercountry adoptees develop an interest in their identity and embark on a search for their origin. This is not surprising considering that it is a fundamental need of every human being to know where they come from. Knowing one's origins gives a person insight into, for example, certain character traits and behavioural patterns. It can contribute to the development of one's identity and personality. Furthermore, it may also be important to know whom one descends from in connection with hereditary diseases that may run in the family.[12] For most people, finding answers to fundamental questions regarding their origins might not be difficult. However, this is different for adoptees, especially those that have discovered inconsistent or incomplete information in their adoption papers.

Numerous adoptees seek to obtain information regarding their background. This has been shown by a study conducted by Statistics Netherlands (CBS), commissioned by the Joustra Committee, which looked into the living situation, well-being and search behaviour of adopted adults in the Netherlands. According to the study results, 51% of the surveyed adoptees have tried to access information about their adoption and origins.[13] Of those who have not done so, 35% indicated that they would (maybe or definitely) want to know more about their adoption in the future. The most common reasons why adoptees tried to obtain information regarding their origins are as follows: wanting to know more about where they come from (82%), their biological family

11 R. Carranza, C. Correa, E. and Naughton, *Reparative Justice: More than Words, Apologies as a Form of Reparation*, New York, International Centre for Transitional Justice, December 2015, https://www.ictj.org/resource-library/more-words-apologies-form-reparation.

12 J.A.E. Van Raak-Kuiper and P. Vlaardingerbroek, *Afstammingsrecht*, Den Haag, Sdu Uitgevers, p. 82.

13 Central Bureau voor de Statistiek (CBS), *Rapport Onderzoek Interlandelijke adoptie in Nederland: Leefsituatie, welzijn en zoekgedrag van geadopteerde volwassenen*, Den Haag, February 2021, para. 5.2.

(69%), whether they resemble family in appearance and character (61%) and whether they have siblings (56%).[14] The CBS study also shows that adoptees regularly discover that certain information and/or documents are incorrect. About 1 in 3 surveyed who gathered additional information about their own background and adoption discovered that the information on their adoption documents, regarding, for example, date and place of birth, name of birth mother/father, and information about the reason for adoption was wrong.[15]

Wanting to know one's origins is part of a natural psychosocial process. However, the moment at which the desire to search for information about one's parents arises can vary from person to person. An adoptee might turn curious about their origins quite early in their childhood. Yet the interest often emerges after important life events, such as the transition to adolescence or young adulthood, becoming a father or mother oneself, the death of an adoptive parent or illness in the family. Adoptees who did not grow up with their birth parents may find the lack of knowledge about their origins very difficult. The popular Dutch television programme *Spoorloos*, which helps individuals find their lost family members, makes this abundantly clear, and from adoption practice and empirical research this has become more than evident.[16] The desire of an adoptee to search for their origins is not necessarily related to (the extent of the) psychological impact they experienced by their adoption. Also, it is not necessarily related to the love and care the person experienced as a child in their adoptive family. Arguably, an adoptee's need to know more about their identity does not depend on the circumstances in which the adoptee grew up (especially whether the adoptee had a happy childhood and development opportunities in the receiving country).

As abuses in intercountry adoptions become more apparent, more and more adoptees begin to look at their adoption differently and want to know more about their origin. Many embark on a search for their origins only to find that the information regarding their identity in the adoption documents is wrong. Quite understandably, they develop an urgent desire to know where they came from and who their birth parents actually are. They want to be able to find out whether they were put up for adoption with the consent of the birth mother and whether their paper identity matches reality by trying to reconstruct the events leading up to their adoption.

14 Ibid., para. 5.2.

15 Ibid.

16 R.A.C. Hoksbergen, 'Waarom het zoeken naar de roots (eigen biologische familie) voor de opgegroeide mens zo fundamenteel is', *Adoptieouders maandblad*, LAVAContact, 2009, https://jeugdbescherming.jimdofree.com/adoptie-en-pleegzorg/identiteit-hechting/.

It is important to verify the truthfulness of the information in the adoption file. It involves investigative acts to verify the information. This includes a search in the country of origin, either independently or with the help of a country-specific organization that conducts roots searches.[17] Adopted individuals should be able to ask the birth parent(s) or other family members directly about the true circumstances regarding their adoption. Also of great importance in the truth-finding process is questioning other persons mentioned in the adoption files who had a role in the adoption proceedings in the country of origin, like midwives, persons who worked in the children's homes, notaries, witnesses and doctors who examined the child's health after birth.

Conducting DNA research has begun to play an important role in the truth-finding process. DNA research has gained more popularity in recent years, also among adoptees. DNA research has long played an important role in crime detection. Many adoptees are also engaged in solving (possible) crimes (e.g. scams, embezzlement of state, kidnapping). Several adoptees were able to trace the individuals indicated on the adoption documents as their birth parent(s), only to discover, after conducting DNA tests, that they were not related.[18] These adoptees then ended up on a huge emotional roller coaster. They are victims of (possible) crimes committed against them.[19] And where is the real mother then? They don't know how and where to look further. All they have is a file with false information. In fact, they then have to rely on any match from a DNA database. This also applies to those adoptees who have only very little information about their origins, and therefore the chances of a successful physical search are virtually nil. The only option, then, is to wait for a DNA match with a relative who also happens to have left his or her DNA in a DNA database.

Many adoptees hit a wall on their search for information about their adoption for various reasons: government institutions and adoption agencies (if they still exist) might work slowly or no longer have crucial data or refuse to share it for privacy reasons, adoptees might be asked to pay for (extra) file information, or adoptive parents withhold important adoption information. Even if the adoptee is able to obtain information from the stakeholders in the receiving country, key questions regarding the true circumstances surrounding their adoption may not be answered solely on

17 E.g. Shapla Community Foundation (Bangladesh), Brazil Baby Affair (Brazil), Chilean Adoptees Worldwide (Chile), Plan Angel (Colombia), Blen-DNA (Ethiopia), Plan Kiskeya (Haiti), DNA India Adoptees (India), MilkboXProject (India), *Mijn Roots* Foundation (Indonesia), Sri Lanka-DNA (Sri Lanka). Roots searching can also imply research with (only) DNA testing.

18 There are adoptees who conducted such a DNA test only after they had been in contact with the persons listed as the mother in the adoption file for years. Because of the stories of cheating that were circulating, they wanted to investigate still further.

19 Much literature can be found on the psychosocial impact of adoption, including attachment issues, but the impact of malpractice is still very much under-researched.

the basis of that information. Rather, extensive fieldwork in the country of origin is necessary to paint a comprehensive picture of the events leading up to the adoption. However, costs for searches in the country of origin are usually high, as money has to be paid for travelling, hiring an interpreter, gaining access to records and having them translated, DNA testing, etc. Some adoptees use the (sometimes costly) services of country-specific organizations that help adoptees find their birth families in the country of origin. If the information in the adoption file appears to be false, the search can be even more complex and expensive. Yet even if an adoptee was able to trace their origins, the journey does not stop there. Many adoptees want their identity restored, which often turns out to be complicated and costly. For example, there are adoptees who have found that they have a different date of birth than the one indicated on the adoption documents. It makes quite a difference if someone is two or even four years older than the age indicated on the birth certificate, and hence many adoptees want the birth date on their documents corrected.

Financial Contribution and Roots Fund

Simply making excuses does not do justice to the suffering that a large group of adoptees have experienced or are still experiencing. Rather, the official apology made by the minister should be effected by financially compensating the individual adoptees. This is also supported by various adoptees and interest groups surveyed by the Joustra Commission.[20] In my view, the Dutch state could set up a roots fund. Any costs incurred by the adoptee on a roots search, with or without the help of a country-specific interest group that conducts roots searches in the country of origin, could be (partially) financed from this.[21] For adoptees from Indonesia, for example, roots searches may involve an allowance of around €3,500 per adoptee. However, there may be adoptees whose search costs may be lower or higher,[22] depending on the country of origin and the amount and quality of information in the adoption file.

In the past, a couple of funds have already been set up in the Netherlands for cases that have been placed outside regular liability law, and a compensation scheme has been put in place for individual victims. The following are some examples:

- Temporary Scheme for Victims of Youth Care: €5,000 per person
- Children of victims of Surcharge affair: €2,000 – €10,000 per child

20 CBS, February 2021.

21 E.g. there are advocacy organizations that have all the knowledge and expertise, for adoptees from Indonesia, Bangladesh, Colombia, Brazil, Sri Lanka, India, Korea and Taiwan.

22 Those who have higher costs in tracing parentage data would then be able to recover the additional costs through a separate liability claim.

- Transgender Act €5,000 per person
- Rawagede victims: €20,000 per person
- Sexual abuse hotline RKK Platform Assistance: €5,000 to €100,000 per person
- Compensation for asbestos victims: €21,269 per person.
- Chrome 6: €4,000 to €40,000.[23]

Such a fund could also be created for intercountry adoptees, regardless of their country of origin and the period in which they were adopted. Compensation should not depend on proof of an illegal adoption. After all, they have the right to know the true circumstances of their adoption. However, in a letter to the *Mijn Roots* Foundation, the Dutch state rejected liability in connection with illegal adoptions of children from Indonesia. According to the foundation, the state had acted unlawfully towards adoptees from Indonesia because they were not adequately protected as children.[24] However, the state denied this and refused to provide support in the form of granting financial assistance to individual adoptees from Indonesia for a roots search.[25]

On several occasions, I have argued that the Dutch state is obliged to assist adoptees to trace their birth families and to compensate for their search expenses. If the adoptee's adoption documents turn out to be false, the state should offer the individual practical ways to have their identity restored. This state obligation follows from the adoptee's right to identity, which I will explore in the following section. On the basis of this right, the Dutch state has recently been ordered to pay damages to victims of an illegal adoption.

The Right to Identity

The 1989 UN Convention on the Rights of the Child (hereinafter UNCRC) was the first human rights treaty to recognize explicitly the right to preservation of the child's identity. Its Article 8 obliges states parties to "respect the right of the child to preserve his or her identity, including nationality, name and family relations as recognized by law without unlawful interference" and when

23 'NJCM roept op tot oprichting rootsfonds voor geadopteerden', *NJCM*, 22 March 2022, https://njcm.nl/actueel/njcm-roept-nieuw-kabinet-op-rootsfonds-op-te-zetten-voor-geadopteerden-uit-buitenland/.

24 Letter of the Association *Mijn Roots* to the Dutch Ministry of Justice and Security, dated 31 May 2018, on file with author.

25 A. van Soest and A. van Eijsden, 'Geen schadefonds voor zoektocht geadopteerden uit Indonesië naar afstamming', *Nederlands Dagblad*, 7 June 2021, https://www.nd.nl/nieuws/politiek/1040098/geen-schadefonds-voor-zoektocht-indonesische-geadopteerden-naar#closemodal.

> a child is illegally deprived of some or all of the elements of his or her identity…to provide appropriate assistance and protection, with a view to re-establishing speedily his or her identity.

Article 8 does not define the concept of identity but only gives three examples of what it includes: nationality, name and family relations.[26] These elements form the base of the child's right to identity and correspond with the elements of the preceding Article 7, which establishes the child's rights to a name, to a nationality, and to know and be cared for by his or her parents. Together, Articles 7 and 8 are crucial for helping displaced children to re-establish contact with their families and also children who are in the care and protection of the state or adopted to have their roots traced at a later stage of their lives. States are obliged not only to provide assistance and protection aimed at restoring the child's identity but also to ensure that it is appropriate to achieve this goal. The UNCRC does not specify what forms of assistance and protection are appropriate.[27]

The European Convention on Human Rights (hereinafter ECHR) does not explicitly enshrine the right to identity. However, the European Court of Human Rights (hereinafter ECtHR or the Court) has recognized this right as an integral part of the right to private life laid down in Article 8. The child's right to obtain information to ascertain his or her parentage (i.e. the circumstances of his birth, events during his childhood, the identity of his parents) is an integral part of the right to identity protected by Article 8(1) ECHR.[28] This right obliges states not only to refrain from arbitrary interference (negative obligation) but also, in certain circumstances, to take active steps to prevent interference by third parties (positive obligation). This positive obligation may include taking measures to ensure respect for private life also in interpersonal relations.[29]

In the Netherlands, some adoptees have initiated legal proceedings against the Dutch stakeholders involved in their adoption proceedings based on the right to identity. For example, in 2019, Patrick Noordhoven sued the Dutch state for damages, arguing that it deprived him of the opportunity to know the circumstances surrounding his illegal adoption and therefore violated his right to identity. Patrick was adopted from Brazil by a Dutch couple in the 1980s, and he later found out that his birth certificate was false: it mentioned his adoptive parents as the biological parents and indicated a wrong

26 S. Besson, 'Enforcing the Child's Right to Know Her Origins: Contrasting Approaches Under the Convention on the Rights of the Child and the European Convention on Human Rights', *International Journal of Law, Policy and the Family*, Vol. 21, No. 1, 2007, 137-159, p. 143.

27 J. Tobin, *The UN Convention on the Rights of the Child: A Commentary*, Oxford University Press, 2019, p. 301.

28 Besson, 2007, p. 141.

29 *ECtHR, Marckx v. Belgium*, 13 June 1979, application no. 6833/74.

birth date. The Dutch authorities had knowledge of 42 illegal adoptions from Brazil (including Patrick's), in which Dutch adoptive parents had passed the adoptees off as their own biological children, but decided to discontinue criminal proceedings against the adoptive parents. In 2021, the Court ruled in favour of Patrick Noordoven, stating that the state had failed to ensure that the man could know his origins, even though it could and should have done so:

> 4.27
> ...The prosecution made the decision not to prosecute the individuals involved, including [plaintiff's] adoptive parents. That decision was within its discretion.
> 4.28
> However, the State was thereby not released from its obligation to protect the rights of [plaintiff] pursuant to Article 8 ECHR. This precisely because it knew that the children concerned, including [plaintiff], had been adopted illegally and were therefore victims of criminal conduct. Those children could not exercise their right under Article 8 ECHR to grow up as much as possible with their biological parents, while it had not been established that the "adoption" by the adoptive parents was necessary and in the children's interest.... There was also a real risk that the adoptive parents would not inform [plaintiff] of his parentage and the circumstances under which he had been illegally adopted. This was all the more true since it had become apparent during the ... investigation that the parents concerned were reluctant to cooperate with the investigation and even resisted it.... In that situation, it was not enough for the State to find that [plaintiff's] adoptive parents had acted criminally culpable, decide that they would not be criminally prosecuted for that, and then close the book. Given the seriousness of the breach that had surfaced and [plaintiff]'s weighty interest as a child to be able to have parentage knowledge, the State had an obligation under Article 8 ECHR to take measures to ensure the right to protect [plaintiff's] identity. It had an obligation towards [plaintiff] to make efforts – as much as possible – to ensure that he would actually receive parentage information and other identity determining information.
> ...
> 4.30.
> Exactly which measures the State had to take, the Court leaves open. The Court deemed it decisive that nothing was done, although the State was obliged to do so, measures were possible and it cannot be said that taking measures would have been a disproportionate burden. For example, it could have done (further) research into the circumstances surrounding the illegal adoption of [plaintiff] with a view to obtaining parentage information, could have decided to retain file information or had research conducted by the

> Child Protection Council with a view to possible child protection measures to safeguard [plaintiff's] right to know his identity.
> 4.31.
> There was every reason for a further investigation in this case, given the fundamental nature of the rights of the children concerned, which had been violated by their adoptive parents. This is all the more true since those children themselves were too young to take action. Hence, the Court is of the opinion that the State could have conducted further investigation into the circumstances under which [plaintiff's] parentage had been made uncertain. Also, the State could have clearly recorded the results of this investigation, so that [plaintiff] could take note of them at a later stage.
> 4.32.
> Another conceivable measure is that the file named "334.33 Brazil / adoption of Brazilian children by Dutch people" with the period indication "1978 – 1982" would have been kept. This file was at the Ministry of Foreign Affairs and was destroyed in 2009. Even if it is assumed that this destruction took place in accordance with the rules, the State thereby denied [plaintiff] the opportunity to take cognizance of the contents of the file. In the opinion of the Court, the State could have reasonably taken into account that [plaintiff] – in order to obtain clarification about events surrounding his childhood – would be interested in the file. After all, the State knew that [plaintiff] (as well as 41 others) had been illegally adopted from Brazil in the period covered by the file. Whether the file actually contained relevant information for [plaintiff] about his parentage is irrelevant.
> 4.33.
> Finally, in the interest of [plaintiff] the State could have taken measures toward the adoptive parents regardless of the criminal context. The State is correct in stating that it is primarily the responsibility of the adoptive parents to provide [plaintiff] with information about his parentage, descent and significant events in his childhood. In this case, however, the adoptive parents were already involved in the crime of embezzlement of state. In these circumstances, the State had an obligation to promote the effective exercise of [plaintiff's] rights under Article 8 ECHR.[30]

In 2019, Dilani Butink, a 28-year-old Dutch adoptee, sued the Dutch state and the adoption agency involved in her illegal adoption from Sri Lanka for damages. The plaintiff had found out that her adoption paperwork was false and had been trying to find her biological parents ever since. She claimed that both the authorities and the

30 Rechtbank Den Haag, 24 November 2021, ECLI:NL:RBDHA:2021:12780 (translated by author).

adoption agency had approved her adoption despite their knowledge of the systemic adoption abuses in Sri Lanka in the 1980s and thereby violated her right to identity. The Court of first instance rejected the claims, arguing that the statutes of limitation had passed.[31] However, in 2022, the Court of Appeal ruled in favour of Dilani Butink. It found that the Dutch adoption agency had violated its obligation to only carry out adoptions that are in the child's best interest and to collect as much information as possible about the child's background in the country of origin. It simply relied on the information provided by the Sri Lankan authorities despite clear signs of abusive practices and, therefore, did not do enough to prevent the uncertainty in which Dilani now finds herself. With regard to the Dutch state, the Court stated the following:

> In the opinion of the court of appeal, the State also failed.... In view of the weighty individual interests of particularly vulnerable individuals that were at stake here and the strict statutory system that was designed precisely with these interests in mind, the State could have been expected to bring its supervision of the execution of this system in line with this, by probing whether the licensed intermediary complied with the statutory norms. The State could and should have reasonably supervised more and better the way in which the agency fulfilled its obligations.... It does not appear that the State asked the agency in what way it established in individual cases that the adoption was in the child's best interest, that placing the child with relatives was not an option, and that the biological mother had relinquished the child in a well-informed and free manner, or how the agency ensured that as much accurate parentage information as possible was collected. The State should have been expected to demand that more be done to collect as much information as possible about the parentage and the mother's reasons for renouncing her child. This could include information about the number of conversations with the biological mother and their content/provision; about the manner in which the contact with the mother was established and on whose initiative; from which it appeared that the mother had voluntarily and well-informed renounced the child and what her reasons were for this renunciation; whether there were also discussions with the family to investigate whether care by the family was possible and if so, what the result of these discussions was and if not, why not; what the name of the father is, and so on. Also, the State should have demanded that to the extent that, according to the agency, this information really could not be found out, even by Probation and the local mediators (e.g., because the mother did not want to give the father's name), it would at least

31 Rechtbank Den Haag, 9 September 2020, ECLI:NL:RBDHA:2020:8735.

> record in the file what efforts had been made to do so and why it had not succeeded.[32]

The courts in both cases recognized that Noordoven's and Butink's fundamental right to respect for their private and family life, their right to (be able to) know their own identity and origin, and their overall personality right and dignity as human beings laid down in Article 8 ECHR were violated, which is why the Dutch state was found liable for damages. In separate proceedings, the damages suffered by both of them and the amount of those damages have yet to be decided (which has not happened at the time of writing this chapter). However, that the state does not feel responsible for the suffering of and the harm done to the adoptees becomes painfully clear now that the state has appealed against the lower court's ruling in the Noordoven case and filed cassation against the higher Court's ruling in the Butink case. Hence, even though the state officially apologized to victims of illegal adoptions, it does not sufficiently recognize the impact on adoptees who want to know where they came from and the complications they may face in their search for parentage information. In my view, the Court's reconsiderations in the cases described previously may well serve to successfully invoke the state's obligation to provide any adoptee with search needs with financial compensation from a roots fund.

The children put up for adoption could not defend themselves at the time of their adoption, and needed the (legal) protection to which a child is entitled, including from the Dutch government. They could not exercise the right enshrined in Article 8 ECHR to grow up with their birth parents as much as possible, while it had not been established that adoption was necessary and in the child's best interests. Respect for 'family life' places an obligation on a state to ensure the right to respect for private and family life. This obligation has been violated by the Dutch state in many cases of intercountry adoption. For many adoptees, it was not established whether it was actually necessary that the child could no longer grow up in the country of origin or whether the adoption was in the child's apparent best interests; it was merely assumed. The Dutch state wrongly assumed the reliability of the adoption documents. This concealed the falsehoods that adoptees now have to detect for themselves.

When the Dutch state became aware that fundamental rights of at least a large group of children from abroad were being violated, it failed to take adequate measures to counteract as many illegal practices as possible in the adoption of children from abroad, such as carrying out stricter controls and monitoring more closely the entry of children or even an adoption ban. Child theft and abduction were even downplayed.

32 Gerechtshof Den Haag, 12 July 2022, ECLI:NL:GHDHA:2022:1248, para. 6.32 (translated by author).

Willingly and knowingly, the risk was accepted that entry into the Netherlands was granted to many children, despite the fact that their identity was fabricated. This violated the fundamental rights not only of children but also of their birth parents, who now depend on their child's will and ability to search for them, because often the parents themselves did not have the necessary means to look for their lost child. They too have lived, or are still living, in uncertainty about the fate and whereabouts of their child whom they have never seen again. Some birth mothers whom adoptees were able to find have stated that they searched for their child for years.

The origins and identity of many children adopted from abroad has been made uncertain because of adoption. It is very likely that they face complications in their search for parentage information as a result. Therefore, in 2017 the *Mijn Roots* Foundation held the Dutch state liable in a letter. Also, it has taken several other actions to persuade the Dutch state to recognize the abuses and get justice restored, such as actively lobbying in politics, in collaboration with similar foundations for adoptees from Colombia (Plan Angel) and Bangladesh (Shapla Community). There is thus, in my opinion, a solid legal basis for obliging the state to support intercountry adoptees in finding parentage information and, where necessary, in restoring their identity, regardless of which country they came from and in which period and whether they had a happy childhood in the Netherlands.[33] This also applies to adoptees who have yet to find out whether mistakes were made in their adoption. The Dutch state has acted negligently. As a result, the rights of many children have been violated. In the case of Noordoven and Butink, the court ruled that the Dutch state had failed in its duty of care to protect them. As a result, their origins have been made uncertain. Arguably, the parentage of many other adoptees has been made uncertain. Many have already found this out, while others are still investigating or may want to do so later. I think all intercountry adoptees should be given a fair chance to obtain information about their origins. Only in this way will they obtain (more) clarity about the true story regarding their adoption and their true identity.

The establishment of a national expertise centre on intercountry adoption that provides psychological support and information to adoptees is not enough.[34] Rather, it is necessary that financial support be offered to adoptees. The Dutch government does seem to be more open to the idea of offering financial support ever since the Joustra Committee published its damning report about illegal intercountry adoptions in the past. For

33 Tracing parentage data can be done through file research and/or a roots search in the country of origin and/or DNA testing.

34 FIOM, Expertisecentrum Interlandelijke Adoptie: Inbedding, Eigenheid en Samenwerking, 's-Hertogenbosch, 25 June 2022, https://www.rijksoverheid.nl/documenten/rapporten/2022/06/10/tk-bijlage-2-plan-van-aanpak-fiom-bestuurlijke-inbedding-expertisecentrum-interlandelijke-adoptie.

instance, to assist adoptees, it set up a grant scheme for country-specific interest groups. However, as I will argue in the following section, such a scheme does not properly meet the needs of individuals doing roots searches.[35]

Group Search Grant Scheme

In a letter dated 10 June 2022, the current minister for legal protection informed the House of Representatives of his intention to provide financial support to country-specific organizations so that they can provide adoptees with general support for searches or organize joint roots journeys:

> Thought could be given to the use of a protocol or practical guidance during a group trip to a country of origin. These roots trips have many common elements. A few key questions: how do I search? What exactly has been the role of the embassy? What can I expect from the embassy? Where should I start? If everyone has to figure this out individually, we are going to duplicate a lot of work. Then adoptees can't help each other either and that's a shame, because they can support each other with knowledge and expertise.[36]

However, the announcement of such a grant scheme makes it clear that there is (still) no recognition of the root cause of the problem and that the minister has no idea of what an investigation into parentage information actually looks like.

Violated Individual Rights

An individual right has been violated, namely that of the adoptee. With this arrangement, however, the right is seen from a collective perspective. However, searching for information about one's parents as well as biological relatives in the country of origin is a complex activity, where what is needed has to be assessed on an individual basis, depending on the quality and amount of information in the adoption file. A search is a personal process and finding the missing pieces of the puzzle can take years.[37] It is not

---

35 See Beleidsregels van de Minister voor Rechtsbescherming van 26 januari 2021, kenmerk 3189058, houdende regels voor tijdelijke subsidiëring van activiteiten van belangenorganisaties van interlandelijk geadopteerden (Beleidsregel subsidie belangenorganisaties interlandelijk geadopteerden), Stcrt. 2021, 4723, https://zoek.officielebekendmakingen.nl/stcrt-2021-4723.html.

36 Kamerstukken II 2021-2022, 31 265, nr. 104.

37 D. Deijle, *Postpakketjes van Overzee: Gelegaliseerde Kinderhandel in Adoptie van Kinderen uit Indonesië*, Steyl, The Netherlands, Uitgeverij Bronsgreun, 2020.

the case that if an adoptee starts searching, they will find something right away. Every country has its own language, culture, customs and taboos, to say nothing about the huge differences within the country itself.

Obstacles for Group Searching

Furthermore, even if adoptees come from the same childcare institution, it does not mean they have the same place of birth. A children's home is not waiting for groups of adoptees on its doorstep, and despite the children's home being the common denominator, each adoptee will continue to go their own way. It may also happen that the adoptee travels to the place of birth but is told that the biological family has moved to another place hundreds of miles away. In that case the adoptee will have to continue their search somewhere else altogether. And if a birth mother or other family member is found (this does not happen automatically during the root journey itself, by the way, and is often preceded by a lot of file and fieldwork research), this should be handled with integrity, also in connection with the privacy of the biological family members. Furthermore, it does happen that the adoptee discovers during his roots search that certain information in the adoption documents is not correct and that they are not searching in the right place at all. The adoptee should then conduct the search elsewhere, but because they are in a group travel, they will be hampered in doing so.

Certain information that does have relevance for a larger group, such as answers to the key questions described by the minister, is already disseminated by country-specific organizations in other ways, such as through their websites, social media platforms and organized meetings. Knowledge and expertise is already shared with and among themselves through other avenues that have been easily accessible to adoptees for years. Precisely with the knowledge and expertise that adoptees have already been able to access through advocacy organizations and perhaps soon through the expertise centre, they can go further in their individual quest. Some adoptees may be much further along in their roots search than others. Also, it excludes large groups of adoptees, as there is no advocacy organization for every country and there are country-specific organizations that focus only on DNA projects and that do not conduct roots searches. Furthermore, there are all kinds of practical obstacles to organizing and conducting group travels for roots searching in the country of origin.

Freedom of Choice and Individual Financial Support

The adoptee who wants to find out the truth surrounding his or her adoption should be able to conduct research independently (both in the Netherlands and in the country of origin), without depending on the root searches of other adoptees. The personal aspect of a roots search means that adoptees should be able to have control over how they want to shape it. The adoptee should have freedom of choice in this.[38] Practical guidance from an advocacy organization may be welcome, but it should be focused on the individual adoptee and his or her personal story, wishes and needs. Adoptees who do want to go on a roots journey together can always organize this themselves or through an interest group.

The need to search for parentage information and the manner in which the adoptee wishes to do so should be appropriately accommodated under the second paragraph of Article 8 ECHR. More concretely, as indicated earlier, the state should support individual intercountry adoptees financially to search for parentage information (both in the Netherlands and in the country of origin and including DNA research) from a roots fund to be set up. Furthermore, the state should contribute to the costs of identity restoration, such as having the name and/or date of birth changed.

Unfortunately, the current Dutch Minister for Legal Protection sees it differently for the time being. I am still in discussion with him on this, so the hatchet has not yet been buried, despite the fact that I have been pleading for financial compensation for several years now with the *Mijn Roots* foundation and then with other interest groups.

Conclusion

The problem with intercountry adoption is that the system has brought with it structural abuses. Not only in the 1970s and 1980s but also in the 1990s and after the ratification of the 1993, The Hague Convention on Protection of Children and Co-operation in Respect of Intercountry Adoption (hereinafter the Hague Adoption Convention), a watertight adoption system free of abuses, could not be set up.[39] It is the Dutch state that failed to prevent abuses in adoptions. While this is not disputed by the Dutch state, there is, unfortunately, insufficient recognition of the overall impact this has had on those that were adopted from abroad.[40] For many adoptees, it is (still) not clear whether their

38 D. Deijle, 'Bezwaar subsidieplan generieke ondersteuning', *OJAU*, 16 August 2022, https://www.ojau.nl/bezwaar-subsidieplan-generieke-ondersteuning/.

39 Argos Medialogica, 'Al red je er maar één', 24 June 2022, https://www.vpro.nl/argos/media/kijk/afleveringen/medialogica/2022/aflevering-3.html.

40 Rijksoverheid, 'Dekker: Bij adoptie uit het buitenland blijft er altijd kans op misstanden', 4 June 2021, https://www.rijksoverheid.nl/actueel/nieuws/2021/06/04/dekker-bij-adoptie-uit-het-buitenland-blijft-er-altijd-kans-op-misstanden#:~:text=Dekker%3A%20Bij%20adoptie%20uit%20het%20buitenland%20blijft%20er%20altijd%20kans%20op%20misstanden,-Nieuwsbericht%20%7C%2004%2D06&text=Er%20blijft%20altijd%20een%20kans,kans%20op%20misstanden%20kleiner%20wordt.

case also involves abuses and irregularities.[41] Those adoptees who want to investigate the circumstances of their adoption should be financially supported to do so. The need is high, and time is running out for many! Birth parents whose children were adopted in the 1970s and 1980s are at an advanced age and may soon pass away.[42] This also applies to other persons who may be able to contribute to the truth-finding process. Crucial information in the countries of origin is disappearing as the years go by.

The past cannot be undone, but the present and the future can be looked at by restoring justice where it is still possible. In my view, a compensation scheme for intercountry adoptees can be seen as part of a broader package of recognition measures, such as the establishment of a centre of expertise and subsidy schemes for interest groups. Reimbursing DNA testing and identity restoration should also be included. The legal ground is already there. However, it is regrettable that, despite the apologies that have been made, the state is protracting costly legal proceedings rather than offering adequate assistance to adoptees. This is a double setback for adoptees, whose best interests are once again being lost sight of.

41 Whether an offence has actually been committed can only be determined after investigation (finding the truth).

42 Especially in developing countries, life expectancy is lower than in the Netherlands.

8 Changing the Historiographical Paradigm: Towards an Alternative Genealogy for Intercountry Adoption

Lies Wesseling

Introduction: Turning a Blind Eye

Discourses on intercountry adoption (ICA) in the later 20th century have modulated from referencing every child's right to a family, to asserting the right of every prospective parent to a child. This discourse of entitlement is often softened by a Romantic vocabulary, representing the emerging tie between adopters and adoptees as a transnational and transracial romance that was 'meant to be'.[1] Concurrently, the adoptee may also be represented as a gift graciously given by the incapacitated birth parent to the deserving adoptive parent.[2]

None of these vocabularies are conducive to raising awareness of the sobering fact that ICA is a market marked by a criminogenic discrepancy between supply and demand. As has been amply demonstrated by now, the excess of demand over supply has generated malpractices such as child kidnapping, child laundering and child trafficking.[3] Additionally, it has turned out that birth parents are not always sufficiently aware of

---

1 E. Wesseling and M. Garcia Gonzalez, 'The Stories We Adopt By: Tracing "The Red Thread" in Contemporary Adoption Narratives', *The Lion and the Unicorn*, Vol. 37, No. 3, 2014, pp. 257-276.

2 E. Wesseling, '"Literature as Equipment for Living": Parental Self-Fashioning in Full-Circle Adoptions', *in* A. Swinnen, A. Kluveld and R. van de Vall (eds.), *Engaged Humanities: Rethinking Art. Culture, and Public Life*, Amsterdam, Amsterdam University Press, 2022, pp. 31-53.

3 D.M. Smolin, 'Intercountry Adoption as Child Trafficking', *Valparaiso University Law Review*, Vol. 39, No. 2, 2004, pp. 281-326; D.M. Smolin, 'Child Laundering: How the Adoption System Legitimizes and Incentivizes the Practices of Buying, Trafficking, Kidnapping, and Stealing Children', *Wayne Law Review*, Vol. 52, No. 1, 2006, pp. 113-200; R. Post, *Romania: For Export Only: The Untold Story of the Romanian' Orphans*, Makkum, Post, 2007; E. Loibl, *The Transnational Illegal Adoption Market: A Criminological Study of the German and Dutch Intercountry Adoption Systems*, The Hague, Eleven International, 2019 (PhD dissertation, Maastricht University).

the permanent nature of the adoption arrangement.[4] In spite of regular exposures of such malpractices in the media, adoption agencies and adoptive parents are inclined to write them off as incidental aberrations, caused by this or that dysfunctional children's home in a sending country.[5] It is generally believed that the problem can be solved by rupturing ties with this one institution and replace it with another one.[6] In brief, the systemic nature of these crimes is insufficiently acknowledged.

The way in which adoption stakeholders in the receiving countries understand the *history* of ICA is one of the sources sustaining this denial of the systemic nature of adoptive malpractices. Historical accounts of how ICA has come into being play into the discourses of white saviourism, transnational romance and the adoptive gift, which turn a blind eye to the potential injustices inflicted on birth parents and adoptees. This chapter provides a critical account of the historiographical paradigm that shapes Western genealogies of ICA. It also sketches the contours of an alternative approach to the history of separating children from their birth families in the global South, to transport them to the other end of the world.

This chapter takes its cue from North American historiography of ICA, to trace how it has influenced European histories of this social practice, with a special interest in France and the Netherlands, two formidable former colonial powers with comparable colonial histories in adjacent regions. It has been designed as a literature review of seminal book-length histories of ICA, as monographs and edited volumes are still the most authoritative forms of publication in academic history, as opposed to the social sciences, where the peer-reviewed journal article carries the most weight. Its approach has been inspired by Michel Foucault's genealogical method, whose forays into the past are intended to provide a critique of the present. In my case, this means that an examination of the conditions of ICA's emergence will create a non-innocent perspective on ICA, exposing its roots in colonial governance. A history of the present is a first necessary stepping stone towards coming to terms with adoptive malpractices. As many post-conflict regions have come to realize, there can be no 'reconciliation' without 'truth'. To meet this necessary precondition for healing historical trauma, we have to make short shrift with sanitized, idealized versions of ICA's history.

---

4 P. Bos, *Once a Mother: Relinquishment and Adoption from the Perspective of Unmarried Mothers in South India*, PhD Thesis, University of Amsterdam, 2007.

5 P. Bos, W. van Sebille and H. Westra, Perverse prikkels leiden ertoe dat ouders hun kind afstaan voor adoptie [Perverse Incentives Persuade Parents to Relinquish their Children for Adoption], *Trouw*, 17 February 2021.

6 I. Hut, Interlandelijke adoptie en mensenhandel [Intercountry Adoption and Child Trafficking], 9 December 2016, https://www.comensha.nl/actualiteiten/item/column-ina-hut-interlandelijke-adoptie-en-mensenhandel/.

Setting the Historiographical Standard

The United States has persistently topped the list of receiving countries since the 1950s.[7] It has adopted the largest number of children transnationally of all Western nations. Predictably, the United States also dominates scholarship on ICA. This does not only apply to social science and law, but also to the humanities, including history. North American scholarly inquiry has set the standard for research into ICA in all relevant disciplines, qualitatively and quantitatively. Sure enough, European countries have also adopted significant numbers of children from the global South, and if one would add up these numbers, they would exceed the figures of the United States. However, since ICA is regulated on the level of individual nation-states, these numbers cannot be added up just like that. Continental European scholarship is equally scattered and less accessible overall because European studies of ICA have been published across a broad spectrum of different national languages. The fragmentation of European scholarly inquiry makes the field of adoption studies susceptible to Anglocentrism, as the only shared frame of reference for scholars in the receiving countries, as I aim to demonstrate below.

Let me therefore begin with an account of the North American historiography of ICA, to subsequently explore how this perspective is refracted across selected European studies. It came into its own with Wayne Carp's seminal *Family Matters: Secrecy and Disclosure in the History of Adoption* (1998). This monograph describes the transition from adoption with sealed records which erases all traces of the birth parents to 'open' adoption which enables adoptees to track down their birth parents if they so wish. Carp's interest is basically in 20th-century legal regulation. He only briefly touches upon adoption's long prehistory of precarious children in workhouses, alms houses, orphanages and adoptive families in the first chapter. Carp does not yet make a clear-cut distinction between domestic and foreign adoption and dwells at length on the social activism of the adoption rights movement which made the transition from closed to open records possible in the United States. Carp's focus on legal regulation explains why there was no comprehensive history of U.S. adoption before: closed records are not only an obstacle for adoptees, but also for historians, barring access to historical sources. Carp's second contribution to the field, the edited volume *Adoption in America: Historical Perspectives* (2002),[8] broadens the historical scope of his monograph considerably in that four out of its nine essays are devoted to 19th-century adoptions. This publication is much more invested in articulating distinct phases in the history of

7 P. Selman, 'The Rise and Fall of Intercountry Adoption in the 21st Century', *International Social Work*, Vol. 52, No. 5, 2009, pp. 575-594.

8 E.W. Carp, *Family Matters: Secrecy and Disclosure in the History of Adoption*, Cambridge, MA, Harvard University Press, 1998; E.W. Carp, *Adoption in America: Historical Perspectives*, Ann Arbor, University of Michigan Press, 2004.

adoption. The essay which Carp himself co-authored with Anna Leon-Guerrero makes the emphatic point that World War II marks a crucial turn in the history of adoption, with adoption practices transitioning from white U.S. children to children from other parts of the world.

Carp's pioneering work set the stage for three landmark studies, namely Barbara Melosh's *Strangers and Kin: The American Way of Adoption* (2002); Lori Askeland's edited volume *Children and Youth in Adoption, Orphanages and Foster Care: A Historical Handbook and Guide* (2006); and Ellen Herman's *Kinship by Design: A History of Adoption in the Modern United States* (2008).[9] Askeland's work differs from the two monographs in that two out of the six essays in this volume dwell on pre-20th-century forms of fostering and adoption. Askeland's essay in this volume delves into the various practices of kinship, fostering and adoption among First Nation Americans and African Americans under slavery,[10] while Marilyn Holt[11] dwells on the so-called orphan trains, i.e., the project of taking 'orphans' (often children with one parent left) out of the urban areas on the East Coast to rural homes across the country. Presumably, this was to safeguard them against urban vice and crime. In the meantime, it also helped to provide much-needed manual labour to farming households. Religious authorities presided over these reallocations, doing their best to ensure children would be placed in decent families by heeding the testimonies of parish priests and ministers. Around the turn from the 19th to the 20th century, these religious authorities were ousted by science-based practitioners of new professions such as social work and family counselling. Their inventions effectively put an end to the orphan train phenomenon.

The studies by Melosh and Herman share a focus on the 20th century with their predecessors, together with the persistent interest in the legal and science-based governance of adoption. All three publications concur, however, that the onset of the 20th century marked a watershed moment in the history of adoption. Melosh clarifies that adoptees in earlier periods were first and foremost sought after for their economic value, i.e., their labour force. By and large, adoptees were little more than unpaid domestic servants, farmhands and construction workers. At best, they were indentured

---

9 L. Askeland (ed.), *Children and Youth in Adoption, Orphanages and Foster Care: A Historical Handbook and Guide*, Westport, Greenwood Press, 2006; E. Herman, *Kinship by Design: A History of Adoption in the Modern United States*, Chicago and London, University of Chicago Press, 2008; B. Melosh, *Strangers and Kin: The American Way of Adoption*, Cambridge, MA, Harvard University Press, 2002.

10 L. Askeland, 'Informal Adoption, Apprentices, and Indentured Children in the Colonial Era and the New Republic, 1605-1850', *in* L. Askeland (ed.), *Children and Youth in Adoption, Orphanages, and Foster Care: A Historical Handbook and Guide*, London, Greenwood Press, 2006, pp. 3-17.

11 M. Holt, 'Adoption Reform, Orphan Trains, and Child-Saving, 1851-1929', *in* L. Askeland (ed.), *Children and Youth in Adoption, Orphanages, and Foster Care: A Historical Handbook and Guide*, London, Greenwood Press, 2006, pp. 17-31.

apprentices. In the early 20th century, however, adoption laws transformed adoptees into full-fledged equivalents of biological children, with the same legal rights and duties. Now they were priced for their sentimental value, with childless couples seeking adoptable children for emotional gratification, a point that was also made before (although not with exclusive reference to adoption) by Viviana Zelizer in her classic sociological study *Pricing the Priceless Child: The Changing Social Value of Children* (1985).[12]

Herman and Melosh agree with Carp in regarding the 1950s as a second turning point in the history of adoption, with Melosh branding it as a period of "redrawing the boundaries" that ushered in transnational and transracial adoption,[13] while Herman even refers to the time segment between 1945 and 1975 as a period of "adoption revolutions".[14] Both authors emphatically position ICA as the successor project to domestic adoption. Elisabeth Bartholet's chapter in Askeland's companion likewise presents international adoption as a new, post-war phenomenon, making no reference whatsoever to the chapters on pre-20th-century patterns of child circulation.[15] The dwindling of domestic adoption is not only imputed to social changes such as the introduction of contraceptives and the growing acceptance of unwed motherhood, which caused a decline of white American adoptable children, but also to the lengthy and laborious procedures for matching prospective adoptive parents to adoptees, with matching periods of an ample six years being no exception. The supposedly new-fangled phenomenon of ICA no longer aspired to the standard of the 'as if begotten' family that the matching procedures of domestic adoption tried to meet, by searching for maximum resemblances between adopters and adoptees as to skin colour, overall outward appearance, IQ, religion and class. Clearly, adoptees from Korea or China could never pass for 'our very own',[16] so striving after resemblance no longer made sense. Rather, ICA aspired to high-flown humanitarian ideals of saving orphaned children from the chaos of armed conflict or of preventing mixed-race children or children born out of wedlock from falling victim to the societal discrimination that was going to be their lot in their birth countries. Given the possibly life-threatening circumstances in which Korean War orphans and mixed-race children had to fend for themselves, it was felt that there was no longer time for lengthy adoption procedures.[17] The victory

12 V. Zelizer, *Pricing the Priceless Child: The Changing Social Value of Children*, New York, Basic Books, 1985.

13 Melosh, 2002, p. 158.

14 Herman, 2008, p. 195.

15 E. Bartholet, 'International Adoption', *in* L. Askeland (ed.), *Children and Youth in Adoption, Orphanages, and Foster Care: A Historical Handbook and Guide*, London, Greenwood Press, 2006, pp. 63-79.

16 J. Berebitsky, *Like Our Very Own: Adoption and the Changing Culture of Motherhood 1851-1950*, Lawrence, University Press of Kansas, 2000.

17 B. Holt, *Bring My Sons from Afar: The Unfolding of Harry Holt's Dream*, Eugene, Holt International Children's Services, 1980.

over the 'old' science-based adoption regime is largely imputed to highly mediagenic individuals such as Pearl S. Buck, the Doss family and the Holt family, who knew quite well how to publicize their humanitarian mission via radio, TV and bestselling novels, autobiographies and memoirs.

The studies under discussion share an almost exclusive focus on the adoption practices of the United States, even though all modern Western nations have participated in ICA, which begs for international comparative approaches. Scholars do provide a motive for this methodological nationalism, most notably Barbara Melosh. While describing the transition from an instrumentalizing to a sentimentalizing valorization of (adoptable) children, she claims the following:

> The emergence of modern adoption required a radically different understanding of family, one that overturned deeply held beliefs about blood and nurture, obligation and love, choice and chance. It was no accident that the United States was the crucible of this kind of adoption: in its repudiation of the past and its confidence in social engineering, adoption is quintessentially American.[18]

Ellen Herman agrees, noting that adoption is eminently compatible with cherished American values and traditions related to migration and mobility.[19] Carol J. Singley develops a comparable argument in *Adopting America: Childhood, Kinship and National Identity in Literature* (2011),[20] while analysing fictional representations rather than historical practices, claiming that "broken and reformed genealogies define the American child, family, and nation".[21] The cardinal contrastive foil for American exceptionalism is provided by Great Britain, which priced lineage and blood ties above all other forms of family making, and only passed its first adoption law in 1926, 75 years after the United States.

Europe Follows Suit

It is quite remarkable that the leading insights of the works discussed above also resonate in the scant and scattered histories of ICA in European nation-states, in spite of their persistent emphasis on American exceptionalism. Most notably, the claim that ICA

18 Melosh, 2002, p. 15.

19 Herman, 2008, p. 6.

20 C.J. Singley, *Adopting America: Childhood, Kinship and National Identity in Literature*, Oxford and New York, Oxford University Press, 2011.

21 Singley, 2011, p. 4.

is a completely unprecedented, late-20th-century phenomenon reverberates in most historical overviews of ICA, as can be illustrated by some tell-tale examples.

Yves Denéchère's *Des enfants venus de loin: Histoire de l'adoption internationale en France* (2010),[22] the first and only comprehensive history of domestic and international adoption in France so far, largely abides by the periodization schemes of North American scholarship. Like his North American colleagues, he also begins in the 20th century. Denéchère does not breathe a word about possible pre-20th-century forms of adoption. As he sees it, adoption only came into its own in the wake of the calamities of the two world wars. Given the high mortality rates of French soldiers during World War I, many children became dependent on the French state for support, and the state entitled itself to make these wards of the state available for adoption via legislative measures. On 27 July 1917, a law was passed to facilitate their adoption, and, on 18 June 1923, this law was extended to include all French minors in need of a family. On 29 July 1939, a law was passed to enable adoption with a complete rupture of all legal ties to the birth family (*adoption plenière*, as opposed to *adoption simple*, in which both forms of filiation existed side by side). For the first time in French history, this law established children subjected to full adoption as equals of legitimate children born in wedlock. After World War II, the French state concerned itself with children of French soldiers and German mothers during the allied occupation of post-war Germany. If these children were neglected or abandoned abroad, their adoption by French families was facilitated.

Denéchère locates the incipience of ICA in the 1950s, dwelling at length on the pioneering role of the French-American artist Josephine Baker. In the overall atmosphere of post-World-War II universalist humanitarianism – so persuasively captured by the MoMa photographic exhibition *The Family of Man* in 1955 – Baker set out to adopt children from diverse races and religious persuasions with her husband Jo Bouillon in 1954, when she had moved passed her prime as a performer. Her *Tribu Arc-en-Ciel* as she called her adoptive family came to include twelve children in all, from Korea, Columbia, France, Algeria, the Ivory Coast, Venezuela, Marocco, Belgium and Japan. Baker designed her transracial and transnational 'tribe' as a model family that was to prove to the world that complete harmony between different nationalities, races and religions was indeed possible. She used all available media of her time to propagate this message with the image of her family, including onsite visits to the castle *Milandes* where they lived together at the time. Clearly, Baker stylized herself as a French equivalent to the mediagenic pioneers of intercountry adoption in the United States, i.e., Pearl S. Buck, together with the Doss and Holt families. According

22 Y. Denéchère, *Des enfants venus de loin: Histoire de l'adoption internationale en France*, Paris, Collin, 2011.

to Denéchère, she helped pave the way for humanitarian organizations that aimed to ensure every child's right to a family worldwide, such as *Terre des Hommes*, founded in December 1963, and *L'Association pour la Protection de l'Enfance au Laos*. *Terre des Hommes* brought young victims of wars and other catastrophes from whatever part of the world to European countries, where they would be received by families willing to raise them, while keeping their birth names, nationalities and religions until they had reached adulthood and would be allowed to choose their own affiliations. As was the case in the United States, these initiatives were responses to emergency situations and preceded state regulation, which would only emerge in the 1970s. Denéchère provides a detailed record of all the regulations that were put into place since then up to 2010, including those that were meant to combat child kidnapping, trafficking and fraud with the birth certificates of adoptees.

Another equally detailed and impressively comprehensive history of intercountry adoption in one particular receiving country is provided by René Hoksbergen for the Dutch case, called *Kinderen die niet konden blijven: Zestig jaar adoptie in beeld* (2011, Children Who Could not Stay: A Picture of Sixty Years of Adoption).[23] The title of the book already gives the timeframe away. Hoksbergen's history of adoption in the Netherlands goes back to 1956, when the first adoption law was passed, to regulate the adoption of mostly children of single mothers. Together with Portugal, the Netherlands was the last country in Europe to introduce adoption legislation. Single motherhood was quite an issue in post-World War II Dutch society. Often enough, this pertained to Dutch women who had had a fling with Canadian soldiers who had liberated the Netherlands from German occupation or with German soldiers during occupation. The Church and the State conspired to put pressure on these women to give their children up for adoption. This law enabled *adoptio plena/adoption plenière*, to prevent birth parents from demanding their child back at a later stage in their lives.

Hoksbergen uses the periodization schema of 'generation' to organize the history of Dutch adoption, distinguishing between five different generations of adopters, namely the traditional/closed generation of adoptive parents (1956-1970), the open/idealistic generation (1970-1980), the calculating/realistic generation (1980-1991), the prepared/optimistic/demanding generation (1991-2005) and the generation who is aware of controversies and contradictions (2005-2010). From the 1980s onwards, Hoksbergen also includes the perspectives of the first and second generations of adoptees, clearly limiting these perspectives to those who were adopted internationally, a practice that only began to gather momentum in the 1970s as Hoksbergen sees it. He explains the transition from domestic to intercountry adoption by sociocultural changes in the

23 R. Hoksbergen, *Kinderen die niet konden blijven: Zestig jaar adoptie in beeld*, Soesterberg, Aspekt, 2011.

post-war period. In the course of the 1960s, a greater openness about taboo subjects such as sexuality, unwed motherhood, non-voluntary childlessness, and contraceptives emerged, which decreased the number of single mothers as well as the societal pressure to relinquish children born out of wedlock. This greater 'openness' also implied a stronger international outlook and a growing awareness of the needs of children globally, coupled to a strongly idealistic, activist political climate in which Dutch citizens were held responsible not only for their own well-being but also for the well-being of people in the economically vulnerable regions of this world. In addition to idealistic motives, the increase in prosperity in post-war affluent society and the introduction of television also helped to make Dutch citizens susceptible to intercountry adoption according to Hoksbergen. An increasing number of families had the financial means to take on another child, while TV brought the misery and deprivation of children in Biafra, Vietnam and so on home.

The Netherlands also had their mediagenic pioneers, namely the Dutch middlebrow novelist Jan de Hartog and his spouse Marjorie Mein. De Hartog had had intense exposure to Anglophone language cultures, having lived in the UK and the United States, where he and his wife had become Quakers. Even though they already had children of their own (like the Holts), they decided to adopt two orphaned Korean girls to 'save' them from neglect and discrimination and strongly appealed to Dutch people to do the same in a highly popular television talk show in 1967. Their call did not go unheeded, to say the least.[24] Obviously, the first wave of intercountry adoptions is steeped in 'white saviourism' (although this is not a term that Hoksbergen uses), and the adopters representing the second generation were not necessarily involuntarily childless couples at all. In the shadow of the Club of Rome's alarming report *Limits to Growth* (1972), some deliberately refrained from procreation, choosing to adopt a child that was already there instead. Others felt compelled to add one or several adopted children to their biological children. The early 1970s Dutch adopters were people who wanted to change the world for the better.

In his portraits of five successive generations of adopters, Hoksbergen clearly records the shift from humanitarian efforts to implement every child's right to a family (the second generation) to assertions of every couple's right to a child (the fourth 'demanding' generation, expressing a strong sense of entitlement). The last generation described in this book, however, is not so assertive any longer according to the author. In the course of the 21st century, adoptive parents are growing aware of the developmental challenges

---

24 Andere tijden [Other Times], NPO (Dutch Public Broadcasting Organization], 'Doe mij maar zo'n Koreaantje!' [Let me Have One of those Little Koreans!], 20 September 2006, https://anderetijden.nl/aflevering/383/Doe-mij-maar-zon-Koreaantje.

that adoptees have to deal with, who struggle with identity problems, belonging neither 'here' nor 'there'. Hoksbergen also dwells on adoption scandals, such as Operation Baby Lift that took children out of earthquake-hit Haïti in 2010 while bypassing adoption laws in several respects. ICA seems to have lost its innocence in this period, although it remains unclear how widespread this emergent awareness of adoption issues actually was or is. In any case, it did not deter prospective parents from ICA: the demand for adoptable children went up in the 21st century, rather than down.

To my knowledge, these two monographs are the most comprehensive histories published so far about adoption in European nation-states. Other studies have been written, but they do not necessarily cover the post-war period.[25] Histories of adoption in the Scandinavian countries have not (yet) been written as standalone monographs, or at least not in languages accessible to me, with anthropological studies outweighing historical perspectives. One has to stitch bits and pieces of their histories together from fragments published in studies that employ multinational[26] or multidisciplinary perspectives.[27] Signe Howell, anthropologist of ICA in Norway, offers a comparison between the United States and Norway, two countries with diametrically opposed political cultures, the one favouring the free market, the other the post-war welfare state, promoting state intervention into the lives of citizens from cradle to grave. In spite of this blatant difference, Howell's periodization of adoption follows the standard schema by and large, with adoption laws emerging in the wake of World War I in Norway, while international adoption is introduced to take care of the war orphans of World War II and the Korean War.

As to Spain, which morphed into another major European receiving country in the late 1980s, when the Chinese adoption channel opened up, anthropological research outweighs historical inquiry there as well, with a similar lacunary understanding of the history of ICA as a result. ICA in Spain basically meant the adoption of girls from China. This seemed a relatively innocent alternative as compared to goings-on during the Franco regime, when newborn babies of Franco's political enemies were spirited away by (Catholic) hospital personnel to be made available for adoption by good

25 See, e.g., J.P. Gutton, *Histoire de l'adoption en France*, Paris, Editions Publisud, 1993; J. Keating, *A Child for Keeps: The History of Adoption in England, 1918-45*, Basingstoke and New York, Palgrave Macmillan, 2009; G. Rossini, *A History of Adoption in England and Wales 1850-1961*, Barnsley, Pen and Sword Family History, 2014.

26 See, e.g., H. Altstein and R.J. Simon, *Intercountry Adoption: A Multi-national Perspective*, New York, Praeger, 1991; K. O'Halloran, *The Politics of Adoption: International Perspectives on Law, Policy, and Practice*, Dordrecht, Springer, 2009; P. Conn, *Adoption: A Brief Social and Cultural History*, New York, Palgrave Macmillan, 2013.

27 S. Howell, *The Kinning of Foreigners: Transnational Adoption in a Global Perspective*, New York and Oxford, Berghahn, 2006.

Catholic couples supporting Franco, a form of family formation that was hushed by the *pacto de silencio* which was to make for a new start after the ravages of the Spanish civil war.[28]

Transatlantic Resonances

Comparing North American and European historical studies of intercountry adoption, one may observe the following shared features. First, the history of adoption is generally written as a history of adoption *regulation* by law and by science-based 'psy-experts'. Thus, the timeline of the Adoption History Project initiated by the University of Oregon (https://pages.uoregon.edu/adoption/) begins in 1851, when the first U.S. adoption law was passed, listing a handful of additional 19th-century entries, which multiply exponentially when we enter into the 20th century. Only then did adoption became a 'modern', i.e., science-regulated, practice as a major research object of burgeoning disciplines such as sociology and developmental psychology, generating new professions such as social work, family counselling and family therapy, which were all invested in guiding adoptive families. European historical inquiry shares this preference for *de jure* over *de facto* adoptions. UK histories offer the proverbial exception to the rule which begin in mid-19th century, focusing on de facto adoptions, as the UK only passed its first adoption bill in 1927.[29] It has to be noted, however, that these studies deal with the circulation of children within the UK only. Second, and closely tied in with the first point of convergence, the turn from the 19th to the 20th century is generally thought to be the moment in time at which children came to be sought after for themselves, rather than for the free labour they could be made to provide.

Third, leading U.S. and European adoption historians converge in regarding ICA as a new phenomenon that only came about in the wake of World War II and the Korean war, the second watershed moment in the history of adoption. The revolutionary qualities ascribed to ICA are associated with the fact that it was initially up against the science-based professionals who strove after 'as if begotten' families based on maximum similarity between adopters and adoptees. Since international adoption often also implied a 'transracial' dimension, this standard was no longer tenable. Finally, adoption historians in both Europe and the United States firmly agree that ICA is the successor project to domestic adoption. Only when the numbers of domestically available adoptable children began to dwindle in Western nations, did prospective parents turn

28 J.B. Leinaweaver, 'Papering the Origins: Place-Making, Privacy, and Kinship in Spanish International Adoption', *Genealogy*, Vol. 3, No. 4, 2019.

29 See Keating, 2009 and Rossini, 2014.

their gaze elsewhere, crossing the boundaries between countries, continents and races, or so the argument goes.

Colonial Contexts

There is a huge elephant in this historiographical room. It is called colonial history. Most historians do not see it because of their myopic concentration on *de jure* adoptions and their tendency to postulate a categorical difference between 'modern', 20th-century adoption and affiliated forms of child re-allocation and re-education such as placing out, boarding and fostering. Adoptees, on the other hand, did see it, once they had reached adulthood and entered the premises of the university. Their scholarly work has played a pivotal role in exposing the racial and colonial subtexts of ICA, opening new vistas for interdisciplinary research. Especially the milestone publication *Outsiders Within: Writing on Transracial Adoption* (2006)[30] deserves special mention here, which includes a section with the tell-tale title 'Colonial Imaginations, Global Migrations'. To my knowledge, an essay in this section, Tobias Hübinette's "From Orphan Trains to Babylifts: Colonial Trafficking, Empire Building, and Social Engineering"[31] is one of the first publications to confront the colonial antecedents of ICA in depth.[32] This essay argues quite bluntly that ICA is best conceptualized as

> a mixed project of colonial uplifting, civilizing, and assimilating non-Western children and modernist service professionalization and institutionalization of family intervention so as to regulate, control, and discipline women's reproduction.[33]

For further evidence and arguments for re-contextualizing ICA within a colonial framework, one may glean the continuities between child circulation in colonial times and ICA in the postcolonial period in publications that do not solely focus on ICA in

30 J.J. Trenka, J.C. Oparah and S.Y. Shin (eds.), *Outsiders Within: Writing on Transracial Adoption*, Cambridge, MA, South End Press, 2006.

31 T. Hübinette, 'From Orphan Trains to Babylifts: Colonial Trafficking, Empire Building, and Social Engineering', *in* L. Askeland (ed.), *Children and Youth in Adoption, Orphanages, and Foster Care: A Historical Handbook and Guide*, London, Greenwood Press, 2006, pp. 139-151.

32 Twila Perry, e.g., also touches upon the colonial contexts of international adoption, as one of the many factors creating power hierarchies that compromise the 'fairness' of the transfer of children from the global South to the Global North considerably in T.L. Perry, 'Transracial and International Adoption: Mothers, Hierarchy, Race, and Feminist Legal Theory', *Yale Journal of Law and Feminism*, Vol. 10, No. 1, 1998, pp. 101-164.

33 Hübinette, 2006, p. 147.

the narrow sense of the word, i.e., legal and science-governed full adoption of mostly non-white minors from the global South by mostly white adults in the global North.

Transnational and transracial adoption was definitely not invented in the second half of the 20th century. The reason for this is twofold. To begin with, children were already circulating transnationally and/or transracially throughout the 19th and early 20th centuries as an integral part of empire.[34] Their circulation patterns were determined by the global inequalities of race, class and gender. Great Britain has a long history of placing out home children who were a burden on the state to families in the colonies who could do with an extra pair of hands, or to institutions in the process of erecting schools, hospitals and monasteries in the overseas territories likewise perennially short of labourers. One could argue that the new-fangled settler colonies did not yet have a firmly established working class, so persons of the 'wrong' age, race or gender were made to fill the gap. Between 1860 and 1920, around 90,000 home children were exported to Canada,[35] while around 10,000 children were sent to Australia between the 1920s and 1970s.[36] Lower-class girls were put to work as domestic servants, while boys became farmhands or construction workers. In fact, this mode of child removal is quite similar to the 19th-century orphan trains in the United States, which suggests that both domestic and international adoption are not as dissimilar as is often assumed in adoption historiography. The official rationale for these displacements was that socially disadvantaged children might have better opportunities for building a good life for themselves in overseas territories where the stigma of British class prejudice would not apply. In actual practice, they received little to no education, being put to work upon arrival, which condemned most of them to a lifetime of menial labour. In addition, without the protection of their families, they were easy victims of physical and sexual abuse.

While the British metropole emptied its children's homes by packing its inmates off to the colonies, boarding schools in the settler colonies filled up with indigenous and mixed children who were removed from their birth families and birth villages in a sustained effort to inculcate Western values and lifestyles in native youth. Margaret Jacobs (2009) has provided a detailed record of the ways in which white (upper) middle-class women moved into the new profession of social work between 1880 and 1940,

---

34 D.M. Pomfret, *Youth and Empire: Trans-Colonial Childhoods in British and French Asia*, Stanford: Stanford University Press, 2016.

35 K. Bagnell, *The Little Immigrants: The Orphans Who Came to Canada*, Toronto, Macmillan of Canada, 1980; R. Parker, *Uprooted: The Shipment of Poor Children to Canada, 1867-191*, Bristol, Policy Press, 2010.

36 P. Bean and J. Melville, *Lost Children of the Empire: The Untold Story of Britain's Child Migrants*, London, Allen and Unwin, 1989; M. Humphreys, *Empty Cradles*, London, Doubleday, 1994; R. Kershaw and J. Sacks, *New Lives for Old: The Story of Britain's Child Migrants*, Kew, Richmond Surrey, The National Archives, 2008.

imposing Western child-raising standards on indigenous families in the United States, Canada, Australia and New Zealand.[37] The removal of indigenous children continued in the post-war world, as her follow-up study *A Generation Removed: The Fostering and Adoption of Indigenous Children in the Postwar World* (2014)[38] reveals, although children's homes had now fallen out of grace and fostering and adoption had become the preferred means of whitewashing. By the 1960s an estimated 25% to 35% of Indian children had been separated from their birth parents. Similar interventions were implemented in Canada via the residential school system.[39] It is estimated that around 150,000 indigenous children were taken out of their families between 1883 and 1997. Thus, children of the 'wrong' class or race were particularly vulnerable to incursions into their family life as they were subjected to compulsory re-education, which always involved some degree of separation and alienation of their birth families and cultural heritage, in compliance with the infamous motto of the U.S. Carlisle Indian Industrial School: 'Kill the Indian, and Save the Man'. Clearly, the transnational and/or transracial circulation of vulnerable children had thus already taken root in Britain's settler colonies way before the post-war period in ongoing displacements from families to boarding schools and vice versa and from metropole to colony and the other way around. Here again, domestic and international practices of child circulation bear a much closer resemblance to each other than is generally acknowledged.

While the dislocations of indigenous children in the settler colonies of Great Britain have been brought out into the open as the subject of public debates as well as government-commissioned inquiries and apologies, it is far less known that the governments of continental European empires also engaged in child separation projects. Children became particularly central to colonial governance during the last phase of colonial expansion (1890-1940), when colonialism acquired a 'humanitarian' glow, as the British picked up 'the white man's burden', while the French embarked on the '*mission civilisatrice*' and the Dutch embraced the '*ethische politiek*' (Ethical Policy) for the Dutch East Indies. The idea took hold in the later 19th century that one should not merely exploit colonized nations but rather civilize, educate and uplift them. The aims of child separation projects in extraction colonies differed somewhat from the re-education policies in settler colonies, given the different ratios between

---

37 M. Jacobs, *White Mother to a Dark Race: Settler Colonialism, Maternalism, and the Removal of Indigenous Children in the American West and Australia, 1880-1940*, Lincoln and London, University of Nebraska Press, 2009.

38 M. Jacobs, *A Generation Removed: The Fostering & Adoption of Indigenous Children in the Postwar World*, Lincoln and London, University of Nebraska Press, 2014.

39 R.D. Chrisjohn, M. Maraun and S.L. Young, *The Circle Game: Shadows and Substance in the Indian Residential School Experience in Canada*, Penticton, Theytus Books, 2012; J.S. Milloy, *A National Crime: The Canadian Government and the Residential School System*, Winnipeg, The University of Manitoba Press, 2017.

settlers/colonial administrators and indigenous nations. While Australia, for example, embraced the aim of 'breeding out the colour' in its Aboriginal population, a form of cultural genocide one could say, no such aim was feasible in extraction colonies, where Europeans constituted only very small minorities. Here, the aim was rather eventual 'independence' of the colonial dominions as confederate states of the metropolitan centres of empire. Since children were considered to be more malleable than their adult counterparts, they were especially targeted by re-allocation and re-education projects, in the hope of raising new generations of Eurocentric religious leaders, politicians, medics and teachers who could function as intermediaries between the colonial government and its indigenous subjects.[40] Thus, overseas territories could be transformed into extensions or mirror images of European nation-states before they would become independent. This meant that children became central to colonial policies in a way they had never been before.[41] Hence, indigenous and mixed children were separated from their birth families and birth villages in extraction colonies as well, to various degrees of intrusiveness and permanence, via day schools, boarding schools or adoption into white families in colony or metropole.[42] In some colonies, Protestant and Catholic missionaries played a leading role in child separation projects as teachers, doctors and adopters, as in the Dutch and Belgian empires. In the much more centralistic French empire, it was the state that concerned itself with the re-education of, most notably, mixed children.

Christina Firpo has analysed in *The Uprooted: Race, Children, and Imperialism in French Indo-China, 1890-1980* (2016) how *métis* children in Indo-China who had been abandoned by their white fathers and were raised by their indigenous mothers in often poor circumstances became the central preoccupation of so-called French *métis* protection societies for almost a whole century.[43] The protection societies were bent on separating mixed children from their indigenous mothers to re-educate them in boarding schools run by the French state, to bring out the French rather than the Asian 'half' in them. The protection societies did not think highly of the pedagogical qualities of indigenous mothers, to put it mildly, so the idea was that children were better off

40 M. Derksen, '"On Their Javanese Sprout We Need to Graft the European Civilisation": Fashioning Local Intermediaries in the Dutch Catholic Mission, 1900-1940', *Tijdschrift voor Genderstudies*, Vol. 19, No. 1, 2014, pp. 29-55; M. Derksen, 'Local Intermediaries? The Missionising and Governing of Local Colonial Subjects in South Dutch New Guinea, 1920-1942', *Journal of Pacific History*, Vol. 51, No. 2, 2016, pp. 111-142.

41 A.L. Stoler, *Carnal Knowledge and Imperial Power: Race and the Intimate in Colonial Rule*, Berkeley, University of California Press, 2002.

42 G. Mak, M. Monteiro and E. Wesseling, 'Child Separation: (Post)Colonial Policies and Practices in the Netherlands and Belgium', *Low Countries Historical Review*, Vol. 135, No. 3-4, 2021, pp. 4-28.

43 C. Firpo, *The Uprooted: Race, Children, and Imperialism in French Indo-China, 1890-1980*, Honolulu, Hawai'I, University of Hawai'i Press, 2016.

under the tutelage of the French state, which had the means to feed and educate them. This rhetoric strikes the humanitarian chord again, but Firpo reveals quite clearly that young *métis* were also made to serve the interests of the colonial government. For one thing, the government feared these impoverished Eurasians as a potential breeding ground for opposition against the colonial state, so re-allocating and re-educating them was a form of risk management. After World War I, *métis* children in France's colonies were seen as a welcome means to boost the decimated French population and so on. All in all, Firpo estimates that around 10,000 *métis* children have gone through the protection system in Vietnam.

In the Dutch East Indies, mixed children had the same legal status as their counterparts in French Indo-China: if they were recognized by their European fathers, they would receive full citizenship of the Dutch state. But if the father had absconded, then they would grow up in the *kampong* among the rural poor, to the discomfort of the colonial government, who regarded the phenomenon of (semi-)Europeans steeped in poverty with anxiety and embarrassment. In the Dutch case, initiatives for the improvement of mixed children were developed in a less centralist way than in the French case, mostly by humanitarian volunteer organizations and – once again – missionaries. Reformist children's homes were instituted for children who had been found guilty of petty crimes by organizations such as *Pro Juventute*,[44] an NGO concerned with delinquent youth in the Netherlands and its colonies. The children would be kept there for as long as school administrators considered necessary for full reform, regardless of the consent of their indigenous mothers. The Protestant missionary Johannes van der Steur (1865-1945) was particularly instrumental in accommodating Eurasians in his boarding school Huize Oranje Nassau, who were left to their own devices in the *kampong*, or so it was thought. In Oranje Nassau, they would receive schooling and a Christian education, so they would qualify for reasonably well-paid jobs in colonial society. In the course of its existence, Oranje Nassau took in around 7,000 Eurasians. Its founder would go down into history as 'Pa' (Dad) van der Steur, father of 7,000 'Steurtjes' as they were called, many of whom emigrated to the Netherlands after the Dutch regime was defeated in two colonial wars in the late 1940s, as participants in the largest immigration wave in Dutch history ever, bringing around 300,000 Eurasians to the Netherlands between 1945 and 1965.[45]

The second reason why ICA cannot possibly be regarded as a new phenomenon is revealed by recent micro-historical inquiries into the emergence of international

44 A. Dirks, *For the Youth: Juvenile Delinquency, Colonial Civil Society and the Late Colonial State in the Netherlands Indies 1872-1942*, PhD Leiden University, 2011.

45 V. van de Loo, *Johannes 'Pa' van der Steur (1865-1945): Zijn leven, zijn werk en zijn Steurtjes: Biografie*, Den Haag, Stichting Tong Tong, 2015.

adoption channels transferring children from the Asian and African continents to Europe and North America in the post-war period. These studies reveal unambiguously that the first ICA networks developed directly out of the child separation projects in the colonies. When the French empire was dismantled, *métis* children were regarded as potential victims of the new regimes and transported to France to be made available for adoption by French families.[46] Similar insights are provided by the latest book-length study by Yves Denéchère, the edited volume *Enjeux postcoloniaux de l'enfance et de la jeunesse: Espace francophone* (1945-1980),[47] which is devoted to the reverberations of colonial dealings with children and youth in France's dominions in Indo-China and Africa in postcolonial French society. By now, Denéchère seems to have moved away from his Anglocentric and anecdotical focus on the example of charismatic stars such as Josephine Baker to explain the 'invention' of ICA, unearthing its roots in colonial childrearing practices instead. In the same vein, Belgian scholars Assumani Budagwa, Sarah Heynssens and Chiara Candaele have detailed how *métis* children in boarding schools run by Catholic orders were evacuated and transferred to Belgium on the eve of the decolonization conflict in Ruanda-Urundi, where they were made dependent on the benevolence of aspiring Belgian adoptive parents.[48] The same religious orders and even individuals who had run these boarding schools actively promoted intercountry adoption after empire. 'Patriation' of displaced Eurasian and Eurafrican children on the eve of decolonization, then, played an important role in the establishment of international adoption networks during the transition from the colonial to the postcolonial period, with children moving from birth families to boarding schools to adoptive families.

Once in the 'motherland', the new-fangled transnational and/or transracial adoptees were to perform a key role in national imago-building in the postcolonial period. Although few in numbers percentage-wise, their symbolic weight was and still is enormous. With national imagos damaged considerably by the mostly violent decolonization processes, adoptees from Europe's former colonies were emburdened

46 Firpo, 2016, pp. 132-165.

47 Y. Denéchère (ed.), *Enjeux postcoloniaux de l'enfance et de la jeunesse: Espace francophone (1945-1980)*, Bruxelles and New York, Peter Lang, 2019.

48 A. Budagwa, *Noirs-blancs, Métis: La Belgique et la segregation des Métis du Cong Belge et Ruanda-Urundi (1908-1960)*, Céroux-Mousty, Assumani Budagwa, 2014; S. Heynssens, 'Practices of Displacement: Forced Migration of Mixed-Race Children from Colonial Ruanda-Urundi to Belgium', *Journal of Migration History*, Vol. 2, No. 1, 2016, pp. 1-31; S. Heynsens, *De kinderen van Save: Een geschiedenis tussen Afrika en België*, Antwerpen, Polis, 2017; C. Candaele, 'Mother Metropole: Adoptions of Rwandan Minors in Postcolonial Belgium (1970-1994)', *BMGN - Low Countries Historical Review*, Vol. 135, No. 3-4, 2020, pp. 209-233.

with repair work that switched from paternalist to maternalist vocabularies, putting the metropole into the picture as a nonracist, protective and nurturing mother.[49]

Transnational and transracial adoptees were not only vital to national imago-building in postcolonial Europe. There was intense rivalry between the United States and postcolonial Europe on this front, as the United States was taking over global hegemony from the UK while entering into the Cold War with Soviet Russia. Christina Klein has spelled out the political subtext of the symbolic work of adoptees in *Cold War Orientalism: Asia in the Middlebrow Imagination, 1945-1961* (2003). As Europe was losing its colonies, the United States struggled to extend its influence over these very territories, to prevent them from becoming vassal states of the Soviet empire. While old-style European colonialism was written off as harshly exploitative, the United States stylized itself as a new kind of imperial power in the same maternalist mode that also set the trend in postcolonial Europe, as motherly and caring that is, rather than patriarchal and oppressive. ICA went to the heart of this maternalist imago-building, with the United States figuring as an adoptive mother clutching "the homeless, the tempest-tost" to her maternal bosom, with the promise of nurturing deprived people, rather than merely using them for her own needs.[50] In spite of the humanitarian rhetoric of saving children for children's sake, one could argue that the symbolic potential of adoptees was deployed to serve political agendas that did not necessarily benefit the children themselves. This suggests that another watershed moment in adoption historiography was not as watertight as the historians referenced above made it out to be, namely the distinction between pre-20th-century adoption when children were priced for their economic value, and the Century of the Child, when children became 'priceless' and valued supposedly purely for their own sake.

BEYOND INNOCENCE

Recent historical inquiry permits the following conclusions, however fragmented and incomplete it may be. First, it is highly contrived to study international adoption as a unique, standalone phenomenon, isolated from affiliated forms of separating children from their birth families, such as, placing out, boarding, fostering and domestic adoption.

49 L. Briggs, 'Mother, Child, Race, Nation: The Visual Iconography of Rescue in Transnational and Transracial Adoption', *Gender & History*, Vol. 15, No. 2, 2003, pp. 179-200; K. Manzo, 'Imaging Humanitarianism: NGO Identity and the Iconography of Childhood', *Antipode*, Vol. 40, No. 4, 2008, pp. 632-657; M.C. Jerng, *Claiming Others: Transracial Adoption and National Belonging*, Minneapolis and London, University of Minnesota Press, 2010; B. Perreau, *The Politics of Adoption: Gender and the Making of French Citizenship*, Cambridge, MA, The MIT Press, 2014.

50 C. Klein, *Cold War Orientalism: Asia in the Middlebrow Imagination, 1945-1961*, Berkeley, University of California Press, 2003.

The dynamic of child separation is rather characterized by an ongoing give-and-take between families and boarding schools, which is obscured by the persistent focus on *de jure* adoptions over *de facto* adoptions. Second, the idea that the onset of the 20th century signals a new commitment to the 'best interests of the child' stands exposed as somewhat short-sighted. Although adoptees and children more broadly ceased to be economically valuable, this does not mean that they were no longer instrumentalized. It is therefore mistaken to claim that modern, 20th-century adoption manifests a 'humanitarian revolution':[51]

> Whether to ensure the continuation of a family name, or to secure the descent of property rights, or to provide for funeral memorials, adoption was intended to serve the needs of adult adopters. Today, it is universally the case that adoption is understood to serve the needs of children.[52]

However, the pressure to perform emotional or symbolic labour by gratifying parents' (often overwrought) desire for a child or boosting the national imago of receiving countries can also be a hard cross to bear, as we may learn by listening to what adoptees have to say about their own experiences.[53] Third, the assumption that humanitarianism is the opposite of colonialism is likewise mistaken. During the last phase of colonial expansion as well as the Cold War period, humanitarianism fed into colonialism and imperialism.[54] Fourth, the idea of ICA is the successor project to domestic adoption is historically flawed. Rather, ICA is the continuation of the last chapter in colonial history which was written in the key of white saviourism, a potent cocktail of 'uplifting' the newer generations of colonized nations and subjecting them in the same process. Fifth, European adoption historiography is blinded by unwarranted Anglocentrism if it passes over its own colonial histories while tracing the patterns of global child circulation. Last, to impute the 'invention' of ICA to a few charismatic, mediagenic individuals is to sanitize the systemic global inequalities that drive this form of family formation. Taken together, these fallacies combine to place a *cordon sanitaire* around ICA, making it seem more innocent than it ever was or ever could be.

The historical paradigm delineated above is conducive to the tenacious underestimation of the systemic nature of adoptive malpractices. If ICA is understood to be a new, modern, enlightened practice of saving children from the third world, untrammelled by the burden of a contested past, then abusive practices can only be seen as incidental

51 Conn, 2013, p. 92.
52 Ibid., p. 48.
53 See, once again, Trenka et al., 2006.
54 K. Vallgarda, *Imperial Childhoods and Christian Mission: Education and Emotions in South India and Denmark*, Basingstoke, Palgrave Macmillan, 2014.

aberrations from an otherwise luminous path. This is not to say that the genealogy presented in this chapter is the only cause of the willed ignorance of adoption crimes. The focus on the post-adoption process in the receiving countries, as manifested by the ongoing concern with the psychological development of adoptees in the receiving countries, at the expense of inquiry into children's pre-adoption trajectories in the sending countries, in combination with the difficulty of accessing the voices of birth parents, also plays into this conundrum, where scholarly inquiry is concerned. This unbalanced situation has been remedied somewhat by anthropological inquiry into the pre-adoption trajectories of children in the sending countries.[55] Adult adoptees who have managed to retrace and reconnect with their birth parents have also helped to create knowledge and awareness of birth parents' perspectives in the sending countries through scholarly publications and documentary films.[56]

Sustained historical inquiry into the continuities between colonial and postcolonial practices of transracial and transnational adoption, in combination with reinserting adoption into the whole gamut of child separation practices, should serve to question the strong sense of entitlement of prospective parents in the global North to children from the global South. As Laura Briggs and Diana Marre have put in rather sobering terms, transnational adoption may be regarded as a "stratified form of assisted reproduction",[57] meaning:

> a transnational system of power relations that enables privileged women to bear and nurture children while disempowering those who are subordinated by reason of class, race and national origin.[58]

The question needs to be posed, rather than muffled by humanitarian do-goodery:

> who is normatively entitled to expect of others that they will engage in biological reproductive functions for them, while they retain the 'right' to be the providers of the child's nurture and culture?[59]

---

55 Bos, 2007; L. Briggs, *Somebody's Children: The Politics of Transracial and Transnational Adoption*, Durham and London, Duke University Press, 2012; K.A. Johnson, *China's Hidden Children: Abandonment, Adoption, and the Human Costs of the One-Child Policy*, Chicago, University of Chicago Press, 2016.

56 See, e.g., the films directed by Deann Borshay Liem: *Person Plural*. Mu films, 2000; *In the Matter of Cha Jung Hee*. Mu films, 2010; *Geographies of Kinship*, Mu films 2019.

57 L. Briggs and D. Marre (eds.), 'Introduction: The Circulation of Children', *in* D. Marre and L. Briggs (eds.), *International Adoption: Global Inequalities and the Circulation of Children*, New York and London, New York University Press, 2009, pp. 1-29, 15.

58 Ibid., p. 17.

59 Ibid.

For sure, questions such as these are a far cry from the imperative of saving children from the third world, and they throw legitimate doubt on the presumed right of every (Western) prospective parent to a non-Western adoptee child and his or her biological parent. The need to question this sense of entitlement remains urgent, even now that some receiving countries are halting ICA or stopping it altogether, as surrogacy practices taking recourse to baby farms in, for example, India raise similar issues. In the aftermath of countless adoption scandals, the power differences between those who adopt and those who give up their children for adoption should occupy the centre of critical attention, to prevent receiving countries from making the same mistakes over and over again. A non-sanitized history of ICA could help to keep this awareness alive. Claiming others as one's very own is always a risky business, especially if these others are confined to a much more precarious position than the claimant.

9 The Baby and the Bathwater: Resisting Adoption Reform

Sophie Withaeckx

Introduction

In 2021, inquiries into illicit practices in intercountry adoption (ICA) were released both in the Netherlands and Belgium. The Dutch report, first published in February 2021, had found that abuses – like fraud, kidnapping and even 'baby-farming' – were systematic and endemic in both past and present adoption practices. It concluded that the Dutch government and adoption agencies, despite being aware of abuses, did not act to prevent them and were themselves involved in some cases by acting 'contrary to the rules'.[1] It recommended to immediately suspend all intercountry adoptions, alleging that the prevention of illicit practices could not be guaranteed in the current adoption system. Then Minister of Justice, Dekker, followed the advice and announced the suspension of all intercountry adoptions.

In September of the same year, a report was published by an expert panel on transnational adoption which was tasked with examining the occurrence of illicit practices in Belgium and formulating recommendations.[2] In line with the Dutch findings, the report concluded that the current adoption system was not capable of preventing illicit practices, guaranteeing correct procedures and providing the necessary support for victims. It advised a considerable restructuring of the adoption system and recommended a passive attitude regarding adoption, implying that agencies should no longer actively look for children but only respond to demands for support emanating from countries of origin.[3] To enable such a paradigm shift, the panel recommended

---

1 COIA, 'Rapport Commissie Onderzoek Interlandelijke Adoptie', The Hague, February 2021, https://www.rijksoverheid.nl/documenten/rapporten/2021/02/08/tk-bijlage-coia-rapport.

2 Expertenpanel-Inzake-Interlandelijke-Adoptie, *Eindrapport*. Brussels, Agentschap Opgroeien, 2021. Although there is an overarching federal agency registering and controlling all intercountry adoption, the practical administration of adoption in Belgium is delegated to the different communities, which each have their own central authority. The report of the expert panel was commissioned by the Flemish governments, and the ensuing debate only concerned the Flemish community. Hence, the analysis is limited to Flemish (Dutch-speaking) newspapers.

3 The report motivates such a shift by the need for a correct implementation of the subsidiarity principle enshrined in the 1993 Hague Convention on intercountry adoption, which "implies that the system of intercountry adoption should be steered by a demand of countries of origin for potential adoption parents in case local care facilities are lacking" instead of being steered by a demand from countries of origin, as was found to be the case (Expertenpanel-Inzake-Interlandelijke-Adoptie, 2021, p. 17).

a two-year temporary 'adoption pause', which the then minister Beke announced to implement.[4]

In both countries, the publication of these reports was followed by fierce debates and strong indignation. Reactions of shock and anger about the systematic fraud, abductions and corruption found to be endemic in the adoption system might indeed be expected. However, many actors seemed more shocked by the idea that transnational adoption might come to an end. Indeed, such was – and is – the resistance to the research panel's propositions to suspend adoptions, that both countries soon reversed the decision. In June 2022 – a year after the publication of the Dutch report – the newly appointed minister Weerwind announced the resumption of adoption, under conditions that would, according to him, offer solid guarantees that would rule out abuses. In Flanders, the reversal happened even quicker: just a week after announcing his agreement with the panel's recommendation and a temporary stop to adoption, Flemish minister Beke – pressured by his own political coalition parties – reversed the decision, allowing adoptions to continue unabated – although he did stick to his intention to fundamentally restructure the adoption system.

In an op-ed piece, adoptee Shashitu Rahima Tarirga describes her disappointment and astonishment about these responses to the systematic abuses revealed in the reports:

> I had hoped that the publication of that [Dutch] report – and the black on white establishment of abuses and illicit practices – would bring about change. I had hoped that the perspective of all adoptees (both those who are positive and those who are negative about their adoption) and birth parents would finally be taken into account. The opposite appeared to be true. It was solely the intended parents who made it into the media. I had hoped so much that the child would be put central.... Beginning of September, it was Flanders' turn. Minding the debate in the Netherlands, I did not put up my hopes too high.... There was only talk of the adoption stop and how devastating this would be for intended parents and the situation of adoptable children. This decision denies the experiences of adoptees who have to wait long time for answers and who might never get an answer on life-determining questions. And what about birth parents, who involuntarily lost a child through transnational adoption?[5]

4 The author was member of the expert panel and in that capacity produced an individually written report discussing "Ethical Dilemmas in Transnational Adoption" (available in Dutch here https://www.opgroeien.be/nieuws-en-pers/nieuws/rapport-expertenpanel-interlandelijke-adoptie-in-vlaanderen). The final report of the expert panel was the result of a consensus among the members.

5 See https://kifkif.be/cnt/artikel/het-debat-over-interlandelijke-adoptie-komen-wensouders-nog-te-vaak-op-de-eerste-plaats.

As Shashitu rightly notices, rather than welcoming initiatives aimed at preventing fraud and doing justice to victims, in a practice that is, after all, meant to be 'in the child's best interest', propositions to reform or abolish adoption are often met with fierce resistance. Announcements of reform have been accompanied by an outpouring of news reports, mediatized debates and op-ed pieces in which not only the adoptive parents, but also politicians and some adoptees, decry how reforms and (temporary) bans on adoption would deprive millions of orphans of a loving home. While such opponents might (reluctantly) concede that illegal practices should be addressed, propositions for reform are mostly perceived as depriving adoptive parents of the opportunity to raise an abandoned child, and Western nations of the opportunity to exercise their moral duty by taking in children from countries assumedly incapable of caring for them. According to a recurring proverb, the abolishment of adoption would amount to "throwing away the baby with the bathwater".[6] This narrative aptly expresses the belief that adoption protects something of priceless value – vulnerable children – and designates those who criticize adoption as carelessly throwing away those children. But what exactly is feared to be lost when adoption is abolished or reformed? Are there in fact other interests at stake when adoption reform is resisted, as Shashitu's blog seems to suggest? Whose voices and interests become centralized when adoption reforms are contested? And why is it that a child protection measure that is actually already on its retour still provokes such fierce debates and emotions?

This chapter explores the discursive work done by actors expressing resistance to adoption reforms. Using the lens of 'the politics of compassion', I will examine how the affects in these discourses are constitutive of narratives of Western nation-building and subject formation.[7] In postcolonial contexts marked by increasing challenges to Western hegemony and claims for redress of past and present injustices, resistances against adoption reform can be understood as skewed attempts "to refashion postcolonial futures",[8] in which the child to be salvaged becomes a proxy for cherished self-representations built on goodness and compassion.

6 This saying is not just used in the media debates which are the focus of the present chapter, but can also be found in academic scholarship, as in the case of Elizabeth Bartholet, a self-declared 'enthusiast' supporter of ICA and opponent of any reform, who warned that "We have to avoid, as the saying goes, throwing the baby out with the bath water" (see E. Bartholet, 'International Adoption: Thoughts on the Human Rights Issues', *Buffalo Human Rights Law Review*, Vol. 13, 2007, pp. 151-204, 179).

7 L. Berlant (ed.), *Compassion: The Culture and Politics of an Emotion*, New York, Routledge, 2004; J. Butler, *Precarious Life: The Powers of Mourning and Violence*, New York, Verso, 2006; I. Danewid, 'White Innocence in the Black Mediterranean: Hospitality and the Erasure of History', *Third World Quarterly*, Vol. 38, No. 7, 2017, pp. 1674-1689.

8 M. Balkenhol, 'Silence and the Politics of Compassion. Commemorating Slavery in the Netherlands', *Social Anthropology*, Vol. 24, No. 3, 2016, pp. 278-293, 290.

Through a discourse analysis of Belgian and Dutch newspaper articles, I will examine which emotions are mobilized when adoption reforms are publicly discussed, how these feed into particular self-representations, and which kinds of social worlds become constructed – and maintained – in order to safeguard such moral selves. The articles I analysed were published between 1 February 2021 and 31 July 2022 and cover eighteen months of frantic discussion about intercountry adoption, occasioned by the Dutch and Flemish ministers' announcement to stop adoption and the subsequent reversals of these decisions.

In the first section, I will discuss adoption as an expression of humanitarian reason, which gives rise to particular mobilizations of affect and shapes moral subjectivities. Next, I will describe how a humanitarian-compassionate narrative on adoption relies on the constitution of two central figures: the humanitarian saviour and the helpless waif. Lastly, I offer a discourse analysis of Dutch and Flemish newspaper articles discussing the announcements to stop and reform adoptions in 2021 before I conclude this chapter.

Emotions, Affect and Power in the Humanitarian Exchange

Since 2005, the number of transnational adoptions has considerably decreased in the Netherlands and Belgium, in line with global trends in transnational adoption.[9] As a child protection measure, it affects a relatively small number of children worldwide. Why is it then that, despite the reoccurring reports of systematic abuses throughout the history of modern adoption, there seems to be so much reluctance to properly address these or to resort to alternatives? Apparently, adoption seems to touch upon a sensitive nerve, to the extent that challenges to adoption are experienced as challenges to an important moral good that is to be preserved at all costs.

The elements that seem essential to the moral goodness of adoption – saving suffering children, expressing solidarity, displaying love – situate it strongly within the logic of humanitarian reason, identified by French anthropologist and sociologist Didier Fassin.[10] Humanitarianism arises from the contemporary fascination with images of suffering and distress, which are now omnipresent and immediately made available

9 See P. Selman, 'The Global Decline of Intercountry Adoption: What Lies Ahead?', *Social Policy & Society*, Vol. 11, 2021, pp. 381-397 and P. Selman, *Global Statistics for Intercountry Adoption: Receiving States and States of Origin 2004-2021*, HCCH, 2023, https://www.hcch.net/en/publications-and-studies/details4/?pid=5891&dtid=32.

10 D. Fassin, *Humanitarian Reason. A Moral History of the Present*, Berkeley University of California Press, 2012; D. Fassin, 'The Predicament of Humanitarianism', *Qui Parle*, Vol. 22, No. 1, 2013, pp. 33-48.

through both traditional and social media, eliciting compassion and a drive to assist. But much more than just an individual expression of empathy, humanitarianism functions as 'a mode of governing': an institutionalized and politicized practice directed at victims of 'precariousness' (homelessness, unemployment, exile, disasters, famines, epidemics, wars etc.).[11] Practices of humanitarian intervention are not just about providing disinterested aid; rather, they are ways to govern, with humanitarianism providing a language that "serves both to define and to justify discourses and practices of the government of human beings".[12] And this is a language that works remarkably well: wielding humanitarian motivations enables governments to mobilize support for social, political and even military interventions into the lives of citizens designated as 'vulnerable' and in need of assistance – both within and across the borders of the intervening nation-state. Humanitarianism succeeds in justifying such interventions due to its ability to conjure up the ideal of a community of human beings, relating to each other as equals. As images of suffering remind one of the actual inequalities in the human condition, humanitarianism provides the (illusory) conviction that inequalities and suffering can be overcome through solidarity and compassion. Thereby, it offers contemporary societies a secularized version of narratives of redemption and salvation, even though it might cover up some less disinterested motives.[13] Indeed, the language of humanitarianism with its emphasis on suffering and compassion has proven more likely to generate support than invocations of justice.[14]

For collectives, like the nation-state, humanitarianism can bolster nationalistic representations built around moral righteousness, providing credibility and justification for their management of vulnerable citizens. For the individual, participating in this humanitarian logic enables to constitute oneself as a subject who recognizes others – even those who are suffering, less fortunate, living at a distance – as fellow-humans. It also underlines one's 'humaneness': an identification of the self as a 'good' person who is emotionally and literally moved by the suffering of other human beings and who is able to couple such feelings to reason and rational action. Emotions, traditionally despised as the opposite of reason, are here recognized as a 'moving force' underpinning reasonable action. Moral sentiments – "the emotions that direct our attention to the suffering of others and make us want to remedy them" – become the prerequisite for action, and the feeling of the 'right' emotions – empathy, indignation, sadness and so on – becomes a forebode, even a proof, that one wants (and will) 'do good'.[15]

11 Fassin, 2012, p. x.
12 Ibid., p. 2.
13 Ibid., p. xii.
14 Ibid., p. 2.
15 Ibid., pp. 1-2.

A key emotion in humanitarianism is compassion. Dictionary definitions emphasize the 'double' nature of compassion, as a combination of feeling and 'sympathetic consciousness' of others' distress with a will or desire to action.[16] Such definitions also reveal the paradoxical nature of the moral sentiments at the heart of humanitarianism: while proffering an egalitarian, common humanity, it is clear that feelings and actions are not equally distributed. Humanitarianism involves a skewed power relation in which the objects of compassion are mainly 'the poorest, most unfortunate, most vulnerable individuals' while those coming to their aid are enabled to do this precisely because they occupy positions of more power and privilege.[17] Indeed discourses of rescue can "extend in only one direction" as reciprocity is de facto impossible.[18]

Fassin's sociological perspective mainly focuses on the material sociopolitical context in which humanitarianist compassion takes shape, to the detriment of the subjectivities and feelings of superiority/inferiority that are generated through the humanitarian exchange. But from an ethical point of view, the question of moral subjectivities equally deserves critical attention and cannot be so easily separated from the materiality of the social worlds in which they take shape. Questions of moral subjectivity have been central in feminist scholarship on affect, which examines how emotions operate precisely in this intertwinement of unequal societies, skewed power relations and individual understandings of the self. Affect theory has reconceptualized emotions as being not just 'psychological states' arising from an assumed pre-existing, stable interior self; nor are they merely imposed upon us from exterior social worlds.[19] Affect literally implies that our selves become 'affected by' the objects that surround us, with our emotions regulating how we relate and respond to those objects. Objects become recognizable to us as 'other' by investing them with particular affects (fear, love, anger, disgust etc.).[20] It is precisely in that moment that boundaries are drawn between self and other, that both self and other 'come to be' and 'surface' as separate beings. Any encounter with an 'other' then, is a moment in which 'selves' and 'others' become actively constituted through the use of emotions. Emotions then should be understood as 'social and cultural practices', involved in 'world making' and, thus, actively creating the social worlds in which

16 The *Merriam-Webster* dictionary defines it as follows: "sympathetic consciousness of others' distress together with a desire to alleviate it"; "a strong feeling of sympathy and sadness for the suffering or bad luck of others and a wish to help them" (see https://www.merriam-webster.com/dictionary/compassion).

17 Fassin, 2012, p. 3.

18 L. Briggs, 'Mother, Child, Race, Nation: The Visual Iconography of Rescue and the Politics of Transnational and Transracial Adoption', *Gender & History*, Vol. 15, No. 2, 2003, 179-200, p. 197.

19 S. Ahmed, *The Cultural Politics of Emotion*, Edinburgh, Edinburgh University Press, 2004, pp. 9-10.

20 Ahmed (2004) uses the example of a child reacting with fear to the sight of a bear to illustrate how affects are not merely 'in' objects: fear does not arise from some essential quality of the bear, or from assumed pre-existing inner knowledge of the child about bears. The child's image of the bear as an animal to be feared arises from "cultural histories and memories" that have been passed down to the child and shapes how it will respond in a real-life encounter with a bear.

they participate.[21] As they involve the constitution of boundaries and the assignation of social positions to the thus constituted self and its other, such encounters are also reflective and productive of power inequalities: "feelings can (re)produce dominant social and geo-political hierarchies and exclusions".[22]

Adoption and the Politics of Compassion

A persistent narrative about adoption holds that it is the only solution for the 'millions of orphans' worldwide languishing in substandard care facilities or on the streets.[23] Adoption is often presented as an ultimate win-win for all parties involved, with love and gratitude acting as the glue binding the different parties in the so-called adoption triad together: 'birth families' or communities who selflessly give up their children to grant them a better life; adoptive parents driven by their desire to found a family or to provide humanitarian assistance to needy children; and adoptive children who find their salvation in a loving home.

However, this narrative has also been exposed as a fallacious myth, built on the distortion of facts and the refusal to recognize the gendered, classed and racialized injustices that underlie adoption practices.[24] For example, the emphatic invocation of the 'millions and millions' of orphans supposedly waiting to be adopted is commonly inferred from UNICEF estimates. However, UNICEF's definition of an orphan is over-inclusive, defining an orphan as any "child under 18 years of age who has lost *one or both parents* to any cause of death" (emphasis added). Of the 140 millions of these 'orphans', it is a minority of 15.1 million who has lost both parents. Even those children are not immediately 'adoptable' as there are often still other family members, community structures or care facilities around that can provide care.[25]

Moreover, the emphasis on individual and colour-blind love in the adoptive family conceals the pernicious global inequalities and market dynamics shaping intercountry adoption. Such a focus on love, attachment and affection taking place in the intimate space of the family has a fetishist quality to it: it works to conceal the labour that is done by a multitude of actors – states, lawyers, laws and conventions, social workers,

21 Ibid., p. 10.

22 C. Pedwell and A. Whitehead, 'Affecting Feminism: Questions of Feeling in Feminist Theory', *Feminist Theory*, Vol. 13, No. 2, 2012, pp. 115-129, 120.

23 D.M. Smolin, 'Intercountry Adoption and Poverty: A Human Rights Analysis', *Capitol University Law Review*, Vol. 36, No. 2, 2007, pp. 413-454.

24 J. Oreskovic and T. Maskew, 'Red Thread or Slender Reed: Deconstructing Prof. Bartholet's Mythology of International Adoption', *Buffalo Human Rights Law Review*, Vol. 14, No. 1, 2008, pp. 71-128.

25 Ibid., p. 79.

adoption agencies, intermediaries, judges and so on – to produce a child that is 'adoptable', gets transferred into a new family and receives a new identity.[26] But through this concealing, the affective language of adoption is also *productive*: it (re)produces a particular worldview, in which certain social relations and subjectivities surface as just and legible, while others recede from view. The representation of adoption as an act of unconditional love hinges on the surfacing of two centralized figures: 'the humanitarian saviour' and the passive, helpless figure of 'the waif'. In what follows, I further explore how each of these figures relates to the constitution of both individual and collective moral subjectivities.

The Humanitarian Saviour

To what extent has adoption actually been the selfless, benevolent practice it is often presented to be? Adoption practices, both domestic and international, are generally motivated by two main rationales: a humanitarian motive – contributing to a better world by giving an abandoned child a 'better' life – and the desire to create a family, often when efforts to conceive one's own child have failed. However, as an expression of humanitarian governmentality, adoption exceeds individual desires and particular acts of beneficence. The legal figure of adoption as we know it now is the outcome of a deliberate reproductive politics, in which some become recognized as 'proper' parents while others become discredited and therefore 'justly' divested of their rights and abilities to parent – a process in which 'race', class and gender intersect to create privileges and exclusions.[27]

In Western countries, the generous availability of children for domestic adoptions until the 1970s was conditioned by the stigmatization of unwed motherhood and infertility, the inaccessibility or criminalization of contraception and abortion, and the complicity of religious and legal institutions enabling secrecy and the swift termination of ties between mother and child.[28] After the 1970s, the combined effects of feminist and adoptee movements and the granting of reproductive rights to women led to a marked decrease in the availability of adoptable children on the domestic market. From then on, intercountry adoption considerably increased, with children moving mostly from

26 Inspired by psychoanalytic and Marxist understandings of the notion of 'fetishism', Ahmed uses this notion to explain how understandings of emotions as pre-existing states residing in objects conceal how emotions are actually actively produced: "'feelings' become 'fetishes', qualities that seem to reside in objects, only through an erasure of the history of their production and circulation" (Ahmed, 2004, p. 22).

27 S. Patton-Imani, 'Redefining the Ethics of adoption, Race, Gender, and Class', *Law & Society Review*, Vol. 36, No. 4, 2002, 813-862, p. 815.

28 P. Selman, 'Intercountry Adoption in Europe 1998-2008. Patterns, Trends and Issues', *Adoption & Fostering*, Vol. 34, No. 1, 2010, pp. 4-19.

the Global South (Asia, Latin America, and Africa) and poorer regions within Europe (Romania, Russia, Bulgaria, Poland etc.) to richer countries of the Global North.

Adoption from the Global South has been inscribed in preceding patterns of oppression and exploitation marking (neo)colonial politics. Practices of child removal had been a recurring part of colonial policies, aimed at 'civilizing' the children of indigenous communities, seen as lacking the skills of 'proper' parenthood. Child separation took on many forms:

> manumission from enslavement and subsequent fostering; discursive, legal and actual 'orphaning' or 'dekinning'; forced or consensual stay at orphanages and boarding schools; consented or coerced fostering or adoption; or civilising and disciplining programmes at day schools.[29]

Often presented as ways to 'save', 'civilize' and properly 'educate' children, these projects were profoundly moral, as they always involved the imposition of "specific morals and life styles on its subjects" and aimed at transforming the colonized objects of intervention into docile, governable subjects.[30] Such projects, however, not only affected indigenous communities; they also shaped the subjectivities of both colonizers and citizens in the 'motherland'. A self-understanding as 'do-gooder' became entrenched not only through direct involvement in acts of salvation in the colonies but also through indirect exposure to narratives describing the moral uplift caused by colonial intervention.[31]

Present-day adoption agencies operate in narrow institutional continuities with these colonial practices, as the same persons, organizations, practices and financial circuits often became involved in the newly rebranded humanitarian adoption agencies.[32] Moreover, there are important discursive continuities. Colonial practices of child separation were legitimized as "charitable, humanitarian, civilising and/ or Christianising projects in which children were 'rescued' from their own so-called poor, primitive, endangered, enslaved, uneducated, heathen or otherwise deficient conditions".[33] Likewise, contemporary humanitarian representations of transnational adoption routinely represent the measure as 'the only hope' for abandoned children

29 G. Mak, M. Monteiro, and L. Wesseling, 'Child Separation: (Post)colonial Policies and Practices in the Netherlands and Belgium', *Low Countries Historical Review*, Vol. 135, No. 3-4, 2020, pp. 4-28, p. 7.

30 Ibid., p. 4.

31 Ibid., p. 13.

32 C. Candaele, 'Mother Metropole: Adoptions of Rwandan Minors in Postcolonial Belgium (1970-1994)', *BMGN - Low Countries Historical Review*, Vol. 135, No. 3-4, 2020, pp. 209-233.

33 Mak et al., 2020, p. 11.

languishing in substandard care facilities in the Global South. Analogously to the colonial civilizing mission, investment in the humanitarian practice of adoption enables the surfacing of a 'do-gooder', this time through the application of a secularist, postcolonial narrative of rescue. This plays out both on collective and individual levels.

On a collective level, intercountry adoption has become inscribed in a process of nation-building, as the engagement with adoption can be presented as an expression of a nation's 'humaneness', solidarity, cosmopolitanism and generosity.[34] As has been shown for countries like France and Sweden, for example, investment in transnational adoption is a corollary of their self-branding as tolerant, open-minded and marked by colour-blind multiculturalism.[35] This nationalist investment in 'humaneness' through adoption also explains why adopted children have become radically differentiated from other categories of immigrants like asylum seekers, labour migrants or unaccompanied minors.[36] The influx of immigrants from non-Western countries is often presented as a threat to 'Western values' that needs to be limited and contained. The benevolence with which adopted children are welcomed and invited in could, therefore, be seen as rather odd. However, the presence of the immigrant other does not only feed into imageries of fear; politics of immigration can also enable a national subject that can imagine itself as generous and hospitable, provided that the immigrant newcomers behave as 'grateful guests' and do not 'betray' the hospitality granted to them.[37] Expectations of gratefulness are obviously much easier to project onto orphaned children, whose presumed innocence and passivity position them as quintessential objects of compassion. Moreover, adoptees' insertion into an adoptive family, stripped of their original nationality and cut from any ties with a racialized family or community, accords them an immediate status as 'one of us'. Indeed, their childish innocence combined with this 'freestanding' status enables to figure them as "'cultureless' blank slates in which the language and culture of the new family and nation can be inscribed".[38]

On an individual level, humanitarian discourse enables individuals to constitute good moral selves, built on values of selflessness, solidarity and relationality and exteriorized by practices of giving, supporting and saving. But the apparent other-directed 'need

34 S. Roux and A. Fillod-Chabaud, 'Adoption: Les Familles de la République', *French Politics, Culture & Society*, vol. 38, no. 3, 2020, pp. 1-13.

35 T. Hübinette, 'Between Colourblindness and Ethnicisation. Transnational Adoptees and Race in a Swedish Context', *Adoption & Fostering*, vol. 36, no. 3&4, 2012, pp. 97-103; Roux and Fillod-Chabaud, 2020, pp. 1-13; B. Yngvesson, 'Transnational Adoption and European Immigration Politics: Producing the National Body in Sweden', *Indiana Journal of Global Legal Studies*, Vol. 19, No. 1, 2012, pp. 327-346.

36 K. De Graeve and C. Bex, 'Imageries of Family and Nation: A Comparative Analysis of Transnational Adoption and Care for Unaccompanied Minors', *Childhood*, Vol. 23, No. 4, 2016, pp. 492-505.

37 Ahmed, 2004, p. 46.

38 De Graeve and Bex, 2016, p. 494; Yngvesson, 2012, p. 19.

to help' is actually a very self-centred act, serving to fulfil personal needs and desires – like "the desire to be part of something greater than themselves" – and thereby eclipsing the needs of the actual receiver "even at the expense of the targeted group".[39] Moreover, his positing of a Western subject, defined by its benevolence and generosity, implies the 'forgetting' of the prior unequal exchanges that enables the saviour/victim relationship in the first place. It obliterates the political, historical and socioeconomic conditions that have led to the poverty and relinquishment of children in minoritized communities and in which Western nation-states have a responsibility through their historical involvement in colonialism and their current involvement in neoliberal structures of oppression.

This entwinement of selfhood with humanitarian practices and acts makes that self particularly vulnerable for criticism, as challenge to those practices can become an experience of attack on the self. The ostensible other-directedness of this moral self conceals how this self is, for its existence, fundamentally dependent upon the other that is constructed to this end. Such constellations then always involve complex dynamics of power. The other has to become 'fixed' as an object in need of intervention, in order to enable the moral subject to consolidate its subject position by intervening.[40] The necessity of this relation thus gives rise to the second figure needed for the humanitarian exchange in adoption: the helpless, orphaned waif.

The Waif and the Nation

The coming-into-existence of the humanitarian subject in adoption requires a suitable object of intervention: a 'deserving' other on whose behalf the subject can act and thereby enable the act of compassion. In the adoption exchange, the figure of the adopted child is constructed in marked continuity with the trope of the 'orphan child'.

In Western societies, the status of children has considerably shifted from useless burdens to useful economic resources to the contemporary 'emotionally priceless' assets of the nuclear family.[41] In this move, children have become the symbols of innocence and purity, whose assumed helplessness and separation from the 'real' world of politics and economics at the same time necessitate the existence of the protecting adult. No

39 A. Sinervo and K. Cheney, 'Humanitarianism and Childhood in Contemporary and Historical Perspective', *in* K. Cheney and A. Sinervo (eds.), *Disadvantaged Childhoods and Humanitarian Intervention*, London, Palgrave MacMillan, 2019, pp. 1-35, 13.

40 Ahmed, 2004, p. 22.

41 V. Zelizer, *Pricing the Priceless Child: The Changing Social Value of Children*, Princeton, Princeton University Press, 1994.

figure embodies this dynamic better than that of the innocent, helpless, vulnerable and mostly 'othered' (in terms of age, class and 'race') orphan.

Orphans are "often seen as the quintessential children in need of intervention to prevent their suffering".[42] During the 20th century, a discourse of 'orphan rescue' developed in close conjunction with the institutionalization of intercountry adoption. This process started after World War I, when the first large-scale cross-border transportations and adoptions of children affected by wars were organized. In the post-World War II era, the visual trope of the 'imploring waif' has become pivotal in the repositioning of Western nation-states as upcoming hegemonic powers, with humanitarianism providing the justification for interventions in the 'Third World'. The representations of Black and Brown children as suffering and dying – either alone or in the arms of their ailing mothers – equally

> reinforced an ideology of the white heterosexual family as fundamentally caring and committed to the well-being of local non-white and working-class children, as well as infants, youth, and families around the globe.[43]

At the turn of the century, the continuing desire "to 'parent' the children of the Global South" has continued through now secularized and commercialized practices capitalizing on the needs of 'orphans' and poor communities, and on the humanitarian desires of Western individuals to contribute to a better world. Such 'altruistic exploitation' (Rotabi, Roby, & Bunkers, 2017, p. 649) in the form of 'voluntourism' and 'orphan tourism' has devastating effects.[44] Humanitarian narratives of 'orphan rescue' not only commodify orphans and orphanhood but can actually spur the production of 'orphans' "through the pathologization of poverty, the vilification of birth mothers, and the erasure of orphans' life histories before adoption".[45] Through a series of 'legal fictions', 'orphans' can become 'adoptable', i.e., declared as freestanding children who can be uncoupled from their birth country and culture and offered a 'comforting home' where they can be loved by 'generous parents'.[46]

---

42 K. Cheney and S. Ucembe, 'The Orphan Industrial Complex: The Charitable Commodification of Children and its Consequences for Child Protection', *in* K. Cheney and A. Sinervo (eds.), *Disadvantaged Childhoods and Humanitarian Intervention*, London, Palgrave Macmillan, 2019, pp. 37-61, 37.

43 L. Briggs, 'Mother, Child, Race, Nation: The Visual Iconography of Rescue and the Politics of Transnational and Transracial Adoption', *Gender & History*, Vol. 15, No. 2, 2003, pp. 179-200, 182.

44 Rotabi et al. coined the notion of "altruistic exploitation" to capture how altruistic motivations "often result in the exploitation of the intended beneficiaries" (see K.S. Rotabi, J.L. Roby, and K.M. Bunkers, 'Altruistic Exploitation: Orphan Tourism and Global Social Work', B*ritish Journal of Social Work*, Vol. 47, 2017, pp. 648-665, 649).

45 Cheney and Ucembe, 2019, p. 39.

46 S. Roux, 'The Colour of Family Happiness: Adoption and the Racial Distribution of Children in Contemporary France', *Social Anthropology*, Vol. 25, No. 4, 2017, pp. 509-524, 513.

This humanitarian adoption narrative, however, coexists with the other main motivation driving adoption, namely the desire to found a family through adoption, often when heterosexual procreation or assisted reproductive technologies have failed or are inapplicable. The legal figure of full adoption still carries the traces of a recent past in which adoption enabled the construction of an 'as-if-family' that approached as close as possible the ideal of heterosexual procreation within the confines of marriage.[47] This effort has justified practices of secrecy and closed records which, although still current in many countries, have become vehemently contested and given way to an increased acceptance of 'openness' in adoption – all the more so since the rise in transnational and transracial adoptions has made the concealing of differences impossible. 'Roots' travels and the acceptance of (assumed) cultural differences have now become a normalized aspect of the adoptee experience. But the often stereotyping celebration of adoptees' cultural backgrounds has also been seen as catering to adoptive parents' own needs for pleasurable 'culture bites' or assuaging feelings of guilt, rather than acknowledging adoptees' own struggles with racism and alienation in their host country.[48]

Moving Emotions/(Re)building Social Worlds

As described previously, adoption is embedded within a humanitarian politics, which enables the constitution of humanitarian subjectivities – both on collective and individual levels – but is, for that process, dependent on the presence of a deserving object of intervention: the freestanding, helpless orphan child who can be seamlessly integrated in the nation. How are such (self)representations connected to resistances to adoption reforms, as expressed in public discussions?

This section presents the results of a discourse analysis of 173 newspaper articles, published in Belgium and the Netherlands between 1 February 2021 and 31 July 2022. The articles were selected by using the academic databases Nexis Uni and Gopress Academic, which provide access to, respectively, Dutch and Belgian news sources. I used the search terms '*interlandelijke adoptie*' (intercountry adoption) and '*adoptie*' (adoption) to retrieve articles published on the topics in the selected time period. After controlling for overlap and relevance – e.g., articles about adoption of animals were not selected – a total of 173 articles were retained for analysis: 91 Dutch, and 82 Belgian (see Table 1). Next to articles which explicitly covered the announcements and the reactions to the reports and ministerial decisions, the selection also included articles

47 Ibid.

48 T.A. Volkman, 'Embodying Chinese Culture: Transnational Adoption in North America', *Social Text*, Vol. 74, No. 1, 2003, pp. 29-55.

which, occasioned by these debates, explored in a more general way experiences of and attitudes to adoption. The sample thus included a variety of article types: coverage of parliamentary debates, interviews with involved actors (politicians, adoptees, adoptive parents, adoption agencies), editorials, op-ed pieces and readers' letters.

Table 1. Overview of articles per country and newspaper

The Netherlands		Belgium	
Algemeen Dagblad	5	De Morgen	17
De Stem	2	De Standaard	31
De Gelderlander	2	Gazet Van Antwerpen	4
De Limburger	2	Het Belang Van Limburg	3
De Stentor	2	Het Laatste Nieuws	7
De Telegraaf	6	Het Nieuwsblad	13
De Volkskrant	11	Krant Van West-Vlaanderen	5
Friesch Dagblad	3	Metro	2
Het Parool	3		
Leeuwarder Courant	2		
Nederlands Dagblad	8		
Noordhollands Dagblad	3		
NRC	17		
Provinciale Zeeuwse Courant	1		
Reformatorisch Dagblad	3		
Trouw	20		
Tubantia	1		
TOTAL	**91**		**82**

My reading and analysis of the articles were guided by the following questions: which emotions are expressed, by which actors? How is adoption defined and characterized? How are abuses explained? How are propositions to stop adoption evaluated? Who is designated as responsible for abuse? The analysis was done using the program ATLAS.t.i., enabling the designation of codes corresponding to these questions and the identification of discourses by correlating reoccurring patterns and statements. The guiding questions and subsequent coding allowed me to identify the social worlds that actors constructed around adoption and the way they mobilized emotions to constitute themselves as moral actors in the debates and justify their position. In line with the literature review, I was able to identify a discourse of humanitarian compassion, in which the actors involved, usually in favour of continuing adoption, positioned themselves as a humanitarian subject out to save something of priceless value. However, an alternative discourse – which I identified as a social justice discourse – crystallized which challenged the skewed saviour/orphan-binary, by complicating the adoption narrative and bringing in the complex emotional struggles of now adult adoptees.

Compassion: "Let's not throw away the baby"

> "What I feel now, is a mixture of anger and sadness. Immense sadness," S. says. "We are already busy for ten years to compose our family. It's an agony. Suddenly we do not get the opportunity to take care of a second child. It is horrible." (Adoptive parent, BE, *Het Laatste Nieuws*)

Both in the Netherlands and Belgium, the publication of the reports by the expert panels was eagerly awaited. The announcements of both ministers' intention to follow the panels' recommendations to suspend adoption were followed by an outburst of emotions. Very prominent in the news reports is the emotion of shock, dismay and amazement.

By Dutch politicians, the report's conclusions are called 'shocking', 'fierce' (*heftig*), 'extraordinarily shocking', 'beyond comprehension' (*niet te bevatten*). Adoption agencies were said to have been 'startled by the findings of the commission – Joustra', 'unpleasantly surprised' and 'shocked' by a 'draconic' decision which they call 'ill-substantiated'. Adoptive parents are quoted as experiencing the news as 'a bombshell'. The expressions of utter amazement at a decision deemed 'drastic' may in themselves be surprising, since the panels' investigations were long preceded by testimonies of poignant abuse. Moreover, systematic abuses have been a recurring feature of intercountry adoption, have already resulted in numerous temporary moratoria or definitive stops to adoption in different sending countries, and are regularly discussed in meetings and reports related to the Hague Convention's institutions. One might expect adoption agencies and government officials to be informed about such discussions and to *not* be surprised if decisions are taken in order to install the necessary checks and balances or to order reforms in line with the Convention's subsidiarity principle.[49] So what exactly are these actors shocked about?

For adoptive parents, who often have already been waiting for a child for years, the announcement comes as an undesired intrusion into their personal trajectories and family projects, kicking in uncertainty and the spectre of completely having to turn around their life plans.

> This news struck like a bombshell.... I have in this moment no idea whether the planned adoption can proceed.... For me, this is very annoying. I had recently received the announcement that I would be able to adopt a child

49 N. Cantwell, *The Sale of Children and Illegal Adoption*, Den Haag, Terre des Hommes, 2017; D.M. Smolin, 'Intercountry Adoption and Poverty: A Human Rights Analysis', *Capitol University Law Review*, Vol. 36, No. 2, 2007, pp. 413-454.

> between now and two years, so I had started to look forward to it enormously. (Adoptive parent, BE, *Het Nieuwsblad*)

> It's a bit like getting children through an IVF-treatment: lying ready for insemination and then hearing that you will 'respectfully' get another trajectory. That is not respectful. (Adoptive parent, BE, *De Morgen*)

But invocations of shock, surprise and indignation do more than merely expressing dissatisfaction. For many actors, the shock seems to arise from suggestions that they could somehow be (co)responsible for abuses, an allegation that does not align with an understanding of their investment in adoption as solely arising from good intentions. Hence, many reactions involve a distancing from the allegations of abuse – by situating abuses in the past or in countries they are not involved in – or by discrediting the panels' reports, which are said to cater only to the complaints of a minority of unsatisfied adoptees, based on invalid data, or downright 'fake news':

> The adoption agencies say to have been shocked about "what the commission considers as the most relevant source material". They especially criticize the lack of the right to a fair hearing, because the commission Joustra has written in the letter that it has recorded signals without validating them. "If Trump would have said this, we would have called it fake news," says B. (Representative of four Dutch adoption agencies, NL, *De Telegraaf*)

Adoptive parents, agencies and politicians are quick to underline that in their own cases, all procedures were 'pure', that abuses only happened in the past and are ruled out now ever since the implementation of the Hague Convention and that it would be unfair to 'punish' them for abuses that have nothing to do with them.

Expressions of shock then seem to conjure up the idea of an unjustified, violent blow to a previously peaceful social world, peopled by actors driven by good intentions, unknowing of and therefore necessarily *not* involved with abuses. Endowed with the best intentions, such actors present themselves as innocent of the malpractices that *others* – in the past, in faraway countries, in other organizations – might have been up to. Preventing them from adopting is, therefore, experienced as an unjust punishment and immorally preventing them from doing their 'moral duty':

> If there are children looking for a warm home and cannot find that in their own country, then it remains our moral duty to receive them here. (Politician/adoptive parent, BE, *De Morgen*)

While substantial attention is drawn to the plight of adoptive parents, adoption agencies and governments, there is also reference to how the decision will victimize children who "will pay the ultimate price" (Politician/adoptee, NL, *Nederlands Dagblad*). However, it appears very difficult to clearly separate the assumed plight of those children from the more self-centred needs of adoptive parents, who claim their "future is endangered" (Adoptive parents, BE, De Standaard) but whose 'conscious' choice for adoption is nevertheless often only a last option after fertility treatments have failed:

> Years ago they (*a couple of adoptive parents*) were just a young couple with a huge child wish. But becoming pregnant in a natural way just wouldn't work. After which there was a switch to fertility treatments. "We stopped fairly quickly with that," relates S … "Worldwide there are 8 to 12 million orphans in institutions. We therefore very consciously chose for adoption, because we wanted to offer a child a warm home." (Adoptive parents, BE, *Het Laatste Nieuws*)

The recurring representations of adoptive parents, agencies and governments as innocent, intrinsically good and compassionate set the stage for an assessment of an adoption stop as unjustly targeting, 'demonizing' and thereby victimizing *them*. Hence, such actors consider the reports as hurtful and insulting, and can go so far as to demand apologies:

> The COIA (*the Dutch expert panel)* has insulted bona fide organisations like World Children and thousands of genuine and honest parents and children and that is insupportable. An excuse of the commission is in its place. (Representative of adoption agencies, NL, *NRC*)

The emotional vocabulary presented above reflects how the news about adoption reforms impacts upon established worldviews. The vocabulary of 'shock' is a telling expression of how a previously stable worldview, solidly built upon the self-representation of a good moral self, can become literally shaken by assessments experienced as challenging and threatening to that state of affairs. Just as an earthquake might reconfigure a natural landscape, 'emotional' shakes might be what are needed precisely to upset a status quo, to induce imbalance in a previously stable situation in order to rebuild and rethink it anew. However, a shock can also be followed by attempts to re-establish the status quo: a shake might not be enough to fundamentally dislodge a practice seen as expressive of a good moral self. While the emotions invoked *are* certainly moving, there is not an equivocal move towards a totally different take on adoption. Certain reactions rather elicit reassurance and the invocation of 'evidence' that it cannot be as bad as the reports seem to suggest. By reaffirming the humanitarian-compassionate discourse, some actors express their desire to safeguard something of priceless value. It is here that the proverbial baby is often evoked, often preceded by references to how 'many adoptions' are 'good'. Evidence of 'good' adoptions seems enough to cancel out the 'bothering' negative information:

> What bothers is that in all publications dedicated to this topic, only the negative results receive attention. Good research into successful adoptions has, to our knowing, not been done. As long as that doesn't happen: do not throw the baby away with the bathwater and keep the possibility of (intercountry) adoption. (Adoptive parents, NL, *NRC*)

Keeping 'the baby' then amounts to safeguarding the status quo and to prevent the occurrence of abuse from discouraging future adoptions:

> As such, despite the unanimous reaction of shock among the Dutch members of parliament and their initial agreement to temporarily stop adoptions, no-one wants to speak in favour of a total ban – not even the very critical Van Toornburg. "I want to put the pieces of the puzzle together first." … "We are all shocked," says Kees van der Staaij. "But we have to be careful not to throw away the child with the bathwater." (Members of parliament, NL, *NRC*)

Social Justice: "We are not children anymore"

> We are numerous and we are not children anymore. We are adults who have been adopted as children. Like no one else, we know how it feels what it is to live as an adoptee in this society and which obstacles and needs that entails. That's precisely why it's important to integrate adoptees in this societal debate…. Being adopted does not stop after your childhood. (Open letter of 124 adoptees, BE, 214)

The invocation of emotions of shock serves to discursively transform a measure intended to protect adopted victims of abuse into an unjust act that is itself victimizing. In this move, the victims are now the two central figures of the humanitarian adoption relation: the good, innocent saviour – driven by good intentions and unaware of abuses; the orphan-children awaiting salvation and facing possible death when left on their own. The re-centring of these figures works to erase the figure of the adult adoptee, fully aware of the abuses suffered through the adoption process, and actively claiming rights and compensation. This figure is indeed difficult to reconcile with the humanitarian adoption discourse that hinges on the intrinsic happiness of adoption and on the supposed gratefulness of an adoptee saved from a life of misery. Such a discourse becomes troubled, however, once adoptees become recognized as speaking actors who may express opinions that critically question the benefits of salvation. Such actors can be considered as "adoptee killjoys": "adoptees who refuse to engage in a politics of gratitude for their adoptions" but instead reveal "the contradictions and violence of adoption including [the] fraudulent creation of orphans and denial of rights to birth parents".[50] They are indeed threatening to the existence of the humanitarian self and therefore preferably silenced and ignored. The repetitive invocation of the figure of the baby then *works* as a way to relegate the 'adoptee killjoy' to the margins of the imagination and to re-centre the compassionate relationship between a humanitarian subject and its powerless object of intervention.

However, the newspaper coverage also enabled the identification of an alternative social justice discourse that presents a very different account of the adoptee experience. Emotions of shock and amazement are mostly, though not exclusively, expressed by adoptive parents, adoption agencies, politicians and some journalists. Among adoptees quoted in the articles, however, invocations of shock are remarkably absent. Unlike the actors mentioned earlier, the revelation of abuse does not come at a surprise for adoptees who have themselves been victims of abuse and have been struggling for years to have their stories heard and taken seriously. For them, the surprise lies in the fact that they are finally being heard. Nevertheless, their experience of being systematically ignored has also made them wary of government's intentions and the possible follow-up.

> After all those years of looking away (from reported abuses) my expectations of the research were low. I was positively surprised when I heard that the report was so critical. (Adoptee, NL, *Het Parool*)

Adoptees are quite divided on the question whether adoption should be stopped altogether, with some deploring and others welcoming this decision, and with the former often invoking the humanitarian-compassionate legitimation of 'saving children' to justify future adoptions. This variety in itself is indicative of how adoptees' accounts offer a very complicated picture of the adoption experience. While there are definitely positive appreciations of adoption as 'a good thing', this nevertheless does not cancel out experiences of suffering and mourning as inherent to the adoption experience, even if their own cases are free of abuse.

> Adoption in my case has been a good thing, let me emphasize that. But the limited stories of success do not weigh up against the battlefield of suffering among a too large number of adoptees and their adoptive parents. A societally

50 K. McKee, 'The Consumption of Adoption and Adoptees in American Middlebrow Culture', *Biography*, Vol. 42, No. 3, 2019, 669-692, p. 674.

> successful adoption does not mean that I don't have challenges. I keep on searching for my place, and mourning about my country of birth, roots, culture and family. (Adoptee, BE, *De Morgen*)

Adoption is presented as a complex experience that cannot be easily aligned along a good-versus-bad binary. Even when adopted by a loving family, feelings of non-belonging and alienation, experiences of racism and discrimination, and the emotional investment involved in 'roots' journeys and possible confrontations with abuse make the adoptee's experience multifaceted. This resonates in the conflicting emotions elicited by the reports, with feelings of joy and sadness alternating in an 'emotional rollercoaster' and adoptees finding it difficult to express exactly how they feel:

> "I had already read some stuff in the report and although it's a confirmation of what I know, some details were very confronting", says the 34-year old Haitian-born. "I just couldn't take it anymore. I think about it all the time, it's a real emotional rollercoaster. The feeling is difficult to describe. It has to land first." (Adoptee, NL, De Telegraaf)

> "There were some tears involved, when the conclusion of the report was published," says B. "It feels for me like a sort of emotional rollercoaster, in a positive way." (Adoptee, NL, *Het Parool*)

The compulsion to salvage adoption as something that is inherently good and of priceless value is conspicuously absent. The proper object of intervention shifts from the (imagined) orphan, passively waiting to be saved, towards older adoptees who have acquired the ability to speak out, to act and to press claims on their own behalf. Nevertheless, their pain and their claims are often not recognized and remain unanswered. In an interview, a 36-year-old adoptee from Sri Lanka denounces the utter lack of understanding he is often faced with when trying to express his grief about the fraud in his adoption and about the loss of his biological mother, who died before he could meet her.

> As a child, I always was told: "You must be grateful. How else would your life have been?" But they must be grateful to *us*. We are the children they wanted so badly. That people continued to say that I should be grateful, is really very painful. People do not understand what it means for us. (Adoptee, NL, *De Gelderlander*)

However, while some deplore the lack of recognition of post-adoption suffering, others criticize how adoptees can also be stereotypically portrayed as "eternal victims", a priori expected to have issues and to long for their "roots", even while "we do not all have the same experience, and we do not all have the same questions" (Adoptee, BE, *De Standaard*). This differentiation in the kinds of subjectivities that arise when simple binaries are rejected is in line with a recognition of adoptees as complex and individual human beings, who do not homogeneously conform to the identity of 'the helpless child'.

Instead of pressing towards a future reprisal or continuation of adoptions, a social justice perspective rather points to pressing problems in the here-and-now of adoptees' lived experiences, which continue to trouble their everyday lives. Many adoptees feel puzzled by the neglect of a government that is quick to come to the rescue of helpless children but refrains from properly responding when these same, now adult children, express their changing needs: financial assistance for family searches, psychological support for distressed adoptees and adoptive families, and the right to identity and access to information about their background. But the lack of response to these needs makes them question the whole of the adoption system, that seems only to have an eye for the start of the process but forgets adoptees once they are here and struggle to survive.

> I've come a long way, but I'm now at a point where I critically question the whole concept of adoption: the whole system, all actors, their internal functioning, both here as in the sending country. For me, the "child faucet" can be closed, if I see how so many adoptees survive instead of live. As long as there is no proper support offered in terms of after-care and assistance in searching, and as long we cannot guarantee that every intercountry adoption occurs 100% correctly, everything here should be put on pause. (Adoptee, BE, *De Standaard*)

By claiming the status of adult citizenship, adoptees insert themselves into the hegemonic liberal understanding of the rights-bearing citizen, whose recognition implies the conferral of the same rights accorded to their fellow-citizens, but hitherto denied to them.[51] Their claims then are embedded in a moral-legal framework concerned with egalitarian redistribution of rights and resources, regardless of one's subjective identification. Hence, the debates about adoption reform and the public revelation of the abuse suffered by them are for these adoptees key moments to claim what they have been denied before.

The right to identity is a right that is seen as key to the well-being of adoptees. Not knowing who you are and where you come from is for many adoptees experienced as a

51 S. Benhabib, 'Reason-Giving and Rights-Bearing: Constructing the Subject of Rights', *Deutsches Jahrbuch Philosophie*, Vol. 4, 2013, pp. 1309-1326.

heavy weight upon their shoulders. Many adoptees struggle with existential questions, but that pain is compounded by a lack of recognition by society, which prefers to see the 'happiness' of the adoption story and ignores the damages done by adoption.

> By stating that most adoptees are doing fine, the existential questions that nonetheless occur are ignored.... I too, consider myself a happy person, although I still carry the pain of the lack of genealogical information. That both the Indian and the Dutch governments refuse to cooperate to obtain genealogical information is also painful. (Adoptee, NL, *De Stentor*)

Many actors point out the juridical foundation of the right to identity, laid down in the UN Convention on the Rights of the Child and enabling adoptees to be 'just like any other' citizen:

> The need for knowledge about one's proper adoption and roots (origin, identity) appears to be big among Dutch adoptees. This is moreover a right. Based on the UN Children's Right Convention they have, just like any other, the right to know, as far as possible, who their parents are. (Adoptee and researchers, NL, *NRC*)

As rights create obligations, the social justice discourse connects the pain suffered by adoptees to the uncooperative attitude of governments, who fail to abide by the Convention they have nonetheless signed and thereby compound adoptees' suffering.

> It's about the question who I am, where I come from. I remember everything, remember exactly how I ended up in the Netherlands and luckily found my mother later. If I had not received support in my search, I think I would have been dead. I was broken by sadness. For other adoptees, I want to continue the struggle for compensation. For me, the struggle is done, I do not trust the government. (Adoptee, NL, *De Stentor*)

Searching for 'roots', for example, requires considerable resources, which adoptees now have to provide for all by themselves. The available funding is channelled towards subsidies for adoption agencies, centres of expertise, and benefits for adoptive parents in the form of tax reductions and adoption leaves, while adoptees "do not receive funding to find out their original identity, no tax advantage and no family reunification leave" (Adoptee, NL, Het Parool). Most adoptees are left to pay themselves for the costs of searching and reuniting with their families, and their numerous pleas for assistance remain ignored. Other invocations of suffering serve to illustrate the lack of psychological assistance for adoptees as specialized care is hard to find.

> What bothers her the most is that she has to organize and finance that search largely herself, just like the psychological support she needed. "It's incomprehensible that we do not know where to get care," D. says. The lack of after-care is an often-heard complaint. (Adoptee, BE, *De Morgen*)

While emotions and invocations of suffering are not absent from a social justice perspective, these serve to subvert the unequal saviour/orphan relationship and are constitutive of a different kind of subject: the once passive, voiceless 'orphans' have turned into agents who assert themselves as rights-bearing citizens, but whose struggle for recognition and visibility remains eclipsed by the preferred image of the victimized 'baby'. It is not hard to see why: while the figure of the suffering waif enables the assertion of an intrinsically good subject expressing itself in the act of salvation, the figure of the adult – that is, assertive and self-conscious adoptee – points out the contradictions of the humanitarian act and calls out the suffering caused by that same 'disinterested' intervention. In a harsh contrast with governments' and adoptive parents' expressed desires to offer warm homes to save children, the now adult adoptees' emotional pleas for reparations, care and support are met with cold rejections.

Conclusion

The announcements of adoption reforms in the Netherlands and Belgium gave rise to intensive public discussions, in which established worldviews and self-representations are not only challenged but also reaffirmed. In Western nation-states, both collective and individual actors have constituted their moral selves through humanitarian acts of 'saving children', and the practice of intercountry adoption has become a powerful symbol of this 'moral duty'. For such actors, announcements of adoption reforms are being experienced as a shock that threatens to break the bond between a compassionate self and a helpless orphan. But instead of moving towards an altered moral landscape, leaving behind the skewed saviour/child relationship, the desire to 'not throw away the baby with the bathwater' reflects the need to hold on to a self-directed humanitarian subject. By reconfirming such compassionate humanitarianism, other relationships and forms of care that might be more relevant when responding to reports of abuse become elided. This narrative avoids the moral responsibilities that ensue once the orphaned child *has* been brought here and expresses needs that go beyond the one-off act of 'salvation'. It does not provide space for a relationship with the grown-up adoptee, who is turned away in favour of the preferred voiceless child.

However, debates about adoption reforms have also revealed a social justice discourse. By claiming rights, recognition and governments' compliance with legal obligations, actors invoking a social justice perspective aim to redraw the skewed compassionate relationship between the humanitarian saviour and the passive child. This more legalistic recourse to rights and obligations is not exempt from affect. However, the invocation of emotions – suffering, pain, disappointment – does not feed into reductive representations of the 'adopted child' but serves to call out the unfulfilled obligations of governments to care for adult adoptees' needs.

While this strategy is effective in challenging the trope of the waif, in favour of centralizing adoptees as complex, individuated human beings who deserve recognition, such a strategy can also come with certain risks. The equalizing and individualistic nature of the liberal rights discourse might well succeed in granting (some) individual rights to adoptees. But its embedding in a Eurocentric and individualistic legalistic framework also risks reducing the adoptee experience to one of mere rights and obligations among freestanding individuals. Once again, this might result in an elision of the broader global, political and economic inequalities that gave shape to the practice of intercountry adoption in the first place. It might also result in a competitive understanding of individualized rights, in which adoptees' claims might not automatically be granted, for example, when the right to identity becomes subordinated to parents' right to privacy. And just as in the humanitarian discourse, the centralizing of some voices and subjectivities can still make other recede from view. It is remarkable how neither of the perspectives enables the hearing of the voices of first parents: we have no clue how *they* feel about adoption, as they are completely elided from the compassionate saviour/child relationship and simply unable to make their claims heard in a social justice perspective. As discussed in this chapter, reforming a taken-for-granted practice like intercountry adoption implies challenging deeply entrenched understandings of 'good' moral selves and their dependence on suffering 'others'. Refashioning postcolonial futures, in which we can truly care for each other, will require therefore a profound shakeup of cherished self-representations of the moral self and a more radical rethinking of our relationships with suffering 'others'.

Part III

Illegal Intercountry Adoptions as Enforced Disappearances

10 Receiving States' Obligations in the Aftermath of Illegal Intercountry Adoptions as Enforced Disappearances

Elvira Loibl

Introduction

In February 2021, Back to the Roots, an association of individuals adopted from Sri Lanka to Switzerland, approached the United Nations Committee on Enforced Disappearances (hereinafter CED). It requested that the cases of illegal adoptions of children from Sri Lanka during the 80s and 90s be recognized as enforced disappearances within the meaning of the 2010 International Convention for the Protection of All Persons from Enforced Disappearance (hereinafter ICPPED).[1] The association based its request on a commissioned study released in 2020 that had revealed systemic abuses and illegal practices in adoptions from Sri Lanka to Switzerland during this period.[2] According to the study, children were obtained illegally from their parents through abduction and deception and their paperwork was falsified identifying them as 'orphans' after which they were placed with Swiss adoptive families. Swiss authorities and adoption agencies failed to take appropriate measures to prevent illegal adoptions, even though the Swiss embassy in Colombo had been sending reports on illicit practices in Sri Lanka linked to international adoptions since the beginning of the 1980s (see Chapter 6).

In May 2021, the CED published its concluding observations regarding its review of Switzerland's implementation of the ICPPED. The observations specifically raised the issue of illegal adoptions of Sri Lankan children based on the facts that were presented to the committee by Back to the Roots and called on Switzerland

* I want to thank Gabriella Citroni for clarifying my questions regarding the ICPPED and André Klip for reading prior drafts of this chapter. The content and views expressed are solely the responsibility of the author.

1 Back to the Roots press release, 'Information Submitted to the Committee on Enforced Disappearances', 26 February 2021.

2 S. Bitter, A. Bangerter and N. Ramsauer, 'Adoptionen von Kindern aus Sri Lanka in der Schweiz 1973-1997: Zur Praxis der privaten Vermittlungsstellen und der Behörden, Historische Analyse betreffend das Postulat Ruiz 17.4181 im Auftrag des Bundesamts für Justiz', January 2020, Zürich, Züricher Hochschule für Angewandte Wissenschaften.

> to conduct thorough and impartial investigations to determine whether children adopted from Sri Lanka during the 1980s and 1990s may have been victims of enforced disappearance and wrongful removal, and whether other offences, such as falsification, concealment or destruction of identity documents were committed in these cases.[3]

It furthermore urged Switzerland to identify the victims and provide them with the support needed to establish their identity and parentage, and to guarantee their right to reparation.[4] The CED's observations are remarkable for two reasons: First, it is the first time that an UN body has prompted a receiving country to investigate past intercountry adoptions. Second, it is the first time that illegal intercountry adoptions are officially considered as a possible form of enforced disappearance within the meaning of the ICPPED. According to Olivier de Frouville, vice-president of the CED, the case of illegal adoptions from Sri Lanka to Switzerland is "clearly a new frontier".[5] Previously, the committee had looked at illegal adoptions in the context of armed conflicts or dictatorships (for example, in Argentina during the military rule or in Spain during the Franco era, where thousands of babies were abducted to be raised according to the regime's ideology) or in the context of colonial or postcolonial genocides, like in North America or in Australia resulting in the 'stolen generation'.[6] In all these cases, the forced removal of children and their subsequent adoption was used as a political tool of suppression. This, however, is different in the case of illegal intercountry adoptions like the ones from Sri Lanka to Switzerland. De Frouville explains:

> [h]ere, we are facing another type of illegal adoption as enforced disappearance, which is rather connected to organised crime with few to no political motives, although sometimes there's a thin line.[7]

Indeed, recent scholarly work has demonstrated that illegal intercountry adoptions can be considered as a form of organized crime.[8] The abuses that occur within the intercountry adoption system are financially motivated and not (at least primarily) used

3 CED, Concluding observations on the report submitted by Switzerland under Art. 29 (1) of the Convention, CED/C/CHE/CO/1, 21 May 2021, para. 40.
4 Ibid.
5 D. Burkhalter, 'UN Body Puts Illegal Adoptions in New, Criminal Light', *SWI*, 30 August 2021, www.swissinfo.ch/eng/un-body-puts-illegal-adoptions-in-new--criminal-light/46905860.
6 Ibid.
7 Ibid.
8 E. Loibl, *The Transnational Illegal Adoption Market: A Criminological Study of the German and Dutch Intercountry Adoption Systems*, The Hague, Eleven International, 2019 (PhD Dissertation, Maastricht University); E. Loibl and S. Mackenzie, 'The Organisation of Crime in the Transnational Adoption Market', *in* H. Nelen and D. Siegel (eds.), *Organized Crime in the 21st Century: Motivations, Opportunities, and Constraints*, Cham, Springer, 2023, pp. 25-41.

as a political tool. The last half century has witnessed the emergence of a transnational adoption market, in which children are obtained illegally and then trafficked for purposes of adoption. This form of organized crime is fuelled by the global imbalance between the demand for and the supply of adoptable children. As of the mid-1970s, more and more involuntarily childless couples from industrialized countries began to consider intercountry adoption as a means to create their own families. However, since the supply of children with the desired characteristics (young and healthy) is low, actors in poor sending countries – motivated by the large sums of Western money involved in the intercountry adoption system – use illegal means to obtain them for adoption.[9]

Currently, cases of illegal intercountry adoption are looked at mainly from the perspective of private international law (1993 The Hague Convention on Protection of Children and Co-operation in Respect of Intercountry Adoption) and international human rights law (1989 UN Convention on the Rights of the Child).[10] These instruments contain guidelines and principles for ethical intercountry adoptions. However, they do not provide specific standards regarding remedies and reparations for illegal adoptions.[11] This, as well as the fact that abusive practices in intercountry adoptions are often seen as an unfortunate evil towards a greater good, is probably why States confronted with signs of illegal adoptions do often not feel obliged to instigate investigations into possible cases of illegal intercountry adoptions and to rectify the harm caused to the victims. According to de Fourville, considering illegal adoptions as enforced disappearances might bring "a new dimension to the issue" as it can strengthen the rights of victims to truth, justice and reparation.[12] The ICPPED obliges States Parties to carry out a prompt, impartial and thorough investigation without delay once a possible enforced disappearance has come to their attention[13] and to ensure that victims of enforced disappearance have the right to obtain reparation and prompt, fair and adequate compensation.[14] Furthermore, considering illegal intercountry adoptions as enforced disappearance might finally send out the important message that illegally obtaining children for intercountry adoption is a serious form of crime. Enforced disappearance has been labelled as "a particularly heinous violation of human rights"[15]

9 Ibid.
10 Burkhalter, 2021.
11 D.M. Smolin, 'The Case for Moratoria On Intercountry Adoption', *Southern California Interdisciplinary Law Journal*, Vol. 30, No. 2, 2021, pp. 501-527.
12 Burkhalter, 2021.
13 Art. 12(1) ICPPED.
14 Art. 24(4) ICPPED.
15 UN High Commissioner for Human Rights, *Enforced or Involuntary Disappearances*, Fact Sheet No. 6/Rev.3, July 2009, p. 1.

and "one of the gravest crimes that can be committed against a human being"[16] that requires a thorough investigation, prosecution, punishment and reparation.

In September 2022, the CED, the Committee on the Rights of the Child, the Special Rapporteur on the Promotion of Truth, Justice, Reparation and Guarantees of Non-recurrence, the Special Rapporteur on the Sale and Sexual Exploitation of Children including child prostitution, child pornography and other child sexual abuse material, the Special Rapporteur on Trafficking in Persons, especially women and children and the Working Group on Enforced or Involuntary Disappearances issued a joint statement on illegal intercountry adoptions stressing:

> Illegal intercountry adoptions may violate the prohibition of the abduction, the sale of, or the traffic of children, and, under specific circumstances, may also violate the prohibition of enforced disappearances. In certain conditions as provided for in international law, illegal intercountry adoptions may constitute serious crimes such as genocide or crimes against humanity.[17]

Existing academic literature discusses under which circumstances illegal intercountry adoption constitutes a form of human trafficking and sale in children.[18] However, so far, there is a lack in scholarly work assessing under which circumstances illegal intercountry adoption can be considered as enforced disappearance. This chapter seeks to fill this gap. It assesses under which circumstances illegal intercountry adoptions fall within the scope of the ICPPED and explains how exactly this could strengthen the position and rights of the victims.

The ICPPED, which entered into force in 2010, is an international human rights instrument that provides the right not to be subjected to enforced disappearance and lays down a number of derivative State obligations and rights that aim to protect this right, whose violation leads to the responsibility of the *State*. Yet, the convention is also an instrument of international criminal law that lays down the rules and conditions for holding *individuals* criminally responsible for the crime of an enforced disappearance.[19]

---

16 Dalmo Abreu Dallari, as quoted in F. Andreu-Guzmdn, 'The Draft International Convention on the Protection of All Persons from Forced Disappearance', *International Commission of Jurists*, Vol. 62, No. 3, 2001, pp. 73-106, 75.

17 UN Human Rights Treaty Bodies, *Joint Statement on Illegal Intercountry Adoptions*, 29 September 2022, para. 4.

18 D.M. Smolin, 'Intercountry Adoption As Child Trafficking', *Valparaiso University Law Review*, Vol. 39, No. 2, 2004, pp. 281-325; Loibl, 2019, pp. 52-59.

19 See L. Ott, *Enforced Disappearance in International Law*, Cambridge, Intersentia, 2011, who describes the difference between the Convention as an instrument of international human rights law and an instrument of international criminal law.

The present chapter focuses on enforced disappearance as a human rights violation and the State obligations that follow from it. The next chapter (Chapter 11) will then zoom in on the individual criminal responsibility for enforced disappearance as a crime.

The chapter only addresses illegal *intercountry* adoptions, meaning illegal adoptions that took place transnationally, and will thus not address illegal adoptions with a purely domestic dimension. Furthermore, this chapter will mainly focus on the obligations of *receiving States* under human rights law in the aftermath of cases of illegal intercountry adoptions that can be considered as enforced disappearances. More and more illegally adopted individuals try to hold the receiving countries responsible for the harm that has been inflicted upon them and their families, claiming that the State authorities knew about the illegal practices in the sending countries but failed to take appropriate measures to prevent them. Yet, the receiving countries are commonly reluctant to investigate possible abuses in past adoptions, let alone to acknowledge any wrongdoing on their part and provide for remedies. This chapter explains that receiving countries are obliged to instigate an investigation when there are reasonable grounds to believe that children have been subjected to enforced disappearance and to provide remedies and reparation to victims.

Illegal Intercountry Adoptions as Enforced Disappearances?

The ICPPED is the first legally binding international legal instrument that creates an autonomous human right not to be subjected to enforced disappearance (Art. 1(1)).[20] It explicitly states that this right is an absolute right, meaning that an interference with this right can never be justified, not even in exceptional circumstances (Art. 1(2)). 'Enforced disappearance' is defined in Article 2 as

> the arrest, detention, abduction or any other form of deprivation of liberty by agents of the State or by persons or groups of persons acting with the authorization, support or acquiescence of the State, followed by a refusal to acknowledge the deprivation of liberty or by concealment of the fate or whereabouts of the disappeared person, which place such a person outside the protection of the law.

20 M.L. Vermeulen, *Enforced Disappearance: Determining State Responsibility under the International Convention for the Protection of All Persons from Enforced Disappearance*, Cambridge, Intersentia, 2012, p. 28.

According to this definition, enforced disappearance essentially has the following elements: (1) deprivation of liberty; (2) direct or indirect involvement of State agents; (3) refusal to acknowledge the deprivation of liberty or the concealment of the whereabouts of the person deprived of their liberty which place the person outside the protection of the law.[21] Article 25 specifically addresses the issue of enforced disappearance of children which thus has to be read in conjunction with Article 2. This section discusses the elements of the definition of enforced disappearance as a human rights violation with regard to illegal intercountry adoptions and explains under which circumstances the latter can be considered as enforced disappearances.

Deprivation of Liberty

The first element of the definition of an enforced disappearance is 'deprivation of liberty', whose scope is rather broad, including a wide spectrum of acts. The definition lists 'arrest', 'detention' and 'abduction' as specific examples of the general term 'any form of deprivation of liberty'.

There are indeed numerous reports documenting the forced removal of children in the form of an abduction within the intercountry adoption system, depriving them of their liberty. Some cases involve the abduction of children either from the streets or their homes, or from orphanages, hostels or schools where they have been placed temporarily by their parents for purposes of education or care.[22] In other cases, children were abducted from the hospital or the maternity clinic right after they were born. The mothers were duped into thinking that their newborn children were stillborn or that the child died shortly after birth, while in reality, the babies were sold for adoption purposes.[23]

There are also reports of cases in which 'lost' or 'missing' children were abducted in the aftermath of a natural disaster or of a conflict situation.[24] For example, it is estimated

21 There is disagreement on whether the element of placing the person outside the protection of the law should be considered as a constituent element of the definition or as a consequence of the other three elements (see M.L. Vermeulen, 2012, pp. 56-58).

22 D.M. Smolin, 'Child Laundering: How the Intercountry Adoption System Legitimizes and Incentivizes the Practices of Buying, Trafficking, Kidnapping, and Stealing Children', *The Wayne Law Review*, Vol. 52, No. 1, 2006, pp. 113-200, 119-123.

23 UNICEF International Child Development, *Intercountry adoption*, Innocenti Digest no. 4, Florence, 1998, p. 6; COIA, 'Rapport Commissie Onderzoek Interlandelijke Adoptie', The Hague, February 2021, p. 71; M. Coline Fanon, *Mama, je ne suis pas mort*, Kennes Editions, 2021.

24 Smolin, 2006, p. 121; UN Human Rights Council, *Report of the Special Rapporteur on the Sale of Children, Child Prostitution and Child Pornography*, 22 December 2016, A/HRC/34/55, para. 56.

that some 400 children might have disappeared in the aftermath of the volcanic eruption in Armero, Colombia, which had killed more than 20,000 people in 1985. Several of the 400 adoptees were able to trace back their biological parents with the help of DNA tests years later, realizing that they were never actually orphans eligible for adoption.[25] Disappearances of children also occurred after an earthquake-hit Haiti in 2010. Several international organizations warned that children should not be placed for intercountry adoption in the immediate aftermath of the natural disaster, as it was impossible to verify their family situation.[26] Nonetheless, some 2,000 children were flown out of the country without any reasonable efforts having been made to trace the child's family and then placed with adoptive families in the US, Canada, France, Germany, the Netherlands and other European countries.[27] As it later transpired, many of these children were not real orphans but had family members who were desperately looking for them.[28] There are also reports of children being abducted during or after a conflict situation.[29]

In other cases of illegal intercountry adoption, the children were removed from their parents' custody by means of deception, which also constitutes a form of abduction. For example, there are incidents in which parents were intentionally provided with false information about the consequences of an adoption in order to obtain physical custody of their children.[30] They were told that their child was only going away temporarily for educational purposes and were promised that they can keep contact with their child, receive payments and letters from the adoptive parents or would be allowed to follow their child to the West once the child has grown up.[31] This made them believe that they were maintaining the parental connection with their child. In other incidents, children were deliberately recruited into a childcare institution on the basis of false pretences (namely that education and care will be provided to them) and then sent

25 COIA, 2021, p. 73.

26 P. Selman, 'Intercountry Adoption After the Haiti Earthquake: Rescue or Robbery?', *Adoption & Fostering*, Vol. 35, No. 4, 2011, pp. 41-49.

27 M. Dambach and C. Baglietto, 'Haiti: "Expediting" Intercountry Adoptions in the Aftermath of a Natural Disaster...Preventing Future Harm', *International Social Service*, The Hague, August 2010, p. 22.

28 K. Joyce, *The Child Catchers: Rescue, Trafficking, and the New Gospel of Adoption*, Public Affairs, New York, 2013, p. 5.

29 K.J.S. Bergquist, 'Operation Babylift or Baby Abduction?: Implications of the Hague Convention on the Humanitarian Evacuation and 'Rescue' of Children', *International Social Work*, Vol. 52, No. 5, 2009, pp. 621-633; P. Fronek and D. Cuthbert, 'History Repeating...Disaster-Related Intercountry Adoption and the Psychosocial Care of Children,' *Social Policy and Society*, Vo. 11, No. 3, 2021, pp. 429-442.

30 UNICEF International Child Development, *Intercountry Adoption*, Innocenti Digest no. 4, Florence, 1998, p. 6; Smolin, 2006, p. 121.

31 Ibid.; Wereldkinderen & Against Child Trafficking, 'Fruits of Ethiopia. Intercountry Adoption: The Rights of the Child, or the "Harvesting" of Children? A Study on Intercountry Adoption in Ethiopia', 2009, on file with author.

abroad for adoption purposes.[32] Sometimes, the parents were urged to sign paperwork relinquishing their parental rights without properly understanding the concept of 'relinquishment'.[33] Or illiterate parents were tricked into putting their thumbprint on blank pieces of legal paper which were subsequently filled in to read as a consent to adoption.[34]

In other incidents, it is not the children themselves who were subjected to enforced disappearance but rather their mother during whose captivity the children were born. For example, in 1987, Sri Lanka suspended intercountry adoptions after an investigative report was released describing widespread abuses in the adoption system, including the phenomenon of so-called baby farms. These are facilities where women are deprived of their liberty and forced to give birth to children who were then appropriated and sold for adoption purposes.[35] According to Article 25, which lists different categories of enforced disappearance of children, these cases would also fall within the scope of the ICPPED.

Having said that, not all cases of illegal intercountry adoption involve an abduction of the child and do thus fall within the definition of enforced disappearance. Criminological literature has identified several illegal means whereby children are obtained for purposes of intercountry adoption. These means do not only include abducting children but also purchasing children from their parents, persuading the latter to obtain their consent for an adoption, falsifying the child's paperwork or bribing government officials to expedite an adoption or to subvert the subsidiarity principle, etc.[36] Even though these means render the resulting intercountry adoption illegal, the latter will not covered by the convention.

Refusal to Acknowledge the Deprivation of Liberty or Concealment of the Whereabouts of the Person Deprived of Their Liberty

In order for the illegal intercountry adoption to meet the definition of an enforced disappearance, the deprivation of liberty must be "followed by a refusal to acknowledge

32 Smolin, 2006, p. 120.

33 D.M. Smolin, 'Intercountry Adoption and Poverty: A Human Rights Analysis', *Capital University Law Review*, Vol. 36, 2007, pp. 413-453, 443.

34 UN Commission on Human Rights, *Report of the Special Rapporteur on the Sale of Children, Child Prostitution and Child Pornography*, 27 January 2000, E/CN.4/2000/73/Add.2, para. 35.

35 COIA, 2021, pp. 89 and 93; such practices were also observed in Guatemala: UN Commission on Human Rights, *Report of the Special Rapporteur on the Sale of Children, Child Prostitution and Child Pornography*, 27 January 2000, E/CN.4/2000/73/Add.2, para. 38.

36 Loibl, 2019, pp. 38-41.

the deprivation of liberty or concealment of the fate of the disappeared person". Also, this constituent element of the definition will probably be met by numerous cases of illegal intercountry adoption that involve the abduction of a child. As has been explained by criminological literature, the transnational illegal adoption market is characterized by the need of a 'laundering process'.[37] Just as crime proceeds and 'dirty money' need to be laundered, illegally obtained children must be purified in order to be profitable.[38] After all, adopters do not want to adopt a child that was stolen or purchased from their parents but an abandoned or relinquished child that is in true need of a family. Hence, the children's birth certificates and adoption-related documents (e.g., relinquishment deeds) are falsified or fabricated with false names and histories so as to hide their illegal origin and to identify them as orphans.[39]

Numerous adoptees have grown up, embarked on a search for their roots in the sending countries and found out that the adoption paperwork identifying them as orphans eligible for adoption was wrong and that they were never given up for adoption by their parents. For example, some learned that the affidavits issued by the orphanage wrongfully stated that they were abandoned by their mother whereas in reality they were abducted. In some cases, it turned out that the woman who officially gave 'their child' up for adoption was not the biological mother but a so-called acting mother, paid to pretend to be the mother of a child put up for adoption. For instance, this practice first came to light in Guatemala in 1997, when the Canadian embassy began carrying out DNA tests on babies and the women indicated by the adoption paperwork as the mothers.[40] In other incidents, the adoptee's birth certificate wrongfully specifies the adoptive parents as the adoptee's biological parents. In numerous reported cases, the adoption paperwork did not only include false information about the adoptee's family status but also about their place and/or date of birth. In some instances, it turned out that the adoptee's birthdate indicated on the documents deviated from the actual birthdate by a couple of days or a week.[41] In other cases, however, the adoptee was made younger by two or three years on the documents.

As a consequence of the adoptees' abduction and the concealment of their whereabouts, the adoptee is being placed outside the protection of the law. The laundering process

37 Smolin, 2006, p. 115; Loibl, 2019, pp. 41-44.

38 Ibid.

39 Ibid.

40 UN Commission on Human Rights, *Report of the Special Rapporteur on the Sale of Children, Child Prostitution and Child Pornography*, 27 January 2000, E/CN.4/2000/73/Add.2, para. 45.

41 For instance, Patrick Noordhoven, an individual from Brazil who was adopted by a Dutch couple in the 80s, found out that his birth certificate wrongly indicated his adoptive parents as the biological parents and specified 21 February 1980 as his birthdate, although he was actually born two weeks earlier, on 6 February.

erases the true identity of the abducted child, essentially severing any link between them and their biological parents – in most cases permanently. The enforced disappearance thus prevents adoptees from knowing the truth about their adoption and their biological identity and family ties.[42] Since their biological identity is not protected, their own personality is not recognized before the law.[43]

Numerous reports of systemic adoption abuses in India,[44] China,[45] Cambodia,[46] Sri Lanka,[47] Guatemala,[48] Haiti,[49] Colombia,[50] Brazil[51] and many other countries suggest that there is a whole generation of individuals adopted illegally to the United States and Europe. However, many of these adoptees and their natural families will probably never

42 J. Sarkin and E.C. Martinez, 'The Global Practice of Systematic Enforced Disappearances of Children in International Law: Strategies for Preventing Future Occurrences and Solving Past Cases', *Catholic University Law Review*, Vol. 71, 2022, pp. 33-103, 37; WGEID, *General Comment on Children and Enforced Disappearances*, 14 February 2014, A/HRC/WGEID/98/1, para. 16.

43 WGEID, *General Comment on Children and Enforced Disappearances*, 14 February 2014, A/HRC/WGEID/98/1, para. 18.

44 D.M. Smolin, 'The Two Faces of Intercountry Adoption: The Significance of the Indian Adoption Scandals', *Seton Hall Law Review*, Vol. 35, 2004, pp. 403-493; A. Dohle, 'Inside Story of an Adoption Scandal', *Cumberland Law Review*, Vol. 39, 2008, pp. 131-185.

45 P.J. Meier and Z. Xiaole, 'Sold into Adoption: The Hunan Baby Trafficking Scandal Exposes Vulnerabilities in the Chinese Adoptions to the United States', *Cumberland Law Review*, Vol. 39, No. 1, 2008, pp. 87-130; B.H. Stuy, 'Open Secret: Cash and Coercion in China's International Adoption Program', *Cumberland Law Review*, Vol. 44, No. 3, 2014, pp. 355-422.

46 T. Maskew, 'Child Trafficking and Intercountry Adoption: The Cambodian Experience', *Cumberland Law Review*, Vol. 35, 2004, pp. 619-638; K. Smith Rotabi, 'Fraud in Intercountry Adoption: Child Sales and Abduction in Vietnam, Cambodia, and Guatemala', *in* J.L. Gibbons and K. Smith Rotabi (eds.), *Intercountry Adoption: Policies, Practices, and Outcomes*, Farnham, Ashgate, 2021, pp. 67-76; J.L. Roby and T. Maskew, 'Human Rights Considerations in Intercountry Adoption: The Children and Families of Cambodia and Marshall Islands', *in* J.L. Gibbons and K. Smith Rotabi (eds.), *Intercountry Adoption: Policies, Practices, and Outcomes*, Farnha Ashgate, 2012, pp. 55-66.

47 COIA, 2021, pp. 91-103.

48 UN Commission on Human Rights, *Report of the Special Rapporteur on the Sale of Children, Child Prostitution and Child Pornography*, 27 January 2000, E/CN.4/2000/73/Add.2l; V. Tadler, *Child Trafficking for the Purpose of Inter-country Adoption, With a Case Study on Guatemala*, Doctoral Thesis, University of Vienna, 2010.

49 S. King, 'Owning Laura Silsby's Shame: How the Haitian Child Trafficking Scheme Embodies the Western Disregard for the Integrity of Poor Families', *Harvard Human Rights Journal*, Vol. 25, 2012, pp. 1-47; K. Joyce, *The Child Catchers: Rescue, Trafficking, and the New Gospel of Adoption*, New York, Public Affairs, 2013, pp. 1-37.

50 S. Hoelgaard, 'Cultural Determinants of Adoption Policy: A Colombian Case Study', *International Journal of Law, Policy and the Family*, Vol. 12, No. 2, 1998, pp. 202-241.

51 C. Fonseca; 'Transnational Connections and Dissenting Views, The Evolution of Child Placement Policies in Brazil', *in* D. Marre and L. Briggs (eds.), *International Adoption: Global Inequalities and the Circulation of Children*, New York, New York University Press, pp. 154-173; A. Cardarello, 'The Movement of the Mothers of the Courthouse Square: "Legal Child Trafficking," Adoption and Poverty in Brazil', *Journal of Latin American and Caribbean Anthropology*, Vol. 14, No. 1, 2009, pp. 140-161; A. Cardarello, 'The Right to Have a Family: "Legal Trafficking of Children", Adoption and Birth Control in Brazil', *Anthropology & Medicine*, Vol. 19, No. 2, 2012, pp. 225-240.

learn about each other's fate and whereabouts. Parents whose children were forcefully removed are often extremely poor and vulnerable and thus lack the voice as well as the capacity to report the abduction of their children and to seek justice.[52] Mothers that were falsely told that their newborn children were stillborn or died shortly after birth might never be aware of the fact that they have been harmed. Also the adoptees themselves will in many cases never know that they were illegally taken from their parents and placed for adoption as 'paper orphans'. The vast majority of children were babies or young toddlers at the time of their adoption and thus too young to realize that they have been victimized.[53]

Despite the hidden nature of abuses in intercountry adoption, numerous victims of illegal adoption have been successful in tracing their natural families, often after many years of searching. In recent years, a number of non-governmental organizations, like Back to the Roots, *Stichting Mijn Roots*, Plan Angel, Shapla Community or *Raices Perididas*, were set up (mostly by adoptees themselves) that help adoptees and their families to reunite by conducting research in the sending countries and doing DNA tests. These organizations have already assisted many families reunify, and in several cases, the reunification revealed that the adoptee was not actually given up freely for adoption or abandoned but was forcefully removed from their parents. In other cases, victims of illegal adoptions were able to find their families via Facebook, a social media platform that some parents use in order to find their kidnapped children. However, there are numerous victims that have already spent years searching and will probably never be able to trace back their families or children. There are quite some adoptees who have strong reasons to believe that their adoption was illegal, as their paperwork contains inconsistent or incomplete information about their family status but were so far not able to find their biological families. The false information about their origins in their adoption documents render it very difficult for many adoptees to trace their origins. This problem is further exacerbated by the fact that authorities in both sending and receiving countries usually hide behind a wall of silence when confronted with adoptees' requests for assistance in their root searches.

Direct or Indirect Involvement of State Agents

As has been shown in the previous sections, several kinds of reported cases of an illegal adoption will probably fulfil the first and third elements of the definition of an enforced

52 D.M. Smolin, 'Child Laundering as Exploitation: Applying Anti-trafficking Norms to Intercountry Adoption Under the Coming Hague Regime', *Vermont Law Review*, Vol. 32, 2007, 1-55, p. 3.

53 Loibl, 2019, pp. 66-67.

disappearance: the child was forcefully removed from their parents that was followed by a laundering process which concealed the child's true identity and whereabouts, placing the child outside the protection of the law. However, these cases can only be qualified as cases of enforced disappearance according to Article 2, if the deprivation of liberty was carried out "by agents of the state or by persons or groups of persons acting with the authorization, support or acquiescence of the State". The Convention excludes non-State actors as possible perpetrators of enforced disappearance if they act without any kind of involvement of the State.[54] Yet, if non-State actors acted with the authorization, support or acquiescence of the State, their acts do fall within the scope of the definition of an enforced disappearance and the State incurs responsibility. Hence, the involvement of the State is a key component in an enforced disappearance.

Based on Article 2 of the Convention, four forms of State involvement can be distinguished that trigger State responsibility: 1. commission by State agents, 2. authorization by State agents, 3. support by State agents, and 4. acquiescence by State agents. In the first form of involvement, the State directly commits the deprivation of liberty through State agents. In the other three forms, the State indirectly commits the crime, in the sense that State agents support, consent to or acquiesce the commission of this crime by non-State actors.[55]

Numerous reports suggest that illegal intercountry adoptions are not the work of single actors but of a number of actors both from the private and the public sector that cooperate in illegally obtaining children and then laundering them.[56] The following paragraphs describe the network of individuals and organizations that are commonly abducting children for adoption purposes and then falsifying their identity documents, and then explains to what extent actors of both the sending and the receiving States are involved in these activities.

Direct Perpetrators of Abducting Children for Adoption

From documented cases we know that the act of abducting children for adoption purposes is commonly carried by non-State actors in the sending States, including attorneys, doctors, orphanage personnel and other private actors. Motivated by the large sums of Western money involved in intercountry adoption, they would set up a system for illegally obtaining children and then processing them as 'orphans'. Smolin explains:

54 Vermeulen, 2012, p. 54.
55 Ibid., p. 253.
56 Loibl and Mackenzie, 2023.

> These systems usually involve persons at the head of the conspiracy who possess the language and literacy skills, and the financial and social position, to interact with first-world adoption agencies and prospective adoptive parents. These persons usually send out intermediaries, generally of a lower social station, to serve as scouts or recruiters. The targets of this recruiting are generally the poor of poor societies, who earn less than one dollar per day.[57]

A well-documented case illustrating such a system of illegally obtaining children for adoption is Guatemala. Between 1990 and 2007, this country was one of the most significant suppliers of children for international adoption, peaking at 4,851 children adopted in 2007.[58] The majority of international adoptions were processed under a 'notarial system: Adopters would hire a private attorney for around US$15,000-20,000 who would facilitate a swift adoption, representing all members of the adoption triad. The primary review of the adoption case was then conducted by the Guatemalan Solicitor General's Office.[59] Numerous reports document the serious and large-scale adoption abuses that took place in Guatemala. For instance, in 2000, the UN Special Rapporteur on the sale of children, child prostitution and child pornography released her report on the mission of Guatemala concluding that legal adoptions were "the exception rather than the rule"[60] and that

> in the majority of cases, intercountry adoption involves a variety of criminal offences including the buying and selling of children, the falsifying of documents, the kidnapping of children, and the housing of babies awaiting private adoptions in homes and nurseries set up for that purpose.[61]

According to the report, Guatemalan attorneys played a key role in adoption procedures. They would hire a network of recruiters who would seek out vulnerable mothers in markets, doctor's offices or hospitals and persuade them to give up or sell their children or resort to threats or baby-stealing if they could not be persuaded.[62] After the children were obtained illegally, false paperwork would be set up in order to identify them as abandoned and eligible for adoption. Some lawyers, in collusion with others, even set

57 Smolin, 2006, p. 118.

58 P. Selman, 'Global Statistics for Intercountry Adoption: Receiving States and States of origin 2004-2022', HCCH, 2024, https://assets.hcch.net/docs/a8fe9f19-23e6-40c2-855e-388e112bf1f5.pdf.

59 Smolin, 2006, pp. 163-174.

60 UN Commission on Human Rights, *Report of the Special Rapporteur on the Sale of Children, Child Prostitution and Child Pornography*, 27 January 2000, E/CN.4/2000/73/Add.2l, para. 13.

61 Ibid.

62 Ibid., para. 38.

up houses (referred to as 'crib houses' or 'fattening houses') where the illegally obtained children were kept until the adoption procedure was finalized.[63]

In other incidents, the systems set up to procure children illegally and profit from intercountry adoption were headed by personnel of charitable organizations. For example, in a number of documented Indian cases, the directors of (mostly well-respected and State accredited) orphanages headed the system of purchasing and stealing children from poor families. One case, for instance, concerned *Missionaries of Charity*, a religious Indian organization, which ran an orphanage in Delhi, authorized to place children for intercountry adoption.[64] In 1999, a group of German adoptive parents discovered that the children they adopted as 'orphans' from India have actually been stolen from their parents. The children involved in these cases were already older and, after having learned some German, informed their adoptive parents that their mother was alive and had not consented to their adoption. As it turned out, personnel of the orphanage run by *Missionaries of Charity* had obtained children from their parents for temporary care or schooling and then processed them through the adoption system without their consent and knowledge.[65]

In the majority of publicized cases, citizens of the sending country operated the scheme of obtaining children through purchase or abduction. However, in some cases, it was citizens of the recipient State that headed the conspiracy of illegally procuring children for intercountry adoption. One such case involved two US citizens, Lauryn Galindo and her sister Lynn Devin, who sent out recruiters in Cambodia to purchase and steal children from their parents and then placed them with adoptive families in the US through their agency 'Seattle International Adoptions' as well as other US agencies.[66] Due to the involvement of US citizens, the US government extensively investigated and ultimately pursued a criminal prosecution in this case. This is also why the Cambodian adoption scandal is one of the best documented instances of illegally obtaining children for adoption. As the US government's investigation 'Operation Broken Heart' revealed, the recruiters approached vulnerable families in their local village and then employed methods of deception in order to obtain physical custody over their children: They would, for instance, tell the natural families that their child was being cared for by reputable non-governmental organization or be sent abroad for education purposes but that they can have their child back at any time.[67] After the children were obtained,

63 Ibid., para. 29.

64 B. Wacker, *Verbrechen und andere Kleinigkeiten. Der Fall „pro infante. Action: kind in Not e.v." und seine Konsequenzen*, Osnabrück terre des hommes Deutschland e.V., 1994.

65 Ibid.

66 Smolin, 2006, pp. 135-146.

67 Maskew, 2004, pp. 633-634.

a false paper trail was created in order to erase their true identities and render them untraceable for their parents.[68]

Indirect Involvement of State Actors

As can be concluded from the previous section, the crime of abducting children for adoption purposes is commonly committed by private actors in the sending countries, including lawyers, orphanage directors or, in exceptional cases, personnel of Western adoption agencies. Yet, as stressed above, an abduction for adoption purposes carried out by these private actors can only be considered as an enforced disappearance within the meaning of Article 2 of the Convention for which the State incurs responsibility, if State actors were at least indirectly involved in committing the crime, either through authorization, support or acquiescence. Is there anything to suggest indirect State involvement in cases of illegal intercountry adoption that would bring these cases within the scope of the ICPPED and thus trigger State responsibility?

As was explained above, an important feature of the illegal adoption market is the need of a laundering process. Children that were illegally obtained for adoption purposes are not traded clandestinely, but they are passed through the same legal channels as children that are actually eligible for intercountry adoption.[69] Illegal adoptions are thus embedded within a legitimate system and rely on its official procedures: the children's birth need to be registered, they need to be declared relinquished or abandoned and eligible for adoption, an official adoption decision needs to be rendered and a visa or passport application needs to be approved. Even cases of illegal adoption in which the adopters circumvent the official adoption procedure by passing off the illegally obtained child as their biological child largely depend on official procedures: a birth certificate needs to be issued as well as paperwork allowing the child to leave the country of origin. All these bureaucratic steps are commonly carried out or monitored by State actors, i.e. government officials, judges, diplomats, etc. whose approvals and services are necessary for an adoption to be able to take place. Even in countries in which the adoption placement is privatized, like in South Korea (see Chapter 2) or in Guatemala (see above), a State authority is responsible to officially sanction an adoption. The State actors involved in these procedural steps ought to act as gatekeepers in the system that monitor and control the adoption process and make sure that only those children that are truly eligible for international adoption enter the system. However, in an illegal adoption, the checks and balances done by State actors failed.[70] It is imaginable that there are single cases in which State actors unknowingly approved the adoption of a

68 Ibid., p. 634.
69 Loibl, 2019, p. 68.
70 Ibid., p. 43.

stolen child whose paperwork has been fabricated or falsified by private actors. However, in incidents where adoption abuses took place on a large scale, there is a strong basis to presume the involvement of State officials, whose stamps were after all required for an adoption to be finalized.

Indeed, a number of investigations into intercountry adoption found that the State authorities involved in the adoption procedure had acquiescence of abusive practices. For example, in 2010, the UN International Commission Against Impunity in Guatemala released a report in which it assessed a large sample of adoption cases that were pending when the moratorium on intercountry adoptions was announced by the government in 2007.[71] It was the first inquiry ever carried out looking into past illegal intercountry adoptions and, most notably, the involvement of the sending State therein. The commission's inquiry essentially confirmed the findings of the UN Special Rapporteur's report on Guatemala mentioned earlier. It concluded that in Guatemala, intercountry adoption turned into a lucrative business in which criminal trafficking networks revolving around lawyers resorted to coercion, deception and abduction to obtain children and then processed them through the adoption system with false identities. Most notably, the inquiry found that Guatemalan State authorities were to a large extent involved in illegal adoptions:

> The quantitative and qualitative dimensions of irregularities in international adoption formalities, which have been tolerated by the public authorities responsible for monitoring them, leads to the conclusion that they have not been exceptional, but rather a systemic practice.
>
> The number and severity of these irregularities obviously means that *irregular adoptions would not have been possible without the participation or at least the acquiescence of State authorities.* [emphasis added] These are, in particular, the authorities of the institutions responsible for public oversight of adoption proceedings, such as the Solicitor General of the Nation, the Immigration Bureau, Court for Children and Adolescents, municipal registers of vital statistics and the National Adoption Council.[72]

As recent inquiries in Switzerland and the Netherlands revealed, also State actors of the receiving countries may have been implicated in past illegal intercountry adoptions.

71 CICIG, 'Report on Players Involved in the Illegal Adoption Process in Guatemala since the Entry into Force of the Adoption Law', 1 December 2010, Decree 77-2007, translated English version available at https://www.cicig.org/history//uploads/documents/informes/INFOR-TEMA_DOC05_20101201_EN.pdf.

72 Ibid., p. 74.

In 2019, the Dutch Minister of Justice and Security established the 'Committee Investigating Intercountry Adoption in the Past', led by Tjibbe Joustra (hereinafter short Joustra Committee). The committee's mandate was to examine possible abuses in intercountry adoptions within the period of 1967 to 1998, focusing on Bangladesh, Brazil, Colombia, Indonesia and Sri Lanka, as well as to assess the extent to which the Dutch government had knowledge thereof. The commission was set up after a number of Dutch adoptees had requested access to government documents which contained information suggesting the involvement of Dutch officials in illegal intercountry adoptions. In addition, a number of media reports documenting abuses in intercountry adoptions increased the pressure on the government to finally inquire into this issue. The report of the Joustra Committee released in 2021 not only uncovered systemic abuses in past intercountry adoptions from the mentioned countries, including abduction and purchase of children, bribery and document falsification. Most notably, it concluded that officials at the Dutch government were well aware of these practices but failed to take appropriate measures to prevent them. For example, with regard to adoptions from Sri Lanka, the commission found:

> The Dutch government, specifically the Ministries of Justice and Foreign Affairs, repeatedly took detailed notice of abuses from Sri Lanka starting in the early 1980s. The existence of baby farms and even "outright child robbery" was raised by concerned parties. No action was generally taken against this. Even when Dutch diplomats abroad raised the alarm, there was no follow-up. Despite this knowledge, and the desire for a stricter approach, the Netherlands continued to refer to the Sri Lankan authorities for solutions.... In Sri Lanka, the Dutch government itself was not involved in abuses, but was regularly aware of them. The government did not act when there was reason to do so.[73]

Also, in 2019, the government in Switzerland commissioned Zurich University of Applied Sciences (*ZHAW*) to conduct an extended study on adoptions from Sri Lanka from 1973 until 1997, focusing on the role of Swiss private adoption agencies and authorities therein (see Chapter 6). In 2017 and 2018, the Dutch TV documentary series *Zembla* had revealed widespread abuses in adoption from Sri Lanka in the 1980s.[74] This had raised alarm bells in Switzerland, which had approved the adoption of 955 Sri Lankan children between 1970 and 1999 alone and led to political inquiries to investigate past adoptions from this country. The study report documents widespread

73 COIA, 2021, p. 104.

74 BNNVARA, Zembla, 'Adoptiebedrog Deel 1', 17 May 2017, https://www.bnnvara.nl/zembla/videos/289823; BNNVARA, Zembla, 'Adoptiebedrog Deel 2', 20 September 2017, https://www.bnnvara.nl/zembla/artikelen/adoptiebedrog-deel-2; BNNVARA, Zembla, 'Adoptiebedrog Deel 3', 28 March 2018, https://www.bnnvara.nl/zembla/artikelen/adoptiebedrog-iii.

abuses in adoptions from Sri Lanka, including the abduction of children from their parents, and concludes that Swiss authorities had knowledge thereof:

> It is striking that the authorities at the federal level and in the cantons were aware of the commercial and partly illegal nature of the adoption placements at an early stage. Nevertheless, children from Sri Lanka were able to enter the country without their birth parents' consent to adoption....[75]

Following this inquiry, the Federal Council released an official statement recognizing that Swiss authorities and adoption agencies failed to take appropriate measures to prevent several illegal adoptions, even though, the Swiss embassy in Colombo had been sending reports on illicit practices in Sri Lanka linked to international adoptions since the beginning of the 1980s.[76]

For a long time, the narrative of authorities in the receiving countries was that the responsibility to control whether an adoption is in compliance with the legal standards rests with the authorities in the sending countries and that they had no other option than to trust the integrity of the foreign adoption system and the reliability of the information provided about the children.[77] This narrative was seriously challenged by the commissioned inquiries in the Netherlands and Switzerland. Both reports concluded that the Netherlands and Switzerland were well aware of the danger that children sent for adoption from the investigated countries were obtained illegally, including by means of abduction. Despite recurring media reports as well as warnings by the States' diplomatic staff in the sending countries, the States allowed the placement of children from these countries to continue. Not all cases of illegal intercountry adoption described in the report involve an abduction of a child and thus constitute an enforced disappearance. However, those that did, potentially fall within the scope of the convention considering that they took place within the acquiescence of the State authorities in the receiving countries. The latter failed to take necessary and appropriate measures to control the adoption placement procedures and to prevent the adoption of disappeared children.[78] They thereby violated their positive obligation of

75 Bitter et al., 2020, p. 256.

76 Bundesrat, 'Illegale Adoptionen von Kindern aus Sri Lanka: historische Aufarbeitung, Herkunftssuche, Perspektiven: Bericht des Bundesrates in Erfüllung des Postulats 17.4181 Ruiz Rebecca vom 14.12.2017', 11 December 2020, p. 66.

77 E. Loibl, 'The Aftermath of Transnational Illegal Adoptions: Redressing Human Rights Violations in the Intercountry Adoption System with Instruments of Transitional Justice', *Childhood*, Vol. 28 No. 4, 2021, 477-491, p. 478.

78 DPLF, 'Non-State Actors as Perpetrators: Precedents from Inter-American Jurisprudence and Their Applicability to Disappearance Cases', Washington DC, February 2022, www.dplf.org/en/resources/non-state-actors-perpetrators-precedents-inter-american-jurisprudence-and-their.

prevention and protection which is why they incur responsibility for the cases of illegal adoption which can be considered as enforced disappearances within the meaning of the convention.

Receiving States' Obligations in the Aftermath of Enforced Disappearances

As mentioned above, the ICPPED is the first legally binding universal instrument that creates an autonomous and non-derogable right not to be subjected to enforced disappearance. A number of derivative obligations and rights found in Part I of the ICPPED aim to realize and protect this right, relating to criminalization, prosecution and penalties (Arts. 4-8), jurisdiction and investigation (Arts. 9-12), extradition and judicial cooperation (Arts. 13-16), prevention (Arts. 17-23) and redress for victims (Arts. 24). Article 25 specifies these State obligations with regard to enforced disappearances of children. The following sections zoom in on and discuss the obligation to investigate as well as to repair that receiving countries have which incur responsibility for an illegal adoption that originates in an enforced disappearance. Before doing that, however, we will take a look at the temporal scope of the convention, in particular the question as to whether States are responsible for violations that occurred before the convention entered into force.

Temporal Scope of the ICPPED

The ICPPED is a relatively recent international legal instrument: it was adopted by the United Nations General Assembly on 20 December 2006 and entered into force on 23 December 2010. So the question is whether the convention and the State obligations laid down in it apply to cases of enforced disappearances that took place decades prior to the entry into force. Can States be considered responsible according to the ICPPED for enforced disappearance that took place years before the convention entered into force? As a general rule, international legal instruments do not have a retroactive effect. Article 28 of the 1969 Vienna Convention on the Law of Treaties stipulates that a treaty shall not be applied to events that took place before the State ratified it:

> Unless a different intention appears from the treaty or is otherwise established, its provisions do not bind a party in relation to any act or fact which took place or any situation which ceased to exist before the date of the entry into force of the treaty with respect to that party.

However, enforced disappearance has a continuous nature that does not cease to exist until the victim's fate or whereabouts are established. This follows, *inter alia*, from Article 24(6) which obliges States to investigate cases of enforced disappearance "until the fate of the disappeared person has been clarified". The continuous nature of enforced disappearance was furthermore stressed by the Working Group on Enforced or Involuntary Disappearance in one of its general comments:

> Enforced disappearances are prototypical continuous acts. The act begins at the time of the abduction and extends for the whole period of time that the crime is not complete, that is to say until the State acknowledges the detention or releases information pertaining to the fate or whereabouts of the individual.... [T]he Working Group considers that an enforced disappearance is a unique and consolidated act, and not a combination of acts. Even if some aspects of the violation may have been completed before the entry into force of the relevant national or international instrument, if other parts of the violation are still continuing, until such time as the victim's fate or whereabouts are established, the matter should be heard and the act should not be fragmented.[79]

Hence, when a State is recognized as responsible for having committed (directly or indirectly) an enforced disappearance that began before the entry into force of the ICPPED and which continued after its entry into force, the State should be held responsible for all violations that result from the enforced disappearance, and not only for violations that occurred after the entry into force of the instrument.[80] This would arguably mean that the receiving States may be responsible for enforced disappearances that commenced in the 70s or 80s (hence decades before the ICPPED went into force), and may incur the State obligations provided in the ICPPED until the fate of the illegally adopted individuals and the whereabouts of their biological parents are established.

However, according to Article 35, the jurisdiction of the Committee on Enforced Disappearance to handle and investigate past abuses is limited. The committee is a body of ten independent experts,[81] responsible for overseeing the implementation of the ICPPED. In particular, it is responsible for reviewing States Parties' reports and issuing comments, observations or recommendations (Art. 29), registering requests for urgent action (Art. 30) and deciding upon individual and inter-State complaints that a States Party is violating the convention (Arts. 31 and 32). According to Article 35,

79 WGEID, *General Comment on Enforced Disappearance as a Continuous Crime*, 26 January 2011, A/HR/16/48, para. 1.

80 Ibid., para. 3.

81 Art. 27 ICPPED.

the committee only has competence in respect of enforced disappearances which commenced after the entry into force of this convention. Hence, the committee is not able to adjudicate cases of illegal adoptions that took place before the ICPPED entered into force.

Yet, in a statement from November 2013 regarding the committee's limited *ratione temporis* jurisdiction, the committee stressed that even if it is precluded from examining individual cases of disappearances that commenced before the entry into force of the convention for the State concerned, it ought to question States on present compliance with their obligations under the convention, even in relation to past disappearances.[82] This is what happened, with regard to the issue of illegal adoptions of Sri Lankan children to Switzerland during the 80s and 90s, mentioned in the introduction of this chapter. The committee was not able to handle individual complaints about particular illegal adoptions, but called on Switzerland to comply with the convention's obligations, in particular, the obligation to investigate past adoptions from Sri Lanka and to provide the victims of enforced disappearances with remedies and reparation.

Investigation

Article 12 ICPPED obliges States Parties to carry out a prompt, impartial and thorough investigation without delay once a possible enforced disappearance has come to their attention. It clarifies that 'any person' has the right to report the facts of an alleged enforced disappearance to the competent authorities. An investigation has to be initiated, also *ex officio* – i.e. without there being a formal complaint – when there are 'reasonable grounds' to believe that a person has been subjected to enforced disappearance.[83]

In numerous cases of intercountry adoption, there are reasonable grounds to believe that the children were subjected to enforced disappearance: they were adopted from countries and during a period in which systemic abuses were notorious and are well documented, and their adoption documents contain information that is inconsistent or does not add up. For example, Dilani Butink, a Dutch adoptee from Sri Lanka who sued the Dutch government in 2020 for having approved her adoption despite consistent reports about illegal practices in the Sri Lankan adoption system, has strong reasons

82 Referenced in O. de Frouville, 'The Committee on Enforced Disappearances', *in* F. Mégret and P. Alston (eds.), *The United Nations and Human Rights: A Critical Appraisal*, Oxford University Press, 2020 (2nd edition), pp. 579-600.

83 Art. 12(2) ICPPED; see WGEID, Guiding principles for the search for disappeared person, CED/C77, which describe good practices with regard to searching for disappeared persons.

to believe that she was adopted illegally.[84] Her adoption papers – more specifically, her birth certificate and the deed of relinquishment – do not contain an exact address of her birth mother, only her mother's place of residence which is far away from her place of birth, which, according to Dilani, does not make sense. In addition, the hospital at her birth place does not have a copy of her birth certificate and the biological mother listed on that certificate was never registered as a patient at that hospital. It is furthermore striking that the birth of another child is registered with the municipality under the number of her birth certificate. Also, forensic investigations, that Dilani had commissioned, found that the signature on the birth certificate and the one on the waiver stemmed from different persons.[85] In 2021, the report of the Joustra Committee confirmed that adoption abuses did take place systemically in Sri Lanka and that the Dutch government had knowledge thereof.[86]

Upon complaints of adoptees like Dilani, who suspect that they have been adopted illegally, the receiving countries – in this case, the Netherlands – would be obliged, based on Article 12, to initiate an investigation. However, the State must also start an investigation without such a complaint if there are reasonable grounds to believe that individuals adopted in the past were subjected to enforced disappearance. Numerous reports as well as studies provide detailed and thorough documentation of widespread and systemic abuses in past adoptions from several countries of the Global South.[87] Extreme poverty and high levels of corruption provided fertile ground for illegal adoption practices, including the forceful removal of children from their parents, which took place on a structural level. Arguably, such reports about systemic abuses cast doubt on the legitimacy of all international adoptions from these countries. Receiving States that arranged adoptions from countries in which children were obtained illegally for adoption purposes on a large scale are therefore obliged to *ex officio* instigate an investigation into past adoptions from these countries.

The ICPPED includes two kinds of state obligation with regard to investigating enforced disappearances. First, the convention obliges States to carry out an investigation with the purpose of prosecuting individuals implicated in this crime and holding them criminally responsible. This obligation will be analysed in the following chapter (Chapter 11) concerning individual criminal responsibility under the ICPPED. Second, ICPPED obliges its State parties to investigate possible cases of enforced disappearance with the purpose of establishing the whereabouts or fate of the disappeared person. Article 24(2) thereby plays a central role, which explicitly provides victims of an

84 Rechtbank Den Haag, 9 September 2020, ECLI:NL:RBDHA:2020:8735.
85 Ibid., para. 5.25.
86 COIA, 2021, pp. 103-104.
87 See literature references in footnotes 44-51.

enforced disappearance with the right to know the truth (also referred to as the right to the truth):

> Each victim has the right to know the truth regarding the circumstances of the enforced disappearance, the progress and results of the investigation and the fate of the disappeared person. Each State Party shall take appropriate measures in this regard.

This right has been recognized in several international instruments[88] and by intergovernmental mechanisms, and it is closely linked with other rights, such as the right to an effective remedy, the right to legal and judicial protection, the right to family life, etc. and even the right to be free from torture and ill-treatment.[89] The right to know the truth is an absolute right that cannot be subjected to any limitations or derogations. Hence, no legitimate aim or exceptional circumstances can be invoked by the State to restrict this right.[90] According to the Working Group on Enforced or Involuntary Disappearance: "This absolute character also results from the fact that the enforced disappearance causes 'anguish and sorrow' … to the family, a suffering that reaches the threshold of torture…".[91]

The right to know the truth implies "knowing the full and complete truth" regarding the circumstances of the enforced disappearance as well as the fate and whereabouts of the disappeared person.[92] Article 24(3) provides that States Parties are obliged to "take all appropriate measures" to search for and locate disappeared persons. Article 25(2) contains a similarly worded obligation with regard to children subjected to enforced disappearance. Article 24(6) clarifies that the obligation to investigate is a continuous obligation that applies until the fate of the disappeared person has been clarified.

Numerous adoptees have an urgent need to find out where they come from and what has happened to them. However, currently, receiving countries do little to assist adoptees in their root searches. Many adoptees feel that they are left to investigate the

---

88 See; e.g., UN Commission on Human Rights, *Updated Set of principles for the protection and promotion of human rights through action to combat impunity*, 8 February 2005, E/CN.4/2005/102/Add.1, Principles 1, 2 and 4; Additional Protocol to the Geneva Conventions, of 12 August 1949, and relating to the Protection of Victims of International Armed Conflicts, Article 32; UN Commission on Human Rights, *Guiding Principles on Internal Displacement*, 11 February 1998, E/CN.4/1998/53/Add.2, Principle 16.

89 UN High Commissioner for Human Rights, *Promotion and Protection of Human Rights, Study on the Right to the Truth*, 8 February 2006, E/CN.4/2006/91, para. 9.

90 WGEID, *General Comment on the Right to the Truth in Relation to Enforced Disappearance*, 26 January 2011, A/HR/16/48, para. 4

91 Ibid.

92 UN High Commissioner for Human Rights, *Promotion and Protection of Human Rights, Study on the Right to the Truth*, 8 February 2006, E/CN.4/2006/91, para. 59.

adoption abuses that they think they have become victims of, a task that is actually the responsibility of the State. In the absence of State assistance, adoptees are required to spend large sums of money to investigate the circumstances of their adoption placement. Unfortunately, States often do more to cover up than to clarify, for example, by refusing to make documents available that could help the adoptee's quest. This clearly violates the State obligation to investigate possible cases of enforced disappearances under the ICPPED. Based on Article 24, States are obliged to ensure that individuals that believe that they are the victims of an illegal adoption receive the assistance they need to know their origins and true identity.[93] States are required to take all appropriate measures to investigate the specific circumstances of a possible illegal intercountry adoption and to search for and identify the family members of the adoptee.[94] Such measures include examining relevant documentation, doing fact-finding investigation in the sending countries and creating or coordinating with a genetic data bank, referring potential cases of illegal adoption to this bank for DNA testing.[95] States should establish independent commissions of inquiry or truth commissions that resolve potential cases of enforced disappearance and help victims trace back their families. These commissions should support and rely on the efforts of existing organizations. As already mentioned above, a number of non-governmental organizations have emerged in recent years with the goal to help adoptees and their families reunite. Many of these organizations have years of experience with seeking the truth concerning illegal intercountry adoptions and should serve to educate and train government agents and institutions charged with investigating cases of enforced disappearance.[96]

Considering the transnational scope of illegal intercountry adoptions, it is vital that the authorities both in the receiving and sending countries assist each other in searching for, identifying and locating victims of illegal intercountry adoptions. Articles 15 and 25(3) contain an explicit obligation for international assistance and cooperation in that regard. For this purpose, States are obliged to conclude bilateral and multilateral agreements. Alternatively, they may rely on the mechanisms provided by the Hague Convention on Intercountry Adoption. As mentioned before, the convention lacks specific procedures for responding to individual cases of illegal adoption. Yet, it obliges States to set up central authorities who can potentially be relied on for processing claims relating to the illegal intercountry adoption of children.

93 UN Human Rights Treaty Bodies, *Joint Statement on Illegal Intercountry Adoptions*, 29 September 2022, para. 15.

94 Ibid.

95 WGEID, *General Comment on Children and Enforced Disappearances*, 14 February 2013, A/HRC/WGEID/98/1, para. 25.

96 Ibid.

Reparation

Article 24(4) ICPPED obliges States Parties to ensure that victims of enforced disappearance 'have the right to obtain reparation and prompt, fair and adequate compensation'. Article 24(5) ICPPED specifies that this right to reparation covers:

> material and moral damages and, where appropriate, other forms of reparation such as:
> (a) Restitution;
> (b) Rehabilitation;
> (c) Satisfaction, including restoration of dignity and reputation;
> (d) Guarantees of non-repetition.

The categories of reparation mentioned in Article 24(4) and (5) mirror the 2005 UN Basic Principles and Guidelines on the Right to Remedy and Reparation for Victims of Gross Violations of International Human Rights Law and Serious Violations of International Humanitarian Law (hereinafter UN Basic Principles).[97]

Based on Article 24(5), victims of an illegal intercountry adoption that constitute an enforced disappearance have the right to obtain reparation covering "material and moral damages". The UN Basic Principles refer to this form of reparation as *compensation* which should be made available "for any economically assessable damage, as appropriate and proportional to the gravity of the violation and the circumstances of each case" (UN Basic Principle 20). In order to live up to the obligations following from this right, receiving States should provide for a compensation fund that covers both economic damages that victims of enforced disappearance had suffered (e.g., due to expensive root searches) as well as moral damages caused by the human rights violations.

Another form of reparation that receiving countries should provide to victims of enforced disappearance is *restitution*. Restitution refers to measures that restore victims, in as much as possible, to the original situation before the gross human rights violation(s) occurred. This includes "restoration of liberty, enjoyment of human rights, identity, family life and citizenship, return to one's place of residence, restoration of employment and return of property" (UN Basic Principle 19). This obligation also follows from the right to identity laid down in Article 8 of the UN Convention on the Right of the Child (paragraph 1), which obliges States to re-establish the identity of a child who has been "illegally deprived of some or all of the elements of his or her

97 For a more detailed discussion of the UN Basic Principles see Loibl, 2021.

identity" (para. 2). Article 25(4) ICPPED specifically acknowledges and substantiates the State's obligation to re-establish a child's identity in the context of an adoption that originated in an enforced disappearance:[98]

> Given the need to protect the best interests of the children [wrongfully removed from their parents] and their right to preserve, or to have re-established, their identity, including their nationality, name and family relations as recognized by law, States Parties which recognize a system of adoption or other form of placement of children shall have legal procedures in place to review the adoption or placement procedure, and, where appropriate, to annul any adoption or placement of children that originated in an enforced disappearance.

Based on Article 25(4), receiving States are thus obliged to set up legal procedures to review and, if appropriate, annul any adoption if there is an indication that the adoptee was forcefully removed from their biological parents. Article 25(2) furthermore requires States to return children subjected to enforced removal to their families of origin, in accordance with legal procedures and applicable international agreements. Of course, these measures must serve the best interests of the child and might not always be appropriate. Finally, States should assist victims with obtaining proper documentation and pertinent corrections in all relevant registries.[99]

Illegally adopted individuals should also have access to *rehabilitation*, which "should include medical and psychological care as well as legal and social services" (UN Basic Principle 21). The forceful removal of children from their parents is a serious crime. The Working Group on Enforced or Involuntary Disappearance has repeatedly stressed that the enforced removal of children constitutes an extreme form of violence against children which "has specific and especially serious effects on their personal integrity that have a lasting impact, and causes great physical and mental harm".[100] Indeed, many illegally adopted individuals report feelings of loss, abandonment, grief and anger as well as uncertainty in cases where they were not successful to trace back their families.[101] Receiving States, thus, have to "appropriate and comprehensive psychological care" to

98 J. Tobin, *The UN Convention on the Rights of the Child: A Commentary*, Oxford University Press, 2019, pp. 284-285.

99 WGEID, *General Comment on Children and Enforced Disappearances*, 14 February 2013, A/HRC/WGEID/98/1, para. 31.

100 Ibid., p. 6.

101 L. Long, 'ICAV Perspective Paper Illicit Intercountry Adoptions: Lived Experience Views on How Authorities and Bodies Could Respond', July 2020, https://intercountryadopteevoices.com/wp-content/uploads/2020/07/Illicit-Adoptions-Responses-from-Lived-Experience.pdf.

ensure "children's physical and psychological recovery and social integration".[102] Also, they have the duty to reimburse the victims for all expenses in cases where third parties provided psychological care.

The third category of reparation listed in Article 24(5) is *satisfaction* which includes a broad range of measures, ranging from establishing and publicly disclosing the truth, acknowledging wrongful conduct, accepting responsibility to issuing judicial and administrative sanctions against those persons involved in the violations as well as a public apology (UN Basic Principle 22). A truth commission can serve as an important measure of satisfaction. Its objective is not only to assist victims in finding the truth about their origins and re-establishing their true identity (see above), but also to make a credible historical record of what has happened.[103] After all, the right to the truth is not just an individual right of the victims and their families but also a collective right of society as a whole.[104] Publicly disclosing the truth should be accompanied by remedies including an official apology as well as public acknowledgement and remembrance of illegal intercountry adoptions.[105]

Finally, reparation according to Article 24(5) should include *guarantees of non-repetition*. These are measures that serve as safeguard against the repetition of human rights violations and abuses. Measures include meaningful reforms of the intercountry adoption system or banning intercountry adoptions altogether (UN Basic Principle 23).

CONCLUSION

More and more receiving countries decide to commission inquiries into past intercountry adoptions due to signs of illegal practices and pressure from adoptees requesting to look into them. In 2019, the Dutch Joustra Commission released its report regarding intercountry adoptions from Bangladesh, Brazil, Colombia, Indonesia and Sri Lanka to the Netherlands in the period of 1967 to 1998. In the same year, a study commissioned by the Swiss government examining adoptions from Sri Lanka to Switzerland from 1973 until 1997 was published. Also the Swedish, French and, recently, the Norwegian governments announced an intention to set up commissions to investigate intercountry

102 WGEID, *General Comment on Children and Enforced Disappearances*, 14 February 2013, A/HRC/WGEID/98/1, para. 34.

103 UN Human Rights Treaty Bodies, *Joint Statement on Illegal Intercountry Adoptions*, 29 September 2022, para. 18.

104 WGEID, *General Comment on Children and Enforced Disappearances*, 14 February 2013, A/HRC/WGEID/98/1, para. 35.

105 Ibid.

adoptions. Hopefully, more receiving countries will follow suit. Both the Dutch and the Swiss reports essentially confirmed the findings of numerous previous studies and reports that have documented large-scale abuses within the intercountry adoption system, including the forced removal of children in the form of an abduction. Most notably, however, the inquiries found that the authorities in the receiving countries had acquiescence in those practices but did do little to prevent the adoption placement of illegally obtained children. This finding is remarkable as it contradicts the previously held position of the authorities in the receiving countries that have emphasized again, and against that, they were unaware of the abuses in the sending countries.

Following the release of the inquiries, both the Dutch and Swiss governments have acknowledged their responsibility for past illegal intercountry adoptions and promised reforming the adoption system. The Dutch government has even offered an official apology to the victims. However, so far, they have done little to investigate the specific circumstances of illegal intercountry adoptions and to search for and identify the family members of those adoptees that could have been affected by abusive practices. It seems that the governments want to close this chapter of the past and move on. However, the findings of the inquiries only mark the beginning of a reappraisal. The conclusion that the authorities in the receiving States had acquiescence of the adoption abuses abroad potentially brings many cases of illegal intercountry adoption, namely those that include an abduction of a child, within the scope of the ICPPED, for which the receiving States incur responsibility. According to the convention, the receiving States are obliged to instigate investigations with the purpose of establishing the origins and identity of adoptees who are reasonably believed to they have been subjected to an enforced disappearance. Enforced disappearances are continuous crimes that do not cease to exist until the victim's fate or whereabouts are established. Hence, the State obligation to investigate continues to apply until the specific circumstances of a possible illegal intercountry adoption are clarified and the true identity of the adoptee is established. Only after potential cases of enforced disappearance have been investigated properly and the harm inflicted upon the victims have been repaired can governments of the receiving countries consider moving on.

11 Individual Criminal Responsibility for Illegal Intercountry Adoptions Following the Crime of Enforced Disappearance

André Klip

Introduction

Chapter 10 focused on enforced disappearance as a human rights violation. It explained under which circumstances illegal intercountry adoptions fall within the definition of enforced disappearance as a human rights violation and discussed the obligations that incur on receiving states in the aftermath of such a violation. Yet, as has been explained in the previous contribution, the ICPPED is not only an international human rights instrument. It is also an instrument of international criminal law that lays down the conditions under which states should criminalize individuals responsible for the crime of an enforced disappearance.[1] The CED's interpretation of illegal adoption as a crime of enforced disappearance is:

> States shall prohibit illegal intercountry adoptions as a continuing offense under criminal law. They shall establish appropriate sanctions that reflect the gravity of this offense and guarantee a prompt and effective judicial remedy. In the case of illegal intercountry adoptions resulting from enforced disappearances, States shall consider as an aggravating factor that the person who disappeared was a child, taking into consideration that enforced disappearances or the wrongful removal of children in the context of enforced disappearance are an extreme form of violence against children.[2]

---

1 See L. Ott, *Enforced Disappearance in International Law*, Cambridge, Intersentia, 2011.

2 Committee on Enforced Disappearances, *Joint Statement on Illegal Intercountry Adoptions.* Issued by Committee on the Rights of the Child (CRC), the Committee on Enforced Disappearances (CED), the Special Rapporteur on the Promotion of Truth, Justice, Reparation and Guarantees of Non-recurrence, the Special Rapporteur on the Sale and Sexual Exploitation of Children including child prostitution, child pornography and other child sexual abuse material, the Special Rapporteur on Trafficking in Persons, especially women and children, and the Working Group on Enforced or Involuntary Disappearances on 29 September 2022.

The present chapter focuses on the individual criminal responsibility for the crimes of enforced disappearance introduced by the convention. It discusses the elements of enforced disappearance as a crime, clarifies who might be considered as a perpetrator thereof and explains under which circumstances an illegal intercountry adoption can be considered as a crime of enforced disappearance. Furthermore, it explains which state has jurisdiction to instigate a criminal investigation and prosecute the perpetrators and whether enforced disappearances that were committed before the ICPPED entered into force can still be prosecuted.

The interpretation of the criminal law dimension of the convention is seriously handicapped by the fact that there is not a single case reported in which a crime under the convention has been prosecuted.[3] The very few references to judgements in which enforced disappearances play a role come from international criminal tribunals who decided these on the definition of enforced disappearance as a crime against humanity under their Statute and in which the attack on the civilian population resulted in many casualties. The interpretation of the convention thus relies much on the author's experience with other conventions on international crimes.

THE ELEMENTS OF THE CRIME OF ENFORCED DISAPPEARANCE

It is clear that the drafters of the convention intended to cover situations in which a state policy either directly or indirectly followed a practice of letting individuals disappear as a tool of suppression. The qualification of enforced disappearance as a crime against humanity and several other aspects of criminal responsibility, such as superior responsibility which were borrowed from the ICC Statute, are evidence of that. However, at the same time, it was also intended to have enforced disappearance as an ordinary crime, to protect individuals outside the context of an attack on the civilian population.[4] In its reviews of the implementing legislation, the Committee emphasizes the need for

3 Schniederjahn reports a handful of national cases of criminal prosecution for enforced disappearance as a crime against humanity (see N. Schniederjahn, *Das Verschwindenlassen von Personen in der Rechtsprechung internationaler Menschenrechtsgerichtshöfe*, Berlin, Duncker & Humblot, 2017, Schriften zum Völkerrecht Band 225, pp. 250-276).

4 See on the coming into being of the Convention, E. Decaux and O. de Frouville (eds.), *La Convention pour la protection de toutes les personnes contre les disparitions forcées*, Bruxelles, Bruyland, 2009. More elaborated on the developments under international law of the human right to be protected against enforced disappearance, as well as the criminal offence; Schniederjahn, 2017, pp. 44-47.

an autonomous offence, and rejects criminalization by existing partial offences.[5] There is an underlying presumption that the act of disappearance as such takes places within the context of one state. However, gradually the transnational aspects came to the fore, when it concerned enforced disappearances of migrants, citizens from one country who have gone missing abroad, or trafficked individuals.[6]

Article 4 obliges states parties to take the necessary measures to ensure that enforced disappearance, defined in Article 2, constitutes an offence in domestic criminal law. According to Article 5, the crime of enforced disappearance has to be qualified as a crime against humanity as defined under international criminal law if it constitutes a widespread and systemic practice. Article 25, which specifically deals with the enforced disappearance of children, obliges states parties in subparagraph 1 to take the necessary measures to prevent and punish under its criminal law (a) the wrongful removal of children subjected to enforced disappearance or whose mother, father or legal guardians were subjected to enforced disappearance, or who were born during the captivity of a mother subjected to enforced disappearance and (b) the falsification, concealment or destruction of documents attesting to the true identity of the those children.[7] Hence, the ICPPED provides for four different criminal offences:

5 The Committee noted on 15 October 2014 concerning Belgium, a party since 2 July 2011, that the State party has begun a legislative process aimed inter alia at defining and criminalizing enforced disappearance in its Criminal Code as a separate offence, and asked the country to step up the pace in drafting the legislation (see Concluding observations on the report submitted by Belgium under Art. 29, para. 1, of the Convention, 15 October 2014, CED/C/BEL/CO/1, paras. 11-12). On 26 April 2021, the country reported that the bill was pending in Parliament (see Additional information submitted by Belgium under Art. 29 (4) of the Convention, 7 May 2021, CED/C/BEL/AI/1). The Committee also noted on 3 November 2021 concerning Brazil, a party since 29 December 2010, that it has yet not adopted an autonomous offence (see Concluding observations on the report submitted by Brazil under Art. 29 (1) of the Convention, 3 November 2021, CED/C/BRA/CO/1, paras. 14-15). The same problem was established for Burkina Faso, Chile, Costa Rica, Cuba, Czech Republic, Gabon, Germany, Mexico, Mongolia, Montenegro, Morocco, Niger, Nigeria, Serbia, Spain, Tunisia and several other states. Some states have implemented an autonomous offence following the request from the Committee.

6 M.C. Galvis Patiño, *The Work of the Committee on Enforced Disappearance Achievements and Jurisprudence Ten Years after the Entry into Force of the International Convention for the Protection of All Persons from Enforced Disappearance*, Geneva, Geneva Academy, August 2021, https://www.geneva-academy.ch/research/publications/detail/607-the-work-of-the-committee-on-enforced-disappearances, p. 15.

7 Art. 25 was added at a later stage. It was not included in the first draft for the convention. See UN Economic and Social Council, Commission of Human Rights, Sub-Commission on Prevention of Discrimination and Protection of Minorities Fiftieth session, Item 9 of the agenda, Working Group on the Administration of Justice, The Administration of Justice and Human Rights, *Report of the Sessional Working Group on the Administration of Justice*, E/CN.4/Sub.2/1998/19, 19 August 1998. It was inserted in 2005 on proposal of the chairperson. However, the report does not state any debate about the relation with the main criminalization (see Report of the Intersessional Open-ended Working Group to elaborate a draft legally binding normative instrument for the protection of all persons from enforced disappearance, E/CN.4/2005/66, 10 March 2005). However, Art. 20 of the Declaration on the Protection of All Persons from Enforced Disappearance adopted by the General Assembly of the United Nations in its resolution 47/133 of 18 December 1992, already saw a link between adoption and enforced disappearance.

- enforced disappearance (Art. 2);
- enforced disappearance as a crime against humanity (Art. 5);
- the wrongful removal of a child subjected to enforced disappearance or whose parents or legal guardians were subjected to enforced disappearance, or who was born during the captivity of a mother subjected to enforced disappearance (Art. 25(1)(a));
- identity concealment or substitution (Art. 25(1)(b)).

Enforced disappearance (Art. 2)

The ICPPED provides for the definition of enforced disappearance in Article 2:

> For the purposes of this Convention, "enforced disappearance" is considered to be the arrest, detention, abduction or any other form of deprivation of liberty by agents of the State or by persons or groups of persons acting with the authorization, support or acquiescence of the State, followed by a refusal to acknowledge the deprivation of liberty or by concealment of the fate or whereabouts of the disappeared person, which place such a person outside the protection of the law.

The previous chapter discussed the elements of the definition of enforced disappearance as a human right (see Chapter 10). This chapter analyses the elements of enforced disappearance as a crime and explains which individuals can be considered as perpetrators thereof.

In the context of the specific focus on the relevance of the convention for illegal adoptions, it is important to assess who is protected by the criminal norm Article 2 of the convention. Looking at the definition of the ordinary crime of enforced disappearance in, it immediately raises the question of who is the person that has disappeared (and for whom?) that is protected by the criminal provision? Is it the mother (or also the father), or is it the child and is the disappearance of the child dependent on a mother that has disappeared? There are several situations possible: the mother was pregnant when she disappeared and the child is born when her whereabouts were unknown. The child may also have been conceived when the mother was in captivity and she may have given birth during disappearance. In these situations, both the mother and the child must be regarded as an enforced disappeared person.

The crime of enforced disappearance within the meaning of Article 2 has four elements. The first element is the *arrest, detention, abduction or any other form of deprivation*. The very few cases that exist are all from international criminal tribunals and in the context of the crime against humanity. However, they are useful in that they describe what kind of conduct amounts to the crime. In the 1970s, in Cambodia, the whole population was to be re-educated by the Khmer Rouge regime. Many people that did not obey (or were thought to disobey) the rules of the regime disappeared. The Extraordinary Chambers in the Courts of Cambodia (ECCC) described the act as follows:

> The main modus operandi of enforced disappearances consisted of the authorities of Democratic Kampuchea putting in place measures designed to conceal the fate of individuals who had disappeared by ensuring that witnesses did not reveal information about them, for example by taking victims away at night so that others would not know how or when they disappeared and also by using loudspeakers to mask the sound of executions. None of the witnesses mentioned any system of recording or registering the personal details of the persons taken away that would have been accessible to the public, or any other procedural protections during the arrest, abduction or detention of those who disappeared, such that the families of these individuals did not know what subsequently happened to them.[8]

The second element is *by agents of the State or by persons or groups of persons acting with the authorization, support or acquiescence of the State*. The deprivation of liberty is done by state agents, if the authorities performing the act above are employed by the

8 ECCC, Closing Order, *Prosecutor v. Nuon Chea, Khieu Samphan, and Ieng Thirith*, Case No. 002/19-09-2007-ECCC/OCIJ, Office of the Co-Investigating Judges, 15 September 2010, paras. 1472-1473, *in* A. Klip and S. Freeland (eds.), *Annotated Leading Cases of International Criminal Tribunals-ILIV-375*, Cambridge, Intersentia, 2015.

state.[9] It is intended to apply a very broad definition when it comes to the potential perpetrators. From the very broad formulation of the necessary link with the state, as compared with the 1984 UN Convention against Torture and Other Cruel, Inhuman or Degrading Treatment or Punishment, I conclude that a formal contractual position as a public official is not required. Any person or group of persons in whatever organization that performs the act with some form of knowledge and implicit approval as the lowest standard is enough. It is clear that there must be some knowledge with state officials of the practice. For the individual perpetrator, it means that s/he must have the intent to be (or work with) such a state agent. The formulations raise countless questions on which, due to lack of any practice, only a few answers can be given.

The third element of the crime of an enforced disappearance is *the refusal to acknowledge the deprivation of liberty or by concealment of the fate or whereabouts of*

9 I. Giorgou, 'State Involvement in the Perpetration of Enforced Disappearance and the Rome Statute', *Journal of International Criminal Justice*, Vol. 11, 2013, pp. 1001-1021 stated: "Enforced disappearance is, in essence, a state-related crime." International tribunals also held this for enforced disappearance as a crime against humanity, see ICC, Decision Pursuant to Art. 15 of the Rome Statute on the Authorisation of an Investigation into the Situation in the Republic of Côte d'Ivoire, Case No. ICC 02/11, P.T. Ch. III, 3 October 2011, para. 77, *in* A. Klip and S. Freeland (eds.), *Annotated Leading Cases of International Criminal Tribunals-LVII-220*, Cambridge, Intersentia, 2020: "For the crime of enforced disappearance the perpetrator must have arrested, detained or abducted one or more individuals or refused to acknowledge their arrest, detention or abduction, or to give information on the fate or whereabouts of the relevant individuals. Therefore, the arrest, detention or abduction must have been followed or accompanied by a refusal to acknowledge that the individual has been deprived of his or her freedom or to give information on the fate or whereabouts of those concerned. Moreover, the arrest, detention or abduction must have been carried out by, or with the authorisation, support or acquiescence of, a State or a political organisation." However, the Appeals Chamber of the ECCC held that in 1975: "enforced disappearances and forced transfer had not yet crystallised into separate categories of crimes against humanity. Indeed, such crystallisation would occur only many years later, as eventually evidenced by their inclusion as separate categories of crimes against humanity in Art. 7(1)(d) and (i) of the ICC Statute. Accordingly, enforced disappearances or forced transfer did not, in 1975, form discrete categories of crimes against humanity, nor did enforced disappearances and forced transfer have specific legal definitions and elements. For that reason, stipulating elements of enforced disappearance or enforced transfer as though they constituted separate categories of crimes against humanity was anachronistic and legally incorrect, whereas subsequently analysing the conduct under the same sub-headings as 'legal findings', among other discrete crimes against humanity, was, at a minimum, confusing." (See Appeal Judgment, *Prosecutor v. Khieu Samphan and Nuon Chea*, Case No. 002/19-09-2007-ECCC/SC, SC. Ch., 23 November 2016, para. 589, *in* A. Klip and S. Freeland (eds.), *Annotated Leading Cases of International Criminal Tribunals-LXV-693 and 694*, Cambridge, Intersentia, 2021). However, enforced disappearances were regarded as an "other inhuman act" as a crime against humanity against persons that were confronted with others that were disappeared. (See ECCC Case 002/02 Judgement, *Prosecutor v. Nuon Chea and Khieu Samphan*, Case No. 002/19-09-2007-ECCC/TC, T. Ch., 16 November 2018, para. 1427, *in* A. Klip and S. Freeland (eds.), *Annotated Leading Cases of International Criminal Tribunals-LXVIa-462*, Cambridge, Intersentia, 2022: "The Chamber finds that the acts described above caused serious mental suffering to the victims, namely those who disappeared and those who were left behind at the worksite, and constituted a serious attack on their human dignity. These disappearances made workers at the construction site live in constant fear of being arrested and disappeared, and made them wonder when their day would come."

the disappeared person, which must be regarded as the most distinguishable element of the disappearance. The outside world simply does not know where they are, whether they are still alive and what will happen to them. The person disappeared may know that s/he is detained, but not necessarily where and by whom and cannot contact the outside. The ECCC described this element as follows in the circumstances of the re-education and working camps in Cambodia:

> Aside from withholding information, the authorities provided evidently false reasons to justify the absence of those who disappeared, stating for example that they had been sent "to see Angkar", sent "to a meeting", or sent "to the Ministry of Foreign Affairs to become diplomats", sent to "study" or sent for "re-education". Regarding the *mens rea*, the perpetrators were aware of the factual circumstances that establish the gravity of their acts, as demonstrated by evidence which shows that intentional measures were taken in order to conceal the fate of people who had disappeared who, in most cases, were killed thereafter.[10]

The perpetrator complying with this element will either give knowingly false information on the whereabouts, or refuse to give information, whilst knowing the truth.

The fourth and last element of the crime is placing the disappeared person outside the protection of the law. The fact of being outside the protection of the law is the consequence of the uncertainty on the fate of the disappeared person. The individual cannot undertake legal action himself; no lawyer can seek remedies if there is no acknowledgement of the person being held. There is no definition as to how long the victim must be outside the protection of the law. Various writers interpret this as that a "prolonged period" is required.[11] This element is not subject to the intention of the perpetrator,[12] but it must be regarded as a consequence of the crime of enforced

10 ECCC, Closing Order, *Prosecutor v. Nuon Chea, Khieu Samphan, and Ieng Thirith*, Case No. 002/19-09-2007-ECCC/OCIJ, Office of the Co-Investigating Judges, 15 September 2010, paras. 1473-1475, *in* A. Klip and S. Freeland (eds.), *Annotated Leading Cases of International Criminal Tribunals-ILIV-375*, Cambridge, Intersentia, 2015.

11 See authors referred to by Ott, 2011, pp. 186-187.

12 Concluding observations on the report submitted by Paraguay under Art. 29, para. 1, of the Convention, 20 October 2014, CED/C/PRY/CO/1, para. 14: "The Committee recommends that the State party take the necessary measures, including the provision of suitable training for judges and prosecutors, to ensure that the phrase 'placing them outside the protection of the law' that appears in article 236, paragraph 1, of the Criminal Code be considered a consequence of the commission of the offence of enforced disappearance rather than an intentional element (animus) that would have to be present in order for the act to constitute criminal conduct."

disappearance that must also be proven.[13] This element makes the crime a continuous offence: "as long as the fate and whereabouts of the disappeared person remain unknown, the offence is ongoing".[14] The Committee itself describes continuous as:

> that enforced disappearance is a unique and consolidated series of acts which continues during the entire time until the victim's fate or whereabouts are established, and is not a series of single acts.[15]

To convict a perpetrator as a principal for the crime of enforced disappearance, it is required that he has personally intentionally committed all first three elements of the offence and has knowledge of the consequential fourth element. A perpetrator who does fulfil fewer elements himself may be regarded as an accomplice to the crime. For instance, the person abducting the victim may be somebody else than the person refusing to give information on the whereabouts.

Enforced Disappearance as a Crime against Humanity (Art. 5)

It is noted that the convention requires states to criminalize both offences of enforced disappearance: as an ordinary crime and as a crime against humanity.[16] In general, the situation in which illegal adoptions that have the potential to be laundered by applying formal adoption procedures may take place are far away from complying with a state

13 See specifically on this element: G. Citroni, 'La position des États', *in* E. Decaux and O. de Frouville (eds.), *La Convention pour la protection de toutes les personnes contre les disparitions forcées*, Bruxelles, Bruyland, pp. 77-80; see also Concluding observations on the report submitted by Portugal under Art. 29 (1) of the Convention, 5 December 2018, CED/C/PRT/CO/1, para. 12.

14 T. Scovazzi and G. Citroni, *The Struggle Against Enforced Disappearance and the 2007 United Nations Convention*, Leiden, Nijhoff, 2007, p. 310.

15 Concluding observations on the report submitted by Montenegro under Art. 29 (1) of the Convention, 16 October 2015, CED/C/MNE/CO/1, para. 10.

16 It is likely that the crime be considered as an obligation *jus cogens*. The ICTY qualified enforced disappearance as "other inhuman acts" amounting to torture. (See ICTY, Judgment, *Prosecutor v. Kupreškić*, Case No. IT-95-16-T, T. Ch. II, 14 January 2000, para. 566, *in* A. Klip and G. Sluiter (eds.), *Annotated Leading Cases of International Criminal Tribunals-IV-825 and 826*, Cambridge, Intersentia, 2002; ICTY, Judgment, *Prosecutor v. Kvočka et al*, Case No. IT-98-30/ 1-T, T. Ch., 2 November 2001, para. 208, *in* A. Klip and G. Sluiter (eds.), *Annotated Leading Cases of International Criminal Tribunals-VIII-622*, Cambridge, Intersentia, 2005; see also J. Sarkin, 'Why the Prohibition of Enforced Disappearance Has Attained Jus Cogens Status in International Law', *Nordic Journal of International Law*, Vol. 8, 2012, pp. 537-584).

policy or widespread attack on the civilian population, as the definition of crimes against humanity requires.[17]

A crime against humanity is one of the few crimes for which the International Criminal Court is competent on the basis of the Statute for the International Criminal Court. It belongs to the most serious crimes of mankind, with only genocide regarded as the more superior crime. As a result of this, the requirements for a crime against humanity are not easy to meet. Although individual acts of murder, rape and enforced disappearance could be qualified as such a crime against humanity, they must take place in the context of *a widespread or systematic attack against the civilian population* of a country. Whilst there must be an attack on the civilian population, the individual perpetrator must not necessarily have initiated or planned the attack as a whole. What is needed is that there is awareness that an individual criminal offence forms part of the context of the attack. The few criminal cases of international criminal tribunals in which enforced disappearance is recognized as a crime against humanity all dealt with a massive attack on the civilian populations in which thousands of people were killed.

It is undisputed that for states parties to either the ICC Statute, the ICPPED or both, there is an obligation to criminalize enforced disappearance as a crime against humanity. However, it may be so that before those conventions were adopted, the existence of a *jus cogens* obligation to criminalize such conduct may have existed already. The importance of the question whether enforced disappearance has obtained *jus cogens* status under international law is that it would then require states to follow it. However, when enforced disappearance had obtained the status of *jus cogens* under international law is unclear. It was not in 1975, so the ECCC decided. But, was it then in 1992, when the UN General Assembly adopted a Resolution, or 1998 when the ICC Statute was adopted or only in 2006 with the conclusion of the convention itself? If

17 This may be different concerning the policy Russia has implemented since 2022 in Ukraine. The ICC issued an arrest warrant against Putin concerning war crimes (see https://www.icc-cpi.int/news/situation-ukraine-icc-judges-issue-arrest-warrants-against-vladimir-vladimirovich-putin-and: "Mr Vladimir Vladimirovich Putin, born on 7 October 1952, President of the Russian Federation, is allegedly responsible for the war crime of unlawful deportation of population (children) and that of unlawful transfer of population (children) from occupied areas of Ukraine to the Russian Federation (under articles 8(2)(a)(vii) and 8(2)(b)(viii) of the Rome Statute)." However, such a large-scale practice may also amount to enforced disappearance as a crime against humanity of Art. 7(1) (i) ICC Statute. The large-scale and systematic approach may be seen as part of a broader Russian attack on the civilian population of Ukraine. For enforced disappearance as a crime against humanity, the individual act must form part of an attack against the civilian population. The ICC has held that this element is decisive for its jurisdiction: "Isolated acts that differ in nature, aims and consequences from other attacks that occur during an attack, fall outside the scope of Article 7(1) ICC Statute." (See ICC, Decision Pursuant to Art. 15 of the Rome Statute on the Authorisation of an Investigation into the Situation in the Republic of Côte d'Ivoire, Case No. ICC 02/11, P.T. Ch. III, 3 October 2011, para. 89, *in* A. Klip and S. Freeland (eds.), *Annotated Leading Cases of International Criminal Tribunals-LVII-222*, Cambridge, Intersentia, 2020; see further Ott, 2011, pp. 165-176).

this is an issue for enforced disappearance as a crime against humanity, it is even more the case for enforced disappearance as an ordinary crime that cannot be regarded as a *jus cogens* crime. This is relevant for the obligations the Committee imposes upon states parties vis-à-vis offences that occurred before the convention entered into force. However, even if there would have been a *jus cogens* obligation to criminalize enforced disappearance, it triggers state responsibility only. There is no individual criminal responsibility without a criminalization at the time of the offence. That is not different when the state should have criminalized the conduct.

Wrongful Removal of a Child (Art. 25(1)(a))

The crime laid down in Article 25(1)(a) protects three categories of children. The first category concerns children who themselves have been subjected to enforced disappearance as they were abducted or, in case they were already older, arrested or detained. The second category concerns children who have not forcefully disappeared themselves, but whose parents or legal guardian(s) were subjected to enforced disappearance. The third category encompasses children born in captivity of their mothers subjected to enforced disappearance. For some, their potential existence might be known to the outside world as the pregnancy of the mother was known when she disappeared. For others, this may not have been known, or the mother only became pregnant in captivity.

The use of the term *wrongful removal of children* brings several messages. The first is that it does not limit the type of removal to a specific (legal) basis of the situation, but it describes what happens in a factual way: a removal without right. It does not mention adoption and the explanation can be found in the word wrongful. A wrong must have been committed in the act of removing the child from their parents. That can be anything violating the rights and interests of the child and/or the parents, it may be adoption, and if so, the adoption must be a wrong vis-à-vis the child. This means that all illegal adoptions may be regarded as complying with the element wrongful removal. It becomes then relevant to prove that there has been a crime committed in the process of adoption. This may be deception of the parents in order to obtain their content to adoption, falsification of the child's documents, bribing an official/judge. etc., in other words: any interest that the Hague Adoption Convention and the UNCRC aim to protect. Whilst the act that may amount to 'wrongful removal of the child' can be anything, there must always be a nexus with an enforced disappearance. The child must fall in one of the three categories of protected children.

In the first ten years of its existence, the Committee clearly required that there must be a link of the illegal adoption with an enforced disappearance.[18] McCrory states:

> Article 25 of the convention is a provision dedicated solely to the issue of enforced disappearance of children, whether they are subjected to it as individuals in their own right or as victims of their parents' enforced disappearance, including where they are born during their mother's captivity.[19]

Patiño writes on the inclusion of Article 25:

> Situations were discussed in which perpetrators of enforced disappearances have appropriated the children of disappeared persons, or in which children are born while their mothers are victims of enforced disappearances and are then given up for adoption, thus losing their identity.[20]

An illegal adoption must be considered as a wrongful removal of a child. In the context of adoption, this is possible concerning disappeared mothers giving birth in captivity and the subsequent adoption of the child.[21] Such an adoption can only be regarded as illegal and leading to a situation that the child has no knowledge about its real identity. An example of such an adoption is described by Citroni:

> In one case (i.e. Mr Guido Carlotto), the disappeared person was born while his mother was being held captive in Argentina; he was wrongfully removed and grew up under a false identity, as part of a systematic practice under the military dictatorship that affected more than 500 children. At the time of the relevant proceedings in Italy (i.e. 2000), the fate and whereabouts of Mr Carlotto remained unknown, but he was presumed to be alive. On 5 August 2014, Mr Carlotto was found and his biological identity was ascertained through DNA testing. In his case, proceedings revolved around the crime of kidnapping and were therefore declared time-barred. Bearing in mind that he

18 Galvis Patiño, 2021, pp. 73-74.

19 S. McCrory, 'The International Convention for the Protection of all Persons from Enforced Disappearance', *Human Rights Law Review*, Vol. 7, 2007, pp. 545-566.

20 Galvis Patiño, 2021, p. 73.

21 For instance, under the dictatorship in Chile: "The Committee takes note of the information provided by the State party regarding investigations into the removal and/or irregular adoption of 341 children, 279 of which allegedly occurred during the dictatorship. The Committee also notes that a special file has been opened in relation to the detention during the dictatorship of 10 pregnant women, whose children might have been born in captivity and survived. The Committee notes that those children could have been particularly vulnerable to becoming victims of identity substitution (art. 25)" (see Concluding observations on the report submitted by Chile under Art. 29 (1) of the Convention, 8 May 2019, CED/C/CHL/CO/1, paras. 30-31).

was properly identified in 2014, it is disputable that the permanent nature of the crime and the corresponding consequences were adequately applied by Italian courts.[22]

Identity Concealment or Substitution (Art. 25(1)(b))

The second offence of Article 25 under b) has the following elements: The first is that the act must relate to a child referred to in Article 25(1)(a).[23] Hence, the child must fall in one of the three categories of children described above. The second is that there must be an act of laundering the child through falsifying, fabricating or destroying documents attesting to the child's true (e.g., birth certificate).[24] As a result of this, the child does not know its real identity.[25] There are various ways of hiding the true identity of a child and given the human right at stake, namely the right to identity laid down in Article 8 UNCRC, it is likely that it was intended by the drafters to interpret this element rather broadly.

POTENTIAL PERPETRATORS OF THE CRIME AND THE REQUIREMENT OF INTENT

As a convention criminalizing conduct, it does not only describe the act that is prohibited, but also stipulates which individuals may be held criminally responsible by the state. The convention follows other treaties on international crimes and applies the same categories

22 See G. Citroni, 'Consequences of the Lack of Criminalization of Enforced Disappearance at the Domestic Level: The Italian Experience', *Journal of International Criminal Justice*, Vol. 19, 2021, p. 689. Apparently, Italy did not see the need to criminalize the international crime separately and simply took the view that it was already covered by its provision implementing the ICC Statute.

23 Mexico was criticized for not having implemented Art. 25 fully: "The Committee takes note of the recent General Act on Enforced Disappearance, which incorporates specific offences regarding the wrongful removal of children. However, it notes with concern that this piece of legislation only provides for offences committed against children born during the period of concealment and does not cover the first two provisions of Art. 25 (1) (a) of the Convention, i.e. 'the wrongful removal of children who are subjected to enforced disappearance, or children whose father, mother or legal guardian is subjected to enforced disappearance'" (see follow-up observations on the additional information submitted by Mexico under Art. 29 (4) of the Convention, 6 September 2019, CED/C/MEX/FAI/1, para. 40). The Committee found an almost absolute impunity in Mexico for enforced disappearances (see Report of the Committee on Enforced Disappearances on its visit to Mexico under Art. 33 of the Convention, 18 May 2022, CED/C/MEX/VR/1 (Findings), paras. 25-27).

24 D.M. Smolin, 'Child Laundering: How the Intercountry Adoption System Legitimizes and Incentivizes the Practices of Buying, Trafficking, Kidnapping, and Stealing Children', *The Wayne Law Review*, Vol. 52, No. 1, 2006, pp. 113-200, 115.

25 Please note that also in regular intercountry adoption proceedings, biological parents do not receive information on the whereabouts and potential new identity of the child.

for individual perpetrators for all four crimes. Article 6 stipulates the various modalities of individual criminal responsibility that states must provide: Any person who commits, orders, solicits or induces the commission of, attempts to commit, is an accomplice to or participates in an enforced disappearance.[26] We can thus distinguish the principal perpetrator, the aider and abettor, the inciter and the person who attempts the offence. The convention does neither require the criminal responsibility of legal entities nor of the state (or its organs). For crimes against humanity, an additional responsibility must be criminalized for commanders.

What does this mean for enforced disappearance in the context of illegal adoption? There are numerous potential perpetrators that may have committed the offence as a principal or as an accessory. The parents, any relatives or other caregivers; any notary, civil servant or other authority attesting a situation in a document; any doctor, nurse or other person in a hospital; a person in the adoption organization in the state of origin; any court official of (or lawyer in) the state of origin; a person in the adoption organization in the state of receipt; any court official of (or lawyer in) the state of receipt; the adoptive parents. It may be so that there is general knowledge of the illegality with all involved in the chain of adoption. It may also be the case that the illegality successfully laundered the child and that individuals further down the chain, closer to the adoptive parents, have no knowledge of it. This raises the question to what extent they should have known. It may also be that knowledge about an act of illegality committed in the process of adoption is discovered only decades after the placement of the child. Which individuals do now conceal the true identity of the child? We will use this panoply of potential suspects to further identify the problems that may exist when determining the state that has jurisdiction over the crimes committed. The answer to all these questions depend fully on the specific circumstances of the case applicable to the individual at the moment s/he acted. It is especially the continuing character of the crime here that poses challenges. It may result in criminal responsibility at a later stage because of knowledge obtained later, where the same person did not have the knowledge years before.

What all offences have in common is that they require intent and knowledge. This can be read from the use of words describing the act of Article 2 (arrest, detention, abduction or any other form of deprivation of liberty). This can only be done intentionally and knowingly. This also applies to the other elements of involvement of state agents and the refusal to share the whereabouts which can only be committed with special intent.

26 Art. 6 is a provision similar to other conventions that create an international crime. It refers to commonly accepted notions of the general part of criminal law. It is likely that states will meet the requirements under this provision, albeit in their own national way.

There must be knowledge on the consequences of being outside the protection of the law. For enforced disappearance as a crime against humanity also intent is required as well as knowledge of the fact that the crime takes place in the context of an attack against the civilian population. Intentional conduct is also required for the two crimes of Article 25. This may have consequences for the criminal responsibility of the individuals involved in the chain of events leading to placement of a child in an adoptive family. The various relevant acts and omissions may take place at different moments at different places/countries by different persons. For instance, a receiving state may initially have assessed documents as genuine. However, 25 years later, it may appear that a key document, such as the consent of the birth mother or the birth certificate is false. Who is now concealing the true identity?

JURISDICTION OVER THE CRIME OF ENFORCED DISAPPEARANCE IN THE CONTEXT OF AN ILLEGAL INTERCOUNTRY ADOPTION

There is only criminal responsibility if the state party has criminalized the conduct as provided under the convention in its national legislation. How states do that, whether they adopt a specific act or put it in the general Penal Code, is for each individual state to decide. What counts is the outcome which must comply with the obligations from the treaty. However, when a state has not (fully) complied with the criminalization, it cannot directly apply the convention to prosecute.[27] This is a problem as it appears that not all states have criminalized appropriately.[28] The Committee has recommended that the offence of enforced disappearance be defined in both its forms: as a separate offence, in line with Article 2 of the convention, and as a crime against humanity, in line with Article 5 of the convention and the two separate offences of Article 25. The Committee

27 Criminal law may only be used if the citizen is able to know what conduct is prohibited. This requires a provision in the national code written in the national language(s).

28 See above under the heading "The elements of the crime of enforced disappearance" and Galvis Patiño, 2021, pp. 16-17.

wants states parties to criminalize the conduct of Article 25 in a specific provision in the criminal legislation.[29] Germany opposed this:

> The Federal Government permits itself the remark that Article 25 paragraph 1 lit. a) of the Convention does not itself establish any obligation for the States Parties to create a specific criminal offence for the conduct referred to in this Article. The provision contains merely a general duty to punish.[30]

In going through all the reports of the Committee, we did not encounter a single state party that has specifically legislated both offences of Article 25 (Mexico did b, but not a).

The Characterization of the Crime of Enforced Disappearance

The Committee attaches much weight to the state parties implementing the conduct to be criminalized exactly as stipulated in the convention and labelling it as enforced disappearance.[31] Whilst, as such, this is understandable as it is evidence of the fact that the state is willing to combat this specific crime. At the same time, there is also value in the argument made by many states that the conduct of Article 2 of the convention is already covered by various existing penal provisions and therefore the added value of a crime of enforced disappearance is merely symbolic.[32] The crime of enforced disappearance is not an easy crime to prove as it has many elements and there is not a sufficient state practice yet on its prosecution. It may be far easier to prove that somebody committed individual

29 Concluding observations on the report submitted by Armenia under Art. 29 (1) of the Convention, 15 March 2015, CED/C/ARM/CO/1, paras. 28-29; Concluding observations on the report submitted by the Plurinational State of Bolivia under Art. 29 (1) of the Convention, 24 October 2019, CED/C/BOL/CO/1, paras. 40-41; Committee on Enforced Disappearances, Concluding observations on the report submitted by Austria under Art. 29 (1) of the Convention, 6 July 2018, CED/C/AUT/CO/1, paras. 24-25. In 2020, Austria reported that it is currently examining the possibility to review its criminal legislation with a view to incorporating the acts described in Art. 25(1) of the Convention as specific offences (see Information received from Austria on follow-up to the concluding observations on its report submitted under Art. 29 (1) of the Convention, 2 August 2020, CED/C/AUT/FCO/1, para. 14). Of many states, the Committee noted that a specific criminalization of the conduct of Art. 25 was absent: Burkina Faso, Colombia, Cuba, Czech Republic, France, Germany, Iraq, Japan, Kazakhstan, Lithuania, Mali, Mongolia, Montenegro, Morocco, the Netherlands, Niger, Nigeria, Norway, Panama, Paraguay, Peru, Portugal, Senegal, Serbia, Spain, Tunisia, and Uruguay. This list is certainly not exhaustive as the Committee does not always mention Art. 25 in its Concluding Observations. It is evidence of how states parties have collectively interpreted this treaty provision.

30 Information submitted by Germany in response to the concluding observations, 23 April 2015, CED/C/DEU/CO/1/Add.1, para. 19.

31 Concluding observations on the report submitted by Gabon under Art. 29, para. 1, of the Convention, 10 October 2017, CED/C/GAB/CO/1, para. 12.

32 Whether new legislation was necessary was already in dispute when negotiating the convention (see Citroni, 2009, p. 84).

serious offences such as torture, cruel or inhuman treatment, false imprisonment and the detention, confinement or concealment of a minor, as has already been criminalized in the Penal Code of the country, than the offence of enforced disappearance. In other words, striving for criminalization and prosecution of the autonomous offence may be far more risky and have less deterrent effect than opting for an offence that partly covers the conduct of enforced disappearance. A few states, like Germany openly question whether the specific legislation may be regarded as an obligation deriving from the convention:

> However, the Federal Republic of Germany does not see how Article 4 can be interpreted as giving rise to an obligation to create a separate criminal offence of "enforced disappearance". The Federal Government considers the offences already defined in German criminal law, combined with the provisions of other acts, to be sufficient for the adequate investigation and punishment of cases of enforced disappearance.[33]

Whatever states have done, it has direct consequences for their jurisdiction. On that, Article 9 obliges states to establish jurisdiction on the basis of several jurisdictional principles.

There are four potential jurisdictional situations that heavily depend on whether the two states involved (state of origin of the child and the receiving state) are a party to the convention. It is only through ratification of the convention that the obligation to criminalize the offences emerges. When neither state is a party, they are not under the obligation to criminalize the conduct, and it is then most likely that their criminal justice systems do not know the crimes. In a situation where both states are a party to the convention, they are both under the obligation to criminalize the conduct. If both have done so in compliance with the convention, all conduct related to an illegal adoption connected to enforced disappearance will fall under the jurisdiction of either one or both states. The two remaining situations will create more difficulties by definition.[34] One is that the state of origin is a party and the receiving state is not. The other is that the state of origin is not a party, but the receiving state is. Obligations to criminalize only exist for state parties. However, as we will see below, it may relate to conduct that took place abroad.

---

33 Information submitted by Germany in response to the concluding observations, 23 April 2015, CED/C/DEU/CO/1/Add.1, para. 3.

34 Especially in cases of accomplices, the aider and abettor, to a crime committed by somebody else, states may require jurisdiction over both the accomplice and the principal. If this applies, it would rule out prosecution in the receiving state of an individual who helped or profited from what the principal did abroad.

The jurisdictional provision of the convention is Article 9. Its wording is identical to the jurisdictional paragraphs of many other conventions of international criminal law, which does not indicate that the specific jurisdictional aspects of enforced disappearance, let alone of international adoption, have specifically been taken into account. The first jurisdictional basis provided for in Article 9 is *territorial*. When the offence takes place on the territory, the state is competent.[35] Concerning the crime of abduction, it seems likely that there will be jurisdiction on this basis for the state of origin only. Even when regarding the disappearance of an abducted child as a continuing crime, the definition of Article 2 places the concealment thereof in relation to the state by/in which the child has been abducted. For the two other crimes, wrongful removal and identity substitution, depending on the circumstances, one may imagine acts being committed in either state. It is important to note that there may be situations in which a child was abducted and disappeared in the state of origin. That state has then territorial jurisdiction over this offence. If subsequently the child is adopted and the child's true identity is concealed by falsifying documents in the receiving state, the latter has jurisdiction over the latter act, as only that offence was committed there.

The second jurisdictional basis is *active nationality* of the perpetrator. Here, the location of the criminal act is, as such, not relevant. What counts is that the perpetrator has the nationality of the state that starts an investigation against him. The principle is widely accepted and based on a longstanding tradition in states applying civil law. However, especially those states often apply the principle with the reservation that the conduct must also be criminalized in the state where it was committed.[36] The convention does not rule out that national law may apply such a limitation. This plays out when a national of the receiving state that is a party to the convention is involved in one of the offences on the territory of a state of origin that is not a party.

The third principle is *passive nationality*. What matters here is that the disappeared person has the nationality of the state.[37] This will often lead to the jurisdiction of the state of origin, as the disappeared child may have its nationality. When the child has later been adopted, it is most likely that it has obtained the nationality of the receiving state (and it may have lost the original nationality at the same time). There are three issues that may create problems in the application of this principle: 1) national law may

35 Also the jurisdictional principles of Art. 9 need to be implemented into national law. In addition to that, para. 3 indicates that states have the discretion to vest wider jurisdiction than they are obliged to under paras. 1 and 2 of Art. 9.

36 See, e.g., Report submitted by Benin under Art. 29 (1) of the Convention, due in 2019, 4 January 2022, CED/C/BEN/1, paras. 28-40.

37 Please note that there is a difference between the definitions of *disappeared person* and of *victim*. The latter as found in Art. 24 is broader.

stipulate rules on whether the nationality must be there at the moment of the offence or at the moment of the prosecution. Children obtaining the nationality of the receiving state will never have that at birth, but get it later as one of the legal consequences of adoption; 2) the nationality may be withdrawn as a result of complying with the obligations deriving from Article 25(4) when the adoption is annulled. This may cause a lack of jurisdiction on this basis; 3) last and not least, the formulation of subparagraph c 'when the state party considers it appropriate' is very weak. This cannot be seen as an obligation, but it is a mere suggestion. It also leaves open whether the state may consider legislation or the exercise of jurisdiction in the individual case appropriate. In other words, in many states, there will not be jurisdiction based on passive nationality.

The fourth principle is the *aut dedere aut judicare* principle.[38] The state must create jurisdiction over an individual if it refuses to extradite or surrender to a state wanting him. This principle of jurisdiction has had very little impact in creating a new basis for jurisdiction.[39]

In some of its Concluding Observations, the Committee has suggested applying the principle of *universal jurisdiction* to enforced disappearance.[40] If the principle of universal jurisdiction applies, the state may prosecute offences committed across the globe, regardless where and by whom committed. We have not found evidence of any state having implemented this suggestion. However, it is likely that some states that have implemented the ICC Statute will have universal jurisdiction over enforced disappearance as a crime against humanity.

---

38 The Committee held on this principle: "27.The Committee is concerned that the State party may not exercise jurisdiction over the offence of enforced disappearance when the alleged perpetrator, who is a foreign national or a person who does not have any nationality and does not have permanent residence status in the State party, is present in its territory, is not extradited or surrendered, and the country in which the enforced disappearance was allegedly perpetrated does not specifically criminalize enforced disappearance (art. 9). 28. The Committee recommends that the State party ensure that no conditions which are not provided for in the Convention, such as double criminality, affect the exercise of jurisdiction by its courts in compliance with Art. 9 (2) of the Convention" (see Concluding observations on the report submitted by Czech Republic under Art. 29, para. 1, of the Convention, 23 September 2022, CED/C/CZE/CO/1, paras. 27-28).

39 The main problem is that reasons to refuse extradition are often also reasons that stand in the way of executing jurisdiction. In addition, by definition, in such a situation, the state exercising jurisdiction has to cooperate with an unwilling other state.

40 Concluding observations on the report submitted by Slovakia under Art. 29 (1) of the Convention, 24 October 2019, CED/C/SVK/CO/1, para. 13.

Temporal Aspects of the Crime of Enforced Disappearance

The International Convention for the Protection of all Persons from Enforced Disappearance was concluded on 20 December 2006 and entered into force for its first twenty parties on 23 December 2010. As of 3 January 2023, 69 states have ratified. It entered into force for the European part of the Netherlands on 22 April 2011 and for Switzerland on 2 December 2016.[41] Obligations to criminalize and vest jurisdiction only commence when the treaty enters into force for the state. Applying the prohibition of the non-retroactivity of criminal law,[42] only conduct that took place after the national criminalization was enacted can be prosecuted. In general, this means that all conduct that took place before 23 December 2010 does not fall under the definition of the crime of enforced disappearance. More specifically, the individual moment of entering into force for each specific state determines whether the criminalization and jurisdiction may be there. However, this is very much dependent on whether there is national implementation. This may especially have severe consequences for the abductions that took place before 2010, followed by adoptions. A major question then is whether such a child may be considered as a person still disappeared. As the key element of the crime is the abduction and the disappearance is the consequence, it seems that the moment determining when the offence took place is the moment of abduction.

Article 8 on the statute of limitations asks states to apply lengthy periods.[43] The continuing nature of the crime may help as it means that the offence in cases of enforced

41 Declarations and Reservations made by the States Parties to the Convention give no information on the provisions relevant for criminal law. By and large, they relate to Arts. 31 and 32 on the individual complaints and the competence of the Committee, some to Art. 42 and Arts. 17 and 18. Its legislative history is well documented in Galvis Patiño, 2021.

42 This is different for enforced disappearance as a crime against humanity.

43 The Committee advised that the limitation term should begin to run from the moment the enforced disappearance ceases in all its elements, that is, from the moment the disappeared person is found alive or his or her remains are located and identified – in case he or she is found lifeless – or from the moment the identity of a child who has been the victim of appropriation is re-established, see Galvis Patiño, 2021, p. 28. In the context of stolen babies, the Committee held: "that, according to the information provided during the dialogue, the terms of limitation applicable in cases of child abduction may vary depending on whether the abduction is treated as a case of enforced disappearance or as an alteration of paternity. It is concerned that, according to the case law referred to, in neither case does the term of limitation commence from the moment when the child's identity is restored. It is concerned in particular about the decision handed down by the Provincial Court of Madrid, which was endorsed by the Supreme Court and according to which the term of limitation in cases involving "stolen babies" commences from the moment when "the situation of deprivation of liberty ceases, which the Court understood to be [the day on which the] child reaches the age of majority, in accordance with art[icle] 132 (1) of the Criminal Code (arts. 8, 12 and 25)." (See Concluding observations on the additional information submitted by Spain under Art. 29 (4) of the Convention, 4 November 2021, CED/C/ESP/OAI/1, para. 27).

disappearance that commenced prior to its entry into force but continued thereafter is not subject to any limitations.[44]

The moment of entrance into force of the convention is relevant for the state party concerned, as its obligation to live up to the convention starts from that day onwards. Given the fact that enforced disappearance is a continuous crime,[45] the obligation to criminalize this conduct may likely result in a situation in which the initial disappearance took place before the convention entered into force, but continues after the state ratified. Also other obligations from the convention apply to continuing disappearances, such as the obligation to investigate, to compensate victims and to annul illegal adoptions. However, the character of the crime as a continuing crime cannot prevail over the principle of legality and the non-retroactivity of criminal law. Whereas for state responsibility, one may attribute conduct of state organs that took place before the convention entered into force after ratification, because this allows the unlawful situation of enforced disappearance to continue and the obligations for the state do not depend on implementing the crime in its penal legislation. Conduct of individuals before criminalization cannot be regarded as criminal. This is not different when the conduct resulted in a situation that has later been criminalized. However, individuals that intentionally contribute to the concealment of identity after its criminalization can be held criminally responsible because they act now, after the criminalization. In other words, the qualification by the Committee of enforced disappearance as a continuing crime has more impact on state responsibility than on individual criminal responsibility. The continuing character of Article 2 crimes has de facto no consequence because states have not criminalized the conduct as a continuing crime, neither at the time, nor now.

Also the wrongful removal of the child must be regarded as have taken place when the child was adopted/removed to another country. This may be different concerning the crime of identity substitution. Falsification, concealment and destruction may take place before and after the removal of the child. Especially in situations in which the now adult (formerly adopted child) is trying to find more information on his/her identity, s/he may be confronted with acts of new falsification, concealment and or destruction. Those acts would undoubtedly fall under the crime definition. Is this also the same for the use of documents previously falsified? It seems that the legislator focused on the producers of the documents more than on the users. However, this does not rule out any involvement as an accomplice, inciter, aider or abettor to the main offence.

44 See Concluding observations on the report submitted by Brazil under Art. 29 (1) of the Convention, 3 November 2021, CED/C/BRA/CO/1, paras. 14-15.

45 Committee on Enforced Disappearances, Concluding observations on the report submitted by Albania under Art. 29 (1) of the Convention, 3 July 2018, CED/C/ALB/CO/1, paras. 22-23.

IMPLEMENTATION IN THE NETHERLANDS AND SWITZERLAND

The Netherlands implemented the convention in its Act on International Crimes (*Wet Internationale Misdrijven*). It included forced disappearance in Article 4 on crimes against humanity. In addition, it created a new Article 8a, criminalizing enforced disappearance as a separate crime (outside the context of crimes against humanity). In its explanatory memorandum to the convention, the government discusses elements of the crime exclusively in the context of the crime against humanity and the ICC Elements of Crime. According to the Netherlands' government, enforced disappearance does not occur in the Netherlands.[46] In its most recent submission to the Committee, the Netherlands merely stated that there was no updated information available on adoption and international disappearance, without stating reasons for the absence of that information.[47] The Committee criticized the Netherlands for not having included all elements of the crime:

> While commending the State for having included enforced disappearance as an autonomous crime in the International Crimes Act, the Committee is concerned that, insofar as the definition of enforced disappearance in section 4 (2)(d) applies also to the autonomous crime, the definition does not include the "concealment of the fate or whereabouts of the disappeared person" as a possible element and does not mention that the crime should be committed by "agents of the State or by persons or groups of persons acting with the authorization, support or acquiescence of the State" but by or with the authorization, support or acquiescence of a "State or political organization". The Committee takes note of the position of the delegation that removal from the protection of the law is regarded as a consequence of the crime of enforced disappearance and not as a constitutive element of that crime (art. 2).[48]

46 See Kamerstukken II, 2009-2010, 32208, nr. 3, p. 2; on Art. 25: "Artikel 25 Deze bepaling strekt tot (strafrechtelijke) bescherming van kinderen die het slachtoffer zijn van gedwongen verdwijning, wier vader, moeder of voogd slachtoffer daarvan is dan wel die in gevangenschap worden geboren. Het wederrechtelijk weghalen van deze kinderen is strafbaar gesteld in de artikelen 279 Sr (onttrekking minderjarige aan het wettelijk gezag), 280 Sr (geheimhouding verblijfplaats minderjarige), en 282 Sr (opzettelijke vrijheidsberoving). Onze adoptiewetgeving voorziet in de toepassing ervan die rekening houdt met de specifieke belangen van kinderen die het slachtoffer zijn van gedwongen verdwijning" (see Kamerstukken II, 2009-2010, 32 251 (R1905), nr. 3, p. 10).

47 Additional information submitted by the Netherlands under Art. 29 (4) of the Convention, 14 April 2021, CED/C/NLD/AI/1, para. 37.

48 Concluding observations on the report submitted by the Netherlands under Art. 29, para. 1, of the Convention, 10 April 2014, CED/C/NLD/CO/1, para. 14.

The Netherlands answered by stating:

> It is true that the International Crimes Act does not contain the exact same wording as the Convention as it states that the crime should be committed 'by or with the authorization, support or acquiescence of a State or political organization' instead of "by agents of the State or by persons or groups of persons acting with the authorization, support or acquiescence of the State'. However, the term 'State' must be interpreted broadly and encompasses agents of the State, as is explicitly set out in the explanatory memorandum to the law giving effect to the Convention. In addition to anyone who acts with the authorization, support or acquiescence of the State, the definition in the International Crimes Act also refers to anyone who acts with the authorization, support or acquiescence of a political organization. This addition is derived from the definition of enforced disappearance contained in article 7 (2) (i) of the Rome Statute of the International Criminal Court. In this regard, the International Crimes Act contains a broader definition than the Convention and thus offers greater protection.[49]

This raises an interesting issue. On the one hand, the government is right, by not including this element of the crime, the Dutch offence can more easily be proven. On the other, such a criminalization denaturizes the original description of the crime of enforced disappearances.

Also the Swiss government started by stating that the crime does not occur in Switzerland:

> *Der Begriff des Verschwindenlassens bezeichnet ein globales Phänomen: Eine dem Staat unliebsame Person wird von staatlichen Organen oder dem Staat*

49 Additional information submitted by the Netherlands under Art. 29 (4) of the Convention, 14 April 2021, CED/C/NLD/AI/1, para. 13.

> *nahestehenden Organisationen festgenommen und an einen unbekannten Ort verschleppt.*[50]

Switzerland resists to criminalize the autonomous offence of Article 25:

> The conduct described in article 25 (1) (a) of the Convention is already covered by the Criminal Code (see paragraph 147 of the report of Switzerland), although no specific offence is defined. Establishing this conduct as a separate offence is therefore not necessary, as it would only have symbolic value, which would make little sense in the Swiss context.[51]

A similar finding as to the Netherlands applies to Switzerland. The existing separate offences will require less evidence and will thus also offer more possibilities in the case of illegal adoption. A link with an enforced disappearance will no longer be required.

CONCLUSIONS ON THE POSSIBILITIES FOR PROSECUTION

Depending on the circumstances of the case, illegal intercountry adoption may amount to a crime of enforced disappearance. Whereas the convention has already constructed a rather complicated crime definition with many intertwined elements to prove, a legal basis for prosecution may often be lacking because states have not implemented the convention well in their national legislation. This applies to the main crime of Article 2 and the situation is even worse for the crimes of Article 25. On enforced disappearance as a crime against humanity states seem to have it criminalized already as a result of ratifying the Rome Statute. In addition, because of the required nexus with an attack,

50 BBl 2014 453, Botschaft zur Genehmigung und zur Umsetzung des Internationalen Übereinkommens zum Schutz aller Personen vor dem Verschwindenlassen, p. 457. On p. 463: "In der Schweiz sind bisher keine Fälle von Verschwindenlassen bekannt geworden. Doch leben auch in der Schweiz Angehörige von Personen, die im Ausland Opfer eines Verschwindenlassens wurden." The message of the Swiss government is that its legislation is already in order. On p. 481 it states: "Die Schweizer Rechtsordnung wird diesen Anforderungen bereits gerecht: Bei einer unrechtmässigen Entziehung von Kindern können verschiedene Bestimmungen des Strafgesetzbuchs zur Anwendung gelangen: Artikel 183 Absatz 2 StGB schützt Personen unter 16 Jahren ausdrücklich gegen Entführung. Zudem stellt Artikel 220 StGB die Entziehung einer minderjährigen Person und die Weigerung, eine minderjährige Person dem Inhaber des Obhutsrechts zurückzugeben, unter Strafe. Schliesslich deckt Artikel 219 StGB Fälle ab, in denen jemand eine minderjährige Person unter Verletzung der Fürsorge- oder Erziehungspflicht in ihrer körperlichen oder seelischen Entwicklung gefährdet. Dokumente, welche die wahre Identität einer Person bescheinigen, sind zudem als Urkunden zu betrachten, deren Fälschung oder Unterdrückung (inkl. Vernichtung) gemäss den Artikeln 251-254 StGB strafbar ist. Auch ausländische Dokumente fallen unter diese Bestimmungen (Art. 255 StGB)."

51 List of issues in relation to the report submitted by Switzerland under Art. 29 (1) of the Convention, Addendum, Replies of Switzerland to the list of issues, 23 January 2020, CED/C/CHE/RQ/1.

illegal adoptions as a crime against humanity offer no possibility for those that were adopted to the Netherlands and Switzerland.

In sum, for criminal prosecution of illegal intercountry adoption as an enforced disappearance, the chances are slim for those that have been adopted before 2011. For later adoptions, the position is slightly better, however, the fact that in a sending state, authorities were involved in illegal adoption may also make cooperation in criminal matters very cumbersome. It would require states to deliver evidence in an individual criminal proceeding that at the same time might disclose that the state violated its human rights obligations and/ or that an official of that state committed a serious crime. Such a situation is not conducive to revealing the truth about the identity of children.

The reviews of the Committee may create more difficulties in allocating the offence to a specific jurisdiction and to subsequently proving the offence. The Committee seems to have as a primary goal that states implement the offence of enforced disappearances in exactly the same way as in the convention. The dilemma is that in doing so, it will result in an offence which only in rare cases can be proven in criminal proceedings. The Committee acts predominantly as a human rights body focusing on state responsibility.[52] However, individual criminal responsibility is a different matter with its own dimensions and states following the Committee's demands will automatically reduce the possibilities for prosecution. These specific dimensions were described in this contribution, but have not yet been recognized by the Committee. States have demonstrated '*peu d'enthousiasme*' at all stages of the convention: in drafting, negotiating, ratifying, implementing, reporting to the Committee, investigating and prosecuting.[53]

52 It appears that the Inter-American Court of Human Rights regards criminalization as an important tool to give effective protection to victims and that it is also relevant to criminalize exactly the conduct that is undesirable. This is how I interpret Schniederjahn when she discusses the need to create criminal provisions, see Schniederjahn, 2017, pp. 236-240.

53 See E. Plate, 'La campagne pour la ratification', *in* E. Decaux and O. de Frouville (eds.), *La Convention pour la protection de toutes les personnes contre les disparitions forcées*, Bruxelles, Bruyland, 2009, p. 143; F. Andreu, 'La mise en oeuvre de la convention', *in* E. Decaux and O. de Frouville (eds.), *La Convention pour la protection de toutes les personnes contre les disparitions forcées*, Bruxelles, Bruyland, 2009, pp. 154-155.

About the Contributors

Sabine Bitter is a journalist in the culture programme of the Swiss radio and television channel *SRF 2 Kultur* and a freelance historian conducting research on international adoptions from Tibet, Sri Lanka and India. In 2019, she and her colleague, journalist and freelance sociologist Annika Bangerter carried out an extended study on adoptions from Sri Lanka from 1973 until 1997, focusing on the role of Swiss private adoption agencies and authorities therein, led by Prof. Nadja Ramsauer at the Zurich University of Applied Sciences. The study was commissioned by the Swiss Federal Council of Justice, and its report, released in 2020, led the Federal Council to officially express regret for past illegal adoptions. Currently, Sabine Bitter and her colleagues are conducting a commissioned research project on adoptions from India to Switzerland, on behalf of the cantons of Zurich and Thurgau, led by Prof. Rita Kesselring at the University of St. Gallen.

Susan F. Branco is a transracial and transnational adoptee from Colombia, South America. She is an advocate for increased adoption-related research and training within counsellor education and is passionate about improving mental health outcomes for transracially adopted persons. Susan is Associate Professor in the Counseling Department at Palo Alto University, CA, USA.

Andréa Cardarello holds a PhD in Anthropology from l'Université de Montréal (Canada) and has taught anthropology and sociology at universities in Canada and Brazil. Her research centres on issues related to kinship, adoption, foster care, poverty, children's rights and immigration. She is a member of the research groups LIELA – *Laboratoire interdisciplinaire d'études latino-américaines*; DIGREG / UFBA – Social Inequalities and Intersectionalities of Class, Gender, Race/Ethnicity and Generations of the Federal University of Bahia; and ANTHERA – International Network for Research on Family and Kinship.

Dewi Deijle was born in Jakarta (Indonesia) and adopted by a Dutch family as a baby. She is a lawyer and represents intercountry adoptees regarding their fundamental rights. In 2017 she wrote a letter to the Dutch state on behalf of the foundation *Mijn Roots* (a country-specific organization that conducts root searches for adoptees from Indonesia), claiming that the Dutch state is liable for (immaterial and material) damages suffered by adoptees from Indonesia as it failed to offer guarantees, adequate control and supervision to protect their fundamental rights. She has been discussing this issue with the ministry and members of parliament for five years now. Currently, she is in contact with the Minister for Legal Protection regarding the need for financial compensation for individual roots searches and truth-finding. In addition, she does humanitarian work and has set up various projects in Indonesia, in particular for children with disabilities who do not have access to education.

André Klip is Professor of Criminal Law, Criminal Procedure and the Transnational Aspects of Criminal Law at Maastricht University. He is a member of the Royal Netherlands Academy of Arts and Sciences and a judge at the Court of Appeal of 's-Hertogenbosch. In 2001 and 2003 he adopted children from South Africa.

Kyung-eun Lee is the founder and director of Human Rights Beyond Borders. She is also an adviser to the Supreme Court's Sentencing Committee and an auditor for Yonhap News Agency. She has extensive experience in human rights as a research professor at the Korean University Human Rights Center and as an adviser to the National Assembly, the National Human Rights Commission and the Ministry of Foreign Affairs. She also served as the director of Amnesty International Korea from 2018 to 2020. From 1995 to 2017, she served as a government officer for the Republic of Korea in a variety of roles, including in the Ministry of Health and Welfare. She holds a PhD in Law as well as a BA, from Seoul National University, and an MA from Fletcher School of Law and Diplomacy at Tufts University. She is the author of 'The Global Orphan Adoption System: South Korea's Impact on its Origin and Development', co-author of 'The Child Selling Country' (written in Korean), and an editor and writer for *The Korea Times*' special column series 'Dialogues with Adoptees'.

Elvira Loibl is an assistant professor in Criminology and Criminal Law at Maastricht University, Faculty of Law. She received her law degree at the University of Vienna and her LL.M. in Forensics, Criminology and Law at Maastricht University. In 2019, she defended her dissertation entitled 'The Transnational Illegal Adoption Market: A Criminological Study of the German and Dutch Intercountry Adoption System', in which she identified and explained the criminogenic weaknesses within the intercountry adoption system that encourage and facilitate illegal adoptions. Her study is frequently cited in commissioned inquiries and studies on illegal intercountry adoption.

David M. Smolin is the Harwell G. Davis Professor of Constitutional Law, and Director, Center for Children, Law, and Ethics, at Cumberland Law School, Samford University. He served as an independent expert for the Hague Conference on Private International Law (HCCH) on intercountry adoption issues and as an external expert for the International Social Service (ISS), on issues related to children's rights, adoption and surrogacy. He is a member of the core expert group that developed the Verona Principles on international standards for surrogacy. He serves as a special adviser for the Swiss NGO Child Identity Protection (CHIP). Many of his publications are available for free download at http://works.bepress.com/david_smolin/, with over 90,000 downloads. He received the Outstanding Scholar in Adoption Award from the

St. John's University Adoption Initiative in 2014. He presented at the 2010 and 2015 Hague Special Commissions on the Practical Operation of the Hague Adoption Convention; the Second International Symposium on Korean Adoption Studies in Seoul, South Korea; the State Supreme Court of Sao Paulo, Brazil; and the NALSAR University of Law, in Telangana, India.

Gonda Van Steen holds the Koraes Chair of Modern Greek and Byzantine History, Language and Literature in the Department of Classics at King's College London. She is the author of five books: *Venom in Verse: Aristophanes in Modern Greece*; *Liberating Hellenism from the Ottoman Empire*; *Theatre of the Condemned: Classical Tragedy on Greek Prison Islands*; and *Stage of Emergency: Theater and Public Performance under the Greek Military Dictatorship of 1967-1974*. Her 2019 book, *Adoption, Memory, and Cold War Greece*, takes the reader into the uncharted terrain of Greek adoption stories that have become paradigmatic of Cold War politics and history. She most recently edited and published *The Battle for Bodies, Hearts and Minds in Postwar Greece: Social Worker Charles Schermerhorn in Thessaloniki, 1946-1951*.

Lies Wesseling is Professor of Cultural Memory, Gender and Diversity at the Faculty of Arts and Social Sciences, Maastricht University, the Netherlands. Her research is in the fields of critical adoption studies and Dutch colonial history. Educative discourses such as reading primers, history and geography textbooks and children's novels have her special attention as sources that shed light on ways in which the re-allocation and re-education of indigenous and mixed children were 'sold' to children in both colony and metropole.

Sophie Withaeckx is Assistant Professor in Philosophy at Maastricht University. Previously, she held the position of coordinator and post-doc researcher at RHEA (Centre of Expertise on Gender, Diversity and Intersectionality at the Vrije Universiteit Brussel), and of lecturer and researcher at Odisee University College. She holds Master's degrees in African Languages & Cultures (UGent) and International Politics (University of Antwerp) and a PhD in Philosophy and Ethics (Vrije Universiteit Brussel). Her research interests concern understandings of culture, gender and morality in experiences with violence; transnationalism, transmigration and social work; how normative understandings of 'humanity' shape public spaces and institutions and, in particular, how diversity and 'decolonization' have become managed in higher education. Her current research examines the ethics of transnational adoption and inquires how taken-for-granted notions of humanness, family and kinship underlie ethics and practice in transnational adoption.

www.ingramcontent.com/pod-product-compliance
Lightning Source LLC
Chambersburg PA
CBHW061353240926
51846CB00007B/1390
* 9 7 8 9 0 4 7 3 0 1 8 8 2 *